Borderline Virginities

How and why did virginity come to play such a crucial part in the Christian Church in the formative and defining period of Late Antiquity? Sissel Undheim analyzes the negotiations over what constituted virginity and assesses its socio-religious value in fourth-century Rome by looking at those at the very margins of virginity and non-virginity. The Church Fathers' efforts to demarcate an exclusively Christian virginity, in contrast to the 'false virgins' of their pagan adversaries, displays a tension that, it is argued, played a larger role in the construction of a specifically Christian sacred virginity than previous studies have acknowledged.

Late fourth-century Christian theologians' persistent appraisals of sacred virgins paved the way for a wide variety of virgins that often challenged the stereotype of the unmarried female virgin. The sources abound with seemingly paradoxical virgins, such as widow virgins, married virgins, virgin mothers, infant virgins, old virgins, heretical virgins, pagan virgins, male virgins, false virgins and fallen virgins. Through examining these kinds of 'borderline virgins' as they appear in a range of textual sources from varied genres, Undheim demonstrates how physical, cultural and cognitive boundaries of virginity were contested, drawn and redrawn in the fourth and early fifth centuries in the Latin West.

Sissel Undheim is Associate Professor of Religious Studies at the University of Bergen, Norway. Her academic work focuses on sacred virginity in antiquity and Late Antiquity, and she has published various articles on this topic, as well as on New Age religion and the didactics of religion. She has edited a collection of translated texts on Roman religion for the Norwegian series Verdens Hellige Skrifter (Sacred Texts of the World).

Borderline Virginities

Sacred and Secular Virgins
in Late Antiquity

Sissel Undheim

LONDON AND NEW YORK

First published 2018 by Routledge

2 Park Square, Milton Park, Abingdon, Oxfordshire OX14 4RN

52 Vanderbilt Avenue, New York, NY 10017

Routledge is an imprint of the Taylor & Francis Group, an informa business

First issued in paperback 2020

British Library Cataloguing-in-Publication Data
A catalogue record for this book is available from the British Library

Library of Congress Cataloging-in-Publication Data
Names: Undheim, Sissel, author.
Title: Borderline virginities: sacred and secular virgins in late antiquity /
Sissel Undheim.
Description: First [edition]. | New York: Routledge, 2017. |
Includes bibliographical references.
Identifiers: LCCN 2017003401 | ISBN 9781472480170 (hardback: alk. paper) |
ISBN 9781315569734 (ebook)
Subjects: LCSH: Virginity–Religious aspects–Christianity–History of
doctrines–Early church, ca. 30-600. | Church history–Primitive and early
church, ca. 30-600. | Virgins–Rome–History.
Classification: LCC BR195.C45 U53 2017 | DDC 248.4/7–dc23
LC record available at https://lccn.loc.gov/2017003401

ISBN: 978-1-4724-8017-0 (hbk)
ISBN: 978-0-367-49598-5 (pbk)

Typeset in Bembo
by Cenveo Publisher Services

Contents

Preface

Every day during my last two years in high school, I passed beneath Jay DeFeo's two monumental paintings that hung on the walls in Kristiansand Katedral School's spacious staircase. The impact of this impressive diptych became even more alluring once I learned what the artist had called her paintings: *The Wise and Foolish Virgins*.

In retrospect, it seems like this is in fact where this book project must have started, in my high school's collection of Beat art. Growing up in protestant, secular Scandinavia, DeFeo's intriguing paintings and their title subtly suggested to me a vast, yet mainly unknown, terrain of cultural history where virginity was inextricably tied to gender, aesthetics, authority, and sexuality, but also to religion; to damnation and salvation.

Several years later, stumbling upon Mary Beard's mind-expanding article "Re-reading (Vestal) virginity" as a Master's student, I discovered some theoretically and methodologically fascinating new approaches to the study of not only Vestal virgins, but also other notions of sacred virginity in the Mediterranean region. In her article, Beard concluded that gendered, social categories of anthropology and sociology may not be enough when analyzing this specific Roman, female priesthood:

> The Vestals […] can be seen not merely as a parade of anomaly, but a focus of negotiation around the category of virginity, a negotiation of the boundary between virginity and non-virginity.

> (1995: 172)

Similar to the effect of DeFeo's stark visual contrast between *The Wise* and *The Foolish Virgin*, Beard turned my attention to the cultural construction of virginity, a much more complex and fascinating field than I had ever imagined. This quote by Beard, then, must therefore be credited as the starting, as well as the pivotal, point for this book's topic. The aim of the following explorations is thus to better understand how the cultural discourses and negotiations over sacred virgins' virginity that Beard saw in the Roman discourses on Vestal virgins, can also shed light on the "virgin craze" of the fourth-century Church Fathers.

The book has been written over the course of a long time span, starting years back with my discovery of the Vestal Virgins as a Master's student in the history of religions at the University of Oslo, and then through my PhD studies at the University of Bergen.

My deepest gratitude goes to my relentlessly encouraging, inspiring, and patient mentor Professor Ingvild Sælid Gilhus, who has contributed to this project in countless ways over the years. This book would never have been completed without her invaluable comments and support.

During my first years at the University of Bergen, as a PhD student, I was so fortunate to be a part of the interdisciplinary Program for the Study of Ancient Christianity (PROAK). This gave me the opportunity to present preliminary texts at a number of seminars and conferences. I therefore wish to thank Professors Einar Thomassen, Jostein Børtnes, Lisbeth Mikaelsson, Tor Hauken, Karstein Hopland, and the late Tomas Hägg, for their comments and support. The same gratitude goes to my then co-fellows at the institute; Jonas Bjørnebye, Mona Farstad, Gina Dahl, Liv Ingeborg Lied, Hugo Lundhaug, Aslak Rostad, Karl Johan Skeidsvoll, and Thea Selliaas Thorsen, with whom I shared many inspiring discussions, as well as the wonderful PROAK excursions to ancient sites around the Mediterranean. Professors Halvor Moxnes and the late Turid Karlsen Seim, as well as Marianne Bjelland Kartzow and Rebecca Solevåg, were, through related projects and seminars, part of PROAK's extended family and the encouraging group of Early Christianity researchers in Norway, from which conversations I profited greatly.

Much of my time working on this project has been spent at the Norwegian Institute in Rome. I would like to thank Professor Siri Sande at the Institute for helping me find my way around the archaeological remains of ancient Rome, and also librarian Germana Graziosi for providing so much help and guiding my search for material at the many libraries of the city. Kristine Kolrud, Pauline Gjøsteen, and Stine Holte made my stay both pleasant and edifying because of their erudite company.

I also spent a few years at Agder University, where I particularly wish to thank Henny Hägg, Årstein Justnes, and Tor Vegge for inviting me to take part in the Early Christianity research group at the university. Thanks are also due to some of my inspiring conversation partners, colleagues, and friends at Agder University: Helle Mellingen, Bjørg Marit Nyjordet, Kristel Jensen, Kari-Mette Walmann Hidle and Irene Trysnes for always expanding my fields of interest with their enthusiasm and knowledge. My long-time friend Frida Forsgren deserves special thanks, not only for making Rome an ever-expanding aesthetic experience for me with her infinite knowledge of art history, but also for bringing DeFeo and Beat art back into my life. Also, at the university library at Agder, Hilde Johannessen and Birgitte Kleivset deserve special thanks for obtaining all kinds of material for me from libraries all over Europe, and for always being supportive when it is needed the most.

Professors Jens Braarvig and Sigurd Hjelde at the University of Oslo played an important part in encouraging me to pursue the project at its earliest stage.

Ingvar Brandvik Mæhle and Liv Ingeborg Lied read Chapters Three and One respectively and provided a valuable response, as did Denise Kimber Buell on an early version of Chapter Four, and I wish to thank them for their very helpful comments. Stig Oppedal diligently proofread and commented on the previous thesis-version of this text, and he also lent me his expertise on ancient history as well as Latin, for which I am very grateful.

I also wish to thank my evaluation committee, Britt Mari Näsström, David Brakke, and Dag Øistein Endsjø for their very productive feedback, both in the written evaluation report and also at the public defence. The same gratitude I wish to convey to Routledge's anonymous reader, whose very generous comments have been very helpful in the process of revision. I am also indebted to the late Professor Tomas Hägg, who kindly read several of my translations and offered suggestions for improvement. The errors that remain now are all mine.

The research for this book has been funded by The University of Bergen. The time I spent in Rome was made possible by the economic support from the University of Bergen, the Italian scholarship under the Cultural Agreements awarded by the Norwegian Research Council and the Meltzer Foundation. I also wish to thank Rasmus Brandt and Marina Prusac who, with their project on Roman Festivals, funded my participation in Erfurt University's Spring School in 2005.

Last, but not least, my thanks go to my husband Svein, for his loving support and endless patience with my incessant urge to always just read one more text, or revise something just one more time. Also to my dearest sons, Magnus and Johannes: you may both have contributed in postponing the realization of this book, but you have made life so much richer by it.

Sissel Undheim
Bergen, 2017

Abbreviations

AE	*L'Année épigraphique*. Paris 1888–
ANF	Ante-Nicene Fathers: http://www.ccel.org/fathers.html
CIL	*Corpus Incriptionum Latinarum*. Theodor Mommsen *et al.*, Berlin 1863–
CLE	*Carmina Latina Epigraphica*. F. Bücheler and E. Lommatzsch, Berlin 1895–1926
EDB	Epigraphic Database Bari: http://www.edb.uniba.it/
EDCS	Epigraphik-Datenbank Clauss/Slaby: http://www.manfredclauss.de/gb/index.html
EDH	Epigraphische Datenbank Heidelberg: http://www.uni-heidelberg.de/institute/sonst/adw/edh/index.html.en
EEC	*Encyclopedia of Early Christianity*. E. Ferguson (Ed.), 2nd edition. Garland Publishing, New York 1999
ICUR	*Inscriptiones Christianae Urbis Romae septimo saeculo antiquiores*. G. B. De Rossi, A. Silvagni, A. Ferrua, *et al.* Officina Libraria Pontifica, Rome 1857–
ILCV	*Inscriptiones Latinae Christianae Veteres*. Ernestus Diehl (Ed.). Weidmann, Berlin, 1961–7
ILS	*Inscriptiones Latinae Selectae*. Hermann Dessau (Ed.). Weidmann, Berlin, 1892–1916
LCL	*Loeb Classical Library*
NPNF1	Nicene and Post-Nicene Fathers, first series: http://www.ccel.org/fathers.html
NPNF2	Nicene and Post-Nicene Fathers, second series: http://www.ccel.org/fathers.html
PIR2	*Prosopographia Imperii Romani saec. I.II.III*, de Gruyter, Berlin, 1873–1950
PL	*Patrologia Latina*: http://pld.chadwyck.com/
PLRE	A. H. M. Jones, J. R. Martindale and J. Morris (Eds). *The Prosopography of the Later Roman Empire*, 4 Vols. Cambridge University Press, Cambridge, 1980–92
TLL	*Thesaurus Linguae Latinae*

1 Introduction

Sancta virginitate: limits and border zones

Holy virginity and that perfect chastity which is consecrated to the service of God is without doubt among the most precious treasures which the Founder of the Church has left in heritage to the society which He established. This assuredly was the reason why the Fathers of the Church confidently asserted that perpetual virginity is a very noble gift which the Christian religion has bestowed on the world. They rightly noted that the pagans of antiquity imposed this way of life on the Vestals only for a certain time;[1] and that, although in the Old Testament virginity is ordered to be kept and preserved, it is only a previous requisite for marriage;[2] and furthermore, as Ambrose writes,[3] "We read that also in the temple of Jerusalem there were virgins. But what does the Apostle say? 'Now all these things happened to them in figure',[4] that this might be a foreshadowing of what was to come."[5]

When Pope Pius XII decided to reaffirm the importance of virginity by issuing the encyclical *Sacra virginitas* in 1954, he turned to the early Church Fathers to underline the unique status of Christian virginity. The Pope, following Ambrose and other predecessors, cast the Roman Vestal virgins as fitting antagonists to the perpetually virginal Christian virgins. The Vestals might, he indicates, have functioned as foreshadowers of the coming of Christian virgins but, according to the Pope, they had only had this way of life "imposed" on them for a certain time. They could therefore, according to Pius XII, gracefully exit the stage, having played their part in the drama leading to the victory of Christianity.

In hindsight, it is tempting to ask what actually made virgins such apt candidates for "the service of God" in Late Antiquity? Late fourth-century Christian theologians' persistent appraisal of sacred virgins constantly evokes a wide variety of virgins that often challenged the stereotypically young, unmarried female virgin. Other textual sources from the period also abound with more or less seemingly paradoxical virgins. In addition to the rather evidently liminal "virgin brides," the Greek and Latin material from the period provide us with married virgins, virgin widows, virgin mothers, virgin martyrs, slave virgins, old virgins, aristocratic virgins, divine virgins, heretic virgins, pagan virgins, gender-bending virgins, male virgins, false virgins, and fallen virgins. By examining these kinds of "borderline virgins" as they appear in a range of textual sources from different genres, and how they again relate to contemporary "stereotype" virgins, this book offers new approaches to the understanding of how fourth-century notions of "sacred virginity" were construed and negotiated in the Latin West of Late Antiquity.

Virginity was indeed a "hot topic" in Late Antiquity,[6] as it has also been in the prolific academic field of Late Antiquity studies over the last three to four decades. One significant and culturally prominent group of Late Antiquity's sacred virgins, the Roman Vestal virgins, has however largely been relegated to the margins of the discussions, both by late antique Christian writers, as well as in contemporary virgin studies. As "proximate others" and part of the common cultural complex that the Christian virgin discourses intersected with, this book argues that virgins such as the Vestals, as well as other contemporary "borderline virgins" that continued to challenge and shape ongoing definitions of what qualified as (sacred) virginity, ought to be more fully acknowledged in studies of virginity in Late Antiquity.

To the extent that Vestal and pagan virgins have been discussed in previous studies, the general tendency in modern scholarship has been to highlight differences between the valuation of sacred virginity among pagans on the one hand and Christians on the other, pointing out that Christian ideals of virginity, which were closely linked to the development of ascetic movements in this period, were part of the innovative, subversive character of early Christianity. These traits were considered specifically "Christian," and institutionalized during the fourth century, as Christianity changed its position from minority group to state religion. According to Pope Pius XII's encyclica, Christian valuation of holy or sacred virginity was something radically different from anything the world had seen prior to Christianity, it was "a very noble gift bestowed on the world" – a mark of the non-comparable and unique status of this new religion. To some extent, this statement accords with the conclusions of a number of scholars who, following Michel Foucault, Peter Brown and now recently Kyle Harper, see the patristic period as representing "the parting of the waters,"[7] the prequel to an epistemic break that laid the foundation for Europe's subsequent history of sexuality. As argued by Kyle Harper, "[…] the transition from a late classical to a Christian sexual morality marked a paradigm shift, a quantum leap to a new foundational logic of sexual ethics, in which the cosmos replaced the city as the framework of morality."[8]

This book does by no means deny the substantial changes brought by Christianity. However, to the extent that scholars have paid attention to "pre-Christian" notions of virginity in the history of sexuality, pre-Christian conceptions and valuations have very often been linked to an understanding of pagan virginity as purely "physical." Although this simplistic notion has indeed been challenged in some recent studies, the Christian cult/ideology of virginity, it is implied, went beyond this purely physical understanding of virginity, and belonged to a spiritual capacity the Romans were commonly supposed to have lacked.

This study's objective is therefore to more thoroughly examine different conceptions of virginity that prevailed and were under continuous construction in Rome and the Latin world in Late Antiquity. Seeing that the polemics of the Church Fathers against the virgins of the pagans reverberates through many of these implicit and explicit comparisons between what is, for the lack of better terminology, here called pagan and Christian virginity, a new look at these virginities and how they were constantly molded, construed and reconstrued against socio-cultural discourses and contexts is called for. These (re-) constructions, it is argued, in turn also became part of the notions of some kind of specific sanctity embodied by consecrated virgins, who, by the middle of the fifth century, we may assume all self-identified as Christians. Thus, in this perspective, "Roman virginity" serves in this study as an overarching category and context that encompassed both sacred and secular as well as Vestal and Christian virgins. In order to understand why sacred virgins and their sacred virginity came to be so esteemed in Late Antiquity, it is necessary to further explore the social and cultural construction of these "Roman virginities." A new way to do so, I argue, is to look for the virgins at the very margins of virginity; the borderline virgins. These virgins are to be found in authoritative theological texts as well as in the fragments of epigraphic material, in poetry and in other literary sources alongside art and archaeological remains. By foregrounding these borderline virgins and the explicit and implicit negotiations over their status as virgins, some of the cultural intersections and hybridizations of the late antique "cult of virginity" will appear more clearly.

The starting point, or indeed the premise, of this study is the fact that the Latin Church Fathers themselves compared Christian and Vestal virgins. Their apologetic efforts to demarcate an exclusively Christian virginity in contrast to the "false virgins" of their contemporary non-Christian co-citizens, highlights tensions that were caused by the ongoing Christian demarcations of "us" versus "them." These tensions have played a larger role in the construction of a specifically Christian sacred virginity than many previous studies have acknowledged. From this comparative starting point, theoretically based in Jonathan Z. Smith's models and "maps," I will proceed to explore how social status, religious ideology and practice, age and gender came to have significance in the conceptions of how virginity was defined in fourth-century Rome. Finally, I will discuss so-called "fallen virgins," those who had allegedly crossed the lines of demarcation, to examine the vocabulary and rhetoric of proposed and effectuated sanctions of such transgressions.

This study's focus on the co-existence of pagans and Christians in the city of Rome in Late Antiquity allows for a socio-cultural approach that discloses how pagans and Christians were joined by common conceptual frames and shared values. This has, for quite a while now, been the dominant approach in studies of Late Antiquity. One delimitation that will soon become rather obvious is the marginalized role Mary, the mother of Jesus, plays in this study. Considering the increasing importance her virginity came to have in Christological debates, Mary's virginity certainly resonated in the ideology that developed around Christian consecrated virgins in the fourth century. Mary was indeed presented as a role model the earthly virgins should try to imitate. The imagery that was used to describe Mary and her sanctity was thus conferred to the consecrated virgins (and also vice versa).[9] The intricate web of divine/superhuman virgins, parthenogenesis, virginal "fertility" and virgin mothers is not only heavily laden with religious ideology but also amply explored from various sides in later Christian theologies.[10] Images of pagan virgin goddesses played an equally important role in the construction of categories of sacred human virgins. The Vestals, for instance, were named after the virgin goddess they were consecrated to serve, and their virginity was said to be in imitation and honor of hers.[11] However, this relationship between imitation and inspiration is one that becomes very complex when the whole firmament of divine and canonized virgins are drawn into the intertextual analysis. These divine and canonized virgins' comparatively rare appearances in the following pages are therefore not due to a dismissive assessment of their role in this process, but to a need to delimit the range of the present study.

Most studies of the early Christian and late antique ideal of virginity have dealt with the ascetic context for its emergence, practice and later institutionalization. Although early Christian asceticism is not treated as extensively and explicitly in the present study as might be expected, it must be clarified that this omission by no means stems from intentions to diminish the importance of this trend in Roman Christianity in the fourth century. The aim of this present study is, however, to shift the focus away from asceticism in order to bring in new perspectives that may supplement and further complicate the picture of Late Antique religious life and virginity as expressions of religiosity. This is done not by replacing, but by adding to the previously dominant approach, where asceticism often has been the main, if not the only, model to understand the period's ardent interest in virginity.

A critical analysis of the complex construction of Late Antiquity's "virgin ideologies" demands a recognition of the social perspective alongside (and as part of) the literary character of the sources.[12] Information regarding class, gender and age will thus (when available) be considered as well as (contesting) ideologies and means of imposing these through rhetoric. Different texts may elucidate struggles for authoritative power to define norms, and these norms may variously reflect concerns regarding social interaction. It is my contention that the inclusion of other textual genres, such as epigraphic material, will better reflect polyphony across a wider span of social classes rather than what initially appears as the univocal, normative stance of the orthodox Fathers. They too, as we will see, often happened to promote quite different kinds of virginities. In this manner, we are presented with an even more complex image of how "the virgin" and her potential for sanctity could be conceived in Late Antiquity.

Defining virginity

Studies of virgins and virginity in Antiquity and Late Antiquity can roughly be divided in two types: those that take "virgin" to be a given and self-evident category, and those that do not. Recent scholarship has tended to favor the second approach, in which the focus becomes the very meaning and construction of virginity as a cultural and social phenomenon and its place within this socio-cultural matrix.

As several scholars have pointed out, virginity is not simply (or even) a physiological trait, but a cultural construction that seems to be under constant evaluation and changing focus.[13] Kathleen Coyne Kelly has convincingly argued that "even at the point at which virginity seems to be most visible, most susceptible to verification, it successfully evades any conclusive confirmation."[14] The many connotations tied to the virgin and his/her intrinsic virginity are nevertheless not without some constancy, although the virgin in the end seems capable of evading any attempt to pin down an exact definition. Words like "ambiguous" and "paradoxical" recur in many studies of the role and function of virgins and virginity in religious, social and literary contexts, and it is indeed in this very multivalent and sometimes contradictory tangle of meanings that the allure of the virgin seems to be embedded. As stated by Hanne Blank, "It is precisely its relativity that makes virginity so troublesome and fascinating."[15]

In the ongoing constructions and negotiations of virginity and its value, the complex and overarching notion of "Roman virginities" thus encompasses the consecrated virgins of both pagans and Christians, making them significant contributors to this construction, at the same time as the understandings of their sacred virginities were "restricted" by already existing discourses and delimitations. By identifying this variety of different "Roman virginities," I argue that it is also easier to understand how these different virginities interconnect with various notions of a sacred virginity, embodied by the consecrated virgins that Vestals as well as Christian virgins may be said to have represented. What qualities specifically linked to virgins and their virginity made it such an attractive state? Or, to put it otherwise: What is it about the virgin that made her (and him?) so extraordinary and apt for a holiness that was not attainable by others? In answering these questions, we also encounter others, such as: How malleable was the conception of virgins and virginity? Which characteristics attributed to virgins are highlighted in the discourses concerning sacred virgins? What kind of imagery is evoked and what semantic fields are in focus in contemporaneous texts that somehow deal with virgins and virginity? How may this imagery in turn, when related to the socio-historical context, elucidate the valuation of virgins in general and sacred virgins in particular? Lastly: What may the virgins at the very borders of virginity teach us about the value attributed to the sacred virgins' sacred virginity?

The Roman *virgo*

Virgo has often been understood as synonymous with *puella* in the sense that both terms refer to a young, unmarried female, thereby focusing on marriage as the social demarcation that would change her into a woman (*mulier*), matron (*matrona*) or mother (*mater*). In this understanding, it is not the sexual experience of the girl that defines her, but her social status as not yet married.[16] We find examples of these kinds of definitions in Servius, whose fourth-century commentaries on Vergil offer a range of different attempts to explain and define words from the Latin vocabulary. Symptomatic of his comments regarding virgins and virginity is that they occur in contexts where the explicit aim is to explain the writings of Vergil. The logic of every particular passage, as well as different views on the matter relevant to the Vergilian passage in question, is thus to be preferred over one single coherent definition of any term. The size of Servius' text should also be taken into consideration, as his definitions rendered below appear in very different books and contexts. Commenting upon Vergil's depiction of *Minerva innupta*, for instance, Servius claims that *innupta* refers to she who never marries, while a *virgo* can marry.[17] However, this distinction is not consistent and we see that *innupta* often functions as synonymous with *virgo* both in Servius' own writings and elsewhere. In his commentary to the eleventh book, for instance, Servius attempts to explain why Camilla, who earlier in Vergil's text had been explicitly said to be a virgin, after a killing frenzy is represented as killing "with the weapons of women," (*muliebribus armis*). Servius therefore provides the following definition:

> It is established usage that we call unmarried (*innuptae*) *virgines*, and married *mulieres*: but among our forefathers, *virgo* was not distinguished from *mulier*. Because both of them only indicate sex, note that he [Vergil] in this place says *armis muliebribus*, even though it is evident that Camilla was unmarried. Likewise, we read in the Bucolica about the "unhappy virgin" when it is clear that Persiphae had begotten offspring from Minos before she fell in love with the bull. Terentius also calls a woman *virgo* after she has given birth.[18]

In the last half of the passage, Servius thus turns the argument upside down and claims that a virgin can naturally be called a woman when a woman – even a mother – can be referred to as a virgin. Similarly, Servius provides several different definitions when he discusses the difference between *matrona* and *mater familias*, including the following, where he asserts that "others call noble virgins *matronae*, while *matresfamiliae* are those who have been married by *coemptio*."[19]

Categorizing virgins according to other groups in Roman society, whether on the basis of gender, age, or social status, seems to have posed occasional problems, not only to Servius but to other writers of the period.[20] The Latin Church Fathers, as we will see, were no less inconsistent in their definitions of *virgo*. In a quite famous passage, Tertullian had two centuries earlier argued extensively and acerbically that virgins represented a sub-category of "woman," just as "youth" was a sub-category of man.[21] Otherwise, Tertullian reasoned elsewhere, the virgin would belong to a third class, "some monstrosity with a head of its own."[22] Ambrose too, when making an exegesis on descriptions of Mary as a woman, stated: "I have said 'he was born' according to the incarnation, but 'of a woman' according to sex; womankind is the sex, virgin is the species: the sex has to do with nature, and virgin with integrity."[23] Classical law also indicates that virgins occasionally were grouped in the same category as "women." However, the very fact that they are mentioned explicitly in such contexts indicates that they were still seen as different from the general notion of "women."[24] On other occasions, it was important to emphasize this very distinction between *virgo* and *mulier*, as was done by Jerome in his treatise on the perpetual virginity of Mary:

> The vessel of election says this; he tells us that there is a difference between the woman and the virgin. Observe what the happiness of that state must be in which even the distinction of sex is lost. The virgin is no longer called a woman.[25]

A virgin, according to Jerome, is thus fundamentally different from "woman." Approaching the definition from a different angle, once again in a comment upon 1 Cor. 7, Jerome sardonically stated that "not every unmarried woman is a virgin. But every virgin is of course unmarried."[26]

Since marriage for most upper-class Roman girls, at least in theory, represented the first sexual encounter, her transition from *virgo* to *mulier* was not just a social change of status, but also perceived as a partly physical transformation. The equation between *puella* and *virgo* that earlier scholarship more or less assumed is undermined by Patricia Watson's study in which she has examined a large sample of texts showing significant differences, as well as a diachronic evolution of the term *virgo* in particular.[27] Watson demonstrates that whereas *puella* appears to describe both very young girls and young women – even young married women and the (by no means obviously virginal) mistresses of elegiac poetry – the term *virgo* has a much more narrow range of reference. According to Watson, the main denominating factors were that a *virgo* was a young, unmarried and freeborn Roman, the daughter of a citizen. She finds that a more physical understanding of *virgo* gradually came into focus. This was also reflected in texts where the term in a metaphorical sense denoted the untouched and pure, and was thus understood as almost equivalent to *purus*. From early imperial times then, the term *virgo* was almost exclusively used to emphasize that the girl in question is unmarried, in the sense *intacta*, that is, sexually "untouched."[28]

However, we should be wary of inferring that the notion of the virgin as *intacta* necessarily affirms that the Romans supported the idea of a hymen as a physical "seal" to her virginity. In her study of the Greek *parthenos*, Giulia Sissa has shown how, in the Greek perception of what virgins were, there was no such physical seal of the virginal body, in contrast to what she finds in her comparative reading of Roman material. This, according to Sissa, "suggests that in Rome, virginity evoked the image of a veil, a fabric curtain, which would explain the polemic of Soranus, a Greek who taught medicine at the turn of the second century in Rome, against the existence of the hymen."[29] Once again, it is Servius who is the main source for this aspect of the virgin's virginity or, more precisely, a text of even more obscure origin that in editions of Servius is referred to as *Servius Auctus* or *Scholia Danielis*.[30] A lengthy passage explaining the expression *pactosque hymenaeos* tells the story of how the young Athenian youth Hymenaeus came to be associated with weddings. At the end, an additional piece of information is added: "There is also another definition of this word: because hymen is said to be this kind of membrane of a virginal girl, and because this is ruptured when she stops being a virgin, weddings are said to belong to Hymenaeus."[31]

Giulia Sissa's theory of a hymenless Greek virginity has later been modified by others, particularly Ann Ellis Hanson, who has noted that the metaphors and descriptions of virgins and their loss of virginity often alluded to a cover of the uterus. According to the medical writers, other signs also clearly gave away the girl's true status in this respect. Her voice, in particular, was believed to change, in analogy with the idea that the widening of "the lower neck" was reflected in a similar change in the upper neck.[32] Although *Servius Auctus* has provided an exceptional description of an exclusively virginal membrane, there were, as Sissa and others have pointed out, obvious conceptions of a particularly physical token, or bodily mark, of virginity. This was not necessarily understood in terms of the hymen.[33] However, the notion that virginity could be physically detected was paralleled with the non-physical sides of virginity that had to be measured, as we will see, by other standards also. This duality of virginity, on the one hand the notions of its very bodily, physical aspect and, on the other, the more socio-cultural (or in other cases identified as spiritual) side that was located "elsewhere," is, as I will argue in the following, what creates both tension and prosperity, and in turn makes the virgin such a potent and multifaceted figure.

Virgo, *virginitas* and variations of chastity

For this and the following chapters it might be useful to distinguish between *virgo* and *virginitas*, as respectively referring to the person(s) said to be virgin(s) and to the quality, i.e. *virginitas*, that such *virgines* are said to possess and somewhat personify or embody. Although this distinction may appear to be artificial, there were, as we will see, some important differences in how the two terms were applied. A pertinent question in that regard is whether a virgin indeed could ever really be distinguished from her virginity. Further, could virginity as a concept actually work separated from the virgins that embodied it? These were questions that seem to underlie many of the discourses of virginity that we encounter in this period, resounding with a particular weight in metaphorical and metaphysical discourses. By exploring some of the norms set up to define and regulate "real" physical virgins and their virginity, we may get a little bit closer to why this came to bear such significance for the Romans in the years before and after the 380s AD. Before we do that, however, some further distinctions need to be made.

Although the term *castitas* (chastity) often seems to substitute *virginitas*, the two terms are not interchangeable, as they do not carry identical ranges of meaning and only partly overlap. This becomes evident when one looks at how and in which contexts they were applied. Unlike *virginitas*, *castitas* does not refer to a state of total abstinence, but could also be used to describe the virtue of widows and married women who had been or were faithful to their partner. The so-called *univira* ideal, the praise and respect bestowed upon the woman who had been with one man only, was an enduring one, as documented by inscriptions as well as literary evidence.[34] Rebecca Langlands refers to Valerius Maximus, according to whom a Roman *matrona*'s mind was particularly uncorrupted (*incorruptum*) "when it did not know how to leave the bed on which her virginity had been laid down."[35] Thus, even when she no longer was a virgin, circumstances regarding her past virginity could be considered significant in defining the character of a Roman woman, distinguishing her as praiseworthy and *pudica*.

Virginity in this respect refers in essence to never having experienced sex, hence claiming present status from a lifetime perspective. In contrast, chastity or celibacy, often used interchangeably with virginity in modern scholarship, refers to the degrees of the present state of renunciation and did not necessarily include any reference to past experiences. Virginity was certainly linked to chastity, and even perceived as the epitome of *castitas*. According to Cicero, for instance, the reason the Vestals had to be virgins was that they, in addition to being able to more easily guard the fire of Vesta, "make women understand that it is possible for the female nature to endure total chastity."[36] They were, as such, living *exempla* that ought to inspire Roman matrons to chastity. Likewise, Valerius Maximus presents the exemplary chastity of the Teutonic women who, when taken captive by the Roman army, committed suicide because they were refused their wish, namely to be handed over to the Vestal virgins. The Vestal virgins and their famed virginity appear in this text as a possible shield and protection against *stuprum*, sexual violation, for these chaste Teutonic women, and the priestesses' virginity serves again as an epitome of honorable *castitas*.[37] Simply stated, the main difference between virginity and chastity would be, to rephrase Jerome, that a virgin had to be chaste to be a convincing virgin, but a woman (and a man) could of course (and according to Jerome probably even ought to) be chaste also without being a virgin.[38]

In many ways, the duality of body and mind that is expressed in the virgin ideology of Late Antiquity is similar to the duality encountered by Rebecca Langlands in her study of the Roman concept of *pudicitia*. Being a moral force, Langlands describes *pudicitia* as "a physical attribute, in direct contrast to moral sensibility, associated with purity, physical state and experience [...] and vulnerable to physical acts," in particular acts of illicit or indecent sexual character.[39] Summing up some of the multifarious aspects of *pudicitia*, Langlands writes as follows:

> It is multidimensional, appearing in the Roman sources as a deity, as core civic virtue, as psychological state, as physical state; it is associated with shame and awareness of social boundaries, with honour and bravery, with reputation, with patriotism, with self-control, with paternalistic authority over the sex lives of other people, with personal vulnerability, and with much more.[40]

In many respects, Langlands' description of *pudicitia* captures some central aspects that also belong to the multidimensional range of virginity, and to why it was valued by Romans.

Sophrosyne, the virtue of self-control that has received much attention (particularly after Veyne and Foucault's influential studies), is also relevant to many a late antique discourse on virgins.[41] Some tensions regarding hierarchical organization as to how the "ignorant" virgin's achievement should be deemed in contrast to the non-virgin's knowing renunciation becomes an occasional issue in Christian texts, tensions that will be explored in the following chapters.

Virginitas, then, is seemingly the specific qualities ascribed to a *virgo*, a young, unmarried girl, freeborn and possibly of some social standing, and who, most importantly, has never had sex. But as the subsequent discussions will show, it was nowhere near as simple as that. Virgins could be old, married and even mothers. Virgins could describe themselves as widows, or be described as such by others. They could also cohabit with men, in "chaste marriages," to which Christian controversies regarding the so-called *subintroductae* attest.[42] Literary representations allowed virgins in the world of fiction to behave against all norms and codes for gender. As recent gender studies have sought to demonstrate, (female) virgins could even "be" male. A perhaps even more interesting question, however, is whether also men could be virgins. This is a question that will be dealt with more extensively in Chapter 3 below.

As virginity for many adherents came to represent a holy way of life in the early Christian church, the semantics of virginity was explored by Christian writers, who found it to be a powerful and titillating image for the ideals claimed by the new religion. Averil Cameron has described the late fourth-century Christian discourse of virginity as one that was "worked by metaphor and paradox, and that boldly exploited the very imagery it was ostensibly denying."[43] There is no doubt that the effects of this rhetoric were momentous, yet the subversiveness of this ideology has often been overstated in recent scholarship. As Kate Cooper has argued, the often deliberate misrepresentation of women in Christian rhetoric has been taken at face value and not seen as rhetorical strategies with ideological purposes.[44] Some of the representations and imagery linked to virginity were attempts to redefine and lay exclusive claim on the virginal status, resulting in contrasting polemics that depended upon a distinction between false virgins and true virgins. According to these definitions, only true virgins could possess the true virginity that, in the end, was attainable only within the confines of the Church.[45] Negotiations over the limits of virginity versus non-virginity thus necessarily had high stakes.

Sacred virgins

A better understanding of the valuation of sacred virgins' virginity should thus be sought among general notions of virginity pertaining to any given historical and cultural context. Distinguishing sacred virgins from plain and simple "virgins," however, is not always as easily done as one might suppose. Indeed, it is in these very "blurrings of categories" that many of the borderline virginities appear.

The actual rite of consecration is perhaps the best starting point in the attempt to identify any distinctions between sacred and secular virgins. In his second century *Noctes Atticae*, Aulus Gellius thoroughly describes the procedures leading to the ceremony called *captio*, in which a Vestal was elected and became a consecrated priestess. Gellius lists several criteria that the future priestess had to fulfill: she had to be between six and ten years old,[46] both her parents had to be alive, and neither of them could be a slave or involved in "sordid business." The girl herself had to be without hearing or speech impediments, nor have any other bodily defects.[47] Several demands were made regarding the legal status of her family, and Gellius also mentions some reasons why girls betrothed or related to someone belonging to any of the other priesthoods should not be elected. According to an old law, 20 virgins fulfilling the criteria for priesthood were to be selected from the people, and the new Vestal was then decided by lot. However, Gellius explains that a different procedure was followed in his days:

> For if any man of respectable birth goes to the pontifex maximus and offers his daughter for the priesthood, provided considerations may be given to her candidacy without violating any religious requirement, the senate grants him exemption from the Papian law.[48]

Gellius explains that the name of the rite, *captio*, is derived from the pontifex literally taking the girl by the hand and leading her from the parent who had the paternal control over the girl, "as if she was taken in war" (*veluti bello capta*).[49] Gellius then quotes Fabius Pictor as his source for the formula pronounced by the pontifex maximus: "As one who fulfills the demands of the law, I take you, Amata, to be a Vestal priestess, and to perform the rites that the law prescribes for the Vestals to perform on behalf of the Roman people."[50] This part of the rite has, as demonstrated by Robin Wildfang, led many scholars to see parallels to the Roman marriage ritual, in which a *raptio* was staged where the girl was taken from her mother's lap.[51] As Wildfang points out, "to say that the rite of the captio was merely a symbolic marriage ceremony is to oversimplify."[52]

The *hieros gamos* theories that scholars have attempted to apply to the Vestal consecration rite were no doubt stimulated by the symbolic marriage that the Christian virgins enacted at their ceremony of consecration. This rite was most commonly known as *velatio*, a name derived from the veil (*velamen*) that the bishop placed on the virgin's head during the ceremony. Our best sources for this ceremony come from Ambrose. Indeed, one of his sermons, *De institutione virginis*, appears to have been originally performed at the consecration of the virgin Ambrosia in 392. Ambrose also refers to the ceremony where his sister Marcellina had been consecrated by Pope Liberius almost 40 years earlier. The part of the text in *De institutione virginis* that renders Ambrose's address for the consecration ritual is dense with nuptial imagery, as exemplified by one of the early passages:

> I ask you [Father], to protect this handmaid of yours, who has taken upon herself to serve you, to dedicate her soul and her zeal for integrity to you. I present her as a priestly sacrifice (*sacerdotali munero offero*), and I entrust her to you with paternal affection, so that you, favorable and protecting, bestow upon her your grace so that she deservedly will see the husband who awaits her in the holiest of the heavenly nuptial chambers, and hear him say: 'Come with me from Lebanon, [my] spouse, with me from Lebanon: you will pass through and pass beyond the principle of faith,' so that you will pass thorough the world and pass beyond this eternity.[53]

Whereas Gellius' rendering of the consecration formula indicates that the Vestals were "taken" to serve on behalf of the Roman people, Ambrose's passage focuses on the virgin's own individual salvation as a result of her consecration.

That the rite of consecration was essential to the virgin's status as sacred is perhaps self-evident but, particularly as regards the Christian virgins prior to the mid-fourth century, the sources that document such formal procedures are scant. Already in 1954, René Metz dismantled much of the evidence for orders of virgins prior to the fourth century, and although virgins appear in the earliest Christian sources all the way back to Paul, their specific status within the community is difficult to establish.[54] Another means to determine the virgins' sanctity is thus perhaps by looking at the terminology used to describe their status as such.

Starting with the Vestal virgins, the literary sources convey that a varied terminology was used in order to classify the members of this public priesthood. The evidence has been systematically gathered by Nina Mekacher.[55] The republican material conveys a penchant for referring to them as *sacerdos Vestae* or *sacerdos Vestalis*[56] but, from the first to the fifth century, the most common denominations were *virgo Vestalis*[57] and *virgo Vestae*.[58] Mekacher has also identified more isolated instances where Vestals in either singular or plural were referred to as *casta virgo*,[59] *sancta virgo*,[60] *virgo prisca sanctimoniae*[61] and *castissima sacerdos*,[62] to name but a few of the examples from the Latin corpus.

Notably, there are also several sources from the entire time span where merely the term *virgo* was applied to refer to one of the priestesses.[63] Of the late antique sources, we find that Symmachus quite often refers to the Vestal virgins as *sacrae virgines*.[64] They are also called *virgines sacri Vestalis antistites*, while we find Macrobius a little later referring to them as *virgines Vestales*.[65] Servius calls them *virgines Vestae*,[66] or merely *virgines*,[67] but when he writes about Rhea Silvia (Rhea Ilia), the mother of Romulus and Remus, she is said to have been a *sacerdos Vestae*, a priest of Vesta.[68]

Greek authors writing about Vestals likewise applied a varied terminology when referring to these Roman priestesses. *Hierai parthenoi*, sacred virgins, appears to be the most common term, and this is also attested in epigraphy.[69] Part of the variation is certainly due to the individual authors' personal preference, as well as rhetorical and poetic ideals and creativity. As Mekacher concludes, however, it is no coincidence that the priestesses' virginity is so prominent in the denomination, since this after all was the most important quality and prerequisite for their ritual services.[70]

Moving to Christian virgins, there is an equal variety in the vocabulary applied. Although context often elucidates whether the particular virgin was thought of as being of the sacred kind, the range of terms may of course cause confusion with other groups of sacred, non-virginal women when *virgo* is not mentioned as a specific part of the denomination. As was the case with the Vestal virgins, Christian virgins also tended to appear under the rather indistinct terminology of *virgines* or *parthenoi*, without further specification of status.[71] According to René Metz, the expression *virgines sanctae* is first to be found in the writings of Tertullian. More cautious and critical in his reading of the sources than most of his predecessors, Metz refrains from deducing that this kind of terminology necessitated some kind of consecratory rite or institutionalized "order of virgins." He also criticizes earlier studies in which terms such as *sponsa Christi*,[72] *ancilla Christi* and *membra Christo dicata*, which appear in the writings of Tertullian and Cyprian, have been understood in the sense that such terms came to bear much later, in the fourth century, when they were gradually (but not exclusively) used to indicate virgins who had undergone some kind of formal consecration. Terms such as *se Deo vovere*, *nubere Christo*, *Christo suam carnem tradere* and *Christo se dicare*, indicated, according to Metz, a private vow and no formal rite of consecration. Even in papal decretals, which did indeed distinguish between those who had gone through a formal consecration and those who remained virgins by private vow,[73] it seems that the categories might be blurred between the different types of *virgines*.

The same problems concerning terminology and dating become evident when we turn to the epigraphic material. Several questions arise such as, for instance, whether every occurrence of a *virgo* in an epitaph should be understood as necessarily indicating "consecrated virgin" or whether we can assume this only in the cases where she is specified as "*sacrata*" or "*sacra*."[74] There might also have been other words that indicated the same status, other expressions that were thought of as synonymous with *virgo sancta*, holy virgin, and the like. Earlier studies of the epigraphic material tended, for instance, to read phrases such as *famula dei/Christi* (God's/Christ's maid-servant), *ancilla dei/Christi* (God's/Christ's handmaid/female slave) and *sacrata puella* (consecrated girl) as terms that indicated that the deceased girl or woman had been a consecrated virgin.[75] To take *famula dei* as an example, there are several examples where this term was also used to describe married women.[76] In the cases where *famula dei* served as an epithet for a deceased virgin, we thus only know of her status as a virgin when this has been explicitly expressed.[77] *Ancilla dei* is another term that also appears in literary sources and that has frequently been taken as an equivalent to *virgo dei*.[78]

Occasionally, we find that several of the terms are combined in one and the same inscription, as the one recorded for the twelve-year-old Praetiosa, *puella virgo* [...] *ancilla dei et Christi*, who was buried in 401.[79] The general impression from the funerary inscriptions is that the virginal status of the girl regularly appears in addition to other expressions of religious devotion. The effect may be that an accumulation of sanctity was conveyed to the reader. To conclude, however, that the virgin in question necessarily had been a consecrated virgin is still a little far-fetched. The formality of the virgin's devotion expressed in the epitaph is impossible to assess. This lack of a fixed terminology thus leaves open the question of the "sacred status" of the virgins who in one way or another were identified as *virgo* on their epitaph.

Christian consecrated virgins are normally thought to have appeared in Rome as a result of Athanasius' sojourn and preaching in the city in the early 340s, which is considered to have inspired several Romans to take up ascetic life. Shortly after Athanasius' visit to Rome, Marcella became the first aristocratic woman to profess ascetic life.[80] From one of the letters of Jerome, we can deduce that Asella, one of the women associated with Marcella, formally became a consecrated virgin in 344.[81] According to the letters of Ambrose, we also learn that his own sister Marcellina had been consecrated in 353 by Liberius, the bishop of Rome. A secular law dated to 354 concerns so-called "sacrosanct virgins," and another given ten years later mentions sacred virgins (*sacratas virgines*).[82] Turning to the epigraphic material, we find that the first "Christian virgin" to appear in the relatively securely datable funerary inscriptions was buried in 295. However, there are several problems in interpreting this Statilia Alexandra as a consecrated virgin. The information regarding the girl's virgin status is scanty, merely stating that she died a virgin, *virgo mortua est*, 14 years old.[83] Another inscription, raised to commemorate the twelve-year-old Rufina, describes the deceased girl as a chaste virgin, "*casta virgo*."[84] Jerome, in his letter, informs us that Asella was only 10 when she was consecrated in 344.[85] If Rufina had indeed been a consecrated virgin, the fact that her epitaph is dated according to the consulate of Marcellinus and Probinus, i.e. 341, would mean that Rufina had been consecrated at least three years before Asella. Still, such conclusions rely on a series of presuppositions that the extant material by no means can univocally affirm. As the cautious René Metz advised in 1954 in his critique of Wilpert's zeal to identify consecrated virgins in funerary inscriptions:

> Mais n'oublions pas que les archéologues sont réduits à de simples conjectures en ce qui concerne la chronologie de ces inscriptions; d'autre part, le terme *virgo* à lui seul ne permet pas de conclure qu'il s'agit d'une personne qui a fait profession de virginité. [86]

Telling the consecrated virgins from the secular ones is thus perhaps less evident than one would initially presuppose.[87] Throughout the following chapters, this will therefore be one of the many themes where the negotiations of virginity and the status of virgins, sacred as well as secular (when we are indeed able to tell them apart), will be considered and further explored.

Comparative virginiology: the echo of the Church Fathers

Before proceeding, some important premises for this "comparative approach" have to be clarified. While the Roman Vestal virgins were of no primary interest to the Christian authors of the first four centuries, these writers were nevertheless the first to compare the Vestals with Christian virgins. Although the Church Fathers' representations of the Vestal virgins vary quite a lot, both according to textual genre, intended audience and contexts, some recurring *topoi* are still discernable in the corpus of Christian virgin writings.[88] One way to approach the Christian authors' representations of Vestal virgins is through the concept of "the proximate other." According to Jonathan Smith, while "the radical 'other' is merely 'other'; the proximate 'other' is problematic, and hence, of supreme interest."[89] In other words, the ones that are radically and obviously different represent no threat. The proximate others, however, do, and are therefore also important as the "other" in group processes of identification. As Smith points out, in religious discourse, shaping a theory of difference *vis-à-vis* the "proximate other" is first and foremost a way to "phrase a theory of 'self'."[90] By this, he clarifies that less than an interest in "the proximate other," what is at stake is actually the construction of identity by means of boundary marking against these proximate others.

Approaching the Church Fathers' references to Vestal virgins from this perspective, we see that their explicit and implicit comparisons with "their own virgins" (*virgines nostrae*)[91] are not just polemical. At least in the cases of Jerome and Tertullian, Vestal virgins and other chaste pagans are presented in a more favorable light as, in fact, examples of chastity, functioning as what Elizabeth Clark has called "shaming devices."[92] In these cases, the audience is likely to be fellow Christians who are sceptic towards, or even opposing, ascetic ideology.[93]

In the apologetic and more polemical texts, however, the authors draw upon various strategies to "devirginize" the Vestals and other famous virgins of pagan history and myth. The Vestals are here presented as the antagonists, indeed the absolute opposite, of Christian virgins. The most notable of these polemical attacks are found in the writings of Ambrose, and the arguments here are even further intensified in Prudentius' long poem *Against Symmachus*, where he explicitly compared "their virgins" with "ours:"

> Our virgins too have their noble rewards: modesty, the face covered with the holy veil, honor in private while their figure is unknown to the public, feasts seldom and slight, a spirit ever temperate, a law of chastity that is discharged only with death.[94]

For the remains of the poem, Prudentius contrasts Christian with Vestal virgins, highlighting how the latter lack dedication, how they are forced into their profession by entering at an age where they cannot choose for themselves, and thus not, as he argues the Christian virgins are, dedicated virgins by their own choice.[95] He further describes how the Vestals have non-virginal minds, wantonly waiting for their period of service to end so that they can marry and, as is more than implied, live out their desires. "[...] their bodies are intact, although they cannot keep their minds intact [...]."[96] In his depictions of the Vestals, he evokes the stereotype of old, sexually voracious women as the effective antagonist to the Christian virgins.[97]

Four main *topi* are discernable in these polemical discourses, all implicitly or explicitly set up as contrasting pairs. Firstly, the Vestals are described as only serving for a limited period, in contrast to the Christian virgins' commitment for life. Secondly, the limited number of Vestal virgins (there were at all times supposed to be six appointed priestesses at the temple) is compared with what is described as a multitude of Christian virgins. Thirdly, and the perhaps most enduring contrast in terms of its *nachleben*, regards the Vestal virgins' forced service versus the Christian virgins' free choice. Finally, the comparisons contrast the moral characters of the respective groups of virgins, depicting the Vestals as greedy, bloodthirsty and wanton, compared with the altruistic, compassionate and in all manners chaste and virginal Christian virgins.[98] By means of these dichotomies, the admirable character of the Christian virgins is all the more highlighted by the unvirginal character and conduct attributed to the Vestals. Ultimately, however, the demarcations drawn in these written depictions of the Vestal virgins marks some of the distinctions between true and false virginity and, by analogy, between true and false religion.

Interestingly, the Church Fathers' rhetorical comparisons have in many respects shaped later receptions as well as studies of Vestal and Christian virginity. First and foremost, there is the very comparison itself. By linking Vestals to Christian virgins, these texts by Ambrose, Jerome and other Christian authors seem to have established a pattern that has proven hard to break, and the two kinds of "sacred virgins" inevitably became conceptually intertwined. Second, later use of the texts by Ambrose, Jerome and their peers as empirical source material – as objective depictions of the Vestals rather than as rhetorical constructions – has strongly influenced later representations of the Vestals. The versions presented by the Fathers have often been given authoritative status. As a result, divergent sources were disregarded or interpreted to "fit" with the patristic texts. Scholars have similarly read these "descriptions" into modern theoretical frameworks, thereby giving the impression that the arguments presented by the Fathers were "factual" rather than rhetorical. A continuity motif was found in the notions that certain pagan practices prefigured Christian virtues, which in turn underline the superiority of Christianity as ultimately demonstrated by its "victory" over paganism.[99] On the other hand, the construction of Christianity as "unique" still demanded a demarcation from the kind of conduct and institutions that might be understood as analogous, or "too-much-like-us."[100]

I will here only dwell on a few examples, simply in order to lay the ground for and legitimize my own approach.[101] Peter Brown, for instance, has contrasted pagan virgin priestesses with Christian virgins in his influential study *The Body and Society*. In order to account for as many aspects of the comparison as possible, I quote at length:

> The chastity of the many virgin priestesses was not a matter of free choice for them. No heroic freedom of the individual will was made plain by their decision not to marry. The city recruited its virgins by dedicating them to the service of the gods. Many virgin priestesses, such as the Vestals at Rome, were free to marry later in life. What had mattered, in their case, was an elaborately contrived suspension of the normal process, by which a girl moved with little interruption from puberty to child-bearing. By not marrying until they were thirty, the Vestal Virgins stood out as glaring anomalies. They were the exceptions that enforced the rule. The presence in some cities of a handful of young girls, chosen by others to forgo marriage, heightened the awareness of all contemporaries that marriage and childbirth were the unquestioned destiny of all other women.[102]

Brown refers to the familiar *topos* of free choice versus forced service.[103] By describing the Vestals as anomalies in Roman society, Brown imposes a very sociological, indeed statistical, interpretation that largely deprives the Vestals of their religious function and all-significant context. The effect is the same in the significant study by Aline Rousselle, who claims that the understanding of asceticism in Late Antiquity is best understood when one looks at "everyday heterosexual relationships between ordinary people of the time," and not "the exceptional behavior of people like the Vestal virgins or a few pagan priests."[104] As Rousselle and Brown both respond to Foucault's project, which likewise had ethics as its prime focus, both give priority to philosophical and medical trends in their respective studies of Christian responses to the body and sexual ethics in Late Antiquity, following the pattern set by Foucault.[105] Nevertheless, their near exclusion of pagan religious valuation of virginity, only explained almost in passing with reference to social norms, becomes remarkable, since the Christian sources they examine so explicitly provide religious/ideological explanations for the Christian ideal of chastity. In this manner, they reflect attitudes that affirm Christian claims of "difference" and subversiveness, and overlook some of the more elitist tendencies in Christian discourses on chastity ideals.

Jo Ann McNamara also cites the limited number, lack of free choice and limited time of service as the main differences between Vestal and Christian virgins. She furthermore alludes to the Vestals' potential for lapsing, which implicitly becomes another distinctive feature in her contrast between Christian and pagan virgins:

> But there were only six of them [the Vestal virgins] at any given time and they were vowed to their posts by their fathers before reaching puberty. They were not volunteers and were not always faithful to their trust. Domitian condemned two Vestals to death at about the same time that he was persecuting both Christians and the followers of Isis. Moreover, after serving thirty years, they were pensioned off and could marry if they wished.[106]

The *topos* of free choice is indeed the most recurring, and to be found even in Robin Lane Fox's otherwise nuanced and thorough chapter on Christian virgins and ideals of virginity:

> Whereas Vestal Virgins were an order, defined by symbolic dress and legal rights and duties, Christian virgins were individual volunteers. Their status was their own choice, not an allotment in childhood.[107]

Maurice Testard actually lists all the three main "factual" differences known from the polemics of the Church Fathers: the difference of numbers, free will and limited time span. In addition he stresses the opposition between the Vestals' luxury and greed with the altruism of the Christian ascetics of Rome, a more moralizing tone of contrast that we recognize from Ambrose and Prudentius' descriptions. Testard also highlights "love" as a demarcation, adding to the virtues of the Christian virgins their ardent love for their spiritual husband:

> Les vestales jouissaient de privilèges et d'avantages financiers, alors que les dames de l'Aventin de dépouillaient de leurs biens en faveur des pauvres obéissant à la parole du Christ au jeune homme riche: 'Va, vends tes biens, donne-les aux pauvres, tu auras un trésor dans les cieux, puis viens et suis-moi'. Enfin et surtout, les vestales, désignées par le sort, n'avaient pas librement choisi leur vie et, après trente années de service, vers trente-six ans au plus tôt, elles pouvaient renoncer au célibat et se marier. Les dames de l'Aventin et leurs semblables, tout au contraire, avaient fait le libre choix de leur consécration à Dieu et ne concevaient cette consécration que comme définitive, en vertu de cet amour irrévocable que l'on appelait, dès cette époque, des "noces spirituelles", pour des femmes que Tertullien avait déjà évoquées comme des épouses du Christ.[108]

The free choice, stressed by the Fathers as a *sine qua non* of true Christian virginity, has, in particular by feminist theologians, been interpreted to indicate that celibate life was an option open to all early Christian women, chosen as a protest against and liberation from Greco-Roman gender hierarchies and social roles. According to Aline Rousselle, "In the ancient Mediterranean world there was no room for choice: a woman did not choose celibacy, she did not choose marriage, and she did not choose remarriage after widowhood."[109]

The idea that Christian valuation of chastity and virginity opened positive avenues of autonomy for early Christian women, bringing a significant change to the existing restrictions on women's range and freedom of action, has now been questioned. Such reconstructions of the autonomy of early Christian women and the notion of equality between the sexes in "the Jesus movement" cannot be understood without referring to the contemporary feminist agenda that initiated these reconstructions. As the cultural turn has permeated Late Antiquity studies, earlier claims founded on the notions of experience and moti- vation are now revised, due to acknowledgement that such issues have little basis in the extant source material.[110] Earlier feminist scholars' attention to free choice is thereby restricted as later research has analyzed the actual restrictions on women's agency in these matters.[111] Although by no means denying that some of these *topoi* stressed in the polemics of the Church Fathers can refer to the "real worlds" of Vestal and Christian virgins, I will also argue that these texts have set up a framework for later comparisons between these two kinds of consecrated virgins. The very attention to these topoi, and their implicit value judgements, will thus in turn open up new approaches that may both bring nuance and clarify many misunderstandings about Vestal virgins that have spilled on to research on the late antique virgin ideal. I will by no means claim to be myself disentangled from this cognitive web of differences and similarities imposed by the Church Fathers' initial comparisons. Many of the restrictions on our under- standing of the position the Vestal virgins and other pagan virgins had in religious cults are no doubt due to the state of the available sources. The historian cannot choose to be too picky, either. As stated, however, a contextualization of the Church Fathers' comparisons and the subsequent *Nachleben* of these comparisons and the intricate ideological meanings they carry,[112] have to be acknowledged before any new attempt to do a comparative virginiology of Late Antiquity.

Fixity, flexity and fluidity

The various strategies to define and describe "true virginity" testify to a widespread rhetorical creativity in the attempts to convey ideals and values attached to virginity. According to Kathleen Coyne Kelly, virginity, as both signi- fier and signified, is shifting and fluid, and this is what makes it a polyvalent and polymorph symbol:

> Just why virginity serves as such a crucial hinge, generating so many signi- fiers in one direction and signifieds in the other, is a complicated question,

and one that may be answered according to the logic of more than one critical paradigm.[113]

What Kelly calls the "crucial hinge," and maybe the reason it serves as such a powerful symbol, is, however, perhaps to be found not in "fixity" as such, but in the constant "desire" for fixity, creating a span between fixity and flexity in which there is a powerful tension between the two. It is within this span that the value of virginity thus becomes constantly negotiated and constructed.

Taking the individual virgin herself as the "signifier," the scope immediately narrows. The relationship between "virgins" and "virginity" has not been considered much in detail in earlier research. The difference will perhaps be more evident when seen in terms of flexity and fixity, where *virginitas*, as an abstraction, clearly represents the most flexible and adaptable concept of the two, whereas *virgo* is the individual person or personification who incarnates the very physical, bodily fixity of *virginitas* and everything virginal. It is my contention that the concept of *virginitas*, as the specific quality possessed by a virgin, gains flexibility through usage. This process, most evident in Late Antiquity, is however always at the potential cost of a departure from fixity, which in turn may compromise its exclusivity and unique value. As Kathleen Coyne Kelly has pointed out, "the many attempts to fix virginity in/on the body are inevitably compromised by recourse to metaphors and metonyms – tropes that make visible not only virginity's construed character, but its gendered and heterosexualized nature as well."[114] Still, in contrast to the *virgo*, who is very much defined by her body (but by no means only so), virginity (i.e., *virginitas, parthenia*), by its very flexity, becomes able to appear and give meaning to discourses where virgins, although always lurking in the background with their "fixity," cannot function in the same manner.[115] It is in this very landscape of "flexity" or potential for elasticity that I will argue that we encounter the "borderline virgins," verging at the point of "rupture," stretching the limits of virginity's socio/cultural/physical fixity.

As regards the terminology, I prefer "flexity" to the generally more favored "fluidity," for the following reasons: "Flexity" indicates something that is flexible in relation to what is "fixed," a situation where the "fixed," despite its alleged character of being immutable, remains changeable and may become something seemingly different from its original position of fixity, or perceived relation to a physical entity or locus. Between "flexity" and "fixity" there is therefore constant tension, caused by external powers inducing deviation in one direction or the other. Fluidity, on the other hand, may, in my understanding of the term, indicate a different relation to its "fixity," in that there is no necessary tension striving to return to the fixed state. In my understanding of the term "fluidity," the forces that cause metamorphosis appear to be something inherent, in that the process seems to operate in itself rather than because of external forces.[116] "Flexity" thus better encapsulates the molding and construction of the virgin and her/his virginity that goes on in relation to the surrounding social and cultural context. When applied to rhetoric and metaphors, my application of the terms "fixity" and "flexity" thus refers to the creative process where authors and/or readers/listeners are able to extend the meaning of a concept without it losing its "core" meaning. The constant correlation between "fixity" and "flexity" comes into focus in a manner that more common terminology of ambiguity or relativity may not grasp with the same accuracy. Virginity is to this extent a very adaptable example, as its "fixity" is so often conceived as very material, in the sense that it is seen as inextricably attached to a bodily "virgin." The symbolic and metaphorical language surrounding the concept nevertheless becomes extremely rich, demonstrating the potential for "flexity" and the eventual unwillingness for definite "fixity."

Another aspect that escapes the terminology of fluidity is the notion that, however "flexible," this flexity is only extendable to a certain point, upon which it may either spring back (or be forced back) to the original "fixed" position, or simply burst, in which case it becomes devoid of meaning. Depending on the necessity of fixity for meaning in any given discourse, this point may vary. Throughout the following chapters I will explore the notions of flexity and fixity of virginity and test virginity's limits of "extension," that is, the different stages or locations where we may be able to discern this very point of "bursting," that is, the "fringes," of borderlines and borderline crossings of Roman "virginitas." In other words, what I will try to identify by this approach are the discourses concerning what a virgin and her/his virginity is by examining the parts of such discourses where the issue is the limits of virginity and the various points where it becomes non-virgin and non-virginity.

My approach is inspired by Denise Kimber Buell, who has employed the terms flexity and fixity in her analyses of understandings of race in early Christianity. Buell refers to Ann Stoler, who has pointed out that narratives that depicted race as initially invested with "fixity" were rooted in biological models of race that assumed some notion of "immutability."[117] This notion of the biological as something "fixed" is perhaps even more clearly expressed when it comes to the virgin. The notion of "hymen," a kind of physical demarcation of virginity to be identified in a virgin, is a conception that, as discussed above, apparently first became explicitly expressed in our written sources from the second and fourth centuries.[118] Whether the notion might have preceded these textual "evidences" remains outside the scope of this study, but the idea of a hymen as a physical "seal" that marks a virgin is at least attested in the period of particular concern here. What is perhaps most note-worthy in this context is the fact that the first known mention of the hymen was only in order to deny its existence (and this was by a medical writer with expertise in gynecology), thus underlining the very instability and uncertainty (or, to keep up the terminology, "flexity") that surrounded the notion of virginity in Antiquity. A desire to "fix" virginity, to make it a concrete and tangible "locus"[119] in the female body, thus marking the enclosed area that is only opened by (sexual) penetration, became increasingly evident as the growing religious significance of virgins made it necessary to verify virginity or the lack thereof. At the same time, this very esteem of virginity – and particularly the soteriological function it came to bear in subsequent Christianity, also for the individual – seems to have created the need for a more elastic concept that made it desirable to also include virgins who were not necessarily defined by this "fixity."[120] This constant oscillation between a "metaphorical" and very "physical" virginity, a distinction that is often impossible to determine due to the array of interpretational possibilities, not to mention all the possible readings and meanings in between these extreme dichotomies, is what I aim to grasp by applying the terms fixity and flexity. In this respect, fixity and flexity may on one level respectively correspond to "bodily" and "spiritual" aspects that were highly important in defining virginity,[121] yet with remarkable differences in the stress laid on them, both by different Church Fathers and in different contexts. To be more specific, fixity and flexity can revolve around sex/gender as one of several issues where the "embodiment of virginity" becomes explicit. To narrow it down then, the question is whether there could be, in the perception of Late Antique Romans, such a thing as a bodiless virginity, that is, virginity existing without being attached to a physical body, and whether this question was first to be raised by Christians or whether it may contain reflections of a wider, cross-cultural and inter-religious concern.

Borderline virginities

Each of the three main sections in this book will discuss different aspects of virginity where these tensions between flexity and fixity are particularly prominent, and where different strategies are applied in order to pin down how "real" and "true" virginity is determined. As already stressed above, virginity is never merely a physical trait or condition, although this certainly is an important aspect of it. However, virginity is evidently just as much tied to cultural and social values, to notions of gender and, by extension, to power and ideology. So inextricably linked to all these aspects mentioned, it also became, in Late Antiquity, an extremely poignant expression of ideas of holiness and sanctity. Thus, in addition to the comparative perspective that attempts to embrace two main categories of sacred virgins in Rome in Late Antiquity, the main concern in this study – the one that eventually ties the different approaches of the different chapters together – is the attempt to identify some of the negotiations at work both at the "core" and at the very fringes of what was understood to be virginity to Latin-speaking Romans in this period. In other words, the task is to identify not only what virginity "was," according to the writers in this period, but also how virginity was identified by what it was not, and where the lines were drawn between the two.

In the second part, I intend to focus on the social context for valuation of virginity. I will look at what might be called the "social dimension" of virginity, that is, the common social context in which I argue that the ideas of Christian and non-Christian (i.e., traditional Roman) consecrated virginity coexisted and also "interacted" within the last half of the fourth century. Arguing that sacred virginity is to be understood in relation to general ideas about virginity and the social position and role of virgins, I will discuss some socially important aspects of virginity that attributed to the elevated and sacred status of the consecrated virgin in Rome in this period – aspects that were at least partially independent of religious affiliation. The material is still largely provided by the so-called Church Fathers, but these texts will now be read together with other types of sources, such as pagan writers (classical as well as contemporaneous), epigraphy and law, in order to outline how virgins were socially and culturally defined in this period. A more socio-cultural perspective will therefore dominate this section. The "virgin" will be approached as a socially and biologically/physically conceived category, and the aim is to examine how the Christian concept of sacred virginity on the one hand was confined by an already existing cultural construction and how some Christian writers on the other hand attempted to develop and expand this construction in their own exegetical and normative writings.

Considering the almost overwhelming interest in female virgins' supposed gender-reversal or gender-ambiguity, as well as several studies on eunuchs that have appeared in recent years, the "male virgin" is surprisingly understudied. As general consensus seems to presuppose that the Christian ideal of virginity applied to men as well as women, and that this partially constituted the decisive change in sexual ethics said to be introduced with Christianity (although variously conceded to be part of a more general trend in Late Antiquity), a more thorough search for male virgins in Christian texts written in Latin in this period will be illuminating. The relationship between virginity as a general ideal and the individual (as well as the symbolic) virgin embodying this ideal will thus appear more complex when perceived through gender as the disturbing lens. The topic for the third chapter is therefore the gender of virgins. However, in contrast to earlier studies' interest in female virgins "becoming male," this chapter will concentrate on the seemingly borderline figure of the male virgin. For this part, my methodological approach will rely on gender-perspectives that particularly focus on the world of ideas, yet not without attempts to glimpse how these ideas were reflected in the "real" world. This is once again done with reference to epigraphic material that may provide means by which to grasp the way relatives and patrons fashioned and understood their deceased beloved ones in accordance with the universal and seemingly genderless Christian ideals of virginity. The lack of studies on male virgins certainly reflects a scarcity of such virgins in the Latin sources and, although they are attested in the sources (however marginal they may appear in comparison with the female virgins), this scarcity nevertheless complicates the concept of virginity as the universal ideal that the Church Fathers undeniably desired it to be. The question, when related to flexity and fixity, is thus whether the notion of a male virgin represented the very bursting point of flexity. Could the notion of *virgo* ever be extended as to also include men?

The fourth chapter provides a discussion of perhaps the most significant demarcation line, namely consecrated virgins' loss of virginity. Again we return to the distinction between "true" and "false" virgins, yet from a different angle than in the previous chapters. Anxiety concerning how one could actually decide whether virginity was present or absent in a girl reflects a desire to fixate what always seemed to evade fixation. In Chapter Four, I will therefore examine some of the different strategies developed in order to identify and deal with so-called fallen virgins, strategies that reveal the religious and social value that was attached to the virginity of these girls. As in Chapter Two, this last chapter will rely on an "intertextual" reading of a variety of texts in which I seek to establish some aspects of the religious/social/cultural context where these negotiations around the fixity and flexity of virginity were particularly crucial, demonstrating not only the difficulty of establishing firm limits, but also the severe and devastating consequences that transgressions of these limits were believed to cause. The problem of determining virginity thus becomes, even at the point where its fixity is thought to be most tangible, seemingly unattainable in the eyes of some of the Christian writers. Like the near impossibility of spiritual virginity, only achievable through the grace of God, and yet so extremely fragile in the human realm, physical virginity likewise turns out to be beyond firm proof. The consequences of these lines of thought would in turn imply that virginity was almost impossible to maintain.[122]

The notion of borderline virginities is indeed inspired by the very ground-breaking work that has been done in the field of Late Antiquity studies over the last four decades. Daniel Boyarin's study *Border lines* will perhaps be the most evident reference,[123] but also, certainly, scholars such as Judith Lieu, Denise Kimber Buell, Elizabeth Clark, Peter Brown, Mary Beard, Jonathan Z. Smith, Virginia Burrus and many, many others who will hopefully be duly credited as the chapters proceed. By relying on these models of shifting and porous border lines, of the discursive constructions and indeed the very hybridity and dynamics caused by the encounters by the many intersecting group identities within (and outside of) the Roman empire in Late Antiquity, we may also identify some hitherto neglected virginities and their importance for Late Antique virgin discourses. In this landscape, the borders are by no means fixed, although many desired them to be so. It is the very negotiations over these borders that may help us better understand what was at stake.[124]

By examining contemporary discourses on how to verify or negate a virgin's virginity, alongside regulations regarding punishment for so-called fallen virgins, I wish to explore some of the tensions arising in the negotiations between closure and openness, indeed – between fixity and flexity – as found in representations of sacred and secular virginity as they were conveyed in historical sources from the Western Roman Empire of Late Antiquity.

Notes

1 Cf. S. Ambros., *De virginibus*, lib. I, c. 4, n. 15; *De virginitate*, c. 3, n. 13; PL XVI, 193, 269.
2 Cf. Ex. XXII, 16–17; Deut. XXII, 23–9; Eccli. XLII, 9.
3 S. Ambros., *De virginibus*, lib. I, c. 3, n. 12; PL XVI, 192.
4 I Cor. X, 11.
5 Introduction to *Sacra Virginitas*, encyclica of Pope Pius XII, 1954. All the four notes above belong to the original document.
6 Goldhill 1995: 2.
7 Foucault 1985, cf. Boyarin and Castelli 2001: 359.
8 Harper 2013: 8.
9 Cameron 1989: 190–2, Cooper 2007, Hunter 2007: 187–8 and passim, Undheim 2012, Lillis 2016.
10 For an overview, see Warner 2000: 34–49.
11 Ov. *Fast*. 6. 283–94.
12 For the literariness of the sources, see Clark 1998a, Clark 1998b, Clark 2004a.
13 E.g. Hastrup 1981, Sissa 1990, Kelly and Leslie 1999, Kelly 2000, Foskett 2002, McInerney 2003, Bernau 2007, Blank 2007, Lillis 2016. The opposite strand is perhaps most dominant in studies of the Vestals, e.g. Staples 1998: 138, Wildfang 2006: 53.
14 Kelly 2000: ix.
15 Blank 2007: 6.
16 In Protestant parts of the world, this equation between *puella* and *virgo*, as well as equivalent terms in Hebrew and Greek, have had obvious Mariological implications. This is a debate that goes all the way back to Antiquity. See, for instance, Jerome's discussions of the Hebrew *almah* from Is. 7:14 as opposed to *betulah*, in Hier. *Adv. Jov*. 1.32 and Hier. *Adv. Helv*. 4. For a recent discussion of the terminology in Greek, see Lillis 2016: 16.
17 Serv. *Ad Aen*. 2.31: *innuptae numquam nubit, nam virgo potest et nubere.*
18 Serv. *Ad Aen*. 11.687: *usus obtinuit, ut innuptas 'virgines', nuptas 'mulieres' vocemus: nam apud maiores indiscrete virgo dicebatur et mulier. utrumque enim sexum tantum significabat, ut ecce hoc loco dicit 'armis muliebribus', cum Camillam innuptam fuisse manifestum sit. item in bucolicis legimus a virgo infelix cum Pasiphaen constat ex Minoe ante amorem tauri liberos suscepisse: Terentius etiam mulierem post partum virginem vocat.* My transl.
19 Serv. *Ad Aen*. 11.476: *alii matronas virgines nobiles dicunt, matresfamilias vero illas quae in matrimonium per coemptionem convenerunt: [nam per quandam iuris solemnitatem in familiam migrant mariti.]* My transl. *Coemptio* was a specific kind of marriage arrangement where the bride was transferred to her husband's household. Consequently, her religious and legal ties to her birth family were dissolved.
20 This slipperiness of the categories then undermines the conclusions of several recent studies on the Vestal virgins, e.g. Staples 1998, Parker 2004: 567, and passim, Wildfang 2006: 53–5, Takács 2008: 81 ("In the end … the Vestal virgins defied all categories"), cf. idem 85–6. These studies have, in my opinion, relied too extensively on what is perceived as rather rigid categorizations in Roman society in order to represent Vestal virgins as either transgressing or comprising all categories.
21 Tert. *De orat*. 21–2: e.g., *Aliud sit vir et investis, si aliud est mulier et virgo.* cf. *Virg. vel*. 4ff. Clark 1999: 313, on Ambrosiaster's distinction between *mulier* and *virgo* in relation to Tertullian. The crux here was Paul's expression in 1 Cor. 7: *Divisa est mulier et virgo.*
22 Tert. *Virg. vel*. 7: *Si caput mulieris vir est, utique et virginis, de qua sit mulier illa quae nupsit: nisi si virgo, tertium genus est monstruosum aliquod sui capitis.*
23 Ambr. *Ep*. 7.18: *Factum secundum incarnationem locutus sum, ex muliere secundum sexum; mulier sexus est, virgo species: sexus generis, virgo integritatis.* Transl. Beyenka 1967: 113. Cf. Ambr. *Inst. virg*. 36–58, arguing why Mary was called *mulier* in the scriptures.

24   Dig. 34.2.25.9 *Ulpianus 44 ad sab. Muliebri veste legata et infantilem contineri et puellarum et virginum pomponius libro vicesimo secundo ad sabinum recte scribit: mulieres enim omnes dici, quaecumque sexus feminini sunt.* Dig. 50.16.13pr. *Ulpianus 7 ad ed. "mulieris" appellatione etiam virgo viripotens continetur.*

25   Hier. *Adv. Helv.* 20: *Vas electionis haec loquitur,' Divisa est', dicens, 'mulier, et virgo.' Vide quantae felicitatis sit, quae et nomen sexus amiserit. Virgo jam mulier non vocatur.* Transl. NPNF2.

26   Hier. *Adv. Jov.* 1.13: *Non omnis innupta, et virgo est. Quae autem virgo, utique et innupta est.* Transl. NPNF2.

27   Watson 1983, cf. Mitchell 1991: 220 on the significance of Vergil's preference for *virgo* over *puella* in the Aeneid.

28   Watson 1983, e.g., Cat. *Carm.* 62, Juv. *Sat.*VI.163 and Juv. *Sat.*VII.87. For the virgin as *integra*, see Ter. *Hec.* 145 and 150.

29   Sissa 1990: 175. For *parthenoi* as priestesses and cultic attendants in Greece see Dillon 2002: 75–7 and Connelly 2007: 33–41.

30   Murgia 2004: 192.

31   Serv. *Ad Aen.* 4.99: *est etiam alia ratio vocabuli: nam hymen quaedam membrana quasi virginalis puellae esse dicitur: qua rupta quia desinat esse virgo, hymenaei nuptiae dictae.* My transl. Cf. Sissa 1990: 107–8.

32   Hanson 1990: 324–30, Hanson and Armstrong 1986, cf. Martin 1995: 234–9.

33   The actual place, shape and indeed existence of such a hymen is still not settled and has received new attention with new options of hymen restoration offered by surgery. See Sissa 1990: 175–7, Blank 2007: 32–57, Bernau 2007: 4–6, Lillis 2016.

34   Treggiari 1993: 232–7 and passim.

35   Langlands 2006: 61, cf. 127–8. I am quoting her translation of the passage from Val. Max. 2.1.3: *qui depositae virginitatis cubile in publicum egredi nesciret.*

36   Cic. *Leg.* II.12.29: [*ei* [*Vestae*] *colendae virgines praesint, ut adviligetur facilius ad custodiam ignis et*] *sentiant mulieres in illis naturam feminarum omnem castitatem pati.* My transl.

37   Val. Max. VI.1 ext. III, cf. Langlands 2006: 141. For the expression "*facere cum virginia (-o)*" as equivalent to *univira (-us)* in funerary epigraphy, see Vogel 1966 and Laes 2013.

38   For another clarification of the relation between *castitas* and *virginitas*, see Kelly and Leslie 1999: 16–17.

39   Langlands 2006: 32.

40   Langlands 2006: 32.

41   Kate Cooper distinguishes between *sophrosyne*, which maintained the social order, and the subversiveness of *encrateia*, continence, which in the Christian ascetic rhetoric was used precisely to disrupt this social order. Cooper 1996: 58. In *Inst.* 6.4, John Cassian distinguishes *enkrate* from *hagnon*.

42   See Clark 1977.

43   Cameron 1994: 174.

44   Cooper 1996: 3.

45   Kelly 2000: 4 and passim, cf. McInerney 2003, Brown 1988.

46   Cf. Suet. *Aug.* 31.3: *Cumque in demortuae locum aliam capi oporteret ambirentque multi ne filias in sortem darent, audiuravit, si cuiusquam neptium suarum competeret aetas, oblaturum se fuisse eam.* The age of Vestals (and Christian) virgins at the time of consecration is discussed below pp. 62–75.

47   Aul. Gell. *N.A.* 1.12.1–6.

48   Aul. Gell. *N.A.* 1.12.12: *Nam si quis honesto loco natus adeat pontificem maximum atque offerat ad sacerdotium filiam suam, cuius dumtaxat salvis religionum observationibus ratio haberi possit, gratia Papiae legis per senatum fit.* Transl. Loeb, with minor changes.

49   Serv. *Ad Aen.* 7.303: *Et sunt propria verba, quae nulla ratione mutantur, ut sacerdotes creari, virgines capi dicimus.*

50   Aul. Gell. *N.A.* 1.12.14: *sacerdotem Vestalem, quae sacra faciat quae ius siet sacerdotem Vestalem facere pro populo Romano Quiritibus, uti optima lege fuit, ita te, Amata, capio.* My transl.

51 For references, see Wildfang 2006: 37–8. cf. Stehle 1989: 149–51.
52 Wildfang 2006: 38, cf. Gallia 2015: 98–102
53 Ambr. *Inst. virg.* 107. My transl. For the role of the Song of Songs in these ceremonies, see Shuve 2016: 109–72 and Henry 1999.
54 Metz 1954, Garrido 1993: 15–34.
55 Mekacher 2006: 20–1.
56 For the use of the Roman term *sacerdos* reflecting a somewhat tentative appropriation of the Greek *hiereus*, see Beard 1990: 43–7.
57 E.g. Macr. *Sat.* 1.17.5, 3.13.11. For further references, see Mekacher 2006: 20–1.
58 E.g. Serv. *Ad Aen.* 1.273, 8.190. 10.288, 11.206. For further references, see Mekacher 2006: 20–1.
59 Arnob. 4.35.
60 Hor. *Carm.* 1.2.27.
61 Tac. *Ann.* 3.69.
62 Cic. *Dom.*144.
63 References are given in Mekacher 2006: 21, note 66. The contexts make it clear in each case that it is the Vestals that are intended.
64 Symm. *Rel.* 3.7, *Rel.* 3.11, *Rel.* 3.17, *Ep.* 9.108.
65 Symm. *Ep.* 2.36, cf. *Ep.* 9.147, Macr. *Sat.* 1.17.15, 3.13.11.
66 Serv. *Ad Aen.* 1.273, 8.190, 10.228, 11.206.
67 Serv. *Ad Aen.* 4.262, 7.153, 7.303.
68 Serv. *Ad Aen.* 1.273, 6.777.
69 IG III 1, 875–7 (rendered in the catalogue of Mekacher 2006: 199–200). For the literary references, see Mekacher 2006: 21, note 83.
70 Mekacher 2006: 21.
71 E.g. Hier. *Ep.* 22.15: *virgo nobilis esse coepisti*, 22.16: *virgo esse voluisti*.
72 See Adkin 2003: 25–6 for instances of *sponsa Christi/ sponsa Domini*.
73 Cf. e.g. note 16 in Ch. 4 below.
74 Metz 1954: 81 and 89–93, cf. Metz 50–1, Pietri 1977: 409–15, and particularly Janssens 1981: 198–210 discuss some aspects concerning how to decide this on the basis of the information given in the epitaphs. For the etymology of the terms *sacer* and *sanctus*, see Rüpke 2007: 8.
75 F g. Wilpert 1892 (upon which Pietri 1977 relies, although with some critical assessments), cf. ILCV 1703: *Leucadia / deo sacrata puella*, ILCV 1704: *Crescentia sacrata deo puellla*, ILCV 1705: *Eusebia sacra do / puella* and the only Roman listed, from S. Praxedis (hypogeo) ILCV 1706 (= ICUR I, 745): *puella virgo sacrata b. m. Alexa[ndra]* (dated as late as 449).
76 The most striking example is perhaps the dedication to Paulina, wife of one of the most prominent pagans in Rome of this period, Vettius Agorius Praetextatus, where, in one famous inscription, Paulina is described as "*famula divis*," handmaid of the gods (CIL 6.1779= ILS 1259).
77 Cf. ILCV 1710: *famula dei Reparata, sacra virgo*, ILCV 1716: *famu/la Xρί Rusticula, virgo de/uota deo*, none of these with provenance in Rome.
78 Literary sources, e.g. Hier. *Ep.* 22.24, Hier. *Ep.* 107.13, Hier. *Ep.* 130.19 (*ancilla virgo*). As becomes clear from the examples listed by Adkin 2003: 217–18, Jerome bestows this title upon a number of women, not just virgins.
79 ICUR pars prima 497: *Pri[di]e [kal.] Jun. pausabet Praetiosa annorum pu[e]lla virgo XII tantum ancilla Dei et Christi, Fl[lavio] Vincentio et Fravito v[iris] c[larissimis] consulibus.*
80 Curran 2000: 269, cf. Hier. *Ep.* 127.5.
81 Hier. *Ep.* 24.2.
82 CTh 9.25.1 and 9.25.2.
83 ICUR pars prima 20: *Statilia Alexandra annorum XIIII virgo mortua es(t) Tusco et Anullino conss. GIII (i.e. IX) Kal. Sept. filia Alexandros* (295 AD), cf. for instance AE 1912, 253 *Urbana … quae virgo vixit*.

84   ILCV 1724: *Rufina, casta virgo, vixit an. XII / et m. (sic) dp. VII id. Martia in pace / Marcellino et Probino conss.* (341 AD). Lizzi 1991: 57–8 also mentions the very fragmented and reconstructed epitaph of a Ioviana who died at the age of 41 in 345. The following excerpt is taken from a longer inscription: ICUR V, 13289 = ILCV 1139: *item Io-/[viniana sanctae m](e)m(oriae) virgo qu(a)e vix(it) an(nos) p(lus) m(inus) XLI fuit mihi / in con[ducto an(nos)] p(lus) m(inus) XXIIII d(eposita) in p(ace) d(ie) VI Kal(endas) Mart(ias) cons(ulatu) / Aman[ti et Al]bini //* …

85   Hier. *Ep.* 24.2.

86   Metz 1954: 77, note 1, where he comments on Wilpert's referral (in Wilpert 1892: 94) to an epitaph which he dates to the third century and which reads *Irene virgo.*

87   Very few of the inscriptions that can be relatively securely dated by means of consular date convey the idea of the sacred or consecrated status of the virgin in question. The first inscription of this kind appears to be a fragmented epitaph in which the name of the deceased cannot be read, but which is dedicated to a *sanctae vircin*[…] and dated to 434 AD (ILCV 1713). The next with provenance in Rome that can be securely dated is from 464, and commemorates the *virgo sacra* Praetextata (ICUR V, 13949). Several of the inscriptions put up for deceased virgins must certainly date to the fourth century, but to derive statistical material from these epitaphs is perhaps a little optimistic. A more flexible approach to both dating and terminology is therefore needed if the aim is to identify "sacred virgins" in Christian epitaphs.

88   For a fuller discussion of these *topoi*, and of their afterlife in modern studies, see Undheim 2017 and Undheim 2011: 63–80. For late antique Christian comparisons between Vestals and Christian virgins, and the Vestals as antithesis to the Christian virgins, see also Leveleux 1995 and Lizzi 1998.

89   Smith 2004: 253.

90   Smith 2004: 246.

91   Ambr. *De virgb.* I.19: *Quanto nostrae virgines fortiores.* Cf. Prud. Contr. Symm. II. 1055: *Sunt et virginibus pulcherrima praemia nostris […].*

92   E.g. Tert. *De mon.* XVII. 2–4, Tert. *De exhort.* cast. XIII, Tert. *Ad ux.* VI, Hier. *Adv. Jov* I. 41–9, Hier. *Ep.* 123. 8.

93   Hunter 2007 has pointed out that those favoring more positive views on marriage and regeneration most likely found larger support among Roman upper-class Christians than those who backed the views of Ambrose and Jerome.

94   Prud. *Contr. Symm.* II. 1055–9: *Sunt et virginibus pulcherrima praemia nostris: et pudor et sancto tectus velamine vultus, et privatus honos nec nota et publica forma, et rarae tenusque epulae et mens sobria semper, lexque pudicitia vitae cum fine peracta.* Transl. Thomson 1949–53.

95   Prud. *Contr. Symm.* II. 1066–70: *ac primum parvae teneris capiuntur in annis, / ante voluntatis propriae quam libera secta, / laude pudicitiae fervens et amore deorum, / iusta mariandi condemnet vincula sexus. / captivus pudor ingratis addicitur aris, /[…].*

96   Prud. *Contr. Symm.* II. 1072: *corporis intacti: non mens intacta tenetur.*

97   Prud. *Contr. Symm.* II. 1080–5, cf. Ambr. *De virgb.* I.15. See also Evans Grubbs 2001: 238.

98   Ambr. *De virgb.* I.14–15. As Duval (1974: 29ff.) has argued, this entire thesis is clearly inspired by Athanasius' treatise on the same topic, cf. Athanasius *First Letter to Virgins* 6, (Transl. Brakke 1995), cf. Athanasius *Apologia ad Constantium*, 33, Ambr. *De virgt.* III.13 (Cazzaniga's edition), Ambr. Ep. 18. 11–12, Prud. *Contr. Symm.* II. 1055–85. For another, and more explicit, deconstruction of Vestal virginity, see Min. Fel. Oct. XXV.

99   Most explicit in Lazaire 1890, but also detectable in later studies.

100   Smith 2004: 245, cf. King 2003: 25, Lieu 2004: 20.

101   See Undheim 2011: 63–80 for a fuller discussion of the impact of these comparisons on modern studies.

102   Brown 1988: 9.

103 The argument of free choice versus force is, of course, heavily loaded with ideology, and was later turned on the Catholic Church by protestant reformists criticizing Catholic monasticism. For two very different yet recent approaches to agency and free will in relation to female chastity in Late Antiquity, see Harper 2013 and Wilkinson 2015.

104 Rousselle 1988: 4.

105 Foucault 1988: 230 saw virginity in Late Antiquity as no longer merely a preliminary period prior to an active, sexual adulthood, but as "a choice, a style of life, a lofty form of existence that the hero chooses out of the regard he has for himself." For Christian ethics in particular, see Foucault 1985 and Foucault 1999. For his influential role in subsequent studies of Greco-Roman and Early Christian sexuality, see e.g., Boyarian and Castelli 2001 and Larmour, Miller and Platter 1998. Cohen and Saller 1994: 37 argued that Foucault's version of Greco-Roman sexual ethics "grossly underestimates the normalizing forces at work in ancient societies," cf. also Langlands 2006: 3–8. According to Goldhill 1995: 93, Foucault's argument for the evidence of a new type of virginal ideal in the Hellenistic novels "depends on a misrecognition of the complex and sophisticated ways in which these fictions [which Foucault refers to as sources for his thesis on the evolution of a virginal ideal] engage with the real, how strategies of mapping the natural are mobilized"; cf. Cartledge 1997. For Foucault's impact on the study of Early Christian sexual ethics, see, e.g., Cameron 1986, Clark 1988, Brown 2003: 5 and 14 for Brown's own dialogues with Foucault on these issues. For feminist critiques of Foucault's project, see, e.g., Richlin 1998 and Oksala 2004.

106 McNamara 1983: 46, indeed reminiscent of Minucius Felix' insinuations in Oct. XXV. For the Vestals' tendency to lapse, see also the not wholly convincing arguments in Wildfang 2006: 105–6. By her comparison, McNamara implicitly indicates that the Christian virgins, on the other hand, were "faithful to their trust".

107 Lane Fox 1988: 362.

108 Testard 1996: 51–2.

109 Rousselle 2000 [1992]: 302, cf. Rousselle 1988: 137.

110 E.g. Corrington 1987: 154, Burrus 1987. For a less optimistic interpretation, see Castelli 1986: 88, as well as the more nuanced discussions of agency and free choice in Wilkinson 2015.

111 E.g. Clark 2004b: 67.

112 Many of the same arguments posed by the Church Fathers against the Vestal virgins (force, depravity, greed and sexual insatiability) were used against the Catholic Church and monastic institutions for females by protestant reformers, as well as critics of the Church. See Kelly and Leslie 1999: 20, Bernau 2007: 46–52, Undheim 2011: 294–309.

113 Kelly 2000: 66–7.

114 Kelly 2000: 11.

115 The significance of this distinction certainly varies from author to author and even within one single author's corpus, so that there may not necessarily be any continuity in the distinction. It is therefore first and foremost a tool in my approach to understand the virgin ideology of the period.

116 This is indicated in the quotation from Kelly above, where the possibility of signifiers seems to be endless as a result of fluidity. There will however still be a "comprehensible" relationship to the signified, which, in my argument, will be determined by the desire for fixity.

117 Buell 2005: 1516.

118 Soranus, *Gynaikeia* 1.17, Serv. *Ad Aen.* 4.99 (see above, note 31) Cf. Sissa 1990. For "the history of the hymen," see, e.g., Kelly 2000: 18ff. Wogan-Browne 2003: 242–5, Blank 2007: 32–41.

119 On "locating virginity," see Kelly 2000.

120   Cf. Clark 2008: 16: "Restricting access to Christ the Bridegroom *solely* to virgins
      ran up against a more egalitarian stream of Christian theology. Depicting Christ as
      married to *all* members of the Church, including the chaste married, challenged
      ascetic elitism."
121   It should perhaps be noted that "bodily" and "spiritual" are concepts that in this
      thesis only refer to textually and socially constructed entities. This does not mean
      that they were not conceived as ontological and physical entities in Antiquity, but
      such a perspective will remain outside of the scope of this study.
122   Cf. Kelly 2000: 67 and McInerney 2003: 78–81.
123   Boyarin 2004, Boyarin 2009.
124   Beard 1995.

2 Roman virginities

Between rhetorics, ideals and "reality"

From a religious point of view, virginity is never merely biological.[1]

Although the scholarly notion of virgin priestesses as something of an anomaly in ancient Greece and Rome is well established, the religious valuation and importance placed on the virginity of these priestesses, however few they might have been in statistical proportion to the population as a whole, did not exist in a vacuum. Regardless of religious context, the sacred virgins' virginity was accentuated by symbols and markers that related to the social world, and indicated a constant process in which the meaning of virginity for consecrated as well as non-consecrated virgins was mutually negotiated, reflecting both religious valuation of virginity as well as its socio-cultural valuation in more general terms.

The gradual erasure of distinctions between specialized disciplines has, over the last three decades, engendered the broader and fruitful scope of "Late Antiquity" as an interdisciplinary approach. Where earlier studies often operated with a terminology that focused on conflict and opposition, and above all on difference, between the Christians and their non-Christian contemporaries, there has been a trend since the 1970s that focuses on common Roman cultural values and ideals, based on the assumption that becoming a Christian did not necessarily mean that one ceased to be a Roman.[2] The concept of *romanitas* encompassed more than merely religious adherence. The Roman nobility of fourth century still anchored many of their common values in their own interpretations of what they conceived as *mos maiorum*, the way of the forefathers, and the cultural legacy of Roman rhetoric, literature and law still persisted, although in new adaptations. Despite sometimes harsh polemical language in contemporary texts, we should still assume that peaceful coexistence rather than conflict between people of different religious affiliations dominated the period after Constantine until the impact of Theodosius' edicts that banned pagan sacrifices in the early 390s. In fact, as late as in 403, Jerome makes a point of the pagan priest Albinus' loving relationship with his daughter, who was a Christian, and his granddaughter Paula, who was dedicated to becoming a virgin of Christ:

> Who could have believed that to the heathen pontiff Albinus should be born – in answer to a mother's vows – a Christian granddaughter; that

a delighted grandfather should hear from the little one's faltering lips Christ's Alleluia, and that in his old age he should nurse in his bosom one of God's own virgins?[3]

We do not know exactly what happened when the college of the Vestals was eventually dissolved, due to Theodosius' legislations in the wake of his defeat of Eugenius and Arbogast in 394. The sixth-century pagan sympathizer Zosimus recounts a story about the last of the Vestals, an old woman who had sought some kind of refuge in the temple of Magna Mater. Serena, wife of the Roman general Stilicho, it is told, visited this temple and discovered a precious necklace adorning the statue of the goddess, which she removed from the goddess' image to place upon her own neck. When the Vestal virgin vehemently protested, she was chased away by Serena's attendants. The old priestess muttered a curse that Serena would bring upon herself and her family punishments as deserved for such an impious act. According to Zosimus, Serena was later haunted by nightly visions predicting her imminent death. Her husband, responsible for similar impieties, also added to the divine retributions, which ended in death for both them and their son. In Zosimus' view, justice prevailed, as the very same neck that Serena so desecratingly had adorned with the goddess' necklace in the end was submitted to strangulation.[4] Although Zosimus' reliability as a historian is disputed, the timeframe still sounds reasonable, given the law's increasing restrictions on traditional cults towards the end of the fourth century. The last of the Vestal virgins, we may thus deduce, lived at least until the early fifth century.

Because the coexistence of Vestals and Christian virgins often disappears from studies of Late Antiquity, where Vestals are only mentioned in passing in the introduction, the impression given is that of a historical "succession" rather than contemporaneity.[5] The fact that fourth-century Rome must at least to some extent have provided a common context, or more specifically "intertexts" and "intersections," against which "virgin ideologies" and the notions of virgins' sanctity were constructed and negotiated, will therefore be a point of departure for the comparisons in this chapter. Bearing in mind the Church Fathers' polemical comparisons mentioned in the previous chapter, it is perhaps apt to consider some of the so-called "facts" established in the antithetical schemata of the Church Fathers: free choice versus forced service, limited time versus perpetual virginity, and the Christian virgins' outnumbering of the pagan ones. However, I will not raise these issues in that particular order, but address them with relation to a wider cultural scope that also accounts for other aspects of virginity, such as social status, age and symbolic signifiers in, for example, vesture and adornment. These aspects were defined by, as well as expressions of, the socio-cultural codes that framed Roman conceptions of what a *virgo* was. Thus, without diminishing the significance of the evident differences between Vestals and Christian virgins, I hope instead by this approach to further complicate the images of sacred virgins in fourth-century Rome. An attempt to relate religious valuation of virginity to its socio-cultural context entails a recognition of this dual aspect of virginity, i.e. its physical as well as non-physical status, in which attempts to pin down a definition, or "fix" the virgin, tend to oscillate between the two aspects but most often settle by favoring one over the other. The increasing tension between flexity and fixity in late fourth-century conceptions and constructions of Roman virgins thus illustrates the religious importance attributed to "the virgin."

As the social, cultural, and religious contexts that form the outset of this chapter's approach are partially overlapping and themselves very complex categories, some notes on the structure of this chapter might clarify the argument. Starting with a key motif, the virgin as bride, I will briefly discuss how this bridal image, as it was expressed in different social contexts, contributed to understandings of the Roman *virgo*. The significance of this motif makes it one that I will return to at various other discussions throughout the following chapters as well. The first part of this chapter thus serves as an introduction to later variations on the relation between virginity and bridal imagery. I will then look at social status in terms of social class, exploring the link between virginity and nobility that is present in the sources. The next part of the chapter concentrates on what I have called "the virgin effect," the perceived qualities attributed to virgins that in turn made virgins appear particularly apt for religious service. I will particularly examine in what respect the virgins' divine connections were understood to be beneficial, and how this was expressed in religious beliefs and rituals. These issues will also reappear in subsequent chapters. I then move on to discuss the age of virgins, a subject that was not only linked to the bridal imagery and the sexual purity of children, but also one that came to play an important part in the discussions of choice and free will. As parents, as well as increasingly younger girls, came to dedicate their daughters or themselves to the service of the Church, the notion of individual choice that the Church fathers had claimed as a significant contrast to pagan virgins' "forced service," encountered new challenges. Towards the end of this chapter, I turn to outward *insignia*, i.e. material symbols and signs of virginal status displayed as particular items of clothing or otherwise recognizable visual markers. As the dress of virgins is widely discussed in recent studies focusing on virgins and gender, this part of the chapter not only anticipates the following chapter on the gender of virgins, but also the last chapter, where these visual markers reappear in the discussion with particular reference to the epistemological concerns regarding fallen virgins. There is thus in this present chapter a move from the social, cultural and religious understandings of what a *virgo* was, to more physical/visual and apparently "fixed" markers of virginal status. This is also where the tension between flexity and fixity perhaps becomes evident, although, as I hope to demonstrate, almost all the material analyzed reveals tensions that pull in both directions.

Virginity at the cultural turn

Before venturing upon some reconstructions of the socio-cultural context for these virgins, some introductory remarks regarding how one can actually access the social context of fourth-century Rome might be called for. Moving from the literary sources' realm of rhetoric and representation to the "real world" entails some epistemological challenges to which historians have chosen different approaches. As Elizabeth Clark has pointed out, "the leap from 'representation' to the extratextual world crosses a wide and ugly ditch whose expanse we historians should take care not to underestimate."[6] The relationship between the textuality of the historians' sources and these sources' function as purveyors of "historical data" has been the subject of a long-standing debate. The so-called "linguistic turn" covers various structuralist and post-structuralist theories that question the value of historians' traditional empirical methodologies, moving away from the "real world," to which we allegedly have only limited (if any) access, to focus on language and rhetoric as the site of social and cultural constructions. Essentialisms and a positivist view of knowledge are replaced with an epistemology that stresses relativity and "gaps and absences," always underlining the frail fundament upon which the researchers' hypothesis and assumptions are made. According to Gabrielle Spiegel,

> No historian, even of a positivist stripe, would argue that history is present to us in any but textual form. But whether the "always ready" textualized character of historical data, its inevitably mediated state as made up of language, necessarily means that it is "made up," foreclosing access to any past other than that we interpretively impose on texts, remains, one hopes, an open issue.[7]

As opposed to the linguistic turn, the "cultural turn" represents a more wide-ranging interdisciplinary approach that is less pessimistic with regard to the existence of a historical social "reality" that is accessible through a cautious analysis of a variety of sources. Gabrielle Spiegel has noted how the cultural turn's "enthusiasm for interpretive approaches and above all the shift in focus of investigation from social phenomena to discourses [...] tended to occlude the differences between the cultural turn and the linguistic turn."[8]

The "cultural turn" in studies of Late Antiquity is defined by Dale B. Martin as referring not to any

> particular theoretical or methodological innovation, but to a broad shift in textual and historical analyses of a newly defined field of study, analyses influenced, to be sure, by cultural anthropology and the social sciences, but more recently by a wide diversity of theories and methods borrowed from poststructuralism [...]. Indeed, the very diversity of new theoretical approaches is one of the most remarkable characteristics of "the cultural turn" in recent late ancient studies.[9]

This kind of "messy theory"[10] that the cultural turn represents, however epistemologically challenged by hard-core post-modernists, nevertheless provides an attempt to cross the aforementioned ditch between representation and "reality," by focusing on ideology and social constructions as well as the importance of the textuality and literary character of the historians' sources.[11] The following chapter on the "social context" and its meaning for the construction of Roman virginity and, as a consequence, "sacred virginity," thus represents an attempt to combine different sources and perspectives without disregarding the complicating "literariness" of the main corpus of sources.

THE SOCIAL VALUE OF VIRGINITY

Virginity in Greco-Roman society is said to be valued only as a commodity that increased the value of the bride in "transactions" and alliances arranged by Roman men, in an exchange of allegiance between families that was formally contracted in the form of weddings.[12] The purpose of women was to marry and ensure that the men had legitimate children who would inherit from them, and if the woman was a virgin at the time she got married, the chances that future children would be legitimate were thought to increase. However, this general notion is complicated by several examples of different practices and attitudes.[13] Sociological interpretations have focused on how the Vestals, as virgin daughters and significant commodities in social interactions, were removed from the important systems of alliances and exchange between Roman (elite) families.

> Vocation to the priesthood of Vesta seems to have been imposed by family ambition rather than by a pre-pubertal girl's desire for celibacy, and in any case, since there were only six Vestals at a time and they could retire after thirty years, virginity was not a statistically significant career. Lifelong celibate women are otherwise practically unexampled as *perpetua virgo*, although nothing can be proved for the lower classes.[14]

Girls from the aristocracy could be married at the age of 12, which was the minimum legal age for girls to marry. Betrothal, however, could be agreed between parents of the future bride and groom at an even earlier stage.[15] Brent Shaw argued in an influential study that most women were married in their late teens and, although this argument is convincing, it leaves us with a time gap that has proven difficult to reconstruct in the lifetime of Roman girls, i.e. that between puberty or menarche (which, according to Plutarch, would normally occur around the age of twelve) and marriage, a time gap that thus coincides with their status as virgins.[16] Functionalist perspectives tend to claim that education of girls from a very early age consisted of preparation for married life, and the general view is that young girls were valued only for their potential as wives and mothers. Epigraphic material seems to support these claims. A striking example is found in the inscription that was raised for Januaria, who had died at the age of fifteen. The epitaph opens by stating that *virgo* ought not to be the title of the girl in question, concluding, after much praise of the girl, that if the fates had only wanted otherwise, the word *mater* should have been the first to be read instead.[17]

A similar epitaph is found in an inscription from Cirta in Numidia in Northern Africa, where the virgin Julia Sidonia had died just before her wedding was planned to have taken place:

> Julia Sidonia, Joy in name only, whose threads (what an abomination!) were snapped by the Fates on the day before her bridegroom lit the hymeneal torch at her wedding; all groaned, the Dryad maidens grieved and Lucina wept at her torches with their fire put out, because she had been a virgin and her parents' only child. She had been a priestess of the rattle-shaking goddess of Memphis; she is buried here silent because of the eternal gift of sleep. She lived nineteen years, four months, fourteen days; here she lies.[18]

As the goddess of childbirth, the image of the weeping Lucina is a clear reference to the children that will now not be born and expresses the grief of the parents now bereft both of their only child and of any hope for future grandchildren. The commemorative inscription for Caecinia Bassa, who died before she reached her eleventh year, does not express any specific notion of loss related to her childbearing prospects. Nevertheless, her death is depicted as Pluto snatching her away from her parents. This is a clear allusion to the rape of Persephone and, as such, may evoke a larger complex of wedding imagery that is not only joyful.[19] This motif, as H. J. Rose has discussed, was not uncommon in Greek funerary inscriptions, where the deceased unmarried girl, *kore*, was often identified with Persephone.[20]

One should however be cautious about reading too much "reality" into this obviously rather conventional motif in epitaphs for young virgins. Mary Harlow and Ray Laurence have illustrated how inscriptions tend to mourn a child's potentiality as an adult, a convention that they argue has perhaps unjustly influenced modern perceptions of how childhood was understood by the ancient Romans.[21] It should also be noted that virgins were mourned and commemorated without reference to unattainable marriage and motherhood. The brief inscription dedicated to 13-year-old Mus may serve as an example:

> Dear to my parents I lived, as a virgin I gave up my life,
> Now here I am, dead and ashes, and ashes is earth
> If earth is a goddess, then I am a goddess, and I am not dead
> I ask you, stranger, do not dishonor my bones.
> Mus lived 13 years.[22]

The father of Vibia Citheris, a *liberta* also described as a *virgo* only 11 years old, records in the memorial monument he raised over his virgin daughter, how he is "writing through tears" over her miserable death.[23] Such inscriptions illustrate that virgins were indeed mourned not only for the loss of their function as childbearing, legitimate wives, but also in other conventional and not so conventional terms that were to characterize and commemorate the deceased virgin.

Felices nuptae: virgin and bride

As has already been indicated, the symbolic and religious imagery surrounding sacred virgins abound with marriage analogies and more or less overt references to weddings, though some general theories regarding so-called *hieros gamos* have occasionally overstated these connections. The idea that ritual enactments of a *hieros gamos* should have taken place between Vestal virgins and the pontifex maximus is most likely a remnant of eighteenth-century imagination[24] and no more supported in present-day scholarship than the idea that a Christian virgin's consecration ceremony entailed any kind of physical intercourse.

Inspired by theories relating to van Gennep's *rite de passages*, scholars have found much food for speculation in Roman marriage symbolism, which appears to have associated the virgin's transition to her new status as wife with violence. According to Macrobius, it seems the virgin is victim of a violent action at the wedding,[25] and his contemporary Augustine derived the name of the goddess Venus from the word violence (*vis*), allegedly "because without violence, a female will not cease to be a virgin."[26] Harlow and Laurence have pointed out that modern scholars' literal interpretation of such textual passages referring to violence has caused a misrepresentation of this notion as specifically Roman.[27] There is of course a symbolical taint to this "violence" that might just as well reflect male concerns as cultural ideology or "real experience." Augustine mockingly described the many gods who, according to Roman tradition, were thought to be present at the wedding night to assist the groom fulfill his conjugal duty:

> Why do they fill the bedroom with a host of gods, when even the bridesmen and bridesmaids withdraw? And this [room] is filled up [with gods], not because their imagined presence is thought to ensure concern for *pudicitia*, but so that the woman, the one of the weak sex and frightened by everything that is new, with their aid may be solved from her virginity without any difficulty. [...] And if the goddess Virginiensis is present to dissolve the virgin's girdle,[28] if the god Subigus is there for her to be subjugated by her husband, the goddess Prema so that she does not move when lying underneath him, what does the goddess Pertunda do there? Let her blush, let her go outside: let also the husband have something to do.[29]

Catullus' epithalamia are excellent examples of what van Gennep termed the group's resistance at the threat of being weakened when members leave it for a new social group by a *rite de passage*.[30] At the same time, Catullus' staging of this resistance in his Carmen 62, by a choir of virgins who counter the seductive arguments sung by a choir of boys or the bridegroom's companions, echoes some of the bittersweet nostalgia for virginhood also expressed in the poetry of his muse, Sappho:[31]

> Like a rare flower grows in a garden enclosed,
> Unknown by the cattle, untorn by the plough,
> The air fondles it, the sun strengthens it, the rain brings it up.
> ***
> Many a boy, and many a girl long for it;
> But once it is picked by a delicate nail, it deflowers,
> No boys and no girls long for it now:
> Such is the virgin remaining intact, while she is dear to her kind
> With the body polluted, she parts with her chaste flower,
> for the boys she is no longer lovely, and she's no longer dear to the girls.[32]

The "intactness" of the virgin referred to in this passage does not necessarily indicate the same as it will when it is applied later, in Christian writings, to describe Mary, nor may the fact that she is described as untouched entail intactness as we may think of it today. However, it is noteworthy that Catullus uses this term, *intacta*, while the preceding poem in this collection contains the somewhat analogous expression *integrae virgines*.[33] Noteworthy is also the idea of the body being polluted (*polluto corpore*) by the act of "defloration," consistently described in terms of the metaphor that frames the stanza.

In the boys' reply to the girls' stanza, the virgin flower is replaced by a widowed vine, depicted as withering alone. They "argue" that "such is the virgin remaining intact; she grows old untended."[34] The boys maintain that if the virgin is married to a fitting husband, she will be dear to him and less of a burden to her parents. Their appeal to this solitary seclusion seems, however, insufficient to convince the virgin bride, and the poem thus ends with an unknown speaker making a final appeal:

> Do not fight, virgin, with such a spouse,
> It is not fitting to struggle against the one to whom your father has handed you,
> Your parents you have to obey!
> It is not entirely yours, this virginity. In part it belongs to your parents.
> One third belongs to your father, one third is your mother's
> And only one third is yours
> Do not fight the two who gave to your husband their rightful part of you
> along with the dowry.[35]

The appeal, then, is no longer to emotions, but to the loyalty towards her parents and to "property" law. Although it is still partially hers, mathematical reasoning is used to argue that her share of her virginity is now smaller than the one her parents have given to her husband, to whom the lion's share of her virginity belongs. Geert Roskam has convincingly argued that Catullus' poem bears no evidence for a Roman virginal ideal similar to that exhorted in early Christianity.[36] What it does indicate, however, is a valuation of virginity that, as a poetic motif, here works upon the psychology and staging of *rites de passages* by evoking nostalgia for virginity and the kind of life it represented.

The importance of the so-called consummation of the marriage seems to have played a role in the festivities held in the wedding celebrations, but a reconstruction of any ritual surrounding this part of the ceremony is evidently difficult to detail.[37] Legally, wedding ceremonies were not necessary for the marriage to be considered valid. According to Justinian's Digesta, Ulpian quoted early law, claiming that "agreement and not sleeping together creates a marriage."[38] The minimum requirement was for the bride to be transferred to her husband's house, and the presence of the bridegroom was by no means mandatory, as a marriage could be valid even with the man *in absentia*.[39] In such cases, a virgin wife would not necessarily be an incongruity. This is what seems to be the background for a statement in Digesta where it is said that "therefore it could happen that a virgin in such a case could both have a dowry and make action for her dowry."[40] Augustus, for instance, is said to have sent back his first wife Claudia, untouched and still a virgin (*intactam adhuc et virginem*) after a falling out with his mother-in-law.[41] Juvenal jokingly has a begging client argue that "though you ignore and disregard my other services, what price do you put on this, that had I not been your true and devoted client, your wife would still be a virgin?"[42] Certainly part of a severe satirical insult aimed at the unmanliness of a patron who is apparently unable to perform his conjugal duties, Juvenal's paradoxical image even of a potential virgin wife scores the point. This, then, is also the context that creates the possibility of the even more seemingly paradoxical virgin widow, which we encounter not only in Christian literature, but also in other contexts.[43]

That marriage necessarily meant the end of the girl's virginity is a logic that Ambrose finds the need to counter in his defense of Mary's perpetual virginity. Arguing against opponents who refer to Mary's marriage to Joseph, Ambrose turns to Roman law and states that "it is not the defloration of virginity that makes a marriage, but the marriage pact."[44] Jerome, on the other hand, comments on Paul (1 Cor. 7:34) and declares that "not every unmarried woman is also a virgin. But every virgin is of course unmarried."[45]

The virgin as bride is necessarily an important image in the Roman conception of virginity, as the wedding in most circumstances would mark the end of a freeborn girl's virginhood, at least in the ideal world. Particular aspects of this transition appear to have occupied male writers, but material that might have shed light upon the bride's experience must unfortunately be accepted as out of reach. What sources nevertheless do express is a kind of nostalgia for virginity, the period in a girl's life that ends with her first marriage, a nostalgia that somehow bestowed certain ideological associations upon this state and that again attributed to the cultural valuation of virgins beyond – although at the same time dependent on – their future role as brides, wives and mothers.

The social status of virgins

That status, in most circumstances, was an even more influential factor than gender has increasingly been acknowledged in current studies on gender in Antiquity. The sources do indeed represent a challenge in this respect, as the upper social classes no doubt dominate the literary sources. However, there is extant material that may still shed some light upon women and men from other social strata in order to, perhaps not balance, but at least disrupt this domination of aristocratic Roman women in present-day scholarship.

According to Patricia Watson's study, one of the traits distinguishing a *virgo* from a *puella* is that the *virgo* is always a Roman citizen, unmarried and free-born. Even in Roman comedy and later in the Hellenistic novels, where this rule apparently did not adhere at first sight, the true status of the virgin in question was revealed at the end of the story, thus affirming her claim to the "title." [46] Caracalla's extension of Roman citizenship to every freeborn inhabitant in the Roman Empire ultimately led to devaluation of citizenship as such, and the third and fourth centuries saw large changes in the distinctions and criteria for membership in the senatorial class. Michele R. Salzman has shown how earlier and quite distinct definitions of *nobilitas*, in terms of senatorial office and family ties, became in Late Antiquity looser and more flexible to interpretation, and hence open for competing claims to such status. [47]

Although, as is often remarked, slaves' living conditions varied remarkably – and, in terms of comfort and economic privilege, they could be far better off than those of the lower social classes – there were fundamental juridical distinctions between slaves, who were considered as property, and free Roman citizens. [48] Carolyn Osiek has pointed out that a female slave in the Greco-Roman culture could "lay no claim to chastity or shame, which have no meaning. In the official view she cannot have sensitivity toward chastity. Her honor cannot be violated because it does not exist." [49] The consequence of Watson and Osiek's observations is thus that neither slaves nor freedwomen could claim the status of a *virgo*, nor would they be rightfully called so by others. A number of questions will emerge from these observations. For instance, to what extent then do we actually encounter virgins from lower social strata, and why and in which contexts are they identified as virgins? How would such social understandings and categorizations affect the nomination of sacred virgins and potential restrictions on who were to achieve this status? Another relevant question is whether giving a female slave or freed-woman status as a sacred virgin potentially would challenge or undermine traditional social structures? And to what extent can we assume that this actually happened?

Since the sacred virgins we know by name, pagan and Christian alike, almost exclusively belonged to the aristocracy or wealthy Roman families, it will be necessary to search not only in the "gaps and absences" but also in material that has so far not been studied with particular attention to social distinctions as far as virgins are concerned. I will therefore stress that my selection of sources by no means reflects a complete overview or any kind of statistical analysis. The material referred to below is rather meant to serve as examples of sources that may support as well as complicate earlier studies that have touched upon these questions.

The social status of Vestal virgins

According to Michele R. Salzman, Christian rhetoric in the fourth century explored how to redefine *nobilitas* in terms of ascetic ideals of piety and – for women – chastity. Her conclusion, nevertheless, is that "even the shaping of the rhetoric of nobilitas as the piety of the ascetic or virgin retained traditional associations with family and secular status."[50] With reference to the Vestal virgins, Salzman points out that Christian authors' ascription of "honour to a noble woman because of virginity was not a totally new concept to the Roman elite."[51] Taking Salzman's observations as a starting point, the following discussion will further explore some of these notions of the "nobility of virginity" and see how this may have affected the use of the term *virgo* in different contexts, especially those relating to sacred virgins.

First of all, the so-called nobility of the Vestals has to be addressed, as there are different opinions among modern scholars on this particular point. This variety of views is mostly based on sources claiming that Augustus opened up the priesthood for daughters of freedmen in 5 AD, commonly interpreted as a response to a crisis in recruiting new priestesses.[52] However, there is no evidence that any priestess was ever elected from this social class, and other sources indicate that daughters from wealthy, aristocratic families continued to be preferred.[53] An alternative interpretation of Augustus' law may therefore be that it was passed in order to appease wealthy freedmen who at the time desired to climb the social ladder by adding traditional signs of nobility to their family.

Aulus Gellius, who wrote in the second century AD, recorded the requirements for those who could be elected for the priesthood. Among the many criteria listed, he stated that neither parent of a potential priestess must have served as a slave, or been involved in "sordid business."[54] The notion that character and virtue were linked to social status permeates Roman writings, where this serves effective rhetorical purposes, for instance when contradicted or confirmed in descriptions of Roman emperors.[55] The Vestal's integrity was thereby supposed to be secured by her family background.[56] Distinctions between plebeians and patricians appear to lose importance towards Late Antiquity, yet this had played a significant role in earlier times. Minucia, who was charged with *incestum* in 329 BC, is said to have been the first Vestal from a plebeian family, although a very influential family that had earlier been patrician.[57] Saquete's prosopography identifies only three Vestals of plebeian families, of which at least two had parents with attested senatorial status. However, José Carlos Saquete's list illustrates how the social status of quite a few of those Vestals we have prosopographical data for still remains uncertain.[58]

That the Vestals were still, in Late Antiquity, being recruited from the Roman nobility and endowed with the traditional values of the Roman elite can be deduced from a passage by Lactantius, where he recounts the martyrdom of a noblewoman and some of her female friends, among whom one is identified as the mother of a Vestal virgin in Rome, a remark that apparently attests these women's claim to nobility.[59] The very reason he appears to mention this Vestal is thus because her status supports his attribution of nobility to her mother. Names of Vestals known from the third and fourth century indicate these girls' and women's aristocratic ancestry, and the inscriptions also clearly demonstrate that family ties were maintained even though the Vestals legally were removed from their family at the time of *captio*. Many inscriptions are put up by close family members of the Vestals. The sister of Coelia Claudiana is, for instance, identified as *c. f.* (*clarissima femina*), while as a brother of Terentia Flavola, Terentius Gerantius describes himself as *v(ir) c(larissimus)*.[60] Fabia Paulina's inscription and statue raised to the *Vestalis Maxima* Coelia Concordia demonstrates ties to the Roman aristocracy in the 380s as well, and also the continuous esteem for these priestesses.[61] A couple of inscriptions were also put up by clients who referred to the Vestals as their *patrona*.[62] According to the fourth-century work with the ambitious title *Description of the Whole World*,

> There are also in Rome itself seven virgins of free birth and senatorial family (*ingenuae et clarissimae*), who for the well-being of the city perform rites for the gods in accordance with ancestral custom; they are called virgins of Vesta.[63]

Symmachus constantly evokes the nobility's link to Roman priesthoods in his famous Relatio 3, and he explicitly describes the Vestals as *nobiles virgines*.[64] There seems to have been a mutual exchange in nobility from the Vestals being recruited from such families and the status of the priesthood as conferring nobility on the priestesses again, so that, even though plebeians and later perhaps other girls from humbler backgrounds (which, as already stated, did not necessarily mean poor, since freed slaves could be among the wealthy and influential) could, through election to the priesthood, even confer some of that nobility on her family.

Christian virgins and the Roman aristocracy

Both Jerome and Ambrose express a certain penchant for aristocratic women, and especially for aristocratic virgins. The delicate balance between nobility and humility is, for instance, expressed by Jerome in his praise of Paula and Eustochium as *unicum nobilitatis et humilitatis exemplar*.[65] In a not so unexpected *praeteritio* in one of his letters to the virgin Principia, Jerome praises Marcella skillfully as he manages to call attention to the very fact he claims he will disregard:

> I will not extol her illustrious family, the splendour of her noble lineage, and the long series of consuls and praetorian prefects who have been her

ancestors. I will praise her for nothing but that which is her own and which is the more noble, because despising wealth and rank she has won higher nobility by poverty and humility.[66]

According to Jerome, Eustochium was the first virgin of noble birth in Rome, but we do not know exactly when she was consecrated.[67] Another virgin, Asella, belonged to the ascetic circle around Marcella (and was perhaps her sister), but even though she was probably consecrated long before Eustochium, she is apparently surpassed by her in terms of virginal nobility.[68] Likewise, in his letter to Demetrias, Jerome envisions her mother and grandmother as they congratulate each other for Demetrias' choice, seeing that now a virgin was "to make a noble household more noble still by her virginity."[69]

Ambrose too preferred to speak of the nobility of virginity when the virgin in question already qualified to secular nobility. The headstrong girl who Ambrose puts forth as having defied her family in order to escape an arranged marriage and who, according to Ambrose, sought refuge at his altar, is described as "noble in terms of our world, now more noble in God," evidently because of her virginal vow.[70] In a much later treatise, he states that "we bishops have a nobility that should be preferred before that of consuls and prefects, that is, the dignity of faith." Interestingly, however, he immediately goes on to "reclaim" his ancestral nobility by reference to his relative Sotheris, "with an exceedingly beautiful face, and a virgin of a noble family, who put the consulates and prefectures of her relatives behind her sacred faith when she was bid to sacrifice but refused."[71] Ambrose's nobility in these two examples is thus not so much a redefinition of nobility as a double claim to nobility, where nobility in terms of traditional standards becomes the base of this "new" nobility in terms of religious office or vocation. His noble virgins are thus always also doubly portrayed as noble in terms of both sacred and secular standards.

Metaphors from royal and aristocratic language (for example, *rex*, *dominus*, etc.) are conferred on the nobility of Mary, presented by Ambrose as an example and teacher of the virgins: "The first enthusiasm in learning derives from the nobility of the teacher. And what is nobler than the mother of God?"[72] The combination of traditional nobility and the nobility of virginity thus leads to an accumulation of *nobilitas* that in turn was conferred both ways, from family to virgin and from virgin to family. According to Salzman, Ambrose "evidently believed that his position would be acceptable to noble families; parents should listen to their daughters' wishes, and they would, like the example of his noble virgin, eventually win over their families."[73]

As in the case of "the virgin," there is a somewhat similar tension in terms of fixity and flexity in Jerome's and Ambrose's rhetorical applications of *nobilitas*. In the attempt to redefine nobility, the term still tends to occur in contexts where such redefinitions are made with reference to "earthly nobility," which "new nobility" then paradoxically both surpasses and still appears to depend upon. Traditional nobility must not therefore be completely devalued, for then the new claim to *nobilitas* is also undermined. Regardless of whether the motivation for the vow was pagan or Christian, the nobility of sacred virgins appears to have been transferred from her blood relations, whose nobility in turn was certified by the virgin's sacred and noble status.

Slave virgins?

That Christianity made virginity into a universal ideal is a general assumption to which we will frequently return. However, it should still be questioned to what extent Christianity opened virginity up as a "profession" for girls and women from other social strata than the aristocracy, as well as to what extent slave girls or girls from lower social strata did in fact achieve the status of sacred virgins and how this, in those cases, was expressed. Although some may have seen this as a specifically Christian leveling of social differences, or perhaps even a new, subversive hierarchical system founded in asceticism, I argue that we also have to consider the extent of what the sources that so predominantly focus on upper-class society might actually reveal. There are indeed many challenges in reading these sources in a modern, emancipatory light.

Rita Lizzi proposes that Ambrose wanted girls also from the lower classes to dedicate themselves to virginity, and that he therefore organized for girls to be invited from Piacenza and Bologna to be consecrated by him in Milan. Lizzi infers that the virgins from Mauritania, who Ambrose makes quite a fuss about having consecrated, were brought to Milan by his brother Satyrus and manumitted for the occasion.[74] Neil McLynn has also suggested that Ambrose's supply of virgins to be consecrated was more or less "shipped in" from Mauritania – perhaps acquired from the slave markets as prisoners of war who had been taken captive after the Romans suppressed a revolt in 375.[75] Whether this staging of consecration ceremonies for exotic foreigners was intended to appeal to the lower classes, as Lizzi suggests, or principally functioned as a form of shaming device directed at the upper social classes among Christians in Milan, the destiny of these Mauritanian virgins is unfortunately untraceable. Rita Lizzi posits that the influx of virgins to Milan under Ambrose's episcopacy might also have initiated the building of the first female monastery in the city.[76] Another possibility is that the virgins were taken in by other families of Ambrose's congregation, as part of the virgin train of the domina or daughter(s) of the household, or perhaps even sent back to North Africa as missionaries for the sake of virginity. Their virginal vocation could thus have provided them with the possibility of making an alternative living to that which would otherwise be the option for freed female slaves in Roman society.

Elizabeth Clark has noted that there are indications that female ascetics brought their slaves along when they joined or founded monasteries.[77] But also those ascetics living in their private houses appear to have surrounded themselves with an entourage of servile virgins. Jerome, for instance, describes Eustochium's sister, the widowed Blaesilla, as so humbly dressed and in appearance that she was only to be distinguished from her virgin slaves by her wavering way of walking, and the way her neck hardly managed to keep up her head.[78] This almost otherworldly walk and frail posture is thus what marks the noble Blaesilla out from the train of servant virgins.

In his letters, Jerome repeatedly advised virgins and widows to "keep with you bands of widows and virgins; and let your consolers be of your own sex. The character of a *domina* is judged by that of her *ancillae*." [79] The consecration of Demetrias is imagined by Jerome to have spurred others on to do the same:

> Many virgins sprouted out at once as shoots from a fruitful stem, and the example set by their patroness and lady was followed by a host of clients and servants. Virginity was warmly espoused in every house, and although those who made profession of it were as regards the flesh of lower rank than Demetrias they sought one reward with her, the reward of chastity.[80]

Although Jerome's panegyric passage that immediately follows betrays his penchant for exaggeration, the idea, and perhaps even expectation, that clients and slaves would follow their patrons and take up an ascetic lifestyle is present in this passage. To Eustochium, Jerome also advises that:

> If any of your handmaids share your vocation, do not lift yourself against them or pride yourself because you are their mistress. You have all chosen one Bridegroom.[81]

The clients and servants following their *domina* Demetrias in the profession as virgins are said by Jerome to have the prerogative of chastity, despite not being equal to her "in terms of the condition of the flesh."[82] Similarly, Jerome stresses that Eustochium's *ancillulae* should be considered equal to her because they all have the same bridegroom. Virginity and chastity thus apparently dissolve the social distinctions. In the Hellenistic story of Joseph and Aseneth, for instance, the seven virgin companions of Aseneth, all anonymous, are described as "all born the same night as she. They were very beautiful, like the stars in the sky, and they had never had anything to do with any man nor with any young boy."[83] When seen in relation to Jerome's band of virgins surrounding the aristocratic ladies, this should alert us to the influence of a literary and mythological *topos*, where anonymous virgins, or better, a whole crowd of virgins, surround the virgin protagonist as if to make her "sparkle" even more. Likewise, Ambrose's choir of virgins adorned his Church and reflected his success as a preacher of virginity.[84] From the female choirs on the bride's side in the traditional epithalamia, to Diana's train of devout virgins in Greek mythology, we see that this motif has an aesthetical, almost ornamental, function, evoking imagery that was elaborated upon in contemporary art and literature.[85] Whatever the status of these virgin companions of Eustochium, Blaesilla, Demetrias and other noblewomen might actually have been in the "real world," their rhetorical — and perhaps also social — function in the texts was clearly to highlight and draw attention to the ascetic achievements and the sanctity of their *domina*, and to affirm her status, not unlike the train of clients that would follow a Roman senator or anyone of some social standing.[86]

If indeed some of these virgin companions, or any virgins pertaining to the "train" of aristocratic widows and virgins, were slaves or emancipated slaves, imitation of their *domina*'s asceticism must have been seen as a true sign of their loyalty to their *patrona*. Jerome further instructs Eustochium on how her relationship to her fellow virgins should be:

> Others ought to be summoned. You should honor the incitement for the other virgins. If you sense that one of them is weaker in her faith, support her, comfort her, coax her, and make her chastity your advantage. But if she pretends in order to escape servitude, read frankly to her the Apostle's words: "It is better to marry than to burn."[87]

Although Jerome insists that Eustochium let them marry if their struggle to remain virgins becomes too difficult, the reality of this "choice," considering the emphasis on virginity and the stern instructions that every devout virgin or widow in these circles must surround herself only with sisters of equally strong ascetic conviction, should at least be questioned. Giving up virginity for marriage could, for a slave or servant, thus entail losing an otherwise privileged position in the *domina*'s train. As Jerome so enthusiastically exclaimed 30 years later, "Which one of the virgins of Christ would not boast if she was associated with this one [i.e. Demetrias]?"[88]

The bodies of women were a commodity that the free as well as slaves had to use for survival and to improve their own living conditions, whether it was through prostitution, performing arts, wet nursing or other professions where their own bodies provided the "qualification."[89] As such, it should be acknowledged that virginity perhaps provided just another way for girls and women to find a safe occupation to sustain a living. It is difficult to ascertain whether slave virgins were emancipated when they joined a monastery supported by their owner, yet even as *libertae* we must assume they would be expected to remain loyal to their former owner, since she would still be their patroness.

Because the language of servitude came to have a specific significance in Christian discourses, we should of course be cautious in reading such references to *ancillae* and *servi* in the literal sense. As already seen, this language was part of a rhetoric communicating the individual Christian's humility and total submission to God. In these passages referred to above, however, the context does suggest owner-servant, or patron-client, relationships that at least should make us question the relevance of the *voluntas*, free will, stressed so insistently by the Fathers elsewhere.[90]

Does the fact that these *ancillae* and *famulae* could figure as virgins thus contradict Watson's and Osiek's observations regarding the status of virgins and slaves? Was the virgin slave first introduced with Christianity? And if a slave could indeed be categorized as a virgin, on what basis and worth was this category assigned in other circumstances? Two passages from Ulpian, a jurist who wrote in the second century and who is quoted in the Digest of Justinian, indicate that the idea of a virgin slave was not necessarily a contradiction. In both cases, Ulpian's hypothetical example is derived from a scenario where a man purchases what he believes to be a virgin, only to discover that she is "a woman:"

> ULPIAN, *Sabinus, book 28*: 1. If, however, I think that I am buying a virgin when she is, in fact, a woman, the sale is valid, there being no mistake over her sex. But if I sell you a woman and you think that you are buying a male slave, the error of the sex makes the sale void.[91]
>
> ULPIAN, *Edict, book 32*: If a man thought he was buying a virgin when in fact a mature woman was sold, and the seller knowingly let him persist in his error, [a jurist believes that] this reason does not justify a redhibition, but that an action on purchase does lie to undo the purchase; the woman should be returned after the price is repaid.[92]

As the examples are used to illustrate different points in the overall arguments, they are a little different. Although it is not grounds for a lawsuit, Ulpian presents this fraud as an understandable cause of indignation. A virgin obviously had a different appeal to the buyer than a "woman," and although not sufficient ground for a legal case, the distinction could certainly be important to the buyer. The purchase can therefore be undone and the woman returned to the seller.

Paulus, another law commentator quoted in the Digest, even considers the juridical consequences of an *ancilla devirginata*, and Ulpian as well, in a context discussing a female slave subjected to *stuprum*, mentions different laws that can be applied, for instance if it is an "immature" (probably to be understood as "underage") virgin that has suffered *stuprum*.[93] Cases of *stuprum* against citizens would be tried according to the Lex Iulia de adulteriis,[94] but slaves were regarded as property, and sexual crimes against anyone else's slave would therefore be punished according to other laws regarding damage or loss of property.[95] However, the two incidents cited above do – in addition to attesting to the potential "existence" of female virgin slaves, that is, the fact that slaves could also be defined as virgins – furthermore indicate that a slave's loss of virginity was estimated differently, and perhaps even regarded as more serious, than other sexual crimes against slaves. Although a slave could not lay claim to chastity or virginity on her own behalf, as Osiek has pointed out, her chastity, and perhaps particularly her virginity, was considered a commodity that could be valued for very different reasons by her owner, and most likely on the same grounds as a bride's virginity, to whom, as Catullus 61 suggested, it would no longer belong when marriage was conducted. The main difference lies in the bride and her husband's option to use this virginity to define her claim to *pudicitia* as a wife, a claim to chastity that a slave girl, when no longer a virgin, would not be able to make.

Early Christian attitudes towards slavery or, perhaps more accurately stated, acceptance of slavery on more or less the same terms as their non-Christian ancestors, has been a somewhat problematic issue for many modern scholars. It is my contention that social status potentially was a greater factor in female ascetic practice than has been acknowledged by recent scholarship. The recognition of these tensions between ideology and reality will thus further complicate the focus on free will that dominates the established narratives of sacred Christian virgins.[96]

Libertae

To find out to what extent the term *virgo* also applied to freedwomen, as the discussion above might entail, we will have to move to inscriptions, where this combination is perhaps best attested. As already stated, inscriptions are highly problematic as sources. They are however still useful in providing a glimpse of how commemorative practices could draw on convention in order to convey certain Roman ideals in terms of which the deceased was identified and characterized.[97] Even though Watson's general observations of the virgin as a freeborn citizen perhaps no longer applied in later imperial times, we could assume that the social denotation still lingered and resounded in its use. A lengthy example may illustrate this:

> To Eucharis, freedwoman of Licinia, a virgin, educated and learned in every skill. She lived 14 years.
>   Ah, as you look with wandering eye at the house of death, stay your foot and read what is inscribed here. This is what a father's love gave his daughter, where the remains of her body lie gathered. 'Just as my life with its young skills and growing years brought me fame, the sad hour of death rushed on me and forbade me to draw another breath in life. I was educated and taught as if by the Muses' hands. I adorned the nobility's festivals with my dancing, and first appeared before the common people in a Greek play.
>   But now here in this tomb my enemies the Fates have placed my body's ashes. The patrons of learning – devotion, passion, praise, honour – are silenced by my burnt corpse and by my death.
>   His child, I left lamentation to my father. Though born after him, I preceded him in the day of my death. Now I observe my fourteenth birthday here among the shadows in Death's ageless home.
>   I beg you when you leave, ask that the earth lie light upon me'.[98]

Unlike some of the epitaphs discussed above, this commemorative inscription does not mourn the unfulfilled adult potential of the girl, defined as wife and mother. Instead, it praises her achievements and her character. As a freedwoman and an actress, Eucharis would have been placed near the bottom of the social hierarchy, yet the elaborate inscription could indicate that the commemorator had a certain wealth. Augustan legislation had prohibited any man of senatorial order or descent from marrying an actress or the daughter of an actor, and the legislation was expanded under Constantine in 336. Slaves and freedwomen were also among those whom men from the senatorial class were prohibited from marrying.[99] Eucharis, however, is said to have "adorned the festivals of the nobility" with her dancing. The appeal to the Muses as her teachers, as well as the characterization of her as a *docta erodita omnes artes virgo* render her as an honorable girl, in spite of her status and profession. Her status as a virgin could then be read as a claim for social dignity and integrity, and not merely inserted to state that she was not yet married when she died. It lends her an aura that perhaps better reflects the genre than her social status.[100]

The fact that Eugamus, who put up the inscription for the fourteen-year-old *virgo* Valeria Sympherusa, identifies himself as *patronus*, might indicate that she was a former slave, or at least that she was in some kind of client-patron relationship with him.[101] Likewise, the daughter of the freedwoman Hilara is described as a virgin who lived to be 15.[102] Another apparent *liberta* is the *virguncula* Julia, daughter of Gaius, who died at the age of 11.[103] Aurelia Prima, commemorated by her brother and *collibertus*, is also denoted as "*virg.*"[104] The epigraphic material thus demonstrates that status as *virgo* was not necessarily exclusive to the upper classes in Roman society. Considering the context in which these *virgines liberate* appear, we may assume that the term has been applied to somehow benevolently characterize the deceased girl, and not merely to state her status as unmarried. If *virgo* indeed was understood as a status mostly confined to daughters of Roman citizens, this might be thought of as an important point to convey in a funerary inscription of some of these *liberti* and their families.

As discussed above, the legal and social status of the virgin companions of ascetic noble women is difficult to ascertain. Ambrose's sister Marcellina lived together with a virgin companion whose sister Candida, according to Ambrose's biographer Paulinus, lived in Carthage, still following the same profession as her then deceased (and anonymous) sister at the time he was writing.[105] Principia was the lifelong companion of Marcella. According to Jerome's letter of consolation, Marcella died in the arms of Principia after the sack of Rome in 410. Asella was another companion, and perhaps even the sister (yet maybe only in the spiritual sense) of Marcella.[106] Principia was the recipient of a couple of letters from Jerome,[107] whereas Candida's anonymous sister is only mentioned in passing by Paulinus and obviously not considered important enough to have been mentioned at all in Ambrose's treatise dedicated to Marcellina.

Redefining noble virginity?

Citizenship, which seems to have been a sort of "minimum requirement" for those qualifying to be called virgins in New Comedy is, in Hellenistic novels, often replaced with nobility (or even royalty, as in Heliodorus' Ethiopian story).

These narratives (where the heroine through many trials maintains her virginity and proves her true ancestral status), and this "literariness" (which constructs "noble," or "aristocratic virginity," together with the nobility and dignity of priesthood), may in turn have affected the usage of the term *virgo* when it appears in other contexts, such as commemorative inscriptions and the Church Fathers' writings. By evoking dignity and chastity, regardless of actual social status, *virgo* retained some kind of honorary connotation that seems to have been important in commemorative contexts as well.

Did Christianity bring any changes to the perception of virginity in terms of social status? Peter Brown has suggested that new hierarchies attributed elite status to virgins and celibate men; that members of both sexes could join this "new elite" by means of their personal choice to renounce sex.[108] Likewise, Kate Cooper explains the appeal of asceticism to women as the possibility to "claim a prestige that was enhanced by factors other than wealth or family status." Although, according to Cooper, social status and wealth could be helpful, the disruptive ideals of asceticism allowed for class mobility.[109] Michele Renee Salzman has, on the other hand, argued that these new Christian claims to *nobilitas* were not as revolutionary as they might appear at first glance. Although Christian leaders attempted to redefine *nobilitas* by claiming it for those who epitomized Christian piety (namely ascetics and, in particular, virgins), their rhetorical strategies reveal that they remained quite loyal to traditional conceptions of *nobilitas*. Virtually all named women who received this praise from the Latin Fathers already belonged to the upper social strata. According to Salzman, this Christian "appropriation of *nobilitas*" was thus brought on by the adoption of rhetorics that eventually diluted any potential and originally subversive implications that a universalized *nobilitas* could have entailed.[110] Correspondingly, in non-Christian contexts, conferring the *nobilitas* of *virginitas* by the identification of deceased girls from lower social strata as *virgines* might explain the examples discussed from the epigraphic material. The entanglement of nobility, sanctity and virginity that was so honored by the Romans made it beneficial to the deceased as well as to the surviving relatives when someone was commemorated as a *virgo*.

THE VIRGIN EFFECT

No matter how important social status was in the Romans' understandings of what a *virgo* could be, the status of the sacred virgins also relied on other factors that more specifically belonged to the realm of religion and sanctity. It is therefore worth looking even more closely at what it was exactly that made virgins so apt for sanctity, and how this sanctity was expressed. What divine benefits and favors were virgins believed to possess and incur better than non-virgins? The scholarship that deals with these questions is voluminous and complex, and some of the valuable qualities attributed to virgins will therefore only be briefly mentioned in passing, such as their alleged receptivity for prophetic gifts.[111] The ornamental function of virginal choirs in ceremonial settings is another religious function virgins could have. Sexual purity and the quality of being "untouched," *intacta*, were certainly underlying factors contributing to virginal sanctity, but how these qualities were transferred to "work" in the realm of ritual and "the sacred" could be expressed very differently. "Virgin effect" thus refers to the specific qualities attributed to virgins, qualities that were believed to benefit not only the individual virgin, but also their relatives and society as a whole. This effect would certainly vary from one context to another, and one explanation alone will rarely suffice when we encounter virgins who are given importance in contexts that are of a religious kind, whether they are consecrated virgins or secular virgins elected for specific occasions to serve in ceremonies and rituals. Some examples of how virgins – both secular and sacred – were believed to work positively on behalf of the community might therefore contribute to an understanding of the sacred virgins' esteem in Roman society.

Roman virgins and religious rituals

There is a general notion that the Vestal virgins represented an exception to the rules in almost every aspect of their being.[112] This, as already argued, does not mean that the religious valuation of their virginity should be seen as an isolated *casus*. In some respects, at least, their priesthood can be understood as an insti-tutionalization of more widespread practices where virgins *per se* were endowed with specific qualities that were thought to be necessary or beneficial in some of the Romans' religious rituals. Festus is our only source to mention the far less-known Salian virgins:

> Cincius says that the Salian virgins are hired. They come to the Salian priests dressed in war gowns and with apexes. Aelius Stilo wrote that they performed sacrifices in the Regia together with the pontifex in the manner of the Salian priests.[113]

Festus does not mention how frequently this ritual was performed, or to which god the sacrifice was made. The male *Salii* were dedicated to Mars, who had a sanctuary in the Regia (just across a narrow street from the temple of Vesta), where the Vestals were also known to sacrifice to the goddess Ops together with a public priest.[114] Mary Beard has proposed that the Salian virgins only held their "priesthood" for a brief period, and that new priestesses were chosen each year. She also assumes they were recruited from families of lower social status, possibly also slaves,[115] a status, as we have now seen, which might have compromised their "virginity" in terms of social standards.

Choirs of virgins performing expiatory hymns were not uncommon in Rome in times of crisis, or on the occasion of big ceremonies and celebrations. In the years 207 and 200 BC, processions consisting of 27 virgins (three times nine) passed through the streets of Rome singing a hymn to Juno. During the celebrations of the *Ludi saeculares* in 17 BC, 27 virgins and the same number of adolescent boys performed the *Carmen Saeculare* by the temple of Apollo.[116] The *Ludi saeculares* were performed after the same pattern as established by Augustus, in the reign of Claudius in 47 AD, Domitian in 88 AD and Septimus Severus in 204 AD.[117] Obsequens describes several episodes from republican times where choirs consisting of 27 virgins performed expiatory hymns after the discoveries of terrifying prodigies that demanded purificatory rites.[118] Choirs of virgins thus had an explicit lustral and apotropaic function in Roman religion, a function that perhaps was added to by the literary *topos* of virgin choirs as discussed above. Although these choirs appear to have been selected for the occasion and were not a permanent institution, their impact at stagings of religious rituals must have been memorable and important in shaping Roman perceptions of virgins. Prudentius refers to the "virgins themselves [the Vestals] and the chaste choirs," indicating that such were still part of the religious ceremonies that were performed in Rome, perhaps as late as the time of Symmachus.[119]

Virginal protection 1

The Vestals were no doubt the most prominent and famed virgins of all, and their sacred status was expressed by the solemn duties they performed and the privileges and honors they were granted. The eternal fire in Vesta's temple had to be tended and kept burning at all times. According to Dionysius of Halicarnassus, the fire was visible to anyone who passed by.[120] If it happened to go out by accident, Festus states that the Vestals were punished by being whipped by the Pontifex, and that the fire then could be rekindled in the old-fashioned manner by means of fertile material (*felix materia*).[121] The fire was renewed ritually once a year, on the first of March, which marked the New Year according to old Roman calendars.[122]

In addition to tending the sacred fire and performing ritual duties at the temple of Vesta, the Vestals had many obligations that were not specifically linked to the cult of Vesta only. As members of a public priesthood and the pontifical college, they participated in many of the public ceremonies and state rituals.[123] Sometimes they were part of the procession of priests, such as at the lustral ceremony of Amburbium,[124] and sometimes they were assigned specific roles, such as in the annual rituals of *Fordicidia* and the *Argei*.[125] Attempts have been made to explain the particular role of the Vestals at these rites, arising from a wish to understand both the specific rite and the more general role of the Vestals in Roman cult. Although the latter attempts tend to rely on rigid categorizations that in the end assume a thorough understanding of the logic of the Roman mind (as if it was unitary),[126] the common themes that seem to persist are purification and fertility. These are both very open categories that perhaps explain very little, apart from the fact that most Roman rituals contained elements that could be described as purificatory and meant to advance fertility and fecundity. The overall role of a Vestal, however, was that which was stated in the formula of her consecration, namely her duty to perform rites on behalf of the Roman people and by this to ensure the gods' benign help and protection.

Another of the much-discussed duties of the Vestal virgins is their making of the *mola salsa*, ground spelt mixed with salt. This was an indispensable ingredient in sacrifices,[127] where the sacrificial animals were consecrated when the priests sprinkled this mixture over them. The term *immolare*, this significant part of the sacrificial rite, was said to derive from *mola salsa*.[128] According to Servius, the Vestals prepared *mola salsa* three times every year in connection with the celebrations of Lupercalia, Vestalia and Iovi Epulum. The spelt had been collected by the three eldest Vestals on certain days in May and then prepared by them.[129] According to Pliny, no sacrifice was made without *mola salsa*, and the Vestals thus apparently provided it for all the public religious ceremonies in Rome.[130]

Vestal virgins were also entrusted with the safekeeping of some of Rome's most precious treasures, the so-called Roman *sacra*. These were surrounded with an aura of mystique and secrecy, and the sources disagree on what these *sacra* actually consisted of. The most famous of the *sacra* was the Palladium, an old wooden statue of Athena that was said to have been brought from Troy to Rome by Aeneas.[131] Like the fire of Vesta, the Palladium was regarded as a pledge and guarantee for Rome's continued well-being and existence. Cicero describes it as "the pledge of our and our empire's vigor."[132] According to Servius, the Palladium was one of Rome's seven *pignora*, sacred pledges, and Pliny also claims that a god by the name Fascinus was kept in the Vestals' charge.[133] Anne Dubordieu has recorded traditions in which the public *penates*, the household gods otherwise connected with the private cult of Vesta at the family hearth, were under the supervision of the Vestals.[134]

Regardless of what these Roman *sacra* actually consisted of, there was no doubt that the Vestals were thought to be in charge of some cult objects believed to be so sacred that all other humans had to be kept away from them. The stories of pontifex maximus Caecilus Metellus, who was blinded by the sight when he had saved the *sacra* from a fire in the temple in 241 BC, were well known and recounted by several ancient authors.[135] In his long passage concerning the sacred objects of the Romans, Dionysius concludes as follows:

> For my part, I find from very many evidences that there are indeed some holy things, unknown to the public, kept by the virgins, and not the fire alone; but what they are I do not think should be inquired into too curiously, either by me or by anyone else who wishes to observe the reverence due to the gods.[136]

Adrienne Staples has described the Palladium as "the symbol of the continuation of power, reaching backwards as well as forwards in time."[137] Staples sees the Vestals' role as analogous to the Palladium, in that they too "were pledges for the continued existence of Rome."[138] Horace applied the image of a single

Vestal climbing the Capitol together with the pontifex (maximus) as a metaphor for the perpetual existence of Rome and thus for eternity.[139] That the
Vestals and Vesta's eternal fire together was a symbol of Rome's continuity is
found scattered everywhere in the sources. Through the story of Rhea Silvia,
the virgin priestesses represented a link to the mythical and historical past and
the origins of the city, at the same time as they were the guarantee for its
continued future existence and well-being, *salus*. By their religious duties, on
which the correct performance was believed to rely on the priestesses' virginity and meticulous dedication, the Vestals protected Rome and its citizens from
all evil fortunes that threatened the city.[140]

Symmachus' appeal to the emperor in 384 AD, where he asked the emperor
to reconsider the legal restrictions placed upon the traditional Roman cults,
explicitly connected the upkeep of the rites and priesthoods with the well-
being of the community. The Roman senator and prefect of the city implied
that the failed harvest that had brought famine upon Rome was a result of
the gods' indignation because of the maltreatment of their own ministers.[141]
The Vestals' contribution in this protection over the inhabitants of Rome is
evident, since they are the only priesthood to be explicitly mentioned.

> Did the provinces ever have to endure such a disaster when the servants
> of the cults were provided for with public reward? When grain was given
> both to the people and to the sacred virgins […]?[142]

Symmachus' insinuation of a link between the famine and the sad economic
condition of the Vestal virgins in particular is very much in line with traditional
Roman conceptions of the public priests' role as maintaining the *pax deorum*
and securing the benevolence of the gods through cult and performance of
ritual. Symmachus' plea to the emperor interestingly stresses chastity and purity
as the very reason for the priestesses' esteem and honor. He only asks the
emperor to restore their immunity from tax, since their poverty makes them
unable to pay, and writes that "a virginity dedicated to the well-being of the
state increases in esteem when there is no (pecuniary) reward."[143]

Although particular rites where the Vestals were involved can often be interpreted in terms of purification or enhancing fertility (of for instance a harvest),
the overall "virgin effect" can be said to be their function as protectors and
guarantors of the eternal welfare and existence of Rome and her inhabitants.
In the mind of the pious Roman, the eternal fire of Vesta, the continued
virginity of Vesta's priestesses, the sacred pledges of the empire under the
virgins' watchful protection and the eternal existence of Rome were all intertwined and interdependent.

Virginal protection 2

In the opening lines of his hymn to the virgin martyr Agnes, perhaps the most
popular of all the virgin martyrs of Rome, Prudentius claimed for Agnes a new

role as protectress of Rome, representing her as guarding the well-being of the citizens – *servat salutem virgo Quiritium* – from her grave.[144] A true virgin, it is indicated, had replaced the false ones who previously served this function.

Similarly, Rita Lizzi has demonstrated how Orosius rewrites and appropriates the famous story of the Vestals' role as guardians and protectors of the Palladium and the Roman *sacra* during the sack of Rome by the Gauls in the fourth century BC. In Orosius' descriptions of Alaric's sack of Rome, a Christian virgin was guarding some sacred vessels of the Apostle Peter when the looting of the city had begun. By a designed encounter with a benevolent Christian Goth, the valuable vessels were brought to safety at St Peter's basilica, along with all the Christian inhabitants of Rome who joined the procession through the city. By leaving out the story of the Vestals' role in the republican sack of the city (as it is present in all of Orosius' sources), Lizzi argues that Orosius deliberately distorts the background in order to introduce a new virgin protagonist, one that replaces the old order that the Vestals represented. As Lizzi points out, traditional religious ideology and Christianity converged in the belief that the well-being of the community could depend on the sacred status held by someone due to their virginal purity.[145]

The protective powers of virgins were apparently not only restricted to Rome. Christian virgins were thought to bring glory and salvation upon the household and even extend their protective effects to the entire community or village. According to Peter Brown, "It was the individual householder who was thought to benefit most directly from the piety of his virgin daughter."[146] Susanna Elm refers to the protective powers of the virgin Piamun who prophesied on behalf of her community and protected her native village from attackers by transfixing them on the spot with her prayers.[147] The pseudo-Athanasian Canons stated that "For the salvation of the whole house is this one virgin. And when wrath cometh upon the whole city, it shall not come upon a house wherein a virgin is."[148] Teresa Shaw also notes that Canons 103 and 104 suggest that a wealthy woman without a virgin daughter could keep one of her virgin maids as her servant.[149] This may indicate, as has already been discussed, that not just daughters, but also servants and slaves were encouraged to dedicate themselves to perpetual virginity, and that their virginal qualities would benefit the whole household. That a consecrated virgin would have redeeming effects on her family's behalf is also conveyed by Ambrose in *De virginibus*:

> You have heard, parents, in what virtues and with what kind of discipline you should raise and instruct your daughters, so that you may have daughters by whose merits your own sins may be forgiven. A virgin is a gift of God, a protection for her family, a priesthood of chastity. A virgin is an offering for her mother, by whose daily sacrifice the divine power is appeased. A virgin is the inseparable pledge of her parents. She does neither trouble them about a dowry, nor forsakes them, nor injures them by word or deed.[150]

Both Jerome and Ambrose state that being the mother of a virgin is almost like being a virgin, and the redeeming effect is surely what they refer to. In the address to her virgin daughters, put in the mouth of the widow Juliana, Ambrose has the mother say:

> I think, for me to be the mother of virgins, is almost like I had preserved virginity myself. Consider, daughters, what mother the Lord Jesus chose for himself when he came to earth. To give salvation to the world he came through a virgin (*per virginem*) and dissolved the sin of one woman by the birth of a virgin: your integrity will also dissolve my sins.[151]

Jerome attempts to reconcile the precept of 1 Tim. 2:15 and his own advocacy of virginity in his treatise against Jovinian:

> For if the woman is saved in child-bearing, and the more the children the greater the safety of the mothers, why did he add "if they continue in faith and love and sanctification with chastity"? The woman will then be saved, if she bears children who will remain virgins: if what she has herself lost, she attains in her children, and makes up for the loss and decay, of the root by the excellence of the flower and fruit.[152]

Jerome alludes to the same notion in his letter to Laeta, the pagan pontifex Albinus' daughter and the mother of a little girl vowed to virginity. Here, Jerome states that Albinus, the unbeliever, is sanctified by his holy and believing family.[153] Jerome reminds Laeta, who has dedicated her infant daughter Paula to virginity, that she has to fulfill her promise. He compares the vow to infant baptism, stating that when children are so young, it is their parents who are responsible for ensuring the salvation of their children. For those who fear that the parents will then be held liable for the sins a child may commit after baptism, Jerome assures that baptism instead will be advantageous to the parents.

> But perhaps you imagine that, if they are not baptized, the children of Christians are liable for their own sins; and that no guilt attaches to parents who withhold from baptism those who by reason of their tender age can offer no objection to it. The truth is that, as baptism ensures the salvation of the child, this in turn brings advantage to the parents. Whether you would offer your child or not lay within your own choice, but now that you have offered her, you neglect her at your peril. I speak generally for in your case you have no discretion, having offered your child even before her conception. He who offers a victim that is lame or maimed or marked with any blemish is held guilty of sacrilege. How much more then shall she be punished who makes ready for the embraces of the king a portion of her own body and the purity of a stainless soul, and then proves negligent of her offering?[154]

Thus Jerome indicates that little Paula is now to be considered betrothed to Christ, and that this is a promise that may not easily be withdrawn. Still, the promise has been made by her parents on her behalf, not unlike other betroth-als in the Roman aristocracy, and by this promise, Jerome strongly insinuates, little Paula's family will benefit too.

Prudentius did not leave Symmachus' connection between the sacred virgins and the prosperity of the city uncountered. In his reply to Symmachus, he argues at length that the barren fields and failure of the crops have nothing to do with the Emperor's deprivation of the Vestal virgins. Prudentius concludes his lengthy comparison between the two types of virgins, stating that

> Our virgins too have their noble rewards – modesty, the face covered with the holy veil, honour in private, while their figure is unknown to the public, feasts seldom and slight, a spirit ever temperate, a law of chastity that is discharged only with death. Hence fruit an hundredfold is brought into their barns, barns never exposed to a thief in the night, for no thief assails heaven, and the seal of heavenly things is never broken by dishonesty; it is on the earth below that dishonesty is planned.[155]

What kind of harvest awaits the Christian virgins of Prudentius? Whether it is earthly or heavenly, as implied in his reference to the impenetrable granaries of heaven, the benefit is certainly one that exceeds the produce of the pagan Vestal virgins with whom they are compared. What is clear from the texts examined above is that the Christian virgins not only were seen to effect their own salva-tion by their virginity, but they also worked upon the salvation of others merely by their presence in the Christian community. The goodwill of God that these human symbols of purity, piety and sanctity incurred was thus expanded to benefit the virgin's closest family and eventually the community as a whole.

Sacrificial imagery

Closely linked to the redeeming role of the consecrated virgins on behalf of the community, is the widespread notion that the virgin somehow represented a sacrifice to God. This image is abundant in Christian texts, and Ambrose in particular returns to the *topos* of the virgin as *hostias Deo* on several occasions.[156] The immediate Christian intertext for this idea of virginity as a sacrifice to God is the letter to the Romans, which recurs frequently in these texts:

> I appeal to you therefore, brothers, by the mercies of God, to present your bodies as a living sacrifice, holy and acceptable to God, which is your spiritual worship.[157]

Most readings of this passage interpret it as applying to all Christians, and not just to consecrated virgins. Jerome, in the "obituary" for Marcella, describes her, for instance, as presenting herself as a living sacrifice in these terms.[158] Allusion to the sacrifice of the martyrs is evidently also part of the complex notions that this image evokes in early Christian writings. The misfortune of Jephta's virgin daughter, who unlike Isaac did not escape the "sacrificial knife," was integrated in Ambrose's defense of the virginal ideal, and became part of his elaborations of the virgin/sacrifice repertoire.[159] Similarly, an anonymous Greek homily named *On virginity* compares a son's vow to chastity as a sacrifice in analogy with Abraham's sacrifice of Isaac and ultimately God's sacrifice of his son.[160]

To Ambrose, it is the parents of the virgin alongside the virgin herself who appear to be the ones who offer this sacrifice to God. In *De virginibus*, she is described as the mother's sacrifice (*Virgo matris hostia est*).[161] Likewise, he opens the sermon he held at the consecration of the virgin Ambrosia by addressing her father, saying that

> the others you raise to have them leave the house and unite with strangers; this one you will always have with you. Also towards the others you will practice the pious duties of fatherhood, but with this one you will be more than a father, you will excel in your promise and zeal to please God. She, who will be the principal guarantee of your promises (*votorum*), she alone will repay that which you owe for her and for all your children.[162]

According to Jerome, there may be many kinds of virgins, "But that virgin is a sacrifice to Christ, whose mind has not been defiled by thought, nor her flesh by lust."[163] Christian sacrificial imagery is of course closely connected to the importance martyrdom was given in these centuries, and asceticism and virginity came to be understood as a daily martyrdom for Christ. Chastity, *pudicitia*, could, according to Jerome, be seen as a kind of martyrdom.[164] The imagery of virgin sacrifice is even more pronounced in Ambrose's highly dramatic account of the anonymous mother and sisters of Pelagia of Antioch at the closing of his third and last book in *De virginibus*. Here baptism, death and martyrdom are mingled as the women, fleeing from persecutors, commit suicide by drowning. According to Ambrose, the last words of the virgins' mother explicitly phrased her valuable sacrifice: "I offer these victims to you, O Christ, as guardians of chastity, guides of our journey, companions in suffering."[165] The willing sacrifice made by virgin martyrs was held up as inspiration and motivation for virgins who no longer had this dramatic possibility to demonstrate their sacrifice. This intertextual web of virgin sacrifice, martyrdom, self-sacrifice and virginity as sacrifice has already generated many interesting studies that also take into account the Greco-Roman context and literary examples.[166]

The "sacrifice" made by the virgin and/or her family upon dedicating her virginity to God thus accentuates the virgin effect that was believed to stem from such a vow. Deprived of the sanctity of martyrdom that had been possible for pre-Constantinian Christians, virginity became the second-best token of devotion and piety: the best way to ensure salvation and a life in eternity.

Chosen by the gods?

In his article from 1930, Arthur Darby Nock pointed at the notion of a Vestal, the *Virgo Vestalis Maxima* Cloelia Claudiana, as chosen by the gods, *a diis electa*, which appeared in one of the inscriptions found at the Atrium Vestae.[167] Nock sees the custom of divine choice, that according to the Romans was revealed through the drawing of lots, as the background for this idea of the Vestal as chosen by the gods. According to Aulus Gellius, the election of a new Vestal was originally done by gathering 20 virgins who fulfilled the criteria for election, and then choosing among them the one who was to become priestess by drawing lots.[168] Nock ties the idea of divine "election" to the cult of the emperor and its function in the official sphere to support and legitimize a ruler. The "rise in religious sentiment" that Nock therefore detects in the third century, as conveyed in the inscriptions dedicated to the *Vestales Maximae*, is taken by Nock to be an expression that coincides with "a new crystallization of monarchic sentiment."[169]

Against Nock, it must be remarked that the inscriptions from the atrium represent no reliable source for diachronic studies of the "religious sentiment" of which the Vestals were recipients. If commemoratory inscriptions were raised in the Atrium prior to 191 AD, when Empress Julia Domna rebuilt the temple and housing area, they are likely to have been destroyed in the many fires in this part of the Forum and in the subsequent restoration of the buildings and area. Rodolfo Lanciani has also commented upon the haphazard selection of remains from sculpture and epigraphy that was found during the excavations.[170] It is therefore difficult to estimate to what extent the surviving inscriptions, of which almost all date from the middle of the third to the beginning of the fourth century, constitute a representative selection of how Vestals were honored in the more than a thousand years the fire was tended in the temple of Vesta at the Roman Forum. The inscriptions that are preserved nevertheless express, as Nock noted, that the Vestals were highly revered in accordance with older notions of the Vestals' excellence, importance and vocation.[171] Their extolled status derived, among many causes, from the fact that their service was for the gods in general, and not merely the goddess from whom they had their title.[172] Although this explicit phrase *a diis electa* remains to my knowledge a hapax in our preserved sources for Vestal virgins, it is too tempting not to point out an author who reveals a similar notion to distinguish the status of a Christian virgin, a little more than a century later. Towards the end of the speech presented at the consecration of the virgin Ambrosiana, Ambrose calls upon her to put on the *stola* as she will assume Christ and as chosen by God (*sicut electa Dei*) to assume compassion, benevolence, humility, patience, etc.[173] D'Izarny sees this notion as part of the wedding analogy, as Christ – God himself – by Ambrose is presented as choosing and calling his own spouses. The role of the bishop is thus to call upon the young virgins in the name of Christ, but the initiator, the one who chooses, is Christ.[174]

Although it is tempting to focus on the honorary idea expressed in both these depictions of two different kinds of sacred virgins as elected by God/the gods, it is important not to underestimate the different settings in which this notion of divine choice is expressed. In the case of Cloelia Claudiana, it is an honorary inscription put up by her sister and brother-in-law, while in the case of Ambrose, we find the image first only as a simile (*sicut*) and, second, appearing within a larger complex of nuptial metaphors where it is the bridegroom who chooses his bride. Jerome makes a point of Matt. 20:16 and 22:14, stating that "many are called, but few are chosen" (*multi vocati, pauci vero electi*) to underline the preciousness of Eustochium's resolution.[175] Later, he cites the Song of Songs, and presents Eustochium as the perfect dove, chosen by her mother, which, according to Jerome, is the Heavenly Jerusalem.[176] Ambrose describes *virginitas* as the gift of a few, while marriage is the gift for the many, thus underlining the exclusiveness of virginity in contrast to the life of the majority.[177]

There is an apparent tension in Christian notions that chastity, although presented as the choice of an individual, could only be maintained by the grace of God. This would in turn indicate a specific status of the individual *vis-à-vis* his or her God, and certainly signal some kind of exclusivity reserved only for a few. Such notions are already found in the gospel of Matthew, and these passages are evoked in the Fathers' writings on virginity to stress this idea of being chosen.[178] John Cassian is the one who perhaps most explicitly elaborated on the notion that chastity could only be maintained by the grace of God, and thus in the end only be the result of a joint collaboration between the individual virgin's own determination and the will of God.[179]

This tension between choosing and being chosen also touches upon the virgins as predestined, or "chosen" by God, portrayed in the erotic language of the Song of Songs as the powers that unite bride and groom in their mutual commitment to each other. Love and devotion are persistent themes in the imagery evoked by the Fathers by their repeated references to the Song of Songs.[180] Socrates had other things than sacred virgins in mind when he asked Euthyphro: "Is that which is holy loved by the gods because it is holy, or is it holy because it is loved by the gods?" yet the final crux is along the very same lines.[181]

The quality of holiness that the consecrated virgins obviously were believed to possess could indeed be explained by a range of virtues, abilities, functions and effects, and whether the virgin and bride of Christ had been elected by the bridegroom, had chosen him for herself or been offered to him by her parents appears therefore to have been a result of the rhetorical strategy of the specific author and text in question. Even if the issue of predestination versus free choice is only lurking at the surface in these pre-Augustinian writings, there is a potential compromising of the free choice so ardently stressed by the Church Fathers in their normative descriptions of the ideal consecrated virgin.

A family affair? The problem of free will

An independent commitment to virginity based on voluntary dedication was regarded as one of the marks that distinguished Christian virgins from pagan virgin priestesses. The biblical cue for this ideal of free will seems to be taken from Paul's refusal to give precepts from the Lord regarding virginity, a passage that is repeatedly quoted by the Fathers.[182] On the other hand, the exegeses of Matthew 19.12 (*Qui potest capere, capiat*) were, as we have seen, often taken as an indication that celibacy and virginity ultimately depended on the grace of God. Although the Church Fathers stress the importance of the virgin's own free will in what was said to be the virgin's own choice, there are other indications in the sources that question the general validity of this distinction.[183] Ambrose, indeed, contrasts the virgin who was dedicated and encouraged by her parents with the one who takes on the virginal vow despite their will:

> It is a good thing, then, if a virgin's parents make an effort to encourage her to be pure, but it is still more glorious if the flame of a tender age betakes itself of its own free will, even without the support of its elders, into the blaze of chastity.[184]

Ambrose glorifies the heroic act of the determined virgin willing to defy her parents, comparing her to the impressive courage displayed by the Christian martyrs, yet he still pleads with the family to reach an agreement. "Parents may object, but they want to be won over," he claims, and a little later he advises the virgin: "Conquer your family feeling first, young woman; if you conquer your home, you will conquer the world."[185]

In their focus on conflict between the will of the individual virgins and their family's plans for the future of their daughters, Ambrose and his contemporaries often represent the family as the obstacle to the virgins' consecration. That the interests might go in the opposite direction is also noted, among others, by Peter Brown, who has pointed out that the will to create a society "based ideally on freedom of choice and not the usual 'organic' bonds of a family based society" did not always correspond to practice, for "children were frequently 'donated' to monasteries and to the clergy with as little respect for their own wills as once they had been married off."[186]

The so-called canons of Basil the Great addressed this problem, observing that some girls had not taken the virginal vow of their own free will, but that this rather was imposed upon them by their own family.[187] Jerome seems to confirm this practice in his letter to Demetrias, where he derides those who dedicate only daughters for whom they otherwise cannot find suitable husbands:

> Poor parents and mothers not filled with Christian faith often consign daughters who are deformed and crippled to virginity because they cannot find worthy husbands for them. So many pieces of glass are esteemed as highly as pearls, as it is said. Assuredly, those who consider themselves very

religious indeed, when they have given to their virgins only little money, and barely enough to nourish them, and lavish all their wealth and property upon their children of the world, both sons and daughters. Recently, in this city, a wealthy presbyter left his two daughters without any resources in their virginal vow, but provided his other children with abundant means for luxury and pleasure. I am grieved when I have to say that this has (even) been done by many women who share our resolution.[188]

As Jerome and Basil indicated, there might have been economic reasons for parents who were unable to raise a proper dowry to instead dedicate a daughter to the Church. Ambrose too notes the economic burden of "purchasing" a son-in-law as part of his attempt to convince parents that their daughters are better off if they remain virgins than if they marry.[189] Peter Brown also refers to a newly discovered letter by Augustine to a widow who had consecrated her daughter to virginity when the girl had been dangerously ill, but who then, when her second child had died, decided to marry off her consecrated daughter with the hope of getting grandchildren. In the place of her daughters' virginity, she wanted to offer a formal vow to remain a widow.[190] As Brown points out:

> The family decided the fate of the girl. If a girl was to remain a consecrated virgin, she had to be hedged around with a heavy sacral language.[191]

Brown draws attention to how, as "a human ex voto," the girl became a gift to the Church – a gift considered both sacred and irrevocable.[192] At the other end of the scale, we encounter martyr acts that heroify young girls who defy their parents and fiancées to become brides of Christ. The story of Thecla's "rebellion" in the acts of Paul and Thecla seems to have become emblematic in this respect. Ambrose, even though he extols this young (and most likely fictional) girl who sought refuge at the altar in his Church, nevertheless argues the importance of her family's final blessing or at least approval of her virginal calling.[193] The image of the headstrong young virgin, being a witness to faith through dramatic martyrdom, is a favored narrative and rhetorical *topos* that, in my view, has been given too much value as "historical documentation" for the rebellious, subversive and "feminist" nature of Christian asceticism in confrontation with what has been presented as traditional Roman misogynist values. As virginity came to be considered a new martyrdom, the determinedness of the martyrs was indeed a fitting image to be conferred on the virgin, and this *topos* was vividly explored in contemporary texts. That these hagiographies should somehow reflect the options and lives of the sacred virgins who lived in the fourth century is, however, not very convincing.

AGE OF VIRGINS

Closely linked to the question of free will, the Christian sources are increasingly preoccupied with how to decide the best possible age for girls to be consecrated to virginity. The almost contemporary arguments found in texts by Basil the Great and Ambrose of Milan could serve as useful points of departure to illustrate diverging opinions and concerns regarding these matters. I will then discuss inscriptions and documents from Church Councils that indicate that there were also other "rules" and practices, eventually rendering an even more complex image of the varied positions on these issues in the late fourth century.

Although presented as fixed and prescriptive, regulations on minimum age seem to have functioned as normative but flexible guidelines where the final decision ultimately was given to one of superior authority within the ecclesiastical hierarchy.[194] A good example is the minimum age given for widows in 1 Tim. 5:9: "Let no widow be taken into the number under threescore years old, having been the wife of one man." This is frequently quoted in the writings of the Church Fathers, although they by no means seem to agree on how strictly this ruling should be endorsed. Ambrose was quite willing to admit not only widows younger than sixty, but also those who had been married twice.[195] Basil of Caesarea, on the other hand, cited this passage as authoritative.[196] The interpretations and endorsements of these guidelines, even those given in the canonical scriptures, thus prove to have been far from fixed in the 370s and 80s. It is therefore interesting to see whether there were, by the end of fourth century, any regulations on the age of consecrated virgins similar to the one that was applied for widows. One of the borders in the delimitation of sacred virginity seems indeed to have been linked to age, and to the agency and free will of the virgin who is to become a sacred virgin. It is therefore relevant to look at different discourses concerning at what age it was considered acceptable for girls or women to be regarded as sacred virgins or to take the formal vow of virginity. In the cases where we find something equivalent to an advised or established minimum age for this type of vow, what were the alleged reasons for such regulations? Conversely, what could have been the motivation for not decreeing limitations on admission based on age?

In order to better grasp Ambrose's arguments regarding a minimum age for virgins at the *velatio* ceremony, it would be clarifying to examine how the issue was handled by Basil of Caesara, who had addressed the same subject just a few years earlier in one of his so-called canonical letters. However, some challenges with this kind of comparison must be acknowledged first. Not only do the sample texts belong to different literary genres, they also represent different cultural and geographical contexts. Basil's canonical letters provide guidelines in response to particular questions that had been presented to him by another bishop. Still, it is likely that these guidelines were intended to have general validity also for a wider audience of bishops. In Ambrose's text, on the other hand, the bishop addressed his own congregation in a sermon. In providing an almost contemporary text, Basil's letters may however elucidate the subject by revealing some significant differences between the teachings and practices of the late fourth century.

The age of virgins at consecration

The so-called canonical letters were written by Basil of Caesarea to Amphilocius, Bishop of Ionucum, between 374 and 375. The three letters are, in the modern editions, called canonical because their main concern is ecclesiastical discipline. Later editors have therefore arranged them into 96 canons after the pattern of Council rulings. In three of these "canons," Basil dealt with various questions concerning virgins; mainly how to sanction those who no longer are virgins, and how to avoid others from falling away from their vow.[197]

In canon 18 of the second canonical letter, Basil describes the virgin as "a spouse of Christ and sacred vessel dedicated to the Lord"[198] and gives his definition of the Christian virgin: "But we must now agree beforehand on this – that she is named a virgin who willingly has consecrated herself to the Lord, and has renounced marriage, and has preferred the life of holiness." He writes further,

> And we sanction their professions from that time at which their age possesses the fullness of reason. For it is not proper to consider children's words entirely final in such matters, but she who is above sixteen or seventeen years, and is mistress of her faculties, who has been examined carefully and has remained constant and has persisted in her petitions for admittance, should then be enrolled among the virgins, and we should ratify the profession of said virgin, and inexorably punish her violation of it.[199]

Basil's primary concern is the penitence prescribed for virgins who had not been able to keep their vow. In order to avoid such shameful behavior in the future, he finds it necessary to set new recruitment guidelines, because changing circumstances had rendered earlier rulings too lenient.[200]

The issue of free will and the independent choice of the girl was, as we have seen, presented by the Church Fathers as a sign of true virginity, in contrast to pagan and heretical practice, where virgins were said to be forced or bribed to make such a vow. According to Basil, the Christian girl had to be past a certain age for him to consider her reason fully developed. Only when she was past this age and her motives had been carefully examined,[201] could her vow be counted as valid and her transgressions thus be subjected to the consequences laid out. Basil explains further why he claims that virgins should be at least as old as 16 when they are consecrated. Because a girl's virginal profession could be beneficial for her family in some worldly way, parents and relatives offered young girls who did not necessarily possess the inner motivation for the virginal vow. These virgins may have been very young and were perhaps dedicated to the Church by families unable to support them. Setting the minimum age at 16, Basil's primary concern is thus to prevent girls unfit for virginity from bringing shame upon themselves and the Church.[202] If economic motivations made poor parents more likely to dedicate their daughters to the Church, Basil's regulations might indicate a general concern that girls from the poorer strata of society were at greater risk of lapsing because, in Basil's words, they did not choose such vocation freely. The moral stereotypes that so often followed social stratifications might, of course, have added to Basil's concerns.

The section of *De virginitate* discussed below is commonly understood as Ambrose's reply to critical voices, most probably from within his congregation, that seem to have arisen in response to his enthusiastic exhortations to virginity and widowhood the year before. In the words of Neil B. McLynn, this "self-defense" that Ambrose presented in *De virginitate* is "a masterpiece in evasion."[203] The text is like a rhetorical roller coaster, as Ambrose rapidly shifts from humbleness to haughty reproach, from satire to prayer, never lingering for long but constantly on the move. However, taking McLynn's point of view and seeing the passage in question as a concrete reply to parishioners' concerns, may help to structure the text. Ambrose discusses the age of virgins at the time of consecration, stating that "there are very many who say that virgins should be older when they are veiled." He continues:

> I do not deny that bishops have to be careful in order to avoid that girls are veiled rashly. The bishop should consider carefully not only her age, but also her faith and modesty. He should consider the maturity of her timidity, he should examine her grey hairs of seriousness, her old-aged conduct, her years of modesty, her chaste soul: then, finally, her mother's cautious protection and the temperate assiduity of her companions. If all these things are present, the virgin does not lack the grey hairs of old age: if they are absent, then the [consecration of the] girl should be put on hold, not as much because of her young age as because of her conduct.[204]

By and large, this line of argument is very similar to Basil's. Like Basil, Ambrose stresses the need to examine the potential consecrated virgin, to make sure she is proper "virgin material." Although Basil does not explicitly state who is to perform this examination, it is plausible to assume that, as Ambrose upholds, this was considered the duty of a bishop.

The passages of Basil and Ambrose, respectively, though read out of context as they have now been, seem to indicate that the two bishops more or less endorse the same point of view on this issue, alluding to the bishop's role in deciding who among the virgins was to be granted admittance. However, Ambrose has elsewhere in his sermon left us with some traces that indicate a rather divergent view on the age of virgins at consecration than that which Basil presents.

Although the accusations Ambrose is defending himself against are only known through his own rendering of them, we may still perceive a difference in opinion between the bishop himself and some of the members of his flock. If "very many people think that virgins should be older when they are veiled," then virgins accordingly, in the eyes of these critics, were too young when they were consecrated. It is impossible to deduce any underlying events behind this critique or whether Ambrose was at this point even aware of Basil's opinion on the age of virgins,[205] but it is not unlikely that this passage reflects general tensions and disagreements within Christian communities of the time.

The fact that Ambrose brings the subject of age and maturity up the way he does, makes it plausible that at least one or maybe more individual virgins from his own diocese were in question.[206] In order to follow his rather dense line of argument, it is necessary to trace his rhetorical exposition, to see whether the composition of this text may clarify his point of view concerning a minimum age for consecrating virgins. Such a reading will also allow us to see how Ambrose's understanding of virginity was potentially bound by a wider, culturally defined web of associations that clustered around the image of the consecrated virgins.

Those who belong to the kingdom of heaven

Ten passages earlier in the text, Ambrose had introduced a discussion on Matthew 19: 12ff., a recurring favorite in writings on virginity and chastity, and a scriptural passage that the bishop here argued was meant to illustrate that the virtue of sexual renunciation is not achieved by half-hearted efforts, "for he that is able to receive it, let him receive it."[207] Ambrose moves swiftly on to the succeeding passage in Matthew, where children are brought forth to be blessed, children who, "free from corruption, by their spotless age (*immaculata aetate*) have preserved the grace of integrity (*integritatis munus*)."[208] Also, with another quote from the same passage in Matthew, "Of such is the kingdom of heaven," he explains:

> that is to say, of those who have returned to a childlike chastity, as if to a state of infancy, unacquainted with corruption. Thus, virginity is certainly recommended by the heavenly Word and, according to the precepts of the Lord, to be desired.[209]

By linking the eunuchs for the kingdom of heaven to the sexual purity of children, Ambrose foreshadows his subsequent authorization of self-dedication to Christ regardless of age. Ambrose hastens on, lamenting the difficulty in making his Milanese congregation offer their daughters to the noble life of virginity, sarcastically rebuking those who fear that their wives might be affected with the ascetic movement ("they can no longer be virgins"[210]), and sardonically consoling worried fathers that their daughters will more easily be married now that so many others are promised to Christ and the competition for those earthly bridegrooms is reduced.[211]

This, then, is where he turns to the issue of age, in the above-quoted passage where he stresses that, no matter what her age is, a virgin can still be too young in her behavior and that age does not necessarily imply maturity. But he has not quite finished his argument. In the following passage, he states that "youth is not to be rejected, but the soul to be examined."[212] He contends that his prime example, Thecla, was not proven by her age but by her virtue, an echo of his appraisal of the 12-year-old virgin martyr Agnes in *De virginibus*.[213] Subsequently, the bishop asks his audience whether it is not so that "any age is appropriate for God, any age perfect in Christ? For indeed, we do not say that age entails virtue, but that virtue entails age."[214] He continues:

> Is it so unbelievable to us that girls of marriageable age[215] should follow Christ to his kingdom, when even children followed him into the desert?[216]

Ambrose finally picks up the line he seemed to have flung overboard so many passages ago and he returns to Matthew 19:14:

> Do not keep the children away from Christ, because they have accepted martyrdom for the name of Christ: 'for to these belong the kingdom of heaven.' The Lord is calling them, and you keep them back? In fact, the Lord says of the same ones: 'Let them come to me.' Nor must you keep away the young girls (*adolescentulae*), of which it is written 'therefore do the young girls love you,' and they will bring you into their mother's house. Do not, then, separate the children from the charity of Christ, those who already in the womb of their mothers bore witness to him with prophetic exultation.[217]

In an almost overwhelmingly condensed citation of the scriptures, Ambrose attacks his opponents who claim that girls should be older when they are consecrated, and he seems to reach some kind of conclusion when he commands them not to keep the children and the young girls away from Christ. It is quite evident that Ambrose applies this passage from Matthew to justify consecration of quite young girls, *adolescentulae*, girls who would be on the edge of or just passed puberty.[218] Unlike Basil, then, Ambrose has not indicated any minimum age for when virgins ought to be consecrated, nor does he, like Basil, deem the words of children to be less valuable than of those who are older. On the contrary, Ambrose's stern warning against preventing the children from approaching Christ indicates that no age limits should be set, if such a limit were to prevent potential virgins from dedicating themselves to Christ.

How are we then to interpret this "conclusion?" Is it primarily a rhetorical device in the argument against those who were not willing to dedicate their daughters to the Church?[219] Or should we also understand Ambrose to have been reluctant to postpone the potential nuptial of future brides of Christ? What seems likely is that Ambrose here not only needs to justify his past actions, he also proposes a standard for the continuation of his consecrations of rather young girls. A relevant question to ask then is what Ambrose might have meant by the terms *pueri* and *adulescentiae*. If what underlies this text is tension resulting from Ambrose's view, or perhaps even practice, of consecrating virgins deemed too young by members of his congregation, or perhaps even others outside of Milan, how are we to understand Ambrose's reluctance to postpone consecration? As already indicated, Ambrose might very well be referring to

actual cases in his own congregation. Admitting a mistake in front of his parishioners could be dangerous at this still early stage in his episcopate. Ambrose
therefore needed to justify his earlier judgments and actions.[220]

A relevant feature to consider is the nuptial analogy in the consecration
ceremony and the bridal symbolism attached to the Christian virgins. As we
have seen, this was not an explicitly Latin phenomenon, as Basil and other
Greek writers express the same image of the sacred virgins of the East.
However, some geographical differences, concerning both the veiling ceremony (which is not nearly as widely attested and stressed in the East) and
common views on the marriageable age for girls, should be considered in this
respect. Neil B. McLynn and Peter Brown have demonstrated the importance
Ambrose put on the veiling ceremony for virgins in his process of consolidating his rather sudden authority as bishop in Milan.[221] His main concern seems
to be the lack of recruits for the virginal choir in his church, a concern that is
raised at several points in his sermons on virgins and virginity. Perhaps the most
important reason is Ambrose's image of the consecrated virgin, the bride of
Christ, which in many respects is presented as an aestheticized conglomerate
of youth, nobility and ethereal beauty. The nuptial analogy might be a reason
why Ambrose thought it was unnatural for women long passed the conventional marriageable age to partake in such a ceremony.

Although Brent Shaw has indicated that the age of Roman girls at marriage
was considerably higher than prior estimations, he still concludes that for girls
of aristocratic families 12–14 years was quite common at their first marriage,[222]
and 12 was also the age at which girls were legally allowed to marry.[223]
To Ambrose, virginity entailed nobility. The consecrated virgin belonged to the
kingdom of heaven, by the throne of Christ and, although humble and ascetic,
her fleeting and covered-up presence gave her an elevated, aristocratic aura,
contrasted and thus enhanced by her youth.[224] The bride of Christ ought to
radiate nobility in every aspect of her appearance. For Ambrose, that would also
include her age at the time of marriage.

Epigraphic evidence and the age of virgins

Ambrose was not the only one who expressed admiration for the unwavering
resolution expressed by very young girls, as in his version of the story of
St Agnes. Jerome likewise drew attention to the tender age of Agnes when he
made her an example for virgins in his letter to the newly consecrated virgin
Demetrias.[225] Jerome also extolled the Roman virgin Asella for having chosen
a life in virginity when she was only 10, and having submitted to a strict
ascetical regime from the age of 12.[226] In his advice concerning a young
virgin's upbringing, Jerome indicates that when the girl reaches the age of
seven, she should learn to behave according to the chastity expected of
virgins.[227] Also Basil's sister Macrina is presented as exemplary in the eulogy to
their brother Gregory, because she displayed such a "firmness surprising in someone of her age" when she, barely 12 years' old, decided to remain unmarried

and a virgin.[228] The purpose of these descriptions is no doubt to make the audience marvel at the young girls' stern conviction, and to inspire fellow Christians to be steadfast in their faith. In this there is a powerful rhetorical construction of the paradox in the "little girl of grey-haired seriousness, of old-aged conduct,"[229] which we also encounter in the popular image of the virgin saints. The *topos* of *puer senex* was not uncommon in Latin commemoration or praise of children,[230] an image that the Christian writers certainly drew upon to describe young, determined virgins.

However, if we were to assume that these texts reflected some kind of reality regarding the age of consecrating virginity, we may, for instance, look to the literary sources that give several examples where girls were dedicated to virginity by their parents even before birth.[231] Although the formal consecration was likely to be postponed until the girl was older, a blurring of the categories is very likely. Since these young, even infant girls were already identified as virgins – and according to Jerome in particular, explicitly so as "virgins of Christ" – the distinction between those who had taken a formal vow and those who were only privately dedicated was not always obvious. Although we should not trust the inscriptions to give the exact age of the deceased girl,[232] they may nevertheless give us some idea of the age span in which girls and young women where characterized as virgins by the Romans. From the inscriptions already discussed above, we see a span between 11 (Citheris and Julia the *virguncula*) and 19 (Julia Sidonia).[233]

We must deduce that most of the Vestals mentioned in inscriptions were older than that. Moving to the Christian inscriptions (identified as such because most were found in the catacombs and recorded in the *Inscriptiones Christianae Urbis Romae*), we find a somewhat larger age span, although most *virgines* seem to have died in their teens. An inscription dated by consular date to 295 AD states that Statilia Alexandra *virgo* died at the age of 14.[234] Rufina, a *casta virgo* who was buried in 341 AD, lived to be only 12.[235] Another very fragmented epitaph, most probably from 398, is dedicated to the *virgo* Crescentia, who was, it seems, only seven when she died,[236] and Gemella *virgo* was no more than three.[237]

Many of the virgins commemorated in funeral inscriptions were in their early 20s, such as Luciferes who was "approximately" (*plus minus*) 19 when she died in 382, and Secunda who died in 362 at the age of 20.[238] Both Agapene, who died in 366, and Rufina, whose inscription is dated to 381, died at the age of 21, while Vervices, who was buried in 395, lived for 25 years as a virgin (*vicsit annos XXV virgo*).[239] Irene, the sister of Pope Damasus, lived to be 20 according to the Philocalean funerary epigram Damasus raised in her memory.[240] Among more mature virgins in this particular period, we encounter Maximilla, *virgo ancilla dei*, who was commemorated in a lengthy inscription when she died in 389 and who lived to be 50, Ioviana who died at 41, and Labinia, buried in 409 after having lived "more or less" 35 years.[241]

Interestingly, we also find infant girls described as *virgines* in the funerary inscriptions.[242] In the case of these infants, as well as with Crescentia Statilia

Alexandra, Rufina and others who all died at a very young age, the vocabulary concerning their presumed religious status is not necessarily unambiguous. Whereas Praetiosa, who died at the age of 12 in 401, is described as *puella virgo ancilla Dei et Christi*[243] – a clear specification of her religious devotion if not necessarily of a formal consecration as such – the vaguer term *virgo* in these other cases could also be read as an indication of the age, character and/or marital status of the girl at the time of death, as we have seen it appear so in non-Christian epitaphs. The term *virgo* in these inscriptions should therefore not necessarily be taken to carry any specific meaning as a title of a religiously devout person or a religious profession.

Hardly any of these epitaphs thus give information that lets us know for certain whether the virgin in question had undergone a formal consecration. The vocabulary is ambiguous and probably by no means standardized. Given the stress that many of the literary sources, and particularly Ambrose, put on the veiling ceremony, we may infer that the identification of the girl as *virgo* had been important to those who commissioned the inscription. The very terminology would then evoke all the implied allusions that the notion carried to Christian readers of the text, and the deceased girl would be commemorated in terms alluding to her status as one of Christ's brides, whatever her or her family's intentions might have been when she was alive. The epitaph would then not only present the girl in terms that evoked favorable virtues such as chastity and *nobilitas*, as the motivation might have been in pagan epitaphs, but also, by explicitly representing a non-consecrated girl as a *virgo* in the epitaph, those who commissioned the inscription might simply have wanted to lend her some of the consecrated virgins' sanctity or even nobility, perhaps with a hope to win some kind of soteriological benefit on her and their own behalf.

The age of Vestals at *captio*: virgins and children

By now we may appear to have moved a long way from the Vestal virgins. Given the significant role age played in the definition of Christian virgins as dedicated by their own free will, and given Ambrose's argument based on the integrity and sanctity of the children, it might add some contextual information to examine Vestal age requirements at the so-called *captio*, and also how children more generally were assigned specific cultic functions in Roman religion.

The Vestals themselves were, by modern standards, no doubt children when they were chosen for the priesthood. Aulus Gellius states that they had to be no less than six and no older than ten years of age, and have both mother and father still alive.[244] The age difference within the order might at times have spanned considerably, as the youngest could be only six and the eldest perhaps even as much as 70 or even more. This could also be what is reflected in some of the coins depicting Vestals, where the difference in size might have been an attempt to render this age gap by showing the youngest Vestals as children.[245]

The lustral role virgins were invested with parallels the role of a different group in Roman rites, namely that of children. Children with ritual duties associated with sacrifices and ceremonies were normally referred to by the term *camilli*. The exact meaning of *camillus* is uncertain. According to Festus, this is the correct designation for a freeborn boy.[246] He specifies further in his description of the Flamen's *camillus*: "*Flaminus camillus* is a freeborn boy whose mother and father are still alive. He assists the Flamen of Jupiter at the sacrifices."[247] Servius likewise calls the girls who assist the *flaminica Dialis camillae*, whereas Festus calls these small priestesses (*sacerdotulae*) *flaminiae*.[248] Varro provides even further information:

> A *camilla* is, according to those who interpreted words, someone who assists (*administram*) – in secret affairs, it should be added. Therefore is he called *camillus* who carries the basket in which the content is unknown to most of those outside the priesthood.[249]

Dionysius of Halicarnassus described a temple for Juno at Falerii, north of Rome, where women served at the sanctuary and an unmarried girl called the basket carrier (*canephorus*) performed the preparatory rites before the sacrifice, and a choir of virgins (*choroi te parthénôn*) praised the goddess.[250]

Camilli (and *camillae*) were required to have both parents living (*patrimi matrimique*), just like the Vestal virgins at their election to the priesthood. Servius' comment that they were *nobiles* indicates also that they were recruited from senatorial families. According to Dionysius of Halicarnassus, the most beautiful girl and boy from families of each *curia* were chosen in those cases where the priests did not have children of their own. These child ministers were then to serve until adulthood; in the case of the girls as long as they remained unmarried.[251] Like the basket-carrying *camilli* at weddings, the Vestals were also entrusted with sacred, secret objects only they were supposed to know. Tacitus relates how the Vestals, together with a group of children, performed purificatory rites in connection with Vespasian's restitution of the temple at Capitol:

> At the advice of the haruspices, the remains of the old temple were removed, and the new one was to be erected at the same spot as the old one, because the gods did not wish the old form to be changed. The space was decorated with garlands and *vittae* […], and the Vestals, accompanied by boys and girls with both parents alive, sprinkled water drawn from rivers and springs.[252]

This coupling of Vestals and children, or virgins and children more generally, seems to combine two aspects. An analogy between their sexual purity and their role in this lustral ceremony can be underscored by Columella, who explains that the necessity of avoiding pollution from sexuality in certain household duties was the reason that young boys or virgins should assist with the handling of food.[253] Their purity would thus in turn guarantee the purification sought by the religious rites they performed.

From a sociological point of view, an additional function of these choirs of virgins, adolescent boys and children could be deduced, in line with the programmatic iconography that art historians in particular tend to read from Augustan art such as the Ara Pacis. As symbolical representations of the prospective growth and future of Rome, these "displays of wealth" are perhaps in turn what triggers Ambrose to so ardently recruit for his seemingly extravagant virginal choir in Milan,[254] as he attacks paganism by attempts to surpass it in this very respect.

A due date for virginity?

The notion that virginity in the Greco-Roman world was "a temporary condition, even in the case of the Vestal virgins,"[255] must, as we have already seen, be said to be a truism in scholarship today. Ann Ellis Hanson points out that Hippocratic gynecology was based on the idea that sexual abstinence was dangerous for a woman's health once she had passed menarche. By the turn of the second century, however, we find that Greek doctors practicing in Rome take a different stand and claim there is no harm for a girl to remain a virgin, apart from the physical effects of an inactive life without children and family to care for.[256]

As has been noted already, the limited time of service set up for the Vestal virgins was one of the favored *topoi* in the Church Fathers' polemical comparisons with their own virgins, and also one that has won ground in contemporary studies. The ancient sources, however, are not as univocal as the Church Fathers. Plutarch, when explaining the priesthood of the Vestals, refers to the legal option that they were allowed to leave the temple after 30 years of service and to marry. Like Dionysius, Plutarch also indicated that the period of service was divided in three terms of ten years each, where the Vestals started out with a period of learning the duties, and then concentrated on performing them before they taught them to new recruits. Seneca, however, referring to the same process of advancement as something obviously well known to fellow Romans, does not mention the ten-year division.[257] Although such a regulated timeline might at first glance appear logical, considering that there were six priestesses who were to serve 30 years each, the calculations posited by the two Greek authors do not account for a few contradictory reflections supported both by their own descriptions as well as other observations regarding the priesthood. First of all, a Vestal could die before her period of service was due and, even though it did not happen very frequently, she could be penalized for breaking her vow. In both cases it would leave a position open that would disturb any rigid division in terms of ten-year periods. Second, both Plutarch and Dionysius state in the very same texts that only a very few Vestals chose to leave the priesthood, and that most continued as priestesses after the first 30 years:

> Then, the 30 years being now passed, any one who wishes has the liberty to marry and adopt a different mode of life, after laying down

her sacred office. We are told, however, that few have welcomed the indulgence, and that those who did so were not happy, but were a prey to repentance and dejection for the rest of their lives, thereby inspiring the rest with superstitious fears, so that until old age and death they remained steadfast in their virginity.[258]

No prosopographic source can document that any of the Vestal virgins actually did choose to marry after her 30 years of service, yet several testify to those who chose to remain Vestals until old age. Tacitus mentions a Vestal named Occia who had served for 57 years when she "retired," and epigraphic remains point in the same direction.[259] The only known epitaph for a Vestal virgin records that the priestess served 11 times her age when entering the priesthood, that is, at least 66 years, and she was apparently still a priestess at the time of her death.[260] Coelia Claudiana appears to have held status as *Virgo Vestalis Maxima* for at least 20 years, according to one of the inscriptions that honor her.[261] Considering these sources, it becomes less plausible that new Vestals were introduced regularly every five or ten years, and we may therefore assume that the transitions between the different grades of learning, doing and teaching were less rigid and more gradual over the years in the priesthood. Dio Cassius, who wrote at the beginning of the third century, interestingly chose the Greek term *aeiparthenoi*, "ever-virgins," to designate the Vestal virgins.[262]

The evidence for Vestals actually marrying after 30 years of service is thus very scant indeed, and no story of such an "unfortunate" bride has survived. However, an undated letter by Symmachus addressed to an unnamed Vestal did express concerns with rumors that circulated in Rome saying that she intended to leave her office before the time was due.

> Everything that is mentioned without an identified author is uncertain, but I cannot accept talk that affects the reputation of a sacred virgin. Therefore, in the capacity as pontifex and by the trust invested in me as a senator, I am advised to bring forth full disclosure. You are said to want to leave the Vestal secret before the years defined by the laws. I never believe in hearsay, but I await an assertion in your own voice which will either confess or refute the doubt of this report.[263]

The further fate of this particular anonymous Vestal is unknown but, combined with the polemics of the Church Fathers writing in the same period, one might get the impression that leaving the priesthood after the minimum years set for service had become a general rule by Late Antiquity. Such conclusions, however, do not find very strong support in a critical reading of the sources.

Jane Gardner has proposed a somewhat prosaic explanation for the Vestals' reluctance to marry when their scheduled time was due. Since the former priestess probably would be passed her child-bearing age when she was allowed to leave the priesthood, she was likely to be prey to potential husbands who were attracted to her wealth rather than her "wifely capacities." The transition from a privileged public life to married life was thus more or less doomed to end in misery.[264] Plutarch and Dionysius, however, imply that religious "superstitions" and fear of evoking the wrath of Vesta and the other gods was a significant reason why the priestesses preferred to continue in the service of Vesta.

Agency, age and the consecration of virgins

Returning again to Ambrose, it is difficult to extract from his writings even an estimate of the age from which he considered it appropriate to consecrate virgins. Although in *De viduis* he stated that "virginity [...] is the fruit of every age,"[265] the way he elsewhere repeatedly links virginity to youth – and also accentuates the purity of children in the context of his discussion in *De virginitate* – makes it tempting to assume that he would have thought the minimum age set by Basil to be at least a couple of years too high. This interpretation, as we have seen, becomes even more likely when his writings are read in light of Ambrose's social and cultural context, where the sexual and ritual purity of children and virgins were connected. That virginity in general was linked to age is, for instance, apparent from the first of Servius' explanations of the term *virgo* in his commentary on the Aeneid, where he merely stated that the term "*virgo* indicates both sex and age. *Virgo* said more than if it had said *femina*."[266]

Ambrose and Basil alike were concerned with defining and consolidating the bishop's authority and status, not only in relation to the consecrated virgins, but also in general terms. However, while Ambrose primarily expressed worry for the (in his view) low recruitment of new virgins, using his sermons to draw more virgins to the Church, Basil's concern was to regulate a group that did not yet seem to be fully under the Church's control. Regarded as the founder of monasticism in Asia Minor, Basil, according to Susanna Elm, "brought order into the chaos of experimentation by creating communities of ascetics and written precepts that were to set the standards for generations to come."[267] To Basil, the possible consequences of consecrating girls not yet aware of what their vow would entail could in the end be more damaging than beneficial to the expanding Church. A minimum age would thus hopefully prevent such embarrassing lapses. Ambrose, on the other hand, reveals his difficulty not only in persuading his parishioners to dedicate their daughters as virgins, but also in separating his image of the consecrated virgin from its entanglement with bridal symbolism. In his mind, the virgin was not only noble and ethereal; she was also the eternally young bride of Christ, "without a blemish, without a wrinkle."[268] The ornamental function of these virgins of the Church is evident in these passages. There are no indications of a maximum age for virgins,[269] although the older a girl was, the less likely would be her claim to the status as virgin. Consecration at a young age would thus, to Ambrose, be the best way to preserve virgins within the Church.

A normative minimum age for the consecration of virgins was by no means settled in the Western Church by the end of the fourth century. Only a couple of years after Ambrose gave his sermon, the council of Saragossa (in 380) set the minimum age of virgins at 40 years, while it was decided in Carthage 17 years later (397) that virgins of the Church should be past the age of 20.[270] Likewise, the local council at Carthage (dated 419) decreed that "deacons should not be ordained, nor virgins consecrated, under the age of twenty-five."[271] The geographic varieties and different opinions of the bishops and monastic leaders attested in the sources thus make it hard to pin down a general regulation on the minimum age for becoming a sacred virgin. This was no less complicated both by the various practices of virginity and the different understandings of sacred virginity and its meaning and function. The explicit tensions between the norms laid down by the authoritative figures of the Church and the practice revealed by their issuing of such norms are thus exemplified by the attempts to establish a minimum age for virgins.[272]

That age was an important issue and closely linked to the question of voluntary dedication is evident from the many sources that address this question through normative rulings. In his treatise *De virginibus velandis*, Tertullian had argued that it was age that determined when a virgin became a woman and should start to wear a veil like other grown women.[273] As already stated, the Vestal virgins were, by modern standards, only children when they went through the rite of *captio*, making them consecrated priestesses. In comparison, we find that, for the Christian virgins, marriageable age seems to have been a minimum limit for most, as the nuptial analogy came to frame so much of Christian virgin ideology. Children could indeed be dedicated by their parents to a future profession in the Church, a dedication that would then be understood, it seems, in analogy with the possibility for a betrothal contracted by parents on behalf of their children. Such dedications, although assumedly hard to oppose by the individual girl in question, would still not count as a lifetime commitment before the formal ceremony of consecration had taken place.

VIRGINAL INSIGNIA

Dio Cassius gives information on the purported background for the Vestals' privilege of being accompanied by a lictor, a privilege that was granted them by the senate in 42 BC:

> They [the senate] also allowed the evervirgins (*aiparthenoi*) to employ one lictor each, because one of them, not being recognized, had been insulted on her way home from a dinner party.[274]

Why was she not being recognized? Was it simply too dark, or were there actually no signs on a Vestal's dress or adornment that marked out her sacred status? The passage might indicate that there was one outfit for official duties, and less severe restrictions on what the priestesses were allowed to wear in private, making it difficult to identify her as a public priestess.

A necessary and important question to establish from the outset is to what degree dress was considered a marker of social status in Roman society. How, for instance, were secular virgins distinguished from *puellae* and *matronae*? Or from prostitutes and slaves? Also, when it came to the Vestal virgins, was there a specific dress or combination of clothes only to be worn by them? The same questions seem to arise when looking at the sources' descriptions of how Christian virgins were expected to dress. Were there any indications in their dress and outward appearance that could distinguish them from other girls or women of the same age? Negotiations over their status as sacred virgins would indeed have been closely linked to their visual appearance. Because clothing, hairstyle and headgear have received increasingly more notice in studies of women in antiquity and late antiquity, it is relevant to map out how virginal status, and particularly sacred virginal status, was communicated and marked by outward insignia.

The official dress of the Vestal virgins

According to Livy, Vestals were on two occasions suspected of un-virginal behavior because of their dress and conduct. This could indicate that Vestals had some individual influence on how they dressed. Nevertheless, decency and modesty were clearly demanded in their appearance.[275] Like the case of Dio Cassius' insulted Vestal, Postumia and Minucia from Livy's recordings of Roman history might have put on a more liberal dress in circumstances where they were not officially performing in the role of priestess.[276]

That there were certain insignia of the Vestals' specific status has already been indicated in the depictions given by Prudentius previously in this chapter. *Vittae* were woolen ribbons that were tied in a person's hair, normally to indicate ritual purity or dedication to the gods. In addition to being a part of the Vestals' appearance, they were tied to altars and sacrificial victims.[277] Unmarried young girls also tied their hair up with *vittae*, according to Judith Lynn Sebesta but, unlike married women, they did not cover them with a veil. The woolen ribbons of religious rites were white, and Sebesta thus infers that the *vittae* of unmarried girls were of the same color.[278] Flaminica, the priestess of Juno and wife of the Flamen Dialis, wore purple *vittae*, *vittae purpureae*, which were similar to those that *matronae* tied to their hair. At funerary rites and periods of mourning, they were dark blue.[279] *Vittae* were also an integral part of the Roman marriage ceremony and, as symbols of ritual purity and inviolability, the brides used them to adorn the doorposts and thresholds of their husband's house before they entered.[280] According to Propertius, *vittae* were worn by the bride,[281] and Sebesta argues that hair tied up by *vittae* was so special that it served as a distinguishing mark of the *matronae*, presumably separated from others who wore *vittae* in distinctive colors. For *matronae* as well as virgins and brides, the *vittae* were meant to symbolize the *pudicitia* of the one who wore it.[282]

Infulae were a different kind of woolen fillets, tied around a Vestal's head. Servius describes it as "a band, in the manner of a diadem, from which *vittae* fall on both sides. Most of them are broad, and they are for the most part twisted and in white and red."[283] *Infulae* were worn by priests and sacrificial animals, indicating that it was an ornament of specific religious significance.[284] Prudentius is our textual source for the Vestals wearing *infulae*, and the iconographical material confirms they did.[285] Scholars have posited that the Vestals' dress probably was the *stola*, the long gown traditionally worn by chaste and good Roman *matronae*.[286] The final characteristic part of the Vestals' outfit was also a headgear, the *suffibulum*. According to Festus, this was a white veil with purple borders that the Vestals wore when they were sacrificing, and Varro explains that the name was derived from the fact that it was fastened with a fibula "below."[287]

Color was an important marker of status, and purple in particular had a clear signification. Ambrose, for instance, had depicted the priestesses as dressed in purple. This may indeed only be a reference to the purple borders of the *suffibulum*, and not the entire outfit. Purple was the color of the stripes worn on the togas of senators and freeborn boys and, as such, it marked nobility and integrity.[288]

Nina Mekacher also mentions Suda, the tenth-century Byzantine encyclopedia, where it is said that the Vestals "were not admitted to wear flowers or unguents or clothing that was not white."[289] Eventually, if there indeed was a prescribed color for their dress, the scarcity of sources on this issue still leaves the question to our imagination.

Thus, according to evidence gathered in these sources, there was not much more than the white *vittae* that distinguished Vestals from the purple ones of *matronae*. The only exception would be when they were wearing the *suffibulum* for sacrificial duties, in which cases there would be no doubt about their official public role as priestesses.[290] One might therefore assume, if Dio Cassius' explanation for the lictor of the Vestals is indeed correct, that the darkness of the night would have erased any features that could have distinguished her sacred status. The Vestals were expected to dress *pudicae*, as was any respectable Roman lady.[291] Their social life in the Roman aristocracy and the ever-shifting fashion might nevertheless have influenced personal taste and caused some Vestals to stray from acceptable appearance.

The most distinctive features of the Vestals' official dress seems thus to have been the headgear. The hair underneath, however, has also caught much attention. Our sources provide several references to shearing and dedications of hair as part of virgins' *rites de passages*, at both weddings and consecration ceremonies. However, there are many difficulties connected to the interpretation of these references. Pliny the Elder mentions a lotus tree called *capillata*, because the hair of Vestals was brought there.[292] Pliny does not provide any information about the frequency or the amount of hair offered by the Vestals, and this has stimulated the field for hypotheses regarding this custom. One suggestion is that the complicated arrangement of the *infulae* functioned as a substitute for the Vestals' hair, based on an argument that Pliny's passage indicated that the Vestals' hair was cut short at all times because of regular hair offerings. La Follette supports this argument with sculptural evidence, where she claims to discern short locks underneath the traditional head coverings of the Vestals.[293] This theory certainly resonates well with general notions of the ambiguous gender of virgins, as they were thought to display male qualities, here symbolized with a male hairstyle. More traditional interpretations of Pliny's *lotus capillata*, however, take this to refer to some kind of initiation ritual, where the shearing of hair is a common motif.[294] Similar customs are known from Greece, where the bride dedicated a lock of her hair as a part of the wedding preparations.[295] The question is thus not only how often, but also how much of the hair that was actually donated at these occasions.

The analogy between Vestals and brides is supported again by a curious and corrupt passage of Festus describing the specific hairstyle known as *seni crines*: "The brides are adorned with *seni crines* because this is the eldest kind of embellishment. Therefore are also the Vestals to be adorned in this manner, whose chastity towards their husbands [* * *] from others."[296] There is general consensus that *seni* is a distortion of the number *sex*, indicating some kind of six-fold braid or arrangement of the hair.[297] Janet Stephens has convincingly reconstructed the Vestal hairstyle, calling attention to the one common feature of the Vestal portraits, namely how the hair is twisted back from the face and around what she calls a structural vitta along the hairline. This particular feature of the Vestals' hairstyle, she indicates, also seems to have inspired different hair style fashions, as seen in the shifting fashions in portraits of Roman upper-class women.[298]

Festus describes a peculiar Roman custom linked to the marriage ceremony called *hasta caelibari* where "the head of the bride used to be dressed with the celibate spear which had been planted in the body of a gladiator thrown aside and killed."[299] For those eager to establish a motif of symbolic mutilation, or even death, the cutting of the hair of the virgin bride/Vestal-to-be fits well in the analogy with the touching of the head with a spear.

It is generally assumed that the Vestals' dress and hair was an imitation of the bride's on her wedding day, yet the question of who "imitated" who remains an open one. The bride was also supposed to carry a *flammeum*, a veil with a characteristic red "flame" color. According to Festus, again, the *flammeum* was part of the required costume of the official priestess *flaminica Dialis*, and it was supposed to ensure good auspices for the bride because the priest of Jupiter, the *flamen Dialis* and his wife the *flaminica Dialis*, were unable to divorce.[300] If the Vestals, on the basis of *seni crines*, were to be regarded as "eternal brides," the same logic would assume *flaminicae* to be in a similar situation. Just as probable is the explanation proposed for the *flammeum*, that the dress of the bride comprised elements thought to bring good luck for the young bride, and that the *seni crines* were formal insignia of chastity and virginity, proper symbols indeed for a bride to display on her wedding day. As for the priestesses, the symbols would in turn acquire new meaning in the interplay with their position in the Roman wedding celebration, rendering any attribution of "original wearer" quite meaningless.

"The garments of Christ"

Originally only a private or perhaps semi-private oath, the vow of the Christian virgins came to be marked with a solemn ceremony, the so-called *consecratio* or *velatio*, in Latin Christian communities by the middle of the fourth century.[301] The virgins were blessed by a bishop who formally put on the veil that marked their new status. The ceremony was modeled after Roman nuptials, and the virgins were described as brides of Christ.

René Metz concluded in his study from 1954 that there was no specific outfit assigned for Christian virgins in the first four centuries.[302] He particularly derives his conclusion from a discussion of Ambrose's remark on the changing of clothes, *vestis mutatione*, mentioned in his account of Marcellina's consecration,[303] and the references to the virgin putting on a *stola* as she puts on Christ in *De insitutione virginis*.[304] According to Metz, these passages must be read allegorically as they signify the Christian virtues with which the virgin from now on will be adorned. There is certainly a clear allusion to the *vestimenta* of baptism in Ambrose's consecration rite, yet whether this also involved an actual change of clothing to mark the important transition is difficult to ascertain. Neil Adkin equally sees the references to garments of Christ in Jerome's writings on virginity as a reference to "putting on" celibacy.[305]

Although Sulpicius Severus' text is a little later, and therefore not necessarily representative of Ambrose's time, a special dress for virgins is indicated in his *Life of Saint Martin*. An ex-prefect named Arborius healed his daughter from agonizing fever by applying a letter from St Martin on her heated body:

> This event had such an influence upon Arborius, that he at once consecrated the girl to God, and devoted her to perpetual virginity. Then, proceeding to Martin, he presented the girl to him, as an obvious living example of his power of working miracles, inasmuch as she had been cured by him though absent; and he would not suffer her to be consecrated by any other than Martin, through his placing upon her the dress characteristic of virginity [306]

Again, the *habitu virginitatis* may have been merely metaphorical speech, but we may also discern a development of an institutionalized dress code. Metz concludes, however, that no existing documents verify that consecrated virgins in this period bore a specific and identical "uniform" to mark their virginal status. He does nevertheless argue that the virgins were expected to dress chastely and in clothes that expressed solemnity, for example by choosing sinister colors, and that this is what Ambrose (according to Metz) refers to in his mention of the *vestis mutatio*.[307]

The colors in Ambrose's description of the virginal garments at the consecration of Ambrosia likewise carry symbolic meaning, and it is very difficult to determine whether they refer to actual clothing or merely elaborate rhetorical points. The purple of the virgin's veil, Ambrose states, is colored by the blood of Christ,[308] and he prays that God dressed his maidservant in clothes that will always be clean, like she will be clean. He turns to the virgin and says with reference to Eccl. 9:8: "May your clothes at all times be white."[309] According to Metz, then, the veil was the only official marker of the status of Christian virgins.[310] However, respectable Mediterranean women in general would also be expected to wear veils.[311] Jerome eventually follows both Tertullian and Cyprian when he advises Eustochium to take care how she dresses: "Let your dress be neither too neat nor too slovenly; neither let it be so remarkable as to draw the attention of passers-by, and to make men point their fingers at you."[312] There is here thus no evident indication of a virginal "uniform," but the encouragement to dress as is fitting according to chastity and for her status.

Just as the hairstyle of Vestal virgins has been a conundrum for modern scholars, the sources' depictions of Christian consecrated virgins' hair have caused some puzzlement. The fourth-century Synod of Gangra declared, "If any woman from pretended asceticism shall cut off her hair, which God gave her as the reminder of her subjection, thus annulling as it were the ordinance of subjection, let her be anathema."[313] Jerome has described a custom among Syrian and Egyptian virgins where they shaved off their hair in secret, mainly for reasons of hygiene, but seemingly also as a renunciation of beauty and vanity.

> It is usual in the monasteries of Egypt and Syria for virgins and widows who have vowed themselves to God and have renounced the world and have trodden under foot its pleasures, to ask the mothers of their communities to cut their hair; not that afterwards they go about with heads uncovered in defiance of the apostle's command,[314] for they wear a close-fitting cap and a veil. No one knows of this in any single case except the shearers and the shorn, but as the practice is universal, it is almost universally known. The custom has in fact become a second nature. It is designed to save those who take no baths and whose heads and faces are strangers to all unguents, from accumulated dirt and from the tiny creatures which are sometimes generated about the roots of the hair.[315]

In his letter to Eustochium written in 384, the same practice was referred to with more disdain, as he reproaches those who overstated their ascetic lifestyle, and falsely so, in order to get praise and credit for their exaggerations:

> Others change their garb and assume the mien of men, being ashamed of being what they were born to be – women. They cut off their hair and are not ashamed to look like eunuchs.[316]

A law passed by Theodosius I in 390 forbade all kinds of women from cutting their hair, and threatened any bishop who allowed women with "shorn hair" to enter their Church or receive communion that they and their "comrades" would also be expelled from the Church.[317]

Hair is in many cultures taken to be a significant marker of gender, and recent interest in gender-bending and gender ambiguity resonates in the focus on virginal hair, whether Christian or pagan. Most likely, the mandatory (yet occasionally discharged, as the discussions of Paul and Tertullian indicated) veils would in Late Antiquity have covered most of the hair of adult women and at least adult virgins. Also, as Jerome remarked with no taint of disdain, on the contrary, the Egyptian virgins did this not to draw attention to themselves, as "no one knows except the shearers and the shorn." Hairstyle could thus not be a public marker of Christian virginity as long as the precept to veil the head was followed. Still, as Jerome himself remarked with reference to the Egyptian nuns, as the practice was said to be universal, it was also universally known. What was hidden under the veil was thus in principle only known to "the shearers and the shorn," and others were left to speculate on what possible secrets the veil hid.

De habitu virginum – or "how to recognize a virgin" 1

In his treatise regarding the dress of virgins, Cyprian had urged virgins to avoid make up and luxurious clothing and to adopt a modest appearance fitting their virginal status. He further stated, "A virgin should not only be [holy in body and spirit], but also be perceived and believed to be so. No one, when they see a virgin, should doubt whether she is one or not."[318] Although things might very well have changed since the time of Cyprian, if we follow Metz we have no certain evidence that consecrated virgins wore a particular type of dress to designate them from other virgins. That there were signs in their appearance and apparel, most probably in the form of a distinguishable veil, is quite probable, considering all indications of such a visible mark of status, but any reconstruction will be highly uncertain and local variation may also have been significant. For instance, Tertullian argued that virgins in second-century Carthage should be veiled in the manner of married women, so that they did not stand out in the congregation with their bare heads.[319]

Macrobius narrates the story of a female slave named Tutela or Philotis, who bravely (and with the senate's approval) headed a delegation of other female slaves, all dressed as *matresfamiliae* and *virgines*, in a scheme that eventually saved the Romans from an enemy that threatened to take all the city's freeborn mothers and virgins.[320] In this passage, we see that status, particularly the differentiation between free women and female slaves, ought to have been discerned by the very outfit of the wearer, yet these markers were taken on by imitators who by their preposterous imitation actually saved the day. That secular virgins were not always recognized by their dress, however, is indicated by a passage from Ulpian, arguing that if anyone should accost virgins, even if they are dressed in slave-clothing, it should be considered a minor sexual sin, but worse than if the woman accosted was dressed as a prostitute and not as a matron.

The point Ulpian appears to be making is that the attire of a woman, in legal terms in any case, is no excuse if she has been insulted or her attendant abducted (!).[321]

A curious legal source that may concern the discussion of a specific dress of sacred virgins is a law that was issued in 394 by the emperor Theodosius:

> We also add to the foregoing provision that actresses of mimes and other women who acquire gain by the wantonness of their bodies shall not publicly wear the dress of those virgins who are dedicated to God. Nor shall a woman or a boy who is known to belong to the Christian religion be tainted by consorting with a man of the stage.[322]

Judith Evans Grubbs finds that the reference to mime actresses and "others who earn their living by the wantonness of their bodies in public" generates interesting questions:

> [1.] Was this some new type of mime devised along the lines of the old adultery mime, depicting the debauchery of Christian virgins as a comic farce? Or [2.] were these mimes dressed as virgins really Christian converts who were trying to abandon their old profession for a life of penitent celibacy?[323]

Evans Grubbs seems to opt for the second question as the soundest hypothesis as it fits her general argument, and she therefore does not linger on the first question. In line with scholarship that has focused on Christian asceticism's appeal to women's agency, she claims that "conversion to Christianity presented an attractive alternative to a degrading and wearying life on the stage."[324] The main argument Grubbs poses is that rulings of both civil and ecclesiastical law suggest that the hagiographical motif of the penitent prostitute (and/or actress) that was particularly popular in the Eastern Church, was more than just a literary *topos*.[325] If this really was a problem, however, and this particular law in question was intended exactly for such girls who tried to leave their earlier non-Christian occupation and present themselves as Christian converts, it still seems highly unlikely that they should wear the dress of consecrated virgins. Their former profession would indeed have made them unfit for status as consecrated virgins in the first place, whether they were "actual" virgins or not, as they were unlikely to ever be regarded as such due to their previous lifestyle (which would have inflicted severe injuries on their spiritual virginity) as well as their low social status.[326]

In my view, Evans Grubb's first suggestion – that these mimes wore costumes of consecrated virgins in order to mock or, perhaps even more plausibly, to play explicitly on suppressed, forbidden sexuality (hence eroticizing the consecrated virgins) – seems to be equally plausible. However, both explanations presuppose that virgins "dedicated to God" wore a dress that made them recognizable as such, both to the public and to those expected to see that the law was implemented. That the untouchable virgins could have such an erotic allure, one that could make them attractive to make a display of on stage, might not come as a surprise, and there are also other sources hinting that this could be a market for prostitutes to specialize in.[327] What nevertheless appears evident here is that sacred virgins by this time wore dress or garments that distinguished them from other women, a distinction that could certainly be misused by anyone with the wrong intentions. Some time had passed since Ambrose wrote his first treatise on virginity, and even more since Athanasius' visit to Rome. That consecrated virgins by the time of 394 wore a dress that marked their status is therefore quite probable. The law of Theodosius thus expresses a need to protect the virgins from impostors, whether they, as Grubb suggests, were remorseful new converts or actual show girls and prostitutes who wanted to make money out of this public display of sacred virginity.

Virginal appearance

Seeing that clothing was used to convey the status of the married Roman *matrona* as distinct from unmarried girls, Lynn Sebesta posed as a rhetorical question: "If the unmarried, adult woman did adopt a different costume, at what age would she have done so?"[328] This, it seems, was exactly Tertullian's concern for the Carthaginian virgins who continued to appear in public without the veil that married women were expected to wear.

There were many reasons why one would want to be able to visually mark out consecrated virgins, and also secular virgins, from other categories of Roman women. But what exactly did virginity "look like"? And how was it to be distinguished from chastity, or *pudicitia*? As Rebecca Langlands has argued, *pudicitia* depended on some type of "display" in order to be valued,[329] and this delicate balance between chaste humility and its need to be displayed to be recognized clearly was a conundrum also in the Late Antique negotiations of virginity. This need for a display of virginity is what apparently makes many of the Christian authors attack those who were insufficiently modest and humble to balance on this edge of demands to modest and virginal appearance on the one hand and the public presentation of it on the other.

The discussions above indicate that virgins could and should indeed be identified as such, but how and by what kind of markers is still not all that clear. Yet, as Cyprian had stated, "No one, when they see a virgin, should doubt whether she is one or not."[330] The only problem is perhaps that this was a normative proclamation, and not a descriptive one. For those who had a lot invested in the virginity of others, the look of virginity was unfortunately not one to be trusted.

The young and noble virgins of Rome

What, then, was a virgin according to the Romans, and how was she recognized as such? In terms of fixity, it seems that social status and, to a lesser extent, age could be indicators, but several degrees of flexity in this respect are still to be found in the texts examined above. The virgin as bride is also a recurring point of "fixity" that emanates a potent and flexible symbolism. These are in turn culturally and socially defined aspects that gave meaning to the notion of sacred virgins, as individuals believed by members of the respective religious communities to have specific qualifications intrinsic to this virginal status. From the comparative perspective, by opposing these religious communities, the question that arises is of course to what extent this chapter merely continues to reverberate the "echo of the Church Fathers."

To a large degree, the *topoi* established by the Fathers – *topoi* that later became heavily laden with ideology on either side of the main religious adversaries in the history of European Christianity – have also been featured here, and some of them have been further explored in this chapter. I do not claim to rise above the limitations set by the Fathers' comparisons and later historical reception of them. Rather, I wish to bring attention to how the terms for comparison that, to some degree, were set in the Church Fathers' polemical texts and how, in turn, later reception and not least religious debate during the Reformation and Counter-reformation have given new meanings to these comparisons. Particularly with the focus on free choice as an important distinction, the recycling of these arguments by reformist Christians resulted in images that still have the most permeating effect today. Depictions from the Reformation of Catholic nunneries as bordellos – and the virgins as forced into them by poor or ambitious parents – portrayed images that again have reflected upon conceptions of sacred virgins in Late Antiquity, pagans as well as Christians.[331]

Facing this complex and ideologically laden history of reception from the Church Fathers until today, I have tried to grapple with some of those polarizations that have been most enduring in the history of comparisons between Vestals and Christian virgins in Antiquity, namely the significance of lifelong virginity versus virginity for a limited period, the Christian wealth of virgins as opposed to the six that the Romans allegedly could barely convince to serve, and the free choice versus forced service. I have attempted to complicate these neat generalizations by drawing attention to how the sources may present a more complex picture when the "testimony" of the Church Fathers as well as the non-Christian sources are scrutinized and questioned. Considering some perspectives that have hitherto been absent from these comparisons, such as social status and age, I have aimed to highlight how "Roman virginities" functioned as fixating, yet by no means fixed, points for the Christians in their efforts to define a specific Christian "virgin," both rhetorically, in the desire for theological flexity, and in the constant returning to fixity. This is seen in the complex bridal imagery, which is so intermingled with conceptions of virginity, in the notions of ("true") virgins as belonging to certain social strata within society, in understandings of virgins as having a privileged connection to the divine sphere, in perceptions of virgins in terms of age, and in terms of symbols and markers that communicated virginal status to the surrounding community.

I have by no means argued that these "criteria" were understood as "fixed" in Roman conceptions of what virgins in general – or sacred virgins in particular – were, but rather that they functioned as fixating denotations, pulling and creating tension as the desire to flex and extend the meaning of virginity became increasingly pressing due to the universal ideals of Christianity.

The Christian virgins should thus not be understood as some kind of crypto-pagan imitation of the Vestals, no more than the Vestals were a prefiguration of Christian virgins. I hope to have demonstrated that the Vestal virgins and the Christian virgins neither were two versions of the same kind, nor that they ought to be compared merely in terms of difference, on their "own terms," outside the historical and cultural context that frame them both. The status they held as sacred virgins would, I argue, necessarily have been negotiated in relation to this shared context, a context in which they both figured and thus in turn mutually attributed to in the negotiations around contemporary conceptions and valuations of their sacred virginity.

The Vestals were Roman public priestesses, the Christian virgins lived privately and preferably secluded. While the Vestals performed their cultic duties in the temple of Vesta at the Forum and elsewhere on public holidays for every passer-by to see, the Christian virgins were told to stay indoors. Still, analogous to what Langlands has shown in her study of *pudicitia*, the value of the virgins' virginity depended upon some kind of "display," whether it was the attention drawn to a veiled face, or the assigned seats at public and religious ceremonies. There are many aspects that could be emphasized in order to draw attention to the difference between these two kinds of consecrated virgins, yet the fact that they were all Romans living in the same period and relating to the same cultural heritage and values makes the model of mere difference or sameness too limited to grasp the complexity of this particular expression of religiosity in Late Antiquity.

Despite the Christian desire to expand and universalize the concept of "virginity" and include virgins of all ages and social statuses, we find that some authors, and perhaps particularly Ambrose and Jerome, in these respects were confined by the fixity of virginity or, more precisely, the already established conceptualization of "the virgin," as she was roughly yet stereotypically sketched in terms of age, social status, and aesthetic imagery. This does not mean that attempts to flex this meaning were impossible – on the contrary. Still, it is clear that no matter how these Church Fathers' language pertaining to the earthly, consecrated virgins displays and elaborates a vivid metaphorical mysticism, the social fixity of virginity – the various points of fixity that constrain the desire for flexity conveyed with such metaphorical density – is revealed as they repeatedly envisage the young, aristocratic bride as beautiful and suitable for the "Prince" of the Song of Songs. Thus, in the tension between soteriological exegesis and the virgins' increasingly elevated place in ascetic hierarchies, a space opens for new borderline virginities, fluctuating between the fixity of the young, female, aristocratic or freeborn "bride", and a religiously motivated need for more flexible notions of virginity.

Notes

1 Visser 2001: 256.
2 E.g. Markus 1998, Brown 2001: 651.
3 Hier. *Ep.* 107.1: *Quis hoc crederet, ut Albini Pontificis neptis de repromissione matris nasceretur: ut praesente et gaudente avo, parvulae adhuc lingua balbutiens Christi Alleluia resonaret, et virginem Dei in suo gremio senex nutriret?* Transl. NPNF2. For Albinus, see Bjørnebye 2007: 199–200, PLRE I s.v. Albinus 8 (Publius Caeionius Caecina Albinus).
4 Zos. *H.N.* 5.38. See also Lizzi 2009 on Roman priesthoods after Theodosius' legislation.
5 The skewed sources of respectively pre- and post-Constantinian times make it difficult to establish exactly how long this coexistence may have lasted.
6 Clark 1998b: 430. See also Clark 1998a: 30 and Jacobs 2000.
7 Spiegel 1990: 76.
8 Spiegel 2005: 8.
9 Martin 2005: 9.
10 Cf. Clark 1998a: 14.
11 For a recent approach to social history that is also attentive to the literariness of the sources, see Osiek and MacDonald 2006.
12 E.g. Treggiari 1993: 105, Pomeroy 1995: 164, cf. Plu. *Lyc. et Num.* IV.
13 For instance, the Roman's seemingly uncomplicated feelings about adoption may indicate that modern scholars have put too much emphasis on the importance of "legitimate heirs" through blood relation in this respect. Likewise, Augustus' marriage to Livia is just one of many examples illustrating that virginity could be of less importance when alliances and good matches had to be made.
14 Treggiari 1993: 83. In a note she refers to one example to explain "practically unexampled," a certain Iaia of Cyzicus who was a contemporary of Varro's and who is mentioned by Pliny in NH 35.147.
15 Treggiari 1993: 125–59.
16 Plu. *Lyc. et Num.* IV, Shaw 1987, Harlow and Laurence 2002: 56–8. According to Eyben 1972, most medical writers claimed that puberty arrived around the age of 14.
17 AE 1916, 00056, cf. de Gubernatis 1916: *Virginis hoc titulo nomen non debuit esse / quae cunctos artes perbibit et cecidit / nunc Ianuaria iaces annos ter quinque sepulta / eripuit miseras invida flamma preces / in te certebat species formata pudore / et studium nitens ad maiora bona / si non fatorum praepostera iura fuissent / mater in hoc titulo debuit ante legi.* For the Romans' habit of commemorating children with funerary inscriptions see King 2000 and Rawson 2003.
18 Courtney, E. 1995: 190, *Musa Lapidaria*, transl. with commentary = CLE 1997. *D.M. memoriae. / Iulia Sidonia, Felix de nomine tantum, / cui, nefas, ante diem ruperunt stemina Parcae / quam procus, heu, nuptiis hymeneos contigit ignes / (ingemuere omnes, Dryades doluere puellae, / et Lucina facis demerso lumine fleuit, / virgo quod et solum pignus fueratque parentum)- / Memphidos haec fuerat divae sinistratae sacerdos; / hic tumulata silet aeterno munere somni. / U(ixit) a. xuiiii m.iii d.xiiii: h(ic) s(ita) e(st).* The goddess of Memphis is Isis Cf. AE 1974, 00260: *Trebia C(ai) f(ilia) Sa/turnina vi/xit annis XIII / mutatum officium est alium sper[ave]rat usum / fax infelicis virginis heu superi / quae thalamis aetas fuerat iam nubilis apta / destituit sponsum flebilis et soceros.* This inscription, dated to the second century and originated in Puteoli, reflects the same theme. The myth of Orpheus and Eurydice appears to be a pertinent allusion.
19 CIL 6.7898 (p 3439) = CLE 01058 (displayed at the Museo Nationale Romano, Terme di Diocleziano): *Hic sum Bassa sita pia fi[lia] / virgo pudica excedens / cunctas ingenio aequalis / cum mihi bis quinos annos mea / fata dedissent undec<V>mum me / non licuit perducere annum / cumque pater materque deos pro me / adularent at saevos Pluto rapuit / me ad infera templa / opside me Parcae finem fecisse videntur / cum ante alios*

vernas tres rapuere mihi / si quis forte mea gaudet de morte iniqua / huic sit iniqua Ceres perficiatque fame / Caeciniae Sex(ti) f(iliae) Bassae.

20   Rose 1925, cf. Dowden 1989: 2 and passim.

21   Harlow and Laurence 2002: 51. They also assume (p. 138) that virgins were somehow treated differently in death, although the nature of this difference is difficult to establish. This is deduced from Dio Cassius' description of the death of the daughter of Sejanus, Dio Cass. 58.11.

22   CIL 6.35887, (=ILS 8168, CLE 1532): *cara meis vixi, virgo vitam reddidi, / mortua heic ego sum et sum cinis, is cinis terrast, / sein est terra dea, ego sum dea, mortua non sum, / Rogo te, hospes, noli ossa mea violare. / Mus vixit annos XIII.* My transl.

23   CIL 3.1128 (=CLE 1565): *Vibia C[ai] l[iberta]/ Citheris/ an[norum]XI h[ic] s[ita] e[st]/ virgo hic sepul/ta fida puella ia/cet ante quidem/ tempus fata rapue/runt mala scripsi / ego per lacrimas/ miserabilis mor/te puellae p[ater] p[osuit]* (From Carnuntum, modern Austria). This could also be a Christian epitaph.

24   Cf. Faroult 2006: 24 on de Sade and his contemporaries' representations of the Vestals.

25   Macr. *Sat.* I.15, 21: […] *ideo tunc vitantur nuptiae in quibus vis fieri virgini videtur.*

26   Aug. *Civ. Dei* VI.9 […] *quae [Venus] ab hoc etiam dicitur nuncupata, quod sine vi femina virgo esse non desinat?* My transl.

27   Harlow and Laurence 2002: 64. For the rape of the Sabine women as important founding myth, cf. Stehle 1989, Beard 1999.

28   For the virgin girdle see, for instance, King 1993: 120–1, Martini 1997b: 487–8 (the nodus Herculaneus) and Panayotakis 2000.

29   Aug. *Civ. Dei* VI.9, my transl. *Pertunda* from *pertundo*: thrust through, perforate. Cf. Sissa 1990: 174–5. The idea of the wedding night as the "first time" for the bride and something that might frighten her is also remarked upon in Seneca's *Contr.* 1.2.22–3 (*Novimus […] istam maritorum abstinentiam qui, etiamsi primam virginibus timidis remisere noctem*). Although Catull asks in *Carm.* 66.15–17: *estne novis nuptis odio Venus? anne parentum frustrantur falsis gaudia lacrimulis, ubertim thalami quas intra limina fundunt?*, he is certain the tears are fake.

30   van Gennep 1981 [1909]: 175ff.

31   On this, see Sappho quoted below, p. 180 and Kelly 2000: 68.

32   Cat. *Carm.* 62.39–47: *ut flos in saeptis secretus nascitur hortis, ignotis pecori, nullo convulsus aratro, / quem mulcent aurae, firmat sol, educat imber, /******/ multi illum pueri, multae opravere puellae; idem cum tenui carptus defloruit ungui, / nulli illum pueri, nullae optavere puellae: /sic virgo dum intacta manet, dum cara suis est; cum castum amisit polluto corpore florem, / vec pueris iucunda manet nec cara puellis.* My transl. *Defloro* used as specific reference to "destruction" of virginity appears to be Christian and particularly favored by Ambrose, cf. TLL, sv. "defloro" and "defloration," e.g. Ambr. *Ep.* 5.11, Ambr. *De Iacob.* 2.7.32, Ambr. *exhort. Virg.* 6.35, Ambr. *Cain et Ab.* 1.10.46, Ambr. *Vid.* 15.88.

33   Cat. *Carm* 61.36–7, cf. Cat. 34.2: *Dianae* […] *puellae pueri inegri*….

34   Cat. *Carm,* 62.56: *Sic virgo dum intacta manet, dum inculta senescit.* Transl. Green 2005: 127, with changes.

35   Cat. *Carm,* 62.59–65: *Et tu ne pugna cum tali coniuge, virgo. / non aequumst pugnare, pater cui traditit ipse, / ipse pater cum matre, quibus parere necessest. / Virgintas non tota tuast, ex parte parentumst; / tertia pars patrist, pars est data tertia matri, / tertia sola toast: noli pugnare duabus, /cui genero sua iura simul cum dote dederunt.* My transl. According to Plin. *Ep.* 14.6–8, a good-looking bridegroom could be a consolation in the exchange with the bride's virginity.

36   Roskam 2000.

37   For an attempt, based on a not always convincing reading of the sources, see Treggiari 1994.

38   Dig. 50.17.30: *Ulpianus 36 ad sab. Nuptias non concubitus, sed consensus faciat.* Transl. from Watson 1998, cf. Gardner 1991: 31–60.

39   Harlow and Laurence 2002: 60, i.e. Dig. 23.2.5 and 6.
40   Dig. 23.2.7: *Paulus 1.S ad l. falcid. Ideoque potest fieri, ut in hoc casu virgo et dotem et de dote habeat actionem.*
41   Suet. *Aug.* 62: *Sponsam habuerat adulescens P. Servili Saurici filiam, sed reconciliatus post primam discordiam Antonio, […] privignam eius Claudiam, Fulviae ex P. Clodio filiam, duxit uxorem vixdum nubilem ac simultante cum Fulvia socru orta dimisit intactam adhuc et virginem.* Cf. Sen. *Contr.* 1.2.22. *Hoc genus sensus memini quendam praetorium dicere, cum declamaret controversiam de illa quae egit cum viro malae tractationis quod virgo esset et damnavit.*
42   Juv. *Sat.* IX.70–3: *Verum ut dissimules, ut mittas cetera, quanto / metiris pretio, quod ni tibi deditus essem / devotusque cliens, uxor tua virgo manerent?* Transl. Loeb, with my amendments. It is a similar insult that is expressed in Cat. *Carm.* 67.
43   Methuen 1997 discusses the figure in Christian writings. This is, however, not an image exclusive to Christian literature. Apuleius, for instance, describes Psyche as a *virgo vidua* in *Met.* 4.32 when drawing attention to her state as unmarried. See also Ignatius, *Smyrn.* 13.1 on "the virgins that are called widows," cf. MacDonald 1996: 225.
44   Ambr. *Inst. virg.* 41: *Cum enim initiatur conjugium, tunc conjugii nomen adsciscitur; non enim defloratio virginitatis facit conjugium, sed pacto conjugalis.* My transl.
45   Hier. *Adv. Jov.* 13: *Non omnis innupta, et virgo est. Quae autem virgo, utique et innupta est.* Transl. NPNF2.
46   Watson 1983, Osiek 2003: 257, cf. Langlands 2006: 209.
47   Salzman 2001.
48   According to Boswell 1984: 16 "By Diocletian's time distinctions between 'free' and 'servile' among the lower classes had become blurred – no longer recognized in many areas." For the new categories of *humiliores* and *honestiores* that were to more or less replace older distinctions based on citizenship, see e.g. Kuefler 2001: 50–4, Evans Grubbs 1999: 5–8. Evans Grubbs 1999: 277 and passim discusses the dissolution of categories and imperial authorities' attempts to reimpose such distinctions through legislation in the fourth century. It is perhaps no coincidence that the concerns for the upkeep of class distinctions are most discernible in legislation concerning marriage and, as such, it also bears relevance to the valuation of *virgines.*
49   Osiek 2003: 255–74 and 257. See also Osiek and MacDonald 2006: 103–5 and Harper 2013: 6–7.
50   Salzman 2001: 384.
51   Salzman 2001: 274, cf. 382–3. For Roman *nobilitas* in Late Antiquity, see Salzman 2002: 17–18, Salzman 2002: 200–19 and Brown 2012: 94–101.
52   Dio Cass. 55.22.5, e.g., Price 2001: 828–9.
53   Mekacher and van Haeperen 2003.
54   Aul. Gell. *N.A.* I.12.5: *item cuius parentes alter ambove servitutem servierunt aut in negotiis sordidis versantur.* Cf. Gardner 1991: 22, who refers to the episode recounted by Tacitus in *Ann.* 4.16.
55   Cf. e.g. Hopkins and Beard 2006: 82 on Commodus, who supposedly was rumored to be the result of his mother's affair with a gladiator (hence his own un-emperor-like behavior).
56   Staples 1998: 140–5 has, in my opinion, made too much out of the juridical peculiarities documented by Aulus Gellius, stating that the Vestal, upon *captio*, (the ceremony of "consecration") left her father's *potestas.* As now thoroughly argued by Gallia 2015, all evidence suggests that the Vestals maintained their family ties, although they were perhaps no longer legally binding.
57   Liv. 8.15, Bauman 1992: 17. Wildfang 2006: 84 claims that Minucia was not necessarily the first plebeian Vestal, but that her status became important in the trial of *incestum*, which according to Wildfang is to be understood in light of the struggle for power between plebeians and patricians.
58   Saquete 2000: 137–43 and 119–27. Cf. Raepsaet-Charlier 1987: 691–2.
59   Lact. *Mort Pers.* 1.40.

60 CIL 6.2140 and CIL 6.2144. The inscriptions are datable to the second half of the third century. For problems on how to understand the term *clarissima femina*, (and *clarissimus*) used to define senatorial status cf. Salzman 2002: 21 and 23. For the importance of the Vestal virgins' family ties, see Gallia 2015.

61 CIL 6.2145 (=ILS 1261) *Coeliae Concordiae virgini / Vestali maximae Fabia Pau/lina C(ai) f(ilia) (or clarissima femina?) statuam facien/dam conlocandamque / curavit cum propter /egregiam eius pudici/ tiam insignemque / circa cultum divinum / sanctitatem tum quod / haec prois eius viro / Vettio Agorio Praetexta/to v(iro) c(larissimo) omnia singulari / dignoque etiam ab huius /modi virginibus et sa/cerdotibus coli statu/am conlocaret.* Cf. Symm. *Ep.* 2.36.

62 CIL 6.2128 (=ILS 4933) and CIL 6.2143. For a (secular) virgin as patrona, cf. CIL 6.12055.

63 *Exp. tot. mund* 55.19–22: *sunt autem in ipsa Roma et virgines septem ingenuae et clarissimae quae sacra deorum pro salute civitatis secundum antiquorum morem perficiunt et vocantur Virgines Vestae.* Transl. Beard, North and Price 1998 Vol. II: 360.

64 Symm. *Rel.* 3.13, cf. *Rel.* 3.7, where Symmachus writes that the emperor Constantius "filled the priesthoods with men of noble birth" (*replevit nobilibus sacerdotia*). Cf. Salzman 2001: 382 for Ambrose's response, claiming true nobility for the Christian virgins.

65 Adkin 2003: 250.

66 Hier. *Ep.* 127.1: *Neque [....] praedicabo; ut exponam illustrem familiam, alti sanguinis decus, et stemmata per Consules et Praefectos Praetorio decurrentia. Nihil in illa laudabo, nisi quod proprium est, et eo nobilius, quod, opibus et nobilitate contempta, facta est paupertate et humilitate nobilior.* Transl. Rebenich 2002: 121. Note that Jerome already in the next paragraph remarks upon the fame of the name of Marcella's husband. Cf. Salzman 2001: 365–7. In a note to his translation of *Ep.* 127 (i.e. note 4 and 5), Rebenich 2002: 197 lists a number of references for, respectively, "Jerome's refusal to praise the lineage of the deceased" and Jerome's "redefinition of nobility."

67 Hier. *Ep.* 22.15: *prima Romanae urbis virgo nobilis esse.* Cf. Hier. *Ep.* 66.3. For the varied suggestions put forth regarding Eustochium's age at the time Jerome wrote his famous letter to her, see Adkin 2003: 8–9.

68 On Asella as possibly Marcella's sister, see Salzman 2002: 168, Lizzi 1991: 56, Sivan 1993: 82. Asella's consecration is normally dated to have taken place in 344 AD. The golden necklace Jerome refers to in *Ep.* 24.3 indicates that she came from a family of some means but, then again, apparently not as noble as that of Eustochium.

69 Hier. *Ep.* 130.6: *Agnoscere in illius proposito mentem suam, et gratulari, quod nobilem familiam, virgo virginitate sua nobiliorem faceret.* Transl. NPNF2, cf. Aug. *Ep.* 150 and Salzman 2001: 370. For Demetrias' nobility, see also Jacobs 2000: 733, who argues that Augustine, unlike Jerome and Pelagius, "deliberately deflated her nobility."

70 Ambr. *De virgb.* I. 65. *Memoriae nostrae puella dudum nobilis in saeculo, nunc nobilior Deo, cum urgeretur ad nuptias a parentibus et propinquis, ad sacrosanctum altare confugit. Quo enim melius virgo, quam ubi sacrificium virginitatis offertur?* My transl. For other references to the nobility of virginity, see *Inst. virg.* 106, *De virgt.* 87.

71 Ambr. *Exh. virg:* 82. *At non sancta Sotheris, ut domesticum piae parentis proferamus exemplum (habemus enim nos sacerdotes nostram nobilitatem praefecturis et consulatibus praeferendam; habemus, inquam, fidei dignitates, quae perire non norunt); at non, ut dixi, Sotheris vultus sui curam gerebat: quae cum esset decora facie valde, et nobilis virgo majorum prosapia, consulatus et praefecturas parentum sacra posthabuit fide, et immolare jussa non acquievit: quam persecutor immanis palmis caedi praecepit; ut tenera virgo dolori cederet, aut pudori.* My transl. For Sotheris, cf. *De virgb.* I. 37–8 and Consolino 1982: 476.

72 Ambr. *De virgb.* II 7. *Primus discendi ardor nobilitas est magistri. Quid nobilius Dei matre?* My transl.

73 Salzman 2001: 380.

74 Lizzi 1991: 69. The wedding analogy of the consecration ceremony could perhaps give a juridical pretence for manumission, as Roman law allowed for younger female slaves to be freed for the purpose of legal marriage.

75 McLynn 1994: 66–8, e.g. Ambr. *De virgb.* I.57 and 59.

76   Lizzi 1991: 69–70.

77   Clark 2005: 39.

78   Hier. *Ep.* 39.1: *Humilitas vestium non (ut in plerisque solet) tumentes animos arguebat: sed cum interiori se mente dejecerat, inter ancillarum virginum cultum dominamque nihil medium, nisi quod in eo facilius dignoscebatur, quod neglectius incedebat. Vacillabant aegrotatione gressus, et pallentem ac trementem faciem, vix collum tenue sustinebat.* See also Undheim 2015: 66–7, Adkin 2003: 268–9.

79   Hier. *Ep.* 79.9: *Habeto tecum viduarum et virginum choros, habeto tui sexus solatia. Ex ancillarum quoque moribus dominae judicantur.* Transl. NPNF2, with my changes. Cf. Hier. *Ep.* 54.14 (to the widow Furia): *Redime virgines, quas in cubiculum regis inducas. Suscipe viduas, quas inter Virginum lilia, et Martyrum rosas, quasi quasdam violas, misceas: pro corona spinea, in qua Christus mundi delicta portavit, talia serta compone.* Hier. *Ep.* 127.3: *Semper in comitatu suo virgines, ac viduas, et ipsas graves feminas habuit.*

80   Hier. *Ep.* 130.6: *Quasi ex radice foecunda, multae simul virgines pullularunt, exemplumque patronae et dominae secuta est clientum turba atque famularum. Per omnes domos fervebat virginitatis professio: Quarum cum impar esset in carne conditio, unum erat praemium castitatis.* Transl. NPNF2. See also Aug. *Ep.* 150.

81   Hier. *Ep.* 22.29: *Si quae ancillulae sunt comites propositi tui, ne erigaris adversus eas, ne infleris ut domina. Unum sponsum habere coepistis.* Transl. NPNF2. Adkin 2003: 268 refers to the similar notion expressed in Aug. *Ep.* 150.

82   Hier. *Ep.* 130.6: *Per omnes domos fervebat virginitatis professio: quarum cum impar esset in carne conditio, unum erat praemium castitatis.* My transl.

83   Joseph et Aséneth. 2.10–11. Other terms indicating these virgins' servile status are found in the text, where, for example, Aseneth is presented as their *kyria* and addressed as *despoina* in 10.6–7. Cf. 17.4–5, 19.1 and 20.2.

84   For Ambrose's "showmanship" see McLynn 1994: 68 and Brown 1988: 260.

85   E.g. Ov. *Met.* 2.426 and Ov. *Met.* 2.441, cf. Ovid's description of Vesta in *Fast.* 6.293–4: *iure igitur virgo est, qua semina nulla remittit / nec capit, et comites virginitatis amat.* Cameron 1989: 182 notes the "ancestors" of the virginal choir in Methodius' *Symposium*. The 11,000 virgin maids of Saint Ursula, as well as the 144,000 (male) virgins in the Apocalypse of John may also be seen as part of this "wealth display" of virgins.

86   Cf. Hier. *Ep.* 22.16 on the derogative description of a Christian noblewoman and her train of "eunuchs" and Hier. *Ep.* 130.19: *Digna res risu, imo planctu, incedentibus dominis, ancilla virgo procedit ornatior, ut pro nimia consuetudine quam incomptam videris, dominam suspiceris.* Aware of Jerome's vivid rhetoric, it is still tempting to linger on this last example, which evokes the wonderful image of a *domina* displaying her humility by dressing conspicuously modestly, while still conveying her social status and wealth through the luxurious dress of her virgin *ancilla*.

87   Hier. *Ep.* 22.29: *Provocentur et aliae. Honor virginum sit invitatio caeterarum. Quod si aliquam senseris infirmiorem in fide, suscipe, consolare, blandire, et pudicitiam illius fac lucrum tuum. Si qua simulat, fugiens servitutem, huic aperte Apostolum lege: «Melius est nubere, quam uri»* [1 Cor. 7:9]. My transl.

88   Hier. *Ep.* 130.6: *Quae virginum Christi non hujus se societate jactavit?* My transl.

89   For wet nursing, see Joshel 1996, Osiek and MacDonald 2006: 100. Prostitution and slavery, see e.g. Harper 2013: 45–52.

90   Metz 1954: 117 gives some examples from the time of Gregory the Great, where rulings stated that it was the slave owner who had the final say when a slave girl wanted to dedicate herself to religious life.

91   Dig. 18.1.11.1 *Ulpianus 28 ad sab.*: *"Quod si ego me virginem emere putarem, cum esset iam mulier, emptio valebit: in sexu enim non est erratum. ceterum si ego mulierem venderem, tu puerum emere existimasti, quia in sexu error est, nulla emptio, nulla venditio est."* (Transl. Watson 1998.) In this first case Ulpian introduces the hypothetical buyer as a blind man. However, it should be noted, for the sake of arguments that we will return to in subsequent chapters, that the next example does not necessitate such a premise.

92 Dig. 19.1.11.5, *Ulpianus 32 ad ed.*: *"Si quis virginem se emere putasset, cum mulier venisset, et sciens errare eum venditor passus sit, redhibitionem quidem ex hac causa non esse, verum tamen ex empto competere actionem ad resolvendam emptionem, et pretio restituto mulier reddatur."* (Transl. Watson 1998.)

93 Dig. 1.18.21 *Paulus l.S. de off. adsess.*: *Praeses cum cognoscat de servo corrupto vel ancilla devirginata vel servo stuprato, si actor rerum agentis corruptus esse dicetur vel eiusmodi homo, ut non ad solam iacturam adversus substantiam, sed ad totius domus eversionem pertineat: severissime debet animadvertere.* Dig. 47.10.25 *Ulpianus 18 ad ed.*: *Si stuprum serva passa sit, iniuriarum actio dabitur: aut, si celavit mancipium vel quid aliud furandi animo fecit, etiam furti: vel, si virginem immaturam stupraverit, etiam legis aquiliae actionem competere quidam putant.*

94 See e.g. Dig. 48.5.6.1, 48,5.35.1, Gardner 1991: 121.

95 Cf. e.g. Gardner 1991: 118–19. For laws concerning sexual relations with one's own slaves, see Evans Grubbs 2002: 173–80, Evans Grubbs 1999 passim, Arjava 1996 passim and Harper 2013.

96 For instance, to what extent could we assume that the *subintroductae* who caused so much trouble for the righteous Church Fathers were slaves or *libertae* of the clerics that they cohabited with? According to the Apostolic Constitutions, male clerics were forbidden to have female house slaves as concubines (Osiek and MacDonald 2006: 116), but it is not certain whether this also entailed keeping female slaves or freed to help with domestic tasks. If these women officially were said to be virgins dedicated to God, this might very well be a measure to enhance the honor and status of the male cleric. As a practical solution, we can imagine that the reasoning behind such cohabitations were exactly that they would at least not impede claims to chastity. According to Clark 1977: 179–80, it is apparent that practical issues like economy and the need for protection of poor women were among the arguments of those who favored such arrangements.

97 Cf. Nielsen 1999.

98 CIL 6.10096 (= ILS 5213): *Eucharis Liciniae l(iberta) / docta erodita omnes artes virgo vixit an(nos) XIIII / heus oculo errante quei aspicis leti domus / morare gressum et titulum nostrum perlege / amor parenteis quem dedit natae suae / ubei se reliquiae conlocarent corporis / heic viridis aetas cum floreret artibus / crescente et aevo gloriam conscenderet / properavit hora tristis fatalis mea / et denegavit ultra veitae spiritum / docta erodita paene Musarum manu / quae modo nobilium ludos decoravi choro / et Graeca in scaena prima populo apparui / en hoc in tumulo cinerem nostri corporis / inf<e=I>stae Parcae deposierunt carmine / studium patronae cura amor laudes decus / silent ambusto corpore et leto tacent / reliqui fletum nata genitori meo / et antecessi genita post leti diem / bis hic septeni mecum natales dies / tenebris tenentur Ditis aeterna domu / rogo ut discedens terram mihi dicas levem.* (Translation from http://www.stoa.org/diotima/anthology/wlgr/wlgr-mensopinions40.shtml with my amendments (last accessed 19 March 2016).)

99 Dig. 23.2.44pr, Cod. Theod. 4.6.3. Cf. Evans Grubbs 2002: 148–9 and 166–8 and Treggiari 1993: 61ff.

100 Then again, epitaphs are in many ways likely to have had fewer restrictions than many other genres.

101 CIL 6.28280: *Valeriae Sympherusae / Eugamus patronus fecit / v(ixit) a(nnos) XIIII dies XXX virgo.*

102 CIL 6.25808 (p 3532) = CLE 01570: *V(iva) Salvidiena Q(uinti) l(iberta) Hilara / Salvidienae Faustillae / deliciae suae / eruditae omnibus artibus / reliquisti mammam tuam / gementem plangentem plorantem / vix(it) an(nis) XV / mensib(us) III dieb(us) XI hor(is) VII / virginem eripuit fatus malus / destituisti vitilla mea / miseram mammam tuam.* See also the inscription for *Vibia Citheris liberta* quoted above in note 23 p. 87.

103 CIL 6.20370: *Iulia C(ai) l(iberta) Ape[***] / virguncula annorum XI de [***] / C(aium) Iulium Apollonidam pia e[t cara viro] / suo et parentibus vixit ann[os ***] / ereptam viro et matri mater me ter[ra recepit] / cum ad mortem matris de gremio rapior / omnibus cara fui viva carissuma(!) matri / adversis quae me sustulit ominibus / desine*

iam frustra mater mea desine [fletu] te miseram totos ex[agitare dies] / tu qui adstitisti mei monumenti [hospes memor] / ambula et te esse hominem fac [perpetuo cogites] // D(is) M(anibus) / Q(uinto) Iunio Chry[***] / et Iuniae Eutyc[***] / Q(uintus) Iunius Lu[***] / patronis b(ene) m(erentibus) f(ecit) et sib[i] / libertab(usque) posterisq(ue) [eorum?].

104 AE 1956, 00235: *Aurelio Onesimo / Aurelio Papirio / Aureliae Prim(a)e virg(ini) / Aurelius Felicissimus / fratri(bu)s et col(l)ibert(is) b(ene) m(erentibus) f(ecit)*. This inscription is from the hypogeum Aurelii in Viale Manzoni, a burial site of disputed religious identification.

105 Paulinus, *Vita Ambr.* 4: *Postea vero cum adolevisset, et esset in urbe Roma constitutus cum matre vidua et sorore, quae virginitatem jam fuerat professa, comite alia virgine, cujus virginis soror Candida, et ipse ejusdem professionis, quae nunc Carthagine degit jam anus.* Cf. Lizzi 1991: 58.

106 Cf. p. 43 above.

107 Hier. *Ep.* 65 and *Ep.* 127.

108 Brown 2000b: 344.

109 Cooper 1996: 86–7.

110 Salzman 2001: 363.

111 For virgins as particularly inclined to possess prophetic skills in the New Testament, see Seim 1994: 180 and 256. Jerome attributes the prophetic grace of the daughters of Philip (Acts 21:9) to their *pudicitia virginalis* in *Ep.* 130.4. Jensen 1996: 194 ff. writes about Philomena, a virgin prophetess in Rome in the last half of the second century. There were also pagan virgins with prophetic gifts, e.g. Suet. *Gal.* 9: *confirmabatur cum secundissimis auspiciis et ominibus virginis honestae vaticinatione, tanto magis quod eadem illa carmina sacerdos Iovis Cluniae ex penetrali somnio monitus eruerat ante ducentos annos similiter a fatidica puella pronuntiata.* Famous pagan virgin prophetesses include, for instance, (the original) Pythia, the Sybil of Cumae and Cassandra. Cf. Parke 1988: 164–5, Potter 1990: 115, and McInerney 2003: 30–5.

112 Brown 1988: 9, Rousselle 1988: 4, Staples 1998: 129: "The Vestal Virgins were Rome's most extraordinary religious phenomenon."

113 Fest. 439: *Salias virgines Cincius ait esse conducticias, quae ad Salios adhibeantur cum apicibus paludatas; quas Aelius Stilo scribsit sacrificium facere in Regia cum pontifice paludatas cum apicibus in modum Saliorum.* My transl.

114 Varro, *L.L.* VI.21: *Opsconsiva dies ab dea Ope Consiva, cuius in Regia sacrarium quod adeo artum, ut eo praeter virgines Vestales et sacredotem publicum introeat nemo. "Is cum eat, suffibulum ut habeat," scriptum: id dicitur u tab suffi⟨g⟩endo subfigabulum.* Ops was identified with Terra, who again was occasionally identified with Vesta, cf. Fest.202, Fest.292, Macr. *Sat.* 1.12.21.

115 Beard 1990: 22–4.

116 Zos. II.1–8, Macr. *Sat,* 1.6.13–14, ILS 5050:147–52, Scullard 1981: 120, Feeney 1998: 28–38.

117 Beard, North and Price 1998 Vol. I: 206.

118 Obseq. 27a: *Virgines tres novenae canentes urbem lustraverunt.* (133 BC); 34: *Virgines ter novenae in urbe cantarunt* (119 BC); 36: *Virgines viginti septem urbem carmine lustraverunt. Reliquum anni in pace fuit* (117 BC); 46: *Per virgines viginti septem cantitatum.* (99 BC); 48: *Cupressea simulacra Iunonis Reginae posita per virgines viginti septem, quae urbem lustraverunt.* (97 BC); 53: *Virgines viginti septem carmen canentes urbem lustraverunt.* (92 BC).

119 Prud. *Contr. Symm.* II.911–12: *quod stipis ipsis virginibus castisque choris alimenta negentur.*

120 D.H. II.66.2.

121 Fest. 94: *Ignis Vestae si quando interstinctur esset, virgines verberibus adficiebantur a pontifice, quibus mos erat tabulam felicis materiae tamdiu terebrare, quosque exceptum ignem cribro aneo virgo in aedem ferret.* Cf. Plu. *Num.* X.3, Fest. 81: *Felices arbores, Cato dixit,*

quae fructum ferunt, infelices quae non ferunt. The so-called *Arbor Felix* serves many ritual functions. Whenever he cut his hair and nails, the Flamen had to bury it under the roots of such a tree (Gell. *N.A.* X.15.15), and his wife had to carry a sprig from an *arbor felix* in her hair (Gell. *N.A.* X.15.28–9). The torches that burned at a Roman wedding were also made of such wood, cf. Stehle 1989, note 13.

122 Macr. *Sat.* I.12.6: *Huius etiam prima die ignem novum Vestae aris accendebant, ut incipiente anno cura denuo servandi novati ignis inciperet.* Cf. Ov. *Fast.* III.135–44.

123 For an overview, see Mekacher 2006: 53–76, Wildfang 2006: 22–33. The Roman republican festivals are thoroughly recorded by Scullard 1981.

124 Scullard 1981: 83 and 233.

125 Fordicidia: Ov. *Fast.* IV.639–40: *igne cremat vitulos quae natu maxima virgo est, / luce Palis populos purget ut ille cinis.* Argei: Plu. *Q.R.* 86, D.H. I.38.3. For the role of the Vestals (or one of the Vestals), see Ov. *Fast.* V.621–2. and Fest. 14: *Argeos vocabant scirpeas effigies, quae per virgines Vestales annis singulis iacebantur in Tiberim.*

126 E.g. Wildfang 2006: 22–33.

127 Cf. Staples 1998: 154.

128 Fest. 124: *Mola etiam vocatur far tostum et sale spasum, quod eo molito hostiae aspergantur.* Fest. 97: *Immolare est mola, id est farro molito et sale, hostiam perspersam sacrare.*

129 Serv. *In Buc.* 8.82: *Sparge molam far et salem. Hoc nomen de sacris tractum est: far enim pium, id est mola casta, salsa — utrumque enim idem significat — ita fit: virgines ter maximae ex nonis Maiis ad pridie idus Maias alternis diebus spicas adoreas in corbibus messuasriis ponunt easque spicas ipsae virgines torrent, pinsunt, molunt atque ita molitum condunt. Ex eo farre virgines ter in anno molam faciunt, Lupercalibus, Vestalibus, idibus septembribus, adiecto sale cocto et sale duro. Igitur quod in sacris mola casta dicitur, ideo Vergilius in quinto Aeneidis farre pio enuntavit; quid enim pium nisi castum?* [...] Cf. Fest. 57: *Casta mola genus sacrificii, quod Vestales virgines faciebant,* and Fest. 152 (*Muries*).

130 Plin. *N.H.* 31.41.89: *maxime tamen in sacris intellegitur auctoritas, quando nulla conficiuntur sine mola salsa. Mola salsa* was also used in private sacrifices, e.g. Plaut. *Amph.* 739–40. It is difficult to estimate how much *mola salsa* was actually needed for the public sacrifices in Rome, but if the Vestals were supposed to provide for all this, it appears to have been quite a lot of grain they would have needed to collect those few days in May.

131 E.g. D.H. II.66.5 and Luc. *Phars.* I.597. For the Palladium, see Ando 2008: 182ff.

132 Cic. *Scaur.* 48: *Palladium illud, quod quasi pignus nostrae salutis atque imperii custodiis Vestae continentur.* Cf. Cic. *Phil.* 11.24: *qui ita conservandus est illud signum, quod de caelo delapsum Vestae custodes continentur; quo salvo salvi sumus futuri.*

133 Serv. *Ad Aen.* 7.188: *septem fuerunt pignora, quae imperium Romanum tenent: # aius matris deum, quadriga fictilis Veientanorum, cineres Orestis, sceptrum Priami, velum Ilionae, palladium, ancilia.* Plin. *N.H.* 28.39: *quamquam religione tutatur et Fascinus, imperatorum quoque, non solum infantium custos, qui deus sacra Romana a Vestalibus colitur.*

134 Dubourdieu 1989: 467 and passim.

135 See e.g. Plin. *N.H.* 7.43.141, Sen. *Contr.* 4.2. The legendary heroic act is also recorded by D.H. II.66.4, Ov. *Fast.* VI.437–54, Liv. *Per.* 19 and Cic. *Scaur.* 48, but the blinding is apparently no issue here. There is an echo here of the story of how Tiresias was blinded as punishment for looking at Athena, see e.g. Call. *Lav. Pall.*

136 D.H. II.66.6. Transl. Loeb.

137 Staples 1998: 153.

138 Staples 1998: 153.

139 Hor. *Od.* 3.30.8–9: *dum Capitolium scandet cum tacita virgine pontifex.*

140 Such misfortunes could actually be interpreted as a sign that Vestals had lost their virginity, particularly under the Republic. Cf Chapter Four below.

141 Symm. *Rel.* 3.16–17.

142   Symm. *Rel.* 3.17: *quid tales provinciae pertulerunt, cum religionum ministros honor publicus pasceret? […] cum populo et virginibus sacris communis esset annona?* My transl.

143   Symm. *Rel.* 3.11: *saluti publicae dicata virginitas crescit merito, cum caret praemio.* Unlike most other priests in official Roman cults, the Vestals were full-time priests and thus dependent on income from the land that belonged to the cult for their survival (cf. Rüpke 2007: 21). Donations and inheritance appear to have been a necessary supplement in Late Antiquity, particularly when imperial legislation withdrew their economic privileges, cf. Lizzi 2007.

144   Prud. *Perist.* XIV 1–6: *Agnes sepulchrum est Romulea in domo, / fortis puellae, martyris inclytae. / conspectus in ipso condita turrium, / servat salutem virgo Quiritium, / nec non et ipsios protegit advenas / puro ac fideli pectore supplices.* Cf. Visser 2001: 236 ff. The *dies natalis* of Agnes (the day commemorating her martyrdom) was recorded in the calendar of Roman martyrs and included in the calendar of Philocalus from 354 AD. For Ambrose and Damasus as sources for this poem of Prudentius, see Palmer 1989: 250–3.

145   Lizzi 1998: 89–92, Oros. 7.39. See also Fox 1986: 370.

146   Brown 1988: 263, cf. Brown 2012: 271 and 303, Fox 1986: 367 and Cloke 1995: 61–9.

147   Elm 2003: 315–16. Curiously, a Vestal's prayer was also believed to have such "transfixing" powers but, in this case, it was a runaway slave that could be stopped, and only provided he or she was still within the city walls. This ability was reported by Plin. *N.H.* 28.3.13: *Vestales nostra hodie credimus nondum egressa urbe mancipia fugitiva retinere in loco precatione.*

148   Shaw 1998a: 226, cf. Elm 2003: 358.

149   Shaw 1998a: 226, note 20.

150   Ambr. *De virgb.* I.32: *Audistis, parentes, quibus erudire virtutibus, quibus instituere disciplinis filias debeatis; ut habere possitis quarum meritis vestra delicta redimantur. Virgo Dei donum est, munus parentis, sacerdotium castitatis. Virgo matris hostia est, cujus quotidiano sacrificio vis divina placatur. Virgo individuum pignus parentum, quae non dote sollicitet, non emigratione destituat, non offendat injuriis.* Transl. Ramsey 1997, with changes. Cf. *De laps. Sus.* IV. 16: *immaculatam praemiserant virginem, hostiam vivam Domino, propitiatricem suorum videlicet delictorum* (quoted in translation below p. 156).

151   Ambr. *Exh. virg.* 26: *Proximum putabo matrem esse virginum, ac si virginitatem tenerem. Considerate, filii, quam sibi veniens in has terras Dominus Jesus matrem elegerit. Salutem mundo daturus per virginem venit, et mulieris lapsus partu virginis solvit: vestra quoque integritas meos solvat errores.* My transl.

152   Hier. *Adv. Jov.* 1.27: *Nam si salvatur mulier in filiorum generatione, et liberorum numerus salus matrum est, cur addidit, si permanserint filii in charitate et sanctificatione cum castitate? Tunc ergo salvabitur mulier, si illos genuerit filios, qui virgines permansuri sunt: si quod ipsa perdidit, acquirat in liberis, et damnum radicis et cariem, flore compenset et pomis.* Transl. NPNF2.

153   Hier. *Ep.* 107.1: *Sancta et fidelis domus unum sanctificat infidelem. Jam candidatus est fidei, quem filiorum et nepotum credens turba circumdat* (with reference to 1 Cor. 7: 13–14).

154   Hier. *Ep.* 107.6: *Nisi forte aestimas Christianorum filios, si baptisma non acceperint, ipsos tantum reos esse peccati, et non etiam scelus referri ad eos, qui dare noluerint, maxime eo tempore, quo contradicere non poterant qui accepturi erant, sicut e regione salus infantium, majorum lucrum est. Offere necne filiam, potestatis tuae fuit (quanquam alia sit tua conditio, quae) prius eam vovisti, quam conciperes) ut autem oblatam non negligas, ad periculum tuum pertinet. Qui claudam et mutilam, et qualibet sorde maculatam obtulerit hostiam, sacrilegii reus est [Deut. 15], quanto magis qui partem corporis sui, et illibatae animae puritatem regis amplexibus parat, si negligens fuerit, punietur?* Transl. NPNF2.

155   Prud. *Contr. Symm.* II.1055–63: *sunt et virginibus pulcherrima praemia nostris; / et pudor sanctus tectus velamine vultus, / et privatus honos nec nota et publica forma, / et rarae*

tenuesque epulae et mens sobria semper, lexque pudicitiae vitae cum fine peracta. / hic decies deni rediguntur in horrea fructus, / horrea nocturno non umquam obnoxia furi, / nam caelum fur nullus adit, caelestia numquam / fraude resignantur;fraus terris volvitur imis. Transl. Loeb. Cf. above p. 16.

156 D'Izarny 1953: 30–7 has collected most of the relevant passages where Ambrose applies this imagery.

157 Rom. 12.1: *Obsecro itaque vos, fratres, per misericordiam Dei, ut exhibeatis corpora vestra hostiam vivantem, sanctam, Deo placentem, rationable obsequium vestrum.*

158 Hier. *Ep.* 127.6: *Sic induta est vestibus, ut meminisset sepulcri, offerens se hostiam rationabilem, vivam, placentem Deo.*

159 E.g. Ambr. *Virgt.* 5–10.

160 Cf. *Homily on Virginity* V.61–2.

161 Ambr. *De virgb.* I.32., see also Hier. *Ep.* 107.6 quoted above, note 154.

162 Ambr. *Inst. virg.* 1: *caeteros enim instituis, ut emittas domo, atque alienis copules, istam semper tecum habebis: in caeteris quoque paternae uteris pietatis necessitudine; in hac ultra patrem procedis, votoque et studio progrederis, ut placeat Deo. Quae cum sit praestantior causa votorum; sola tamen solvat quidquid pro se et pro omnibus filiis debes.* My transl. Cf. *De laps. Sus.* IV.16: *quia immaculatam praemisissent virginem, hostiam vivam Domino, propitiatricem videlicet delictorum.*

163 Hier. *Adv. Jov.* 1.13: *Sed illa virginitas hostia Christi est, cujus nec mentem cogitatio, nec carnem libido maculavit.* Transl. NPNF2.

164 Hier. *Ep.* 130.5: *Habet et servata pudicitia martyrium suum.* Cf. Hier. *Vitae Mal.* 6: *Verte in te gladium. Tua magis mors timenda quam corporis est. Habet et pudicitia servata martyrium suum.*

165 Ambr. *De virgb* III. 7.35: *Has tibi, inquit, hostias, Christe, immolo praesules castitatis, duces itineris, comites passionis.* Transl. Ramsey.

166 E.g. Burrus 1995, Trout 1994, Mitchell 1991, Scodel 1996, Burkert 2001: 75–8, Kelly 2000, McInerney 1999, McInerney 2003, Bowersock 2002, Castelli 2004. See also Parker 1983: 93, where Thenoe's virginal dedication to the gods is seen in analogy to sacrificial animals.

167 Nock 1930, CIL 6.2139(=ILS 04935): *Coeliae Claudianae / v(irgini) V(estali) maximae / a diis electa merito / sibi talem antistitem / numen Vestae reservare / voluit / Coelia Nerviana soror una / cum Pierio coniuge ac liberis / suis orantes ut per tot(a) saecula / facere dii permittant.* Two of the other inscriptions for Cloelia Claudiana, CIL 6.2136 and CIL 6.2137 (=ILS 4936) are dated to 286 AD. See also CIL 6.2138, CIL 6.2140 and CIL 6.32420(=ILS 4937) dedicated to the same Vestal.

168 Nock 1930: 254, Aul. Gell. *N.A.* 1.12.

169 Nock 1930: 296. Nock's argument appears to be based in the "functionalistic" approach to Roman religion, not unlike Zanker's presentation of religion mainly functioning as propaganda for the imperial family. There are many difficulties with this approach, but its survival into modern scholarship is not surprising due to the way it fits with the idea that Christianity brought individual emotions back to the religiously deprived Romans, who did their best to fulfill their emotional void, sadly unsuccessfully, with the mystery religions.

170 Lanciani 1883 refers at several instances (e.g. 1883: 447) to the destruction caused by "Gli scapellini ed i fornaici del medio evo" and to the dismantling of ancient monuments in the Renaissance that destroyed so much of the remains of Ancient Rome.

171 Nock 1930: 252.

172 Nock 1930: 260–1. Scullard's general examination of the rites of the republican calendar (Scullard 1981) demonstrates how the Vestals, as official priestesses, participated in rites and ceremonies for other gods and not just Vesta.

173 Ambr. *Inst. virg.* 102. *Hanc sume stolam, ut induas Christum, (Gal 3:27) atque in ejus agnitione renoveris. Indue ergo sicut electa Dei viscera misericordiae, benignitatem,*

humilitatem, patientiam, modestiam, charitatem, quae est unitatis vinculum (Coloss. 3: 12 et seq.); ut nemini quidquam debeas, nisi ut invicem sororem tuam diligas: nec gratiae ejus invideas, sed quo probatiorem videris, imiteris; ut sit in te pax Christi et gratia, et verbum Dei habitet in corde tuo, atque hujus mundi fugias cogitationes.

174   D'Izarny 1953: 19.

175   Hier. *Ep.* 22.23.

176   Hier. *Ep.* 22.24: *et ille respondeat: "Una est columba mea, perfecta mea: una est matri sua, electa genitrici suae" (Cant. 6:8), coelesti videlicet Jerusalem.*

177   Ambr. *De virgb.* I.35: *Non itaque dissuadeo nuptias, si fructus virginitatis enumero. Paucarum quippe hoc munis est, illud omnium.*

178   I.e. Matt. 19:11–12, (cf. Ambr. *De virgt.* 29), Matt. 22: 14.

179   Brown 2001: 631, Brown 1988: 421–3.

180   Consolino 1984, Clark 2008, Shuve 2016.

181   Pl. *Eupthr.* 10.

182   I. Cor. 7.25, e.g. Athanasius *Ep. de virg.* 18, in Brakke 1995: 279: "Hence [Paul] gave it to the free will of those who desire [virginity] so that its virtue may be for those who have chosen it for themselves." Cf. Adkin 2003: 176.

183   Discussed briefly by, among others, Cloke 1995: 64 and 73, Brown 1986: 434. I should also note that raising these issues is not without larger implications. Many of the arguments used by the Church Fathers in their polemics against pagans and heretics were "recycled" by Protestants in their criticisms of Catholic monastic institutions during the Reformation and sometimes up until this day. This is discussed more fully in Undheim 2011: 294–302.

184   Ambr. *De virgb.* I.62: *Bonum itaque si virgini studia parentum quasi flabra pudoris aspirent: sed illud gloriosius, si tenerae ignis aetatis etiam sine veteribus nutrimentis sponte se rapiat in fomitem castitatis. Dotem negabunt parentes: sed habes divitem sponsum cujus contenta thesauro, patriae successionis emolumenta non quaeras. Quanto dotalibus praestat compendiis casta paupertas!* Transl. Ramsey 1997.

185   Ambr. *De virgb.* I.63: *Contradicunt parentes: sed volunt vinci. ... Vince prius, puella, pietatem. Si vincis domum, vincis saeculum.* Transl. Ramsey 1997.

186   Brown 1986: 432, cf. Garrido 1993: 53–71.

187   Bas. *Ep.* 199.18. Cf. pp. 74–5 below.

188   Hier. *Ep.* 130.6: *Solent miseri parentes, et non plenae fidei Christiano, deformes et aliquo membro debiles filias, quia dignos generos non inveniunt; virginitati tradere. Tanti, ut dicitur, vitrum, quanti margaritum. Certe qui religiosiores sibi videntur, parvo sumptu, et qui vix ad alimenta sufficiat, virginibus dato, omnem censum in utroque sexu, saecularibus liberis largiuntur. Quod nuper in hac urbe dives quidam fecit Presbyter ut duas filias in proposito virginali inopes relinqueret, et aliorum ad omnem copiam filiorum luxuriae atque deliciis provideret. Fecerunt hoc multae, proh dolor, nostri propositi feminae; atque utinam rarum esset exemplum, quod quanto crebrius est, tanto istae feliciores, quae ne plurimarum quidem exempla secutae sunt.* My transl.

189   Ambr. *De virgb.* I.33. Oblation, the medieval practice of the offering of children to the Church or to monasteries, has likewise been explained as a solution to the economic burden any new child could represent for an already poor family with little or no means to raise the child on their own. As such, the dedication of virgins or monks to the monasteries and oblation converge; cf. Boswell 1984: 17ff. He notes, however, that the public sale of children, which seems to have increased in the fourth century, continued throughout the High Middle Ages.

190   Brown 1988: 261.

191   Brown 1988: 260.

192   Brown 1988: 260–1.

193   Ambr. *De virgb.* I. 62–6.

194   Cf. Metz 2001: 58, Thomassin 1865: 178–84.

195   Ambr. *De vid.* 10: Cf. Hier. *Ep.* 123, 3ff. *et al.*

196 Bas. *Ep.* 199.24.
197 Bas. *Ep.* 188.6 (fornication of canonical persons), *Ep.* 199.20 (on women who professed virginity while in heresy and later married) and 199.18.
198 Bas. *Ep.* 199.18. (Transl. Loeb.)
199 Bas. *Ep.* 199. 18. (Transl. Loeb.)
200 Cf. the note in the Loeb translation of *Ep.* 199.18, where it is assumed that Basil is referring to the Council of Ancyra.
201 Susanna Elm reads this passage of Basil as a reference to the establishment of some kind of novitiate, a trial period, that the girl had to subsume before taking on the veil. Elm 2003: 140.
202 Likewise, a minimum age of 16 was set for boys to be accepted as full members of an ascetic brotherhood. See Elm 2003: 71.
203 McLynn 1994: 63.
204 Ambr. *De virgt.* 39: *Aiunt etiam plerique maturioris aetatis virgines esse velandas. Neque ego abnuo sacerdotalis esse cautionis debere ut non temere puella veletur. Spectet plane, spectet aetatem sacerdos, sed fidei vel pudoris. Spectet maturitatem verecundiae, exanimet gravitatis canitiem, morum senectam, pudicitae annos, animos castitatis: tum deinde si matris tuta custodia, comitum sobria sedulitas. Si haec praesto sunt, non deest virgini longaeva canities: si haec desunt, differatur puella moribus quam annis adolescentibus.* My transl. Ed. Cazzaniga.
205 According to Boniface Ramsey, a letter attributed to Basil of Ceasarea (197.2) indicates that Ambrose requested and obtained Basil's help in retrieving the body of his predecessor Bishop Dionysius, who had been exiled for his orthodoxy and, elsewhere, we find Ambrose heavily relying on the writings of Basil in his own compositions, as evident in among others *Exameron, de Tobia, psalmos davidicos, de spiritu sancto, de Nabuthae,* etc. Ramsey 1997: 23, 56, 58, 59, 62 and 177 accordingly.
206 Cf. McLynn 1994: 65.
207 Ambr. *De virgt.* 29: *ut ostenderet hoc non mediocris esse virtutis: 'qui potest' inquit, 'capere, capiat'.* Ed. Cazzaniga.
208 Ambr. *De virgt.* 30: *Et ideo post hoc verbum offeruntur pueri ad benedicendum, qui, corruptelae expertes, integritatis munus immaculata aetate servarint.* Ed. Cazzaniga.
209 Ambr. *De virgt.* 30: *Talium est enim regnum caelorum, qui in puerilem castimoniam tanquam in naturam infantium corruptelae ignoratione remeaverint. Est ergo etiam caelesti voce probata virginitas, dominisque expetenda praeceptis.* Ed. Cazzaniga. My transl.
210 Ambr. *De virgt* 38: *Si qui habent, timere non debent; uxores enim eorum jam virgines esse non possunt.*
211 Ambr. *De virgt* 38: *An fortasse patres pro filiarum coniunctione solliciti moleste ferunt virgines consecrari? Nec hi quod vereantur habent si sequantur consilium. Inter paucas suae citius eligentur.* Ed. Cazzaniga.
212 Ambr. *De virgt* 40: *Non ergo aetas rejicitur florentior, sed animus examinatur.* Ed. Cazzaniga. My transl.
213 Ambr. *De virgt.* 40: *At certe Theclam non senectur, sed virtus probavit.* Cf. Ambr. *De virgb.* I.5–9; I.19: *Aetate utique Agnes minor, sed virtute major.* Pelagia of Antioch, whose martyrdom is recounted in *De virgb.* III.33, is said to have been a 15-year-old virgin when she drowned herself to escape her persecutors.
214 Ambr. *De virgt.* 40: *Et hinc quid plura contextam, cum omnis aetas habilis Deo, perfecta sit Christo? Denique non virtutem aetatis appendicem dicimus, sed virturtis aetatem.* My transl.
215 According to the note to this passage in the version of Patrologia Latina, quite a few MSS have *puellae nobiles* instead of *puellae nubiles* here, cf. the edition of Cazzaniga.
216 Ambr. *De virgt.* 40: *Et quasi incredibile putamus, si puellae nubiles Christum sequantur ad regnum, quem etiam pueri sequebantur in deserto....* Ed. Cazzaniga. My transl.

217   Ambr. *De virgt.* 41: *Nolite ergo a Christo arcere infantes; quia et ipsi pro Christi nomine subiere martyrium: talium est enim regnum coelorum.* (Matt. 19:13.) *Vocat eos Dominus, et tu prohibes? De ipsis enim Dominus ait: Sinite eos venire ad me.* (Matt. 19:14.) *Nolite adolesecentulas arcere, de quibus scriptum est: Propterea adolescentulae dilexerunt te.* (Cant. 1:2.) *Et induxerunt te in domum matris suae.* (Cf. Cant. 8:2.) *Nolite postremo a Christi charitate etiam parvulos separare, quem etiam intra matris uterum adhuc positi exsultatione prophetica fatebantur.* (Luke 1:41.). Ed. Cazzaniga. My transl.

218   For such a definition of *adolescentula*, cf. Ambr. *De vid.* 25: *Sed in illis [viduitate] tardior fructus, in virgine maturior: illas senectus probat, virginitas laus aetatis est; nec adjumenta quaerit annorum, quae omnium est fructus aetatum. Adolescentiam decet, juventutem ornat, amplificat senectutem: omnique aevo habet justitiae suae canos, maturitatem gravitatis, velamen pudoris, quae devotionem non impediat, religionem augeat.*

219   Cf. Clark 1991: 233 on Chrysostom invoking "girls not twenty years old" to shame male audience.

220   McLynn 1994: 64–5.

221   Brown 1988: 356, McLynn 1994: 65–8, Cf. Hunter 2000: 285.

222   Shaw 1987. Cf. Tert. *Virg. vel.* 11: *Tempus etiam ethnici observant, ut ex lege naturae jura sua aetatibus reddant. Nam foeminas quidem a duodecim annis, masculum vero a duobus amplius ad negotia mittunt, pubertatem in annis, non sponsalibus aut nuptiis decernentes.*

223   Shaw 1987: 42, note 42, see also Treggiari 1993: 401–2, contrary Elm 2003: 43, who claims that Macrina, after being engaged at 12, had to wait two years before reaching the legal age for marriage. In the meantime, her betrothed died, and she declared herself a widow and dedicated herself to an ascetic life.

224   Cf. Ambr. *De vid.* 9: *Non quo senectus sola viduam faciat, sed quo viduitatis merita stipendia sint senectutis. Nam utique illa praeclarior, quae calorem adolescentiae, et junioris fervescentem edomat aetatis ardorem; nec mariti gratiam, nec uberiora liberorum oblectamenta desiderans: quam quae effeta jam corpore, frigida senectute, matura aevi, nec calere voluptatibus potest, nec sperare de partu.*

225   Hier. *Ep.* 130.1: *Quanquam puellares annos fidei ardore superarit; et inde coeperit, unde alias desisse, perfectae consummataeque virtutis est.* See also Hier. *Ep.* 130.5.

226   Hier. *Ep.* 24.2.

227   Hier. *Ep.* 128.4.

228   Quoted by Elm 2003: 44.

229   Ambr. *De virgt.* 39.

230   Harlow and Laurence 2002: 49, i.e. Plin. *Ep.* 5.16.2–4.

231   Hier. *Ep.* 107 (to Laeta regarding Paula the younger), and *Ep.* 128 (regarding Pacatula). According to Gerontius' *Vita Melaniae* 1, a daughter of Melania was dedicated to virginity at birth, see Pietri 1977: 415 s.v. 'Filia Melaniae'.

232   Harlow and Laurence 2002: 138.

233   For Julia Sidonia and Citheris, cf. above p. 36.

234   ICUR pars prima 20: *Statilia Alexandra annorum XIIII virgo mortua es(t) Tusco et Anullino conss. GIII (i.e. IX) Kal. Sept. filia Alexandros* (295 AD), cf. ICUR VII, 19015: *Leontia virgo vixit annos / XIIII mensis III dies X* (undated) and ICUR II, 5393: *Mara que vixit virgo/ plus minus XIIII d(e)p(osita)* […], AE 1912, 253: *P. Acilius Victor fecit se vivo sibi et suis parentibus. Posita autem Urbana soror huius quae vixit virgo annos XIIII menses VIII dies XXI; iisdem diebus soror horum posita a nomine Vitalis quae vixit annos X et dies. Libertis libertabusque posterisque eorum.*

235   ILCV 1724: *Rufina, casta virgo, vixit an. XII / et m. (sic) dp. VII id. Martia in pace / Marcellino et Probino conss.* (341 AD).

236   De Rossi, ICUR pars prima 460: *c]ons dn Honari aug IIII [et euty] / [ch]iani vc G idus ian depo[sita] / [est] crescentia virgo quae vi[xit] / ann GI M E N […]* (dated to 398 AD). According to Pietri 1977: 410, she was six. Cf. also ICUR II, 4229 dedicated to six-year-old Aelia Romana.

237 ICUR V, 15283: *Hic est posita virgo Gemella quae/ vixit ann IIII m IIII d XX decess/ III idus octobres in pace.*

238 ICUR V, 13115: *Dep(ositio) Lucifer(a)es birginis XIIII Kal(endas) / Octobris quae vixit annos p(lus) m(inus) XVIIII m(enses) XI / conss(ulatu) Antoni et Svagri,* ICUR Pr. Suppl. I.1505 (p. 46): *mirae bonitatis Secunde, / quae vixit pura fide annos / viginti pudica cessavit / in pace id virgo fidelis / benemerenti quiescent id iul/ palumbo sine felle m et n.* (362 AD.) Pietri 1977: 411 also records a *Basilla virgo* of 20 years.

239 ICUR III, 8723: *Bene merenti filiae / Agapeni vircini in pace / dep(osita) III Kal(endas) Dec(embres) Gratiano et / Dagalaifo co(n)s(ulibus) v(ixit) a(nnos) XXI* (366 AD), ICUR pars prima 304: *infanti(ae) aetas, virginitatis integritas morum grab(i)tas / fidei et reverentiae discipli(n)a (h)ic sita Rufina iacet que uixit anis XXI / deposita IIII nons avg Fl(avio) S(y)gario et Euer(i)o consulibus* (381 AD). ICUR pars prima 428: *Aniciis Ocnid et Provinio cons dp / Vervices XII kal Octobres que vicsit / annos XXV virgo benemenrenti in pace / parentes fecerunt.* (395 AD.)

240 *Epig. Damas* 11, p. 108 = ICUR IV, 12417. Cf. Pietri 1977: 414.

241 Maximilla: ICUR V, 13355. Ioviana, see above note 84, p. 28. Labinia: ILCV 1722: *[hic] iacet Labinia, virgo dei inimitabiles, in pace, que bixit annus / [pl]us minus XXXV. Deposita III nonas Apriles consulate / dd. ññ. Honorio VIII et Teodosio III Augustis cons.* (409 AD.)

242 E.g. ICUR I, 3841 (1 year and 8 months), ICUR III, 9325 (Valeria, 1 year, 10 months), and ICUR VI, 15530 (Gemella, 3 years, 3 months). Cf. Sylloge Inscr. II p. 207. Nero's infant daughter, who died at only four months old, received a posthumous commemoration as *diva Claudia virgo*, cf. PIR2 C1061.

243 ICUR pars prima 497, quoted in note 79, p. 27 above.

244 Aul. Gell. *N.A.* 1.12: *Qui de virgine capienda scripserunt [...], minorem quam annos sex, maiorem quem annos decem natam, negaverunt capi fas esse; item quae non sit patrima et matrima.* For the difference in minimum age for Greek female priesthoods (also for virgin priestesses), see Dillon 2002: 75.

245 Cf. Mekacher 2006: 256 (M6). The representation of the Vestals at the Ara Pacis shows a procession of the six priestesses in which the first of them is depicted as considerably smaller in size than those who follow after her. This might certainly be due to mere aesthetic ideals or as symbolic illustration of status differences within the priesthood, but could also have been a reflection of this age and physical size difference within the priesthood.

246 Fest. 38: *Camillus proprie appellantur puer ingenuus.* My transl.

247 Fest. 82: *Flaminus camillus puer dicabatur ingenuus patrimes et matrimes, qui flamini Diali ad sacrificia praeministrabat.* My transl. Cf. Plu. *Num.* VII.5.

248 Serv. *Ad Aen.* 11.543: *Romani quoque pueros et puellae nobiles et investes camillos et camillas appellabant, flaminicarum et flaminum praeministros.* My transl. Cf. Serv. *Ad Aen.* 11.558: *ministros enim et ministras inpuberes camillos et camillas in sacris vocabant, unde et Mercurius Etrusca lingua Camillus dicitur, quasi minister deorum. In sacris tamen legitur posse etiam opera consecrari ex servis, usque dum solvatur caput hominis, id est liberetur sacrationis nexu* aut enim numen famulae, quam servi significatio condicionis.*

249 Varro *L.L.* VII.34: *Camilla‹m› qui glos‹s›emata interpretati dixerunt administram; addi oportet, in his quae occultiora: itaque dicitur nuptiis camillus qui cumerum fert, in quo quid sit, in ministerio plerique extrinsecus ne‹s›ciunt.* Cf. Fest: *Cumeram vocabant antiqui vas quodam quod opertum in nuptiis ferebant, in quo erant nubentis utensilia, quod et camillum dicebant, eo quod sacrorum ministrum kadmilon apellabant.* My transl.

250 D.H. I.21.2. It should be noted that Dionysius here explicitly strives to prove the Greek cultural predominance in this area, cf. Feeney 2006: 21. For *kanephoroi* in Greek cult, see Dillon 2002.

251 D.H. II.22.

252   Tac. *Hist.* IV.53: *Ab eo contracti haruspices monuere ut reliquiae prioris delubri in paludes aveherentur, templum isdem vestigis sisteretur: nolle deos mutari veterm formam. (XI kalendas Iulias serena luce) spatium (omne quod templo dicebatur) evinctum vittis coronisque, (ingressi milites, quis fausta nomina, felicibus ramis;) dein virgines Vestales cum pueris puellisque patrimis matrimisque aqua e fontibus amnibusque hausta perluere.* My transl. The area was then purified with a *souvetaurilia.*

253   Col. *XII.4.3: His autem omnibus placuit eum, qui rerum harum officium susceperit, castum esse continentemque oportere, quoniam totum in eo sit, ne contractentur pocula vel cibi, nisi au tab impubi, aut certe abstinentissimo rebus venereis. Quibus si fuerit operatus vel vir vel femina, debere eos flumine aut perenni aqua, priusquam penora contingent, ablui. Propter quod his necessarium esse pueri vel virginis ministerium, per quos promantur, quae usus postulaverit.* Cf. Cato *Agr.* 143.2: *munda siet: villam conversam mundeque habeat; focum purum circumversum cotidie, priusquam cubitum eat, habeat.* It is at least not impossible that there is here also a subtle warning about the potential pollution from the activities of the cubitus, in line with the common notion of the necessity of Vestals to tend the *focus* with "chaste hands," i.e. Ov. *Fast.*VI.290, Val. Max.VIII.1, absol.5.

254   See also Brown 1988: 260: "By the end of the fourth century, 'benches in the apse raised on steps, thrones veiled with curtains, processions and the chanting crowds of virgins' were an integral part of the bishop's show of power." The quote is from Augustine (*Ep.* 23.3).

255   McInerney 2003: 52–3, cf. Warner 2000: 48, Hanson 2007: 45, etc. Cf. Dillon 2002: 75: "the priest and woman priest of Artemis Hymnia in Mantineia were, unusually for Greek practice, lifelong virgins."

256   Hanson 2007, cf. King 1993, King 2004.

257   Sen. *Ot. Sap.* II.2: *deinde, ut posit hoc aliquis emeritis iam stipendiis, profligatae aetatis, iure optimo facere et ad alios aucus animum referre virginum Vestalium more, quae annis inter officia divisis discunt facere sacra et cum didicerunt docent.* Cf. Plu. *Num.* X and D.H. II.67.2, who both operate with ten-year terms. Some of the inscriptions from the Atrium mention "degrees" (*omnes gradus sacerdotii*), i.e. ILS 4930, 4931, 4934.

258   Plu. *Num.* X.2, (transl. Loeb) cf. D.H. II.67. Aulus Gellius' description of how the Vestal Taracia was granted the right to marry at the age of 40: *N.A.*VII.7.4: *Praeterea si quadraginta annos nata sacerdotio abire ac nubere voluisset, ius ei potestate exaugurandi atque nubendi facta est munificentiae et beneficii gratia....* In this case, the right to marry seems an exception granted only to Taracia. Gellius does not mention a general rule regarding this in his review of the legal peculiarities regarding the Vestal virgins. In fact, this general rule is only mentioned explicitly by Plutarch who, in turn, seems to rely heavily on Dionysius, although other sources clearly presuppose it, e.g. Symm. *Ep.* 9.108.

259   Tac. *Ann.* II.86: *Post quae retulit Caesar capiendam virginem in locum Occiae, quae septem et quinquaginta per annos summa sanctimonia Vestalibus sacris praesederat.* Junia Torquata, who lived in the first half of the first century, appears to have served at least 64 years (Saquete 2000: 140 (n. 32), cf. CIL 6.2128, Tac. *Ann.* III.69.6.

260   Battaglia 1983: 130: *Undecies senis quod Vestae paruit annis hoc sita / virgo manu populi delata quiescit / L(ocus) D(atus) S(enatus) C(onsulto).* The front reads: *V(irgini) V(estali)/ Cossiniae / L(uci) f(iliae) // L(ucius) Cossinius Electus.*

261   ILS 4937 (*sic XX, sic XXX feliciter*), cf. Mekacher 2006: 206–7 and Lanciani 1883: 452–4. We could perhaps assume that she had served as a Vestal for a number of years before she obtained the status as Maxima?

262   Dio Cass. *H.R.* 37.45.1.3, 47.19.4.1, 48.12.2,2, 48.37.1,2, 54.27.3,4, 56.5.7.2, 56.10.2,4. Cf. Mekacher 2006: 21. The term eventually came to carry a specific Mariological meaning after the Council of Chalchedon in 451.

263   Symm. *Ep.* 9.108: *Omnia, quae sine auctore iactantur, incerta sunt; sed ego in sacrae virginis famam nihil patior licere sermonibus. Quare officio pontificis, fide senatoris admoneor*

proferre conperta. Diceris ante annos legibus definitos vestali secreto velle decedere. Nondum credo rumori, sed adsertionem tuae vocis expecto, quae opinionis dubium aut agnoscat aut respuat. My transl.

264 Gardner 1991: 25.

265 Ambr. *De vid.* 25: *virginitas [...] quae omnium est fructus aetatum.* Transl. NPNF2.

266 Serv. *Ad Aen.* 1. 493: *virgo et sexum ostendit et aetatem. virgo plus dixit, quam si feminam diceret.*

267 Elm 2003: 61.

268 This is one of his favorite *topoi*, from Ephes. 5.27: "That he might present it to himself a glorious church, not having spot, not having wrinkle, or any such thing: but that it should be holy and without blemish." Cf. Ambr. *Ep.* 68, *Exh. virg.* 67, *Inst. virg.* 15: *sine macula, sine ruga.*

269 For *veteranae virgines* see Adkin 2003: 267.

270 Brown 1988: 216 note 7.

271 The Council of Trent agreed on 16 years complete with one year's novitiate as necessarily preceding religious profession, while in 1902 it was ruled that 19 years complete was necessary for solemn profession, for both men and women.

272 Cf. Elm 2003: 29.

273 Tert. *Virg. vel.* 22.8, see also D'Angelo 1995: 144, Dunn 2005.

274 Dio Cass. 47.19.4 (my transl.), cf. Plu. *Num.* X. That Vestals attended dinner parties is also indicated in Macr. *Sat.* 3.13.11. Note, however, that these Vestals, perhaps because it was thought of as more proper, dined in a separate triclinium with other women and not with the pontifices. See also the "Umschlagbild" in Mekacher 2006.

275 Liv. 4.44.11–12: *Eodem anno Postumia virgo Vestalis de incestu causam dixit crimine innoxia, ab suspicione propter cultum amoeniorum ingeniumque liberius quam virginem decem abhorrens. Eam amplitiatam, deinde absolutam pro collegii sententia pontifex maximus abstinere iocis colique sancte potius quam scite iussit.* And Liv. 8.15.7–8: *eo anno Minucia Vestalis, suspecta primo propter mundiorem iusto cultum, insimulata deinde apud pontifices ab indice servo, cum decreto eorum iussa esset sacris abstinere familiamque in potestate habere, facto iudicio uiua sub terram ad portam Collinam dextra uiam stratam defossa Scelerato campo; credo ab incesto id ei loco nomen factum.* Cf. Kelly 2000: 134.

276 A distinction between office and leisure in the lives of Vestals has to my knowledge not been studied, yet there are some indications that there was a difference. In official ceremonies and processions it may be assumed that their priestly insignia were displayed in a different manner than in their more everyday religious duties, not to mention their social life.

277 Serv. *Ad Aen.* 2.133: *Vittae quibus victimae coronabantur.* Cf. Serv. *Ad Aen.* 2.156, 3.81.

278 Sebesta 1994: 48–9. For white as a symbolic color of clothing, see Plu. *Q.R.* 26.

279 *Vittae purpureae*: Sebesta 1994: 52, with note 40, cf. Fest. 485: *caerulae vittae*; Serv. *Ad Aen.* 3.64: *Caeruleis vittis Cato ait, deposita veste purpurea feminas usas cum lugerent.*

280 LaFollette 1994: 63, note 37, e.g. Serv. *Ad Aen.* 4.458: *Moris enim fuerat, ut nubentes puellae, simul venissent ad limen mariti, postes antequam ingredientur, propter auspicium castitatis, ornarent laneis vittis: unde ait 'velleribus niveis': et oleo ungerent, unde uxores dictae sunt, quasi uxores.* Plin. *N.H.* 29.30: *lanis auctoritatem veteres Romani etiam religiosam habuere postes a nubentibus attingi iubentes.*

281 Prop. IV.3.15 and IV.11.33.

282 Sebesta 1994: 48–9.

283 Serv. *Ad Aen.* 10.538: *infula fascia in modum diadematis, a qua vittae ab utraque parte dependent: quae plerumque lata est, plerumque tortilis de albo et cocco.* My transl.

284 Fest. 100: *Infulae sunt filamenta lanea, quibus sacredotes et hostiae templaque velantur.* Cf. Verg. *Geor.* III.486–8: *Saepe in honore deum medio stans hostia ad aram, / lanea dum*

nivea circumdatur infula vitta. LaFollette 1994: 57, note 5, lists other priests who wore *infula.* She also argues, on the basis of a passage from Seneca (*Ep.* 14.11), that *infula* was seen as a protective badge that set apart those who wore it as consecrated to the gods.

285　Prud. *Contr. Symm.* II.1086, II.1094–5.

286　Plin. *Ep.* 4.11.9, cf. Martini 1997b: 486ff. Beard 1980: 16. According to Sebesta 1998: 107, a *stola* was white, as was the *toga virilis.* It should be noted that the only literary source for this kind of dress describes a Vestal at the very moment she is buried alive, and it is therefore perhaps not representative of an "official dress" if there indeed was such a thing for the priesthood.

287　Fest. 475.4: *Suffibulum vestimentum album, praetextum, quadrangulum, oblongum, quod in capite Vestales virgines sacrificantes habeant, idque fibula conprehendebatur.* Varro *L.L.* VI.21: *Opsconsiva dies ab dea Ope Consiva, cuiuc in Regia sacrarium quod adeo artum, ut eo praeter virgines Vestales et sacerdotem publicum introeat nemo. "is cum eat, suffibulum ut habeat," scriptum: id dicitur ut ab suffi‹g›endo subfigabulum.* For the praetexta as an indication that the wearer was "inviolable" (*sacer*), see Sebesta 1998: 108–9.

288　Ambr. *Ep.* 18.11–12: … *purpuratarum vestium murices,… non illa purpurarum insignia,…*.

289　Mekacher 2006: 47, Suda v 515, English translation from: http://www.stoa.org/ (last accessed 10 August 2009).

290　Cf. Martini 1997b: 487–8, quoting Rizzo on the identification of Vestals on the so-called Sorrento base. Martini also argues that Vestals were distinguished by a special *cingulum* analogous to the *nodus Herculaneus* of the bride (i.e. Fest. 55), but this is only attested in sculpture, which represents an unreliable source for the appearance of the Vestals (cf. van Deman 1912). The point of this *cingulum* was, according to Martini, that it remained intact, in contrast to the one of the bride. For the *nodus virginitatis,* see also Panayotakis 2000.

291　Many of the statues from the Atrium Vestae are presented in the veiling "Pudicitia-type."

292　Plin. *N.H.* 16.85: *antiquior, sed incerta eius aetas, quae capillata dicitur, quoniam Vestalium capillus ad eam defertur.* Cf. Fest. 50: *Capillatam vel capillarem arborem dicebant, in qua capillum tonsum suspendebat.* Most scholars agree that the *lotus capillata* of the Vestals was situated in the sanctuary of Juno Licina, where women came to pray for assistance from the goddess at delivery. A curious rule was that they had to avoid any knots on their garments, and their hair had to be untied. Untied, or loose hair, was also demanded of women before baptism.

293　La Follette 1994: 57–9.

294　E.g. Martini 1997b: 477–9 and 481, who reads this rite as an expression of ritual death, cf. van Gennep 1981: 238–40, to whom the cutting of hair represents rites of separation.

295　Dillon 2002: 215 and 225–6, Dowden 1989: 2, viz. Paus. 1.43.4.

296　Fest. 454: *Senis crinibus nubentes ornantur, quod [h]is ornatus vetustissimus fuit. Quidam quod eo Vestales virgines ornentur, quarum castitatem viris suis +sponoe * * * a ceteris.* My transl.

297　E.g. Wildfang 2006: 11.

298　Stephens 2013.

299　Fest. 55: *Caelibari hasta caput nubentis comebatur, quae in corpore gladiatoris stetisset abiecti occisique […].* Transl. La Follete 1994: 60. Cf. Plu. *Q.R.* 87, Plu. *Rom* 15, Arn *Adv. Gent.* II.67 and Ov. *Fast.* 2.560.

300　Fest. 79: *Flammeo amicitur nubens ominis bona causa, quod eo assidue utebatur flaminica, id est flaminis uxor, cui not licebat facere divortium.* Cf. Fest. 82, Sebesta 1998: 111 and Schilling 1979: 154–65.

301　The earliest certain example of a Western bishop presiding over the consecration of a Christian virgin seems to be the consecration of Macellina by Pope Liberius in 353.

302 Metz 1954: 136.

303 Ambr. *De virgb.* III.1: *Namque is, cum Salvatoris natali ad apostolum Petrum virginitatis professionem vestis quoque mutatione signares.*

304 Metz 1954: 136, e.g. Ambr. *Inst. virg.* 102: *Hanc sume stolam, ut induas Christum*, and 110: *His igitur famulam tuam indue vestimentis quae in omni tempore munda sint.*

305 Adkin 2003: 19, commenting on Hier. *Ep.* 22.1: *post Christi tunicam.* Cf. *Homily on virginity* 3.56.

306 Sulp. Sev. *Vita Mart* 19: *Arborius autem, vir praefectorius, sancti admodum et fidelis ingenii, cum filia ejus gravissimis quartanis febribus ureretur, epistolam Martini quae casu ad eum delata fuerat, pectori puellae in ipso accessu ardoris inseruit, statimque fugata febris est. Quae res apud Arborium in tantum valuit, ut statim puellam Deo voverit, et perpetuae virginitati dicarit; profectusque ad Martinum, puellam ei, praesens virtutum ejus testimonium, quae per absentem licet curata esset, obtulit, neque ab alio eam quam a Martino, habitu virginitatis imposito, passus est consecrari.* Transl. NPNF2. For a different view on the dress of consecrated virgins of Gaul regulated in canonical law, see Peyroux 2001: 246.

307 Metz 1954: 137.

308 Ambr. *Inst. virg.* 109: *purpureo Dominici cruoris redimita velamine, mortificationem Domini Jesu in sua carne circumferat; haec sunt enim meliora velamina.* Perhaps as in the color of the bride's and the *flaminica's flammeum*? The exact color of this is not clear, but some kind of red/purple hue is likely, cf. Schilling 1979: 154–65.

309 Ambr. *Inst. virg.* 110: *His igitur famulam tuam indue vestimentis, quae in omni tempore munda sint; mundum enim manet, quidquid nulla interveniens culpa fuscaverit, ut ei jure dicatur: Quoniam placuerunt Deo facta tua* (Eccl. 9:7, 8). *In omni tempore sint vestimenta tua candida,* Cf. Hermas 4.2, where the Church is described as a virgin dressed entirely in white.

310 Metz 1954: 135–6. Optatus (*Schism. Don.* 2.19) mentions a *mitra* that adorns the consecrated virgin's head. D'Izarny 1953: 93 takes this to be the same as what in Latin was called *vitta*. In conversation, I learned from Carolyn Osiek that the Shepherd Hermas describes a virgin wearing *mitra* as part of her dress in vision 4.2.

311 Martin 1995: 233–49, D'Angelo 1995, BeDuhn 1999. Cf. Langlands 2006: 69–77 on what *pudicitia* "looks like."

312 Hier. *Ep.* 22.27: *Vestis nec satis munda, nec sordida, et nulla diversitate notabilis; ne ad te obviam praetereuntium turba consistat, et digito monstreris.* Transl. NPNF2, cf. Tert. *De cult. fem.* II.5: *Haec utique non ad crudam in totum et ferinam habitudinem insinuandam vobis suggeruntur; nec de bono squaloris et paedoris suademus, sed de modo et cardine et justitia corporis excolendi. Non supergrediendum ultra quam simplices et sufficientes munditiae concupiscunt, ultra quam Domino placet.*

313 Canon 17. Transl. NPNF2.

314 1 Cor. 11:5–6.

315 Hier. *Ep.* 147.5: *Moris est in Aegypti et Syriae monasteriis, ut tam virgo, quam vidua, quae se Deo voverint, et saeculo renuntiantes, omnes delicias saeculi conculcarint, crinem monasteriorum matribus offerant desecandum, non intecto postea contra Apostoli voluntatem incessurae capite; sed ligato pariter ac velato. Nec hoc quispiam, praeter tondentes novit et tonsas, nisi quod quia ab omnibus fit, pene scitur ab omnibus. Hoc autem duplicem ob causam, de consuetudine versum est in naturam, vel quia lavacrum non adeunt, vel quia oleum nec capite, nec ore norunt, ne a parvis animalibus, quae inter cutem et crinem gigni solent, et concretis sordibus, opprimantur.* Transl. NPNF2.

316 Hier. *Ep.* 22.27: *Aliae virili habitu, veste mutata, erubescunt esse feminae quod natae sunt, crinem amputant, et impudenter erigunt facies eunuchinas.* Transl. NPNF2.

317 CTh 16.2.27, cf. Evans Grubbs 2001: 228.

318 Cypr. *De hab. virg.* V: *Virgo non esse tantum sed et intelligi debet et credi. Nemo cum virginem viderit, dubitet an virgo sit.* Transl. ANF, with my changes. See also Undheim 2015.

319   Tert. *Virg. vel.* 13.1, Tert. *De orat.* 22.9, cf. D'Angelo 1995: 143ff.
320   Macr. *Sat.* 1.11.38: *ancilla nomine Tutela seu Philotis pollicita est se cum ceteris ancillis sub nomine dominarum ad hostes ituram: habituque matrumfamilias et virginum sumpto hostibus cum prosequentium lacrimis ad fidem doloris ingestae sunt.*
321   Dig. 47.10.15.15 *Ulpianus 77 ad ed.: Si quis virgines appellasset, si tamen ancillari veste vestitas, minus peccare videtur: multo minus, si meretricia veste feminae, non matrum familiarum vestitae fuissent. si igitur non matronali habitu femina fuerit et quis eam appellavit vel ei comitem abduxit, iniuriarum tenetur.* For the prostitute as *togata*, see e.g. Hor *Sat.* 1.2.63, Sebesta 1994: 50–1.
322   CTh 15.7.12.1: *His illud adicimus, ut mimae et quae ludibrio corporis sui quaestum faciunt publice habitu earum virginum, quae deo dicatae sunt, non utantur, et ut nulla femina nec puer thymelici consortio inbuantur, si christianae religionis esse cognoscitur. Dat. III kal. iul. Heracleae Arcadio a. III et Honorio a. II conss.* (394 iun. 29).
323   Evans Grubbs 2001: 238.
324   Evans Grubbs 2001: 238.
325   E.g. Coon 1997 passim, Miller 2005: 90. For the transvestite woman-monk as such a literary *topos*, see Davis 2002 and Vogt 1995.
326   As we have seen above, the inscription commemorating Eucharis, the freed stage performer and virgin, seems very untypical, and the combination of actress and *virgo* is therefore perhaps particularly mentioned as a statement of the girl's honor despite the reputation of her profession.
327   E.g. Hanson 2007: 57, who sees brothels as a probable context and intended "audience" for late antique "medical" treatises that gave instructions on how to fake virginity, and Juv. *Sat* 4.9 (cf. Freudenburg 2001: 259–60) on the excitement of "defiling" a Vestal virgin. Pornographic exploitation of virgins, also consecrated, is a common motif, e.g., Ch. 3 note 17.
328   Sebesta 1994: 50.
329   Langlands 2006: 69–77 on what *pudicitia* "looks like." See also Undheim 2015 for a discussion of the mobility of Christian consecrated virgins and the necessity of virginity on display.
330   Cypr. *De hab. virg.* V: *Nemo cum virginem viderit, dubitet an virgo sit.*
331   Kelly and Leslie 1999: 20, Faroult 2006. See also Undheim 2011: 302.

3 Ungendering virginity?

Virginal paradoxes and paradoxical virginities

So far, there has been hardly any need to specify the gender of the virgins we have encountered. It was never necessary to underline that the Vestals were *female* virgins, because *virgo*, as the definitions so often underlined, was a subcategory of *femina*, female. However, since this appears to have changed with Christianity, it is the construction of a distinct Christian virgin that will be the main focus in this chapter, aiming to explore this purported attempt to redefine *virgo* in terms of gender. Because gender has been an important factor in recent scholarship regarding both Vestal virgins and Christian virgins, this apparent stray away from the "comparative framework" is thus justified, because it is part of the attempt to uncover some of the dynamics in the flexity/fixity of virginity as it was construed and negotiated in this shared context of Late Antique Rome and its environs.

The theoretical framework that in recent years has emerged around questions regarding gender and sexuality has naturally played a large role in studies of virgins and virginity in early Christianity and Late Antiquity.[1] Jorunn Økland has criticized the Anglophone distinction between "gender" and "sex" as one that may not be so helpful when approaching texts from Antiquity. She argues that "by attempting to describe sex, one is already producing gender, one has already made sex part of the structures of meaning that inhabit language, and thus sex in language is always already gender."[2] According to Økland, the fusion of "sex" and "gender" that we find, for instance, in Scandinavian languages and in French, is more in line with ancient Greek conceptions, and is thus also more suitable for grasping the range in the use of terms such as *parthenos*.[3]

That the problem in separating biological sex from the culturally constructed gender becomes particularly evident in the case of the virgin is also pointed out by Kathleen Coyne Kelly, who has argued that "there is no better example of the body exceeding its own physical boundaries than that of virginity, which exists on the cusp between body and culture. By definition, virginity is an abstraction greater than the sum of body parts."[4] The question that arises is whether a definition of virginity could be convincingly made without reference to "body parts," and, then, which bodily parts this would be. In other words, a pressing issue seems to have been whether the physical, bodily aspects so closely associated with virginity could be discharged in favor of a new, bodi-less definition and, then, whether the virgin's body could be a genderless body. Examining some of these cultural negotiations over the gender of virgins and virginity, we will also see how such borderline virginities may in turn have challenged or affected the religious semiotics of "the virgin."

Becoming male? Gender-bending "female" virgins

> While a woman serves for birth and children, she is different from man as body is from soul. But when she wants to serve Christ more than the world, then she shall cease to be called woman and shall be called man.[5]

The *topos* of women "becoming male" as part of the soteriological scheme is well established in feminist studies of Early Christian women. Tales of transvestite saints and "independent widows and virgins," heroically standing up for them-selves in what has been seen as a prequel to modern emancipation, have attrib-uted to the affirmation of this ideal of women "becoming male" as significant in early Christian thinking.[6] The valuation of virginity has particularly been under-stood as an expression of this "becoming male" ideology, as virgins are said to have denied their sexuality and reproductive roles and thereby their "female-ness."[7] The "becoming male" theme thus covers a range of aspects in such a transformation, from an appropriation of virtues that were generally perceived as masculine, to a physical transformation that included the cutting of hair, trans-vestitism and even a change in physical appearance, as a result of stern ascetic practice that would make the female body erase female characteristics and appear "male."[8] Yet, as Teresa Shaw has remarked in her study of fasting and sexuality in the fourth century, "the notion of 'becoming male' can only be taken so far."[9]

There were not only physical limitations to the prospects of salvation by "becoming male." In many respects, the virgin as such was not only gendered female, but also perceived as a highly erotic object and, as such, charged with potent "femininity." The idea that virgins were androgynous and somehow "de-sexualized" is again balanced by other depictions where virgins were represented as attractive heterosexual temptations, with strong erotic allure. John Cassian's *Conlactiones*, for instance, recounts a revelation on the trial of perfect chastity. The ultimate test to see whether all desires are eliminated involved the temptation presented by a naked and beautiful virgin:

> Go, take a naked and most beautiful virgin, and if while you hold her you find that the peace of your heart remains steadfast, and that carnal heat is still and quiet within you, then the touch of this visible flame also shall pass over you gently and without harming you as it did over the three children in Babylon.[10]

The old monk to whom this was revealed wisely refrained from such a test, "guessing that the weight of purity was not yet sufficient to outweigh the force of this trial."[11] That anyone could even sleep beside a virgin and not touch her was simply too inconceivable to Philotis, a character in one of Terentius' plays, who, when she heard such a story, exclaimed: "What is it you tell me? A young man went to bed with a virgin, intoxicated to boot, and was able to restrain himself from touching her! You do not say what's likely; nor do I believe it to be the truth."[12] Both of these examples seem to refer to secular virgins and belong to a world of fiction and revelation. What nevertheless seems to be at play here is the aforementioned aestheticization and eroticizing of virgins that we find exemplified by the legendary virgins in Greek and Roman myths. Many of the narratives in Ovid's *Metamorphoses* testified to how beautiful virgins could evoke and inflame desire to such a degree that even gods were unable to restrain themselves.[13] The virgin goddesses were no less immune to attempted rape, although, as in the stories of virgin martyrs, such attempts were always successfully "circumvented."[14] This, then, was an area where sacred and secular virginity could blur, as it was the personalized, embodied virgin that became the center of attention. Divine or sacred status did not change the virgin's effect on members of the male sex. According to Suetonius, for instance, Augustus had a particular liking for virgins, and his wife Livia supposedly helped to recruit them.[15]

Several scholars have recently pointed out that although the many stories of virgin martyrs that circulated in this period often emphasize the (masculine) virtues of heroic young girls, they still kept a firm focus on the virgin's physical beauty and erotic attraction that often got her into trouble in the first place. The voyeurism exploited in the (narrative) spectacle that led up to the virgin's inescapable death in the arena thus accentuated the virgin martyr as a symbol of the integrity and inviolability of the Church through the popular motif that Kathleen Coyne Kelly has called "circumvented rape." According to Kelly, this "near-rape narrative is a bait-and-switch game that always leaves the audience fully aware of the bait that has been withheld."[16] In this respect, the consecrated and the secular virgin were represented as no different, and there are even indications that a consecrated virgin for some might evoke even stronger desire than one who was more "approachable," a motif that becomes crucial to the narratives relating the martyrdom of virgin martyrs. Juvenal, for instance, seems to imply a cruel conquest motif in the seduction of a Vestal virgin by Crispinus, a libertine and villain in one of his satires.[17] The Theodosian law discussed above could also be taken to indicate that consecrated virgins had an appeal that other women in turn could take advantage of when they wanted to attract men's attention.[18] As with Christian virgins, it is evident that the "androgynity"/"masculinity" attributed to the Vestal virgins has been exaggerated out of proportion. In their analysis of Propertius' elegy on the betrayal of Tarpeia, Paul Allen Miller and Charles Platter have argued that "the Vestal virgins are […] in a sense Rome's most sexual beings."[19] The very focus on the Vestals' obligation to remain virgins thus attests to this heterosexual erotification, and consequently feminization, of these sacred virgins.

Dale Martin has discussed another aspect of the sexuality of virgins and girls on the verge of puberty in general, namely the "widespread opinion at the time [of Paul] that young women at this point of life were especially passionate and eager for copulation."[20] Virginal desire was thus one of the obstacles that had to be overcome by women aspiring for prolonged virginity, and this in turn resulted in a somewhat paradoxical disorder to the gender/asceticism hierarchy. Susanna Elm has remarked that women could achieve some kind of superiority, since "their nature was by definition seen as 'weaker' and softer, their ascetic achievements in comparison to those of men were in effect greater."[21] Such insinuations, particularly when they occur in monastic texts, may indeed fit with the rhetorical strategy Elizabeth Clark identifies as "shaming devices" often directed mainly at a male audience. The prospects, however far-fetched, of an upheaval in the well-known gender hierarchy that such shaming devices could still bring about in the minds of the reader, might however produce a necessity for new negotiations regarding the hierarchies of sanctity in terms of virginity and reversed gender categories as well. For if weak females, prone to give in to any possible opportunity for sex, could surpass men in virtue by remaining virgins, how could Christian men ever reclaim their male authority? No matter how interesting the transvestite female virgin may be, there is another figure that has so far been conspicuously absent from the scene, namely the male virgin.

MALE VIRGINS AND GENDERLESS VIRGINITY

I have never known a woman, and yet I am no virgin.[22]

While the somewhat paradoxical gender ambiguity that has been attributed to some early Christian women, and in particular to consecrated virgins, has been widely explored, male virgins, if such a category or notion did exist at all, have in comparison been more or less neglected in the many studies that have investigated such virginal gender ambiguity.[23] The absence of male virgins becomes even more remarkable considering that almost all scholars who have written on this topic seem to understand the early Christian ideal of virginity as one that was universal and regardless of gender.[24] If such ideals of genderless virginity were indeed part of Early Christian teaching, a logical consequence would be that the source texts reflected an abundance of male virgins alongside the female ones. However, the lack of interest in these particular aspects of gendered virginity, as well as further problematization of gendered issues, is therefore striking when we turn to the ancient Latin material as well as to modern interpretations of it.[25] This chapter will focus on how virginity and virgins might have been understood as asexual and "ungendered," as some of the Church Fathers and modern scholars so often present them, and how this in turn presented some challenges for Christian writers, particularly in the Western Church. While some of them claimed that virginity could dissolve all gendered distinctions, others seem to have been more reluctant to accept the

consequences of such genderless virginity. By examining the texts and specifically looking for the male virgins in them, the negotiations over the limits of
virginity, and what is at stake in the relationship between a virgin and his or
her virginity in terms of gender, becomes more clear.

Many questions follow from this approach. First of all, if virginity was indeed
considered a universal ideal regardless of gender, then where are the male
virgins in our sources? In what circumstances were men explicitly described as
virgins? And where are the virgins explicitly (or implicitly) females? Was the
male virgin simply a "mythical beast," as Maud Burnett McInerney suggests?[26]
Or a rhetorical joke, as Virginia Burrus has suggested?[27] One could of course
ask whether the dominant focus on female virgins in present scholarship is due
to a feminist bias, where the quest to recover historical "women" has simply
created a "blind spot" for male virgins in these sources. As the sources, however,
by no means abound with male virgins, it is perhaps no surprise that it is the
female virgins that have been the focus of scholarship too. It is therefore
reasonable, given the noteworthy dearth of male virgins in the Latin discourses,
to look more closely at whether the borderlines of gendered virginity were
more problematic for males than for females.

As McInerney has called attention to, the notion of virginity as a "guarantee"
for salvation would indeed have had grave soteriological and theological implications if it was actually denied to the male half of the Christian community.[28]
That such a prerogative should be limited to females only would seem strange,
particularly in light of the otherwise rather misogynistic tone in the Fathers'
writings.[29] The tension conveyed in the sources between the physical and the
spiritual aspects of virginity seems to have represented the crux for Latin writers who were eager to convince all Christians to pursue the life of virgins as
virgins (and not merely in imitation of exemplary female virgins). Terminology
will therefore be as important here as in my previous discussions of virginity.
Confusion regarding the terms related to chastity, abstinence and virginity is
certainly one reason why texts concerning male virgins (or their like) often
appear so vague, given that modern studies rarely distinguish virginity from, for
instance, chastity. The terms also appear to overlap in the ancient sources, but
this does not mean that they were synonymous in all respects.[30]

As already stated, my primary concern in this chapter will be instances
where men are explicitly described as virgins, that is, by the terms *virgo* and
parthenos. I will also deal with instances where the derivatives *virginitas* or
partheneia are applied with specific reference to men. Since, however, various
rhetorical considerations certainly motivated the choice of language pertaining
to sexuality, different authors would address different audiences in different
genres, and adapt their vocabulary accordingly, sometimes in order to provoke
and at other times in order to avoid offensive and inappropriate language, all
depending on the genre and purpose of the text. Several Latin writers thus
appear to have opted for some kind of periphrasis in order to specify the sexual
status of the man or boy in question. In this regard it is therefore relevant to
consider other concepts as well, such as *castitas* and *sophrosyne*, and other terms

denoting degrees of sexual purity, even though there were, as I have already underlined, significant distinctions that had to be kept for the virgin only, in order to maintain his or her special sanctity.[31] Eunuchs represent one example of such gender adaptation in language because they occasionally came to function, at least rhetorically, as male counterparts to female consecrated virgins. As in previous chapters, I will stray from my main sources, Ambrose and Jerome, and take several detours as regards chronology as well as literary genres and geography in order to outline the contexts and intertexts for their writings. Through this approach, I also hope to touch upon a range of different attitudes and conceptions that may indicate part of the tension between virginity's fixity and flexity in terms of gendering or ungendering, tensions and complexities that I argue can only be accessible through using a variety of sources.

Male virgins in non-Christian sources?

Recent studies of sexuality and gender in Antiquity all stress how the division between the two sexes reflects the social and cultural importance of this division in classical Greece as well as in Roman times.[32] Nevertheless, as these same studies point out, our sources abound with examples of persons and characters that stretch these categorical divisions and in different ways cross the rather fluctuating lines drawn between male and female.[33] Scholars have unearthed heroic women displaying male virtues as well as "soft men" who have succumbed to feminine vices, and gender seems a theme never to be exhausted of variations. It has been remarked that sexual renunciation, long thought to be a distinguishing mark of early Christianity, was also pursued among some male pagans,[34] yet the concept of virginity is more or less absent in these discourses.[35] The lack of terminology for authors who needed to convey the sexual inexperience of males seems only rarely to have been a problem. Julius Caesar, for instance, solved it appropriately when he described the Germans in his *De Bello Gallico*:

> Those [men] who have remained chaste (*impuberes*) for the longest time, receive the greatest commendation among their people; they think that by this the growth is promoted, and that by this the physical powers are increased and the sinews strengthened.[36]

Caesar has here chosen the word *inpubes*, a term that usually denotes a boy's status before reaching puberty, to render the lack of sexual experience of these young men.[37] Though, to leave no doubt as to what he is referring, Caesar adds that these Germans consider it disgraceful to "have knowledge of a woman" before the age of 20, a statement about the sexual status of these males that might, according to some at least, qualify as "virgins."[38]

An interesting remark is found in the text of the early fourth-century grammarian Nonius Marcellinus, who refers to Varro for the following observation: "Not only females are said to be virgins, but also prepubescent boys, for all who had left adolescence, were said to be devirginized." As evidence for this usage, Nonius quotes a rather obscure passage from Varro's *Peri exagoges* where the possibility of a boy's "devirginization" is discussed.[39] *Devirginare*, "to devirginize," is an uncommon word in classical Latin[40] and Varro appears to be the only one of our extant sources that applies the term to adolescent boys. It is thus impossible to estimate whether Varro's reflections on male virginity represented a widespread idea of male virginity as parallel to female. What appears from this "definition," however, is a different understanding of what terminates male virginity than what Caesar deems to be of significance in his description of the German warrior ideals. We thus encounter the "limits of virginity" that, as we will see, were indeed important in the negotiations concerning the epistemology of virginity, and that become perhaps even more flexible when the virgin becomes ungendered, or even male. The following is by no means meant to be a comprehensive outline of male virgins in the Greco-roman culture, but a few examples to illustrate the variety of genre and context for even writing about male virginity.

Hippolytus

Hippolytus, the devoted follower of the virgin goddess Artemis, is probably the closest we may come to a male virgin in classical Antiquity. The son of an Amazon warrior and the mythic hero-king Theseus, Hippolytus' tragic story of an attempted seduction staged by his stepmother, Phaedra, was retold by a number of classical authors.[41] Servius describes Hippolytus as chaste (*castus*), and writes that it was because of this chastity that the goddess Artemis/Diana rewarded Hippolytus with a shrine and a cult in Aricia under the name of Virbius.[42]

In Euripides' dramatic version of the story from the fifth century BC, Hippolytus is presented as avoiding women and cherishing *sophrosyne*.[43] When his father, Theseus, accuses him of having sexually assaulted his stepmother, Hippolytus declares his complete ignorance when it comes to the sexual act:

> By one thing I am untouched, the very thing in which you think you have convicted me: to this very moment my body is untainted (*hagnon*)[44] by love. I do not know this act save by report or seeing it in painting.[45]

To further emphasize his complete lack of interest in sex, Hippolytus states that he has no desire even to see images of the act, "since I have a virgin soul."[46] Hippolytus' virginity then, is located in his soul, *psyche*, rather than in a part of his body or as a term applied to describe Hippolytus himself. By claiming a virgin *psyche*, Euripides' Hippolytus enhances his claim of indifference towards sex, but, more interestingly, the virgin soul also avoids the problems entailed by making the audience envision a male virgin as such, at the same time as the statement brings attention to the traditionally gendered division.[47] Hippolytus has already come across as an uncharacteristic male, not only in his devotion to

Artemis but also by his devotion to the goddess' (for him) paradigmatic virginity.[48] It is exactly this unnatural and unmanly disinterest in love and sexuality that in the play is punished by Aphrodite, as Hippolytus' anomalous desire to be virginal disrupts her schemes and insults the goddess of love by rejecting her.

Physicians on male virginity

As noted by Caesar when commenting on the practice of the Germans, there were those who believed there were health benefits to be achieved by prolonged virginity and sexual abstinence. Soranus presents different physicians' views on the dangers versus benefits of keeping girls as virgins for too long.[49] Medical texts have turned out to be a rich source for the recent interest in ancient sexualities and conceptions of gender, and different opinions find support here regarding notions of both positive and negative effects of prolonged sexual abstinence.[50] Soranus concludes his discussion on this issue by stating that "unbroken virginity [*dienekés partheneia*] is healthful, in males and females alike."[51] Virginity is thereby understood to be a quality that, in medical theory at least, can be maintained by both sexes, and it is not seen as an exclusively female characteristic. It is however noteworthy how Soranus refrains from applying the term *parthenos* to males, whom he prefers to designate *aphthoros* [*menontes aphthoroi*], i.e. "those remaining incorrupt," to indicate their lack of sexual experience.[52] This passage thus indicates that, in medical terms, virginity (*partheneia*) as a physical state can be applied regardless of gender, yet *parthenos*, at least in this genre, is restricted to females. Soranus and later medical writers' preference for virginity for both sexes should be seen in relation to similar ideas on the benefits of sexual abstinence for men, such as prescribed for athletes and the German warriors mentioned by Caesar.[53]

Greek romance

The so-called Greek novels abound with the kind of gender-bending we also find in Early Christian literature, and these texts have therefore, particularly in the wake of Foucault, become popular as comparative material for scholars of Early Christianity.[54] Virginia Burrus has explored how the concept of virginity in these novels could function as "a site of articulated cultural ambivalence." Her main interest is what she calls "the *impurity* – the *hybridity* – of virginity," of which the male virgins in these texts were a part according to Burrus' reading.[55]

In the story of *Joseph and Aseneth*, both protagonists, male and female alike, are said to be virgins, and their virginity is central to the narrative as they approach a mutual decision to renounce virginity in favor of marriage.[56] Likewise, in Heliodorus' *Ethiopian Story*, the lovers Theagenes and Charikleia carefully guard their respective virginities[57] through their separate and dangerous journeys, which culminate in a crucial scene where both hero and heroine are finally united as captives and are forced to undergo a test of virginity featuring a magical golden gridiron. When the hero Theagenes passes unscathed, the crowd murmurs both approval and surprise that such a virile youth has proved "ignorant of the joys of Aphrodite."[58] Theagenes had, prior to his first encounter with Charikleia, maintained that "he had never been intimate with a woman" and "had never felt anything but contempt for their whole sex … and even for married love."[59] The final test thus proves that he was truthful.

Contrary to Joseph and Theagenes, whose virginity in both novels is explained as a deliberate expression of piety and religious devotion, Kleitophon from the story of *Kleitophon and Leukippe* makes no similar claim to religiosity. Confronted with Leukippe's jealous accusations, however, Kleitophon insists that "I have imitated your virginity – if that word has any meaning for men as it does for women,"[60] and later he similarly states: "If one can speak of such a thing as male virginity, this is my relationship to Leukippe up to now."[61] As Burrus remarks, "Kleitophon's slippery rhetoric here seems to reinstate, with a knowing wink, a traditional sexual double standard, thereby insinuating that the notion of male virginity is indeed no more than a joke."[62] Unlike Theagenes and his own fiancée Leukippe, Kleitophon is not subjected to a test of virginity. As Simon Goldhill has shown, such tests are in this novel jokingly played with by means of cunning rhetoric. When the vengeful husband of Kleitophon's married mistress suddenly appears, she phrases her oath in such terms that she manages to "prove" her chastity. All the readers, however, know she has been unfaithful and are aware of the unreliability of the test that her husband trusts.[63] Daphnis and Chloe, on the other hand, whose burning love but helpless innocence in sexual matters makes for suggestive and sometimes comic effect, are in no need of such tests. In frustration over not figuring out the *techne* necessary to fulfill Eros, Daphnis ends up being "initiated" by an experienced woman, who in turn gives him instructive advice for the deflowering of Chloe.[64]

In different ways, Kleitophon and Hippolytus question the possibility of a male virginity and demonstrate the illogical nature of such a construction. Likewise, the audience of Theagenes' trial in the *Ethiopian Story* marvels at the unbelievable spectacle when the virile youth is proven to be virgin: it is simply beyond their belief. The only male virgin whose virginity is not directly challenged by such gender conventions seems to be Joseph in *Joseph and Aseneth*. However, his virginity appears first and foremost to be a mirror to Aseneth's protagonist virginity, which is a pivotal center in the structure of the first part of this narrative.

Although it might be unwise to draw general conclusions on the basis of such meager material, it is nevertheless tempting to point out that these discourses concerning and also constructing male virginity are almost without exception of Eastern origin, belonging to a Greek linguistic and cultural context. Earlier Latin authors seem to opt for other terms than *virgo* and *virginitas* to describe men prior to sexual experience, as seen in the example from Julius Caesar.

As the story of Hippolytus and the ancient novels demonstrate, male virgins, however rare and "anomalous," could be explained in narratives as religious devotees to certain deities who favored virginity as an expression of their subjects' commitment.[65] The following sections will explore how contemporary and later discourses on Christian ideology tested and explored gendered limitations and the "fixity" of virginity, especially in ideologies where virginity was an expression of religious sentiment, as virgins increasingly became an important manifestation of theological issues and the power of the Orthodox Church.

Like angels on earth

> And now, after all this, it is to you, Father of grace, that I address my prayers; to your kindness we offer immense gratitude, because we see in the sacred virgins the life of angels that we once lost in Paradise.[66]

That being a virgin should be attractive to Christian men as well as to women seems justified by the Church Fathers' identification of virgins as angels on earth, already taking part in the heavenly life. This idea stems from an early equation between virgins and the unmarried in Matt. 22:30: "For in the resurrection they neither marry nor are given in marriage, but are like the angels of God in heaven," a passage that would explain some of the soteriological implications of the virginal ideal. Jerome commented on Matt. 22:30 in his treatise against Jovinian:

> What others in the future will be in heaven, virgins begin to be on earth. If we are promised the likeness of angels (and among the angels there is no difference of sex), then we will either be without sex (*sine sexu*) as the angels are, or at least that which is proved with clarity; when we rise from the grave in our own sex, we will not perform the function of sex.[67]

Jerome states that the angels are without sex, but he appears to have more difficulty in envisioning the afterlife of humans to be without the distinctions of these categories. Therefore, although "we rise from the grave in our own sex," what Jerome stresses is the "function of sex," the belief that there will be no sexual coupling. Jerome's attitude to the sexlessness of Christian ascetics and their aspiration for the angelic life on earth is therefore not as flexible as it may appear to be elsewhere, and he seems ultimately to reject this vision of the afterlife where people are no longer marked by their sex/gender.[68] Several questions thus arise around this assimilation between virgins and angels: If virginal life was to live as angels on earth, what were the implications of this in terms of how gender was perceived? May the notions of the gender of angels clarify points regarding the gender of virgins or vice versa? Given that aesthetics seems important in rhetorical appeals to angels, do the texts reveal anything about how this sexlessness of the angels was perceived? Was one sex favored over the other in the way angels were depicted in text?

The understanding of virgins as worldly equivalents to angels touches upon difficult issues at the core of Christian doctrine, such as bodily resurrection and the creation of man (and woman) in the image of God. It is here not possible to venture upon a discussion of all the different aspects of angels and angelic life that appear in the sources from this period; however, by discussing certain passages where virgins were equaled to angels and where virginity was presented as angelic life on earth, I hope to shed some light upon gendered assumptions and presuppositions that exemplify the tension between fixity and flexity in what is apparently linked to an aesthetics of the virginal/angelic life.

Turning the question around and starting with the gender of these angelic virgins, it is interesting to study the letters and treatises written to and about virgins. As already stated, most treatises on virginity from Late Antiquity were addressed to individual young virgin girls (both prior to and post consecration and, in some cases, such as at least one of Ambrose's sermons, as part of the consecration itself).[69] It is nonetheless evident that the authors had a wider audience in mind as well, as seen in Jerome's famous letter to Eustochium and Ambrose's first treatise on virginity addressed to his sister Marcellina. Only very few of these texts, however, seem to have been reaching out to members of the male sex alongside the female addressees.[70] The cases appear even more exceptional when we restrict the selection of texts to those where men also are explicitly referred to as virgins. There are, as far as I am aware, no treatises on virginity of this period that are addressed to any identified individual male virgin nor to any group of male virgins.

Often, the treatises on virginity open with a general exhortation to chastity (with no restrictions on gender), before the author swiftly moves on to issues particularly and undoubtedly pertaining to female virgins. Cyprian's *De habitu virginum* (*On the dress of virgins*), indisputably directs the initial exhortation at members of each sex:

> And, indeed, let men as well as women, boys as well as girls; let each sex and every age observe this, and take care in this respect, according to the religion and faith which they owe to God, that what is received holy and pure from the condescension of the Lord be preserved with no less anxious fear.[71]

Virginity as such, however, is not stated as the explicit calling, but rather chastity and purity in a more general (and thus more widely accessible) manner. After his opening paragraphs, Cyprian then immediately narrows down his audience and stresses that "now my speech is to the virgins."[72] That these virgins are thought of as female is evident from grammar and from the main argument of the treatise, which attacks women's weakness for jewelry, make-up and adornment.[73]

There were some, however, who did apply the ideal of perpetual "virginity" to all Christians regardless of gender. In his apologetic text *Octavius*, Minucius Felix met accusations of Christians being frivolous and incestuous by stating that their common meals were, on the contrary, chaste and sober, "tempered by chaste conversation and even more chaste bodies" (*casta sermone, corpore castiore*), and he affirms that "several of us are inviolated and enjoy rather than brag about our perpetual bodily virginity."[74] The fact that he characterizes those of his fellow Christians by the term *inviolati*[75] in the masculine plural seems to indicate that he envisions this as a quality pertaining to men (as well as women, we can only assume). His distinction between "you" and "us," as is common in apologetic rhetoric, presents a wide-ranging and inclusive "us" where gender and social status appear to be unimportant, at least in this context. That this "us," although inclusive, might be envisioned as male, was also indicated in Tertullian's contemporary *Apologia*, where he writes:

> A persevering and steadfast chastity has protected us from anything like this: keeping as we do from adulteries and all post-matrimonial unfaithfulness, we are not exposed to incestuous mishaps.[76] Some of us, making matters still more secure, beat away from them entirely the power of sensual sin, by a virgin continence, still boys in this respect when they are old.[77]

Of course Tertullian's twist to the *puer senex* motif gets its meaning from the purity assigned to children, and he uses it again in his description of "our own Proculus, dignified and of a virgin(al) old age and Christian eloquence."[78] It is noteworthy that, just like Euripides and the medical writers, neither Minucius Felix nor Tertullian explicitly describes these men as virgins. Instead, they are invested with virginal qualities, such as a "perpetual bodily virginity," "virgin continence" and "virgin old age."

Although the topic of Jerome's letter to Gaudentius is the proper upbringing of Gaudentius' daughter, who was vowed to virginity by her parents, Jerome also stresses that his advice is not necessarily relevant for all to follow. He makes it explicitly clear, however, that this limitation is not restricted by gender: "What I say I do not say as universally applicable; my treatment of the subject is only partial. I speak of some only, not of all. However, my words are addressed to those of both sexes, and not only to 'the weaker vessel'."[79] In the following passage, the hypothetical "virgin" Jerome addresses is clearly, as given by context and grammar, to be envisioned as male:

> Are you a virgin? Why then do you find pleasure in the society of a woman? Why do you commit to the high seas your frail patched boat, why do you so confidently face the great peril of a dangerous voyage? You know not what you desire, and yet you cling to her as though you had either desired her before or, to put it as leniently as possible, as though you would hereafter desire her.[80]

The passage is apparently directed at men who nurtured what Jerome deems as a too intimate relation with women, as servants, conversation partners or even so-called *subintroductae* or *agapetae*.[81] In a succeeding passage, Jerome turns to the women:

> You too, whether virgin or widow, why do you allow a man to detain you in conversation so long? Why are you not afraid to be left alone with him? At least go out of doors to satisfy the wants of nature, and for this at any rate leave the man with whom you have given yourself more liberty than you would with your brother, and have behaved more immodestly than you would with your husband.[82]

The concern is thus virgins, both male and female, who consort with members of the other sex and thus endanger their virgin state. Virginity does not erase gender distinctions but, in this case, rather calls for stricter division in order to be maintained. It is clear here, however, that to Jerome *virgo* is not a status that only privileges one sex.

While Jerome is the master of provocative and clear-cut language, Ambrose's literal density demands a different analytical approach. Even though he is one of the most ardent proponents of virginity and chastity, his somewhat suggestive play on gender and sexuality remains firmly rooted in traditional gender conventions.[83]

In her reading of *De virginibus*, Virginia Burrus finds that Ambrose's "final narrative of chastity threatened and defended will leave no doubt that the apostle Paul's message concerning the value of virginity is intended not only for one sex but for all."[84] An examining of the text, however, reveals an Ambrose who, despite the telling of a narrative that plays on transvestitism and gender conventions, obviously remains reluctant about extending the gender of virgins in order to include men (if that is even a possibility he has considered at all). Ambrose introduces his tale as an example for everyone, as remarked by Burrus, yet gender is neither specified nor a topic at all in this particular passage. Since Ambrose recognizes that the elevated virgin saints Mary and Thecla may appear as models impossible to imitate, he goes on to recount a story from what he refers to as recent times, namely the story of a girl whom his audience allegedly may find it easier to identify with.[85] This *recens exemplum* is the story of an unnamed virgin of Antioch and the soldier who saved her when her virginity was in grave danger. As in Ambrose's other narratives about virgin martyrs, we encounter a beautiful virgin whose appearance stirs male desire, but whose heroic behavior displays masculine virtues that surpass those of many men. In this particular story, the spectacle is further enhanced by the introduction of transvestitism (one of the rarer instances where a male also dresses as a female).[86] Despite a carnivalesque play with gender roles, the virgin and her soldier savior nevertheless remain solid and traditional examples for their respective genders: the virgin by miraculously remaining virginal, and the soldier by confirming himself as a masculine hero indeed, despite his brief performance in virginal garb. When the virgin is sentenced to serve at a brothel,[87] the soldier appears as her first customer, only to reveal himself as a fellow Christian whose intention is to help her preserve her virginity rather than put an end to it. He suggests they swap clothes so that she can escape, hiding her face and virginal body in his cloak. The soldier emphasizes how this changing of clothes will only strengthen their claim to their respective professions: "Your dress will make me a true soldier; mine will make you a virgin."[88]

The next customer that enters is of course stunned to find the soldier where he had expected the beautiful girl, and exclaims (still according to Ambrose): "Now, this is not that old tale of a hind for a virgin,[89] but what is in truth a soldier from a virgin. And I had even heard, but not believed, that Christ changed water into wine; now, though, he has started to alter the sexes."[90] Although he is presumably still dressed in the virgin's clothes, there is never any doubt about the gender of the soldier. The comic effect of the "sex change" is on behalf of the pagan, whose gendered confusion eventually leads him to conversion and a happy ending.

The soldier is then "sentenced in the virgin's place, he who was captured in the virgin's place."[91] When his death sentence is about to be carried out, the fundamental and indeed markedly gendered difference between the two becomes evident as the virgin suddenly appears at the arena with a plea, or more precisely, a demand. She insists on sharing in the soldier's martyrdom:

> I did not choose you to rescue me from death, but as a bondsman for my chastity. If chastity is what is sought, my sex remains the same (*si pudor quaeritur, manet sexus*). But if blood is demanded, I do not desire a bondsman: I have my own blood, and I will dissolve you from your bond. This judgement, which was sentenced [you] because of me, was sentenced against me. […]. Let me die as an innocent, that I may not die guilty of a crime. There is no middle way in this. Today, I will be condemned because of your blood, or be a martyr in my own (blood). […] There is in a virgin place for a wound, even if there was none for violation (*est in virgine vulneri locus, qui non erat contumeliae*). I rejected the disgrace, not martyrdom (*ego opprobrium declinavi, non martyrium*). I gave up my clothes to you, but I did not abandon my profession. If you deprive me of my death, you have not redeemed me, but deceived me. Be careful, I beg you, not to contest, and be careful, so you dare not speak against me. Do not take away the favor which you did for me. When you refuse me my judgement, you bring back the one that was first sentenced (against me). For this sentence will be abandoned in favor of the first one. If I am not liable to the last one, I am still bound to the first. We can both fulfill our sentence, if you allow me to be killed as the first (of us). Upon you, they cannot inflict another sentence than this, but for a virgin her chastity is always in danger.[92]

In Ambrose's rendering of the tale, the unnamed virgin seems to confirm R. Howard Bloch's statement that "the only good virgin […] is the dead virgin."[93] In her speech she predicts that while the soldier obtains martyrdom, she will be sent back to the brothel if he does not make sure she is killed before he is. When Ambrose has her proclaim that "for a virgin her chastity is always in danger," it is clearly implied that only death can safely preserve her virginity. As also Burrus remarks in conclusion, the virgin remains safely within the gendered hierarchy, eroticized and female.[94] Ambrose's exemplary story of virginity thus becomes an example of how martyrdom, and not virginity as such, is the ideal for all to follow.[95] Through the heroic act of martyrdom, the virgin may be equal to the soldier, since martyrdom seems to erase the gendered distinctions and, as a consequence, the constant danger she is exposed to as a virgin and a woman. As the attentive reader/listener of Ambrose's sermon would have remembered from the exemplary Agnes, whose story Ambrose had recounted in the prior book of the treatise, this anonymous virgin of Antioch too would earn the double crown of martyrdom and virginity, whereas the soldier would have to settle with only one crown, the crown of martyrdom.[96] Thus virginity – despite the soldier's heroic appearance in virginal clothing – remains only the girl's Achilles' heel and, at the same time, exactly because of this, is her privilege alone.[97]

Other passages from Ambrose's writings on virginity generally affirm this gendered notion of virgins.[98] *Exhortatio virginitatis*, for instance, is addressed to the widow Juliana's children, one son and (at least) two daughters. This rather lengthy passage is written as though presented by Juliana herself (yet with the characteristic eloquence of Ambrose),[99] to console her children after their father's death. Throughout the text, Ambrose appears to substitute *virginitas* with *integritas* as his preferred gender-neutral honorary term when this is needed.[100] At one point, it is declared that "only faith does not make distinction between the sexes; it is the wealth of men, and the dowry of virgins."[101] Ambrose seems to imply that a distinction between the sexes is upheld everywhere but in faith, yet, paradoxically, even phrasing this unique absence of gendered distinctions in faith has to be done by these very distinctions, where the rewards are termed differently for men and *virgines* accordingly.

Although, as we have seen, some authors of ascetic treatises address their exhortations to members of both sexes, there are clear sex/gender distinctions to be found in their choice of vocabulary. One of these terms is obviously *virgo*, which only very rarely was used to address an "incorrupt," celibate man or men. Instead, it appears that other terms were preferred when describing these men's sexual "incorruptness," and this again underlines how virgins were fundamentally conceived as gendered and female.[102] Also, the traditional rhetorical structure reveals how these texts tend to sometimes address men and women as one group, and sometimes address them separately (first the man/men, then the women).[103]

Eunuchs and male virginity

And immediately by the instance of the three eunuchs he shows the blessedness of virginity which is bound by no carnal tie.[104]

The biblical passage concerning those who had made themselves eunuchs for the sake of the kingdom of heaven (Matt. 19:12) represented some interpretational challenges to ancient as well as modern exegetes.[105] As already mentioned, eunuchs often functioned rhetorically as the male counterpart to female virgins (and vice versa). An example of how this terminology overlapped and was sometimes confused is to be found in Rufinus' translation of Eusebius' *Historia Ecclesiastica*. Melito, bishop of Sardis, is described by Eusebius as a eunuch, a term which Rufinus in turn renders as *virgo*.[106]

Tertullian had proclaimed voluntary eunuchs and virgins wed to Christ as the feature of the Church's might:

> See here the features of our future strength! We even, as we may be able, excuse our mouths from food, and withdraw our sexes from copulation. How many voluntary eunuchs are there! How many virgins married to Christ! How many, both of men and women, whom nature has made sterile, with a structure which cannot procreate![107]

Tertullian's passage indicates that eunuchs and virgins are gendered categories reflecting notions of chastity that share similar meaning in this context. The "voluntary eunuchs" reappear repeatedly in Tertullian's writings, just as they later did in Jerome's.[108]

However, the difference between eunuchs and virgins was not merely one based on gender. To some, castration would signal "fixity," something very finite, similar to that of perpetual virginity. Also, like virgins, with eunuchs one might never actually achieve absolute certainty regarding their sexual history.[109] Two very significant differences between eunuchs and virgins seem nevertheless to be at play. First, unlike the qualifying requirement for virgins, there was no guarantee a eunuch had not experienced sex prior to castration, in which case (impossible to ascertain) he would not have retained the sexual purity or "intactness" that was assigned to virgins. As Matthew Kuefler has demonstrated, neither was castration itself thought to guarantee complete sexual abstinence or elimination of desire.[110] Eunuchs could still engage in sexual acts, and not only as the "passive" part of a relation between males, but even, possibly, in some cases (depending on the method of castration), be the active penetrator of men as well as women.[111]

Peter Brown among others points out how eunuchs were therefore thought of by some Christians to represent a constant danger for women, particularly for virgins, who might feel a false security surrounding themselves with eunuch servants.[112] Daniel F. Caner argues convincingly that orthodox Christian writers of Late Antiquity came to understand castration as a deceptive signifier, such as Basil of Ancyra who compared the eunuch with a bull: just as a bull would still be a bull even if it had no horns, a man "who has cut off all his genitalia does not become a woman by the loss of these; he is still by nature a man."[113] Second, as McInerney and Kelly stress, there is another fundamental difference between female virgins, who "are, by a definition that comes to us from the Latin, intact, untouched; [and the] male virgins, *spadones voluntarii*, [who] are equally definitely touched, mutilated."[114] Although in this case their reading of male as well as female virgins is certainly very selective, and they overlook the importance of *voluntarii* in this category of eunuchs, they do have a point that seems to partially explain why the popularity of sacred virgins grew sky high into the Middle Ages, while the terminology related to the consecrated eunuch (apart from the explicitly stated *spiritual* eunuch) disappeared from the gradually institutionalized ascetic movement. Virginia Burrus has analyzed how these eunuchs represented difficult images for Ambrose to handle: "The problem, for Ambrose, is that self-castration seems to represent 'a declaration of weakness rather than a reputation of strength'."[115] Male sexuality, Burrus argues, can in Ambrose's view "not be confined to the male genitalia and then simply pared away," yet, on the other hand, virile strength cannot be completely detached from the male organ either.[116]

The efforts to establish the orthodox exegesis of central ascetic biblical passages clearly created gendered tensions as Christian writers sought to stretch and extend terms such as eunuch and virgin in order to dissolve their gendered denotation; thus we find Jerome referring to female eunuchs, which he dubs *eunuchiae*, and the passages from the Gospel of Matthew (22:19) and Isaiah 56:3ff. were occasionally applied to (female) virgins as well as married women.[117] Even more so than male virgins, these female eunuchs must be said to have been exceptionally rare in early Christian literature. Whereas Tertullian's eunuchs were contrasted in terms of gender to virgins wed to Christ, John Cassian at the beginning of the fifth century conflated the two categories in his *Conlactiones* (*Conferences*) when he describes those who have achieved the powers of the body:

> For the true and uncorrupted virgins of Christ, who are considered admirable and honourable eunuchs, are not those who fear fornication and to whom it is not permitted, and who repress impurity, but those who have overcome even the slightest titillation of the mind and the least incitements to wantonness. They have subdued what I might call the feelings of their flesh to such an extent that they are affected not only by no pleasure arising from any movement thereof but not even by the most insignificant titillation.[118]

In the case of eunuchs in early Christian literature, we find that the gendered "flexity" of a concept that at first glance appears so fundamentally "fixed" is partially in line with the theoretical and practical problems that we encounter concerning "fallen virgins" and virginity's strangely indefinable and elusive nature. In this respect, the ascetic interest in figures such as eunuchs and virgins alike signals a desire to control and to "fix" sexuality, as one aspect of an attempt that eventually seems to become an overwhelming task for the Orthodox Fathers, and therefore one that they will return to time and again. In the world of angels and eunuchs and virgins, a high degree of flexity in terms of gender was present, yet the sexlessness attributed to angels did not necessarily entail that they were envisioned as androgynous. Mark Kuefler has pointed out, with reference to the angel that visited Mary, that

> if the virginal ideal was angelic, it was also masculine: angels, who were supposed to be beyond sexual difference, were *mostly* [my italics] imagined as men, as can be seen in the numerous descriptions of Mary's fright at seeing a strange man in her bedroom when the angel Gabriel appeared to her.[119]

Likewise, Tertullian, reading Paul, meant uncovered virgins represented a temptation for the angels, who in turn becomes a threat to the virgins' virginity.[120] These angels, presumably less benign than the one who visited Mary, indicate that the category covered a varied group of creatures. This, however, does not necessarily mean that angels as such were always imagined as men. Female angels are certainly harder to come across in Late Antiquity, but pagan Victoria/Nike iconography appears to have influenced the visual images of angels.

As Shaw stated with regard to maleness, the notion of "being angels" in terms of their acclaimed sexlessness could, of course, only be taken so far when virgins were likened to angels. Other readings of Matt. 22:30 saw the angelic life on earth to be within reach for all those who lived in chastity and who renounced marriage.[121] Like the passage in Matt. 22:30, this advice has no gendered addressee and, as such, it is perhaps best to understand the virgins as a sub-category of those who are chaste.

VIRGINITY, HUMILITY, AND MALE AUTHORITY

> For with what shame has a bishop or presbyter dared to preach integrity or continence to a widow or a virgin, or even to propose the keeping of marital chastity, whenever he himself has been more involved in the begetting of children for the world than for God?[122]

The inconsistencies, elusive vocabulary and internal negotiations that we encounter in discourses where the gender of virgins is implicitly or explicitly an issue, seem to arise from a tension between a general skepticism towards the spiritual abilities of women on the one hand and the unsurpassed virtue displayed by the consecrated female virgins on the other. As McInerney has pointed out, it is therefore relevant to ask whether virginity as a marker of sanctity and guarantee for salvation was only attractive for women, or whether it could equally be perceived as a marker of male sanctity. The tensions between virginity, gender and authority seem to have been negotiated exactly over these soteriological dilemmas that followed in the wake of Christian virgin ideology. This is detectable both in the Late Antique sources, but also as they have been interpreted by modern scholars. Thus, while some scholars have seen virginity as a genderless, or gender-neutral term, others have brought the gendered complexities to the fore.

Jo Ann McNamara focuses on the subversive initiative she claims is found among female ascetics, and argues that male virgins did not represent the same threat to institutionalized authority as the celibate women:

> Though it is clear that men also embraced the life of asexual celibacy, Christian writers do not appear to have perceived them as a challenge to the order of their communities. Since a full range of roles, from pious layman to bishop, was open to men, and a growing party within the Church accepted and even championed the idea of clerical celibacy, male virgins could be readily integrated into the community at every level. Male theologians, however, had serious difficulties in adapting their social and clerical ideas to the existence of celibate women as active components of their congregations.[123]

As McNamara presents this, male virginity and clerical celibacy seem universally accepted, and it is the female virgins that cause difficulties for the male theologians.[124]

Although he does indicate that there was something of a strife in the pursuit of virginity, Peter Brown, too, seems to find male virginity as an imitation of a model so explicitly female to be a very uncomplicated issue, as when he analyzes the hierarchy arranged by Ambrose where

> the virgins came first, the widows second, and the married persons third. This was a universal scale, applicable to both sexes. The virgin state of the woman was hailed as a *norma integritatis*: it was both the pinnacle and the model of a state of sexual intactness that men, and especially members of the clergy, should strive to make their own.[125]

McNamara and Brown do not seem to distinguish between virginity and celibacy[126] and, as we have seen, the distinction could admittedly become blurred in the writings of the Fathers. Still, it should be clear by now that the term *virgo* was applied with relative consistency regarding virginity as superior in its fundamental "intactness," the very reason for its place at the top of the hierarchy. It is my contention that difficulties could arise, at least for some of the Fathers, who, eager to unite or merge different hierarchies of sanctity, came to be restricted by conventional gendered categories. Martyrs, for instance, were generally placed above virgins but, as Ambrose merges these two, the virgin martyr with her double crown becomes a figure of almost unsurpassed sanctity, exceeding her fellow martyrs as twice a martyr. The sanctity of the virgin martyr, although predominantly a female figure, seems to inspire instances where virginity also becomes an enhancement to the virtues of male martyrs, such as in the *Passio* of the bishop Felix. When his sentence was about to be carried out, Felix was said to have declared, "I thank you, God. Fifty-six years I have had in this world. I have maintained my virginity, I have kept the Gospels, and I have preached faith and the truth."[127]

Along similar lines, one might ask whether bishops and priests, holding the highest positions in the "male hierarchy," would be endowed with even more sanctity and power by being, or at least imitating, virgins or widows. Or would such categories, although linked to masculine virtues like self-control, nobility, eloquence and heroic martyrdom still, by the very terminology, be considered too feminine for someone in positions of power, and hence thought to some-how undermine male clerical authority at a stage in history when the specifics of this were still being negotiated.[128] In other words, could the feminine connotations of the term *virgo* be thought to compromise male authority when the concept was expanded to include men as well as women, or might there be other reasons to avoid this term when the subject was men in posi-tions of authority with no experience of sexual encounters whatsoever? Although no univocal answer to this can be extracted from contemporary Christian sources, some different rhetorical strategies and further variations in the understanding of *virgo* might emerge from a closer reading with these questions in mind.

Virginity and clerical celibacy

David G. Hunter has argued that the increasing demand for priestly celibacy should be seen as a reaction to the formalization of the public consecration of virgins. According to Hunter, this process developed in Italy from the middle of the fourth century.[129] That the eventual orthodox position on priestly celi-bacy was not achieved without controversy is demonstrated, for instance, by the massive impact of the teachings of Jovinian.[130] In his reading of Ambrosiaster, Hunter finds that the anonymous Roman presbyter deemed female ascetics as a threat to his clerical authority while, to Ambrose, who was already a bishop and presiding over the veiling ceremony for virgins, the consecration of virgins became a means to strengthen and consolidate his authority.[131]

In her analysis of Ambrose's last treatise on virginity, the *Exhortatio virginitatis*, Franca Ela Consolino has demonstrated how the widow Juliana, in the ficti-tious address to her son and daughters, encourages her son to follow in his father's footsteps and become a priest. The three daughters, on the other hand, are urged to consecrate themselves as holy virgins.[132] This then reflects the options of a life in sanctity that were considered attractive and available for the boy and the girls respectively. What they have in common, according to Ambrose/Juliana, is the necessity of keeping the *integritas* of body and of mind. The topic for the sermon, the concept of virginity, is evidently more elusively related to the male profession than to that of the daughters, who are identified as virgins throughout. As noted above, the son is never explicitly called *virgo* and, in this text, the term is reserved for the girls, as a reference to their gender, their sexual status, their virtues and their consequential sanctity. Although the two professions, *sacerdos* and *virgo*, seem somewhat equaled in Juliana's exhorta-tion, the gendered implications of them reflect a more complicated web of hierarchies, where the virgins, incarnating the highest virtue and angelic life on earth, will nevertheless have to subject themselves to the male authority of the priest, provided, again, that he possesses the *integritas* required by his profession. Again we see that the boundaries between celibacy and virginity, which in writings addressed to women are kept quite distinct, tend to blur when the subject is male. The lack of a proper Latin term to designate virgin status in a male is again apparent and, although Ambrose explores and applies similar vocabulary, his admiration for virginity is shaped by its very gendered fixity as female. The fact that he appears to locate and restrict virginity in and to the female virgin's body is also what, to him, endows virginity with such unique religious value. Ambrose's frequent use of the term *integritas* reveals it to be his preferred choice when he is in need of a more gender-neutral inclusive expression to indicate the untouched pure state of body as well as mind. Nevertheless, *integritas* can never fully cover the range of religious implications imbedded in *virginitas*, the sanctity of which to Ambrose represented the perfect integrity and purity at the very intersection of heaven and earth, of God and humans.

If Ambrose presents the consecration of virginity as the female equivalent to a man's dedication to the priesthood, Jerome applies even stronger rhetorical means to promote clerical celibacy. In an attack on Jovinian and his followers he writes:

> You shall either allow priests to exercise the works of marriage, so that virgins are equal to married people, or, if it is forbidden for priests to touch their wives [which is Jerome's point of view], then they are holy because they imitate virginal chastity. [133]

In a later letter to his friend Pammachius concerning his previous polemics against Jovinian, Jerome marvels at the inconsistency he claims is practiced by Jovinian's followers.

> If men of the world consider it unworthy to be in a position below virgins, I am amazed that clergymen and monks and those that are continent do not praise that which they practice. They cut themselves off (*castrant se*) from their wives in order to imitate the chastity of virgins; and they want married women to be the same as virgins?[134]

In both paragraphs, Jerome describes the celibacy of priests and monks as an imitation of the chastity of virgins or virginal *pudicitia*.[135] In another letter, praising the virgin Asella, he similarly exhorts bishops to look up to the humble virgin's example.[136] These could certainly be taken as examples of women as shaming devices but, unlike Ambrose, as has already been demonstrated, Jerome is not hesitant to apply the term *virgo* to characterize men. His wish would be that all priests were virgins. He admits, however, the difficulties in recruiting new men who fulfill these requirements:

> I do not deny that married men are elected to the priesthood, since there are not as many virgins as is the demand for men to be priests.

Now because the strongest will be chosen for the army, shall not the weaker ones also be accepted, when not everyone can be strong?[...] But how then, will you say, is it that a virgin is so often disregarded when priests are ordained, and one that is married is chosen? Because he might not have the rest of the requirements appropriate for virginity, or he is thought to be a virgin, but is not, or it is an ill-reputed virginity: or yet indeed virginity itself produces arrogance, and while he applauds himself for bodily chastity only, he neglects the other virtues.[137]

After a long list of other possible reasons, Jerome claims that married men maintain partiality for their own kind, as they, being in the majority, elect men who are not celibate, just like themselves. However, Jerome insists that it is exactly thereby that they also demonstrate their own inferiority to virgins.[138] Jerome argues there are male virgins "out there" that should be given positions within the ecclesiastical hierarchy, yet there are several hindrances, as the majority of married clergy in their way needs to be overcome. In his subsequent letter to Pammachius, he also mentions "male widows," or widowers, along with the obviously male virgins, as two predominantly female categories of sanctity that are now used to describe the ideal sexual status of men:

Bishops, priests, and deacons are chosen either as virgins or widowers, or they at least remain chaste for eternity after they are chosen for the priesthood.[139]

Clerical celibacy became a question of authority as ascetic ideals gained lay support. Hunter has argued that "as the public ritual of the consecration of virgins became more prominent in the Western churches, it became increasingly expected that the clergy would embody a similar degree of renunciation."[140] Although the female virgins (and widows) were praised as the embodiments of sanctity among the living, their ultimately gendered status posed no serious threat to the male clergy. According to Hunter:

asceticism and ritual purity functioned as means by which the male clergy in the West established their identity and defended their prerogatives over against ascetic women. Celibacy emerged in the later fourth century partly as a way of defining a specifically male persona, the *sacerdos*, whose role as representative and intercessor for the community set him apart from other Christians, male and female alike.[141]

Jerome and his predecessor Tertullian appear again as the writers whose desire for a concept of virginity that would not be restricted by the cultural gendered fixity of the *virgo* gives new meaning to the term by the authors' flexible adaptation of it. Although they were both prolific writers, they still represent a minority in the Latin patristic corpus when they extend the term to also include men as a rather innovative turn in the cultural and religious history of the sacred virgins. The fact that the term was considered not equally gender neutral in most contemporary Latin sources, but delimited to refer to female virgins, gives an indication of the unease such gender-flexible virgins might have provoked.

Virgin Fathers of the Church?

Considering the rather insistent demand for priests and bishops to be virgins, or at least celibate, that became increasingly pressing in the fourth century, there are surprisingly few Church Fathers who are described as virgins by others, or who actually claim to be virgins themselves.

From the many texts addressed to his wife, we know that Tertullian was married. A large number of the other Church Fathers, however, remained unmarried, but they vary in how they convey their choice of sexual renunciation in their own writings. My following survey of some of the most notable claims to virginity, or – what was apparently more frequent – declarations of an unfortunate lack thereof, is intended to further clarify and complicate these gendered notions concerning celibacy and self-control as well as the complex processes of negotiating the fixity of virginity.

Gregory of Nyssa had mourned his own misfortune as one who could no longer partake in the blessings of virginity:

> Happy they who have still the power of choosing the better way, and have not debarred themselves from it by engagements of secular life, as we have, whom a gulf now divides from glorious virginity [...]. We are but spectators of others' blessings and witnesses to the happiness of another class. [142]

In a similar manner, Jerome famously praised virginity at the same time as he drew attention to his own regrettable lack thereof: "I praise virginity to the skies, not because I have it myself, but because I admire the more that which I do not have."[143] Elsewhere, Jerome had described himself not as a virgin, but as a voluntary eunuch: "Others are made eunuchs by necessity, but I am one by will."[144] Considering these two of his declarations together, we might again discern some seemingly fundamental differences between eunuchs and virgins. The voluntary eunuch, who by not possessing the physical requirements for "real" eunuchs, is in this respect the honorable and virtuous one. Since he does not meet the physical requirements for virginity, it is to Jerome not possible to claim the positive qualities that come with virginity of the will or of the mind. Jerome will not claim the complete intactness of a virgin, but finds the zeal of the eunuch a more appropriate marker of his commitment to celibacy. In this, he once again illustrates the restrictions, or fixity, of virginity, the very same that constitutes its exclusivity.

Ambrose, on the other hand, is more reluctant to reveal any kind of information about this side of his private life, and there are to my knowledge no "confessions" of this sort to be found in his own writings. According to Augustine's observations from his sojourn in Milan, celibacy seemed to be one of the difficult aspects in the bishop's life.[145] That Ambrose found seemingly feminine *pudor* and virgin-like behavior to be laudable qualities even in a man is, however, evident, for instance, in the funerary oration written on the death of his brother Satyrus. According to Ambrose, "it was as if a certain virginal shyness tinged his face, giving away his feeling by its expression, if he incidentally had come upon some female who had suddenly appeared."[146] Satyrus was no different around men, Ambrose claims; in such company he would rarely speak or lift his face or eyes and, if he did, he did it "with a chastity of the mind with which the chastity of his body also coincided."[147] Ambrose further asserts that his brother "kept the gift of the holy baptism inviolate (*intemerata*), with a pure (*mundus*) body and an even purer (*purior*) heart."[148] Again we see how the purity of the heart and body are inseparable, even if the purity of heart is valued as the most important. Traditionally regarded as feminine virtues (but not only so[149]), *verecundia*, *castimonia* and *pudor* are qualities attributed to Satyrus as positive descriptions of his moral character. Ambrose also reveals that his brother never married, and the bishop presents this as Satyrus' wish to remain so, although modesty made him camouflage this desire and give the impression that he merely was postponing marriage.[150] Despite a host of adjectives and other terms describing Satyrus' sexual purity, it is noteworthy that Ambrose never calls him a virgin. The closest he comes is the "as if a certain virginal shyness tinged his face," but once again the male virgin seems to have been a too difficult, if not completely unimaginable, category for Ambrose to use even when describing his own chaste brother.

Modesty and humility are core concepts in this part of Ambrose's depiction of his brother.[151] Genre is of utmost importance here, as exaggerations are one of the characteristics of panegyrics. The funerary oration for Satyrus was composed in 378, the year after Ambrose had written *De virginibus*, and at a time when female chastity still occupied his mind.[152] That he praised his brother for possessing the same qualities that Ambrose had invested so much of his Episcopal authority in elaborating and defining is therefore no surprise. Humility appears to be the very same reason John Cassian presented Basil of Caesarea as having stated that he was no virgin, despite his lack of knowledge of women:

> A puzzling saying of Saint Basil, the bishop of Caesarea, is conveyed. He said: 'I have not known a woman, but I am no virgin.' So well did he understand incorruption of the flesh as being not so much in abstinence from women as in integrity of the heart, which truly preserves the sanctity of the body incorrupt forever by fearing God and by loving chastity.[153]

Doubtless an expression of humility, first and foremost, the attributed quote still challenges the notion of male virginity. A contrary account, on the other hand, is to be found in Gregory of Nazianzus' presentation of his once estranged friend in the funerary oration he wrote for Basil. Here, the Bishop of Caesarea is in fact described as a model for virginity in terms that place him almost next to Christ in this respect.[154] The terms of defining virginity thus reach two very different conclusions when it comes to the virginity of Basil the Great, which ultimately nevertheless will be buried under layers of rhetoric, and where genre, topic and the purpose of the statement are the defining factors. The presentation of Basil as exemplary in Gregory's panegyrics becomes a warning against hybris in Cassian's admonitions to the celibate monks struggling with their vows. But, with hardly any fixity helping to confirm the valuable virginity even of one of the greatest of the Church Fathers, what then is left of the male virgin?

Male virgins in funerary inscriptions

As mentioned repeatedly above, despite the limitations of epigraphy as source material, inscriptions give access to individuals and members of social strata that would otherwise be outside the reach for a historian of Antiquity. When almost all other contemporary texts fail to identify individual boys or men who were regarded as virgins or who described themselves as such, the inscriptions reveal at least a handful of instances where *virgo* functions as an epithet for the deceased male. Such vocabulary is, as we have seen, relatively common in funerary inscriptions dedicated to young girls, and the inscriptions commemorating boys and men closely followed the pattern recognizable from similar inscriptions dedicated to female virgins.

The longest of the funerary inscriptions to be considered here was dedicated by the parents of the newly baptized Theusebius:

> Born April 1.   baptized April 2.
> to Theusebius, virgin and neophyte.
> This is for my son, so pious and dear to me, who is buried here
> Theusebius, who always lived in sanctified modesty.
> He went home to God, after he had lingered one year – two times six months –
> and three times ten days, upon this light.
> Not stained by sin he was buried with a fortunate gift
> having celebrated his birthday and likewise been reborn by Christ,
> Theusebius entered the halls of eternal life
> carrying his virgin crown given by the Lord
>
> Rufinus and Severa, parents of the sweetest and most deserving son,
> made this [i.e. inscription] in the Lord
> Rest in peace. Deposited May 2.[155]

This inscription is found on a child's sarcophagus and is dedicated to Theusebius, who only lived to be thirteen months old.[156] In addition to this dedicatory inscription, there is another text, now barely visible, that has been painted on the bottom frame of the casket. With Ferrua's emendation the text reads, "here is my firstborn son, a virgin dedicated in this virginal place."[157] According to Ferrua, "the virginal place" refers to the fact that the sarcophagus had not been used by anyone else, that it was completely new and previously "untouched."[158] This then gives the commissioner, or indeed, author, of the inscription a chance to once again emphasize the virginity of the deceased. The repeated focus on Theusebius' virginity makes this inscription quite remarkable compared with the other extant dedications to (male and female) virgins. Theusebius' virginity is depicted as a "fortunate gift" (*felix donum*)[159] and later even described as the crown of virginity which is bestowed upon him by the Lord. This is a very strong indication of how highly God was believed to esteem virginity. It seems the thought of their son with this precious gift would have had an appeasing effect for the grieving parents. We do find several examples of similarly young girls who were identified as virgins in funerary inscriptions,[160] and whose virginal state likewise seems to have been thought of as advantageous by those who commissioned and put up the inscription. The relative frequency with which these very young virgins appear in inscriptions cannot, as we have already discussed, merely be explained in terms of the popularity of formal consecration, which would, as we have seen, have been conducted at a considerably later stage in a virgin's life. Rather, this practice of commemorating infants and toddlers as virgins is more likely due to a belief in the beneficial and soteriological value of the virgin state, regardless of formal and institutionalized consecration. In this sense, the notion of border-line virginities and need for flexity may account for why these infants and toddlers were identified as virgins.

The other inscriptions that mention male virgins are all considerably shorter than that of Theusebius, and not as explicit in expressing the value of the virginal state of the deceased. One of them reads as follows: "Hope, to a modest son, who lived 30 years (as a) virgin, well deserving, in peace."[161] Like so many other inscriptions, this does not give any indication of date, and further interpretation is therefore highly problematic. Another, quite fragmented and reconstructed, reads: "To [A]urel(ius) Peter, sweetest son, who l[ived] as a virgin 17 years and 7 months. Parents M[ari]nus Aur(elius) and Ael(ia) Donata of the Pelagians."[162] Similarly, a Pontius Athenagoras is said to have lived as a virgin for 22 years,[163] and a son identified as Felix *virgo de saeculu et neofitus* lived to be 23.[164]

The oldest male virgin to appear in the inscriptions from Rome is perhaps Eugamius, lector (?) and virgin. From the reconstruction of his very fragmented inscription it is indicated that he died at the age of 38.[165] There is also an inscription dedicated to "Eusebius virgin."[166] Another brief fragment we have only consists of *virgo et a lege n*[eo]*fitus*,[167] yet the masculine grammatical form of *neofitus* may allow us to identify even one more rare male virgin. Even more suggestive is *Alessander virg*[o ...], found in Rome, but undatable and indeed open to emendation and interpretation.[168] Lastly, we should also include the catechumen Victor, whose Greek commemorative inscription identifies him as a *parthenos*.[169]

Outside of Rome, at Lyons, we find a father describing himself as *Romanus*, commemorating his virgin son Eutychianus, who only lived to be eight, in an undated epitaph. The religious sympathies of the father cannot be stated, but the reference to the dedication *sub ascia* and *quieti aeterna* do indeed complicate any attempt to identify a specific religious ideology to explain why this boy's virgin status is mentioned in the epitaph.[170] Another inscription, from Naples, identifies Iulius Marturius, a citizen of Constantinople and a "faithful and spiritual virgin" (perhaps in the tradition of Hippolytus), who lived to be around 50 years old.[171]

Since hardly any of these inscriptions can be dated with much precision, there is always the possibility that the religious ideals and conceptions they may be said to represent belong to the period after 410 AD. On the one hand, then, the existing inscriptions have actually enabled us to identify men and boys who were described as virgins by those who commissioned their epitaphs. On the other hand, such a low number of male virgins[172] in the vast corpus of Christian funerary inscriptions does not represent very firm and convincing support of a universally acclaimed and pursued ideal of genderless virginity. Like the rest of the material discussed in this chapter, the relative scarcity of inscriptions commemorating male virgins seems to confirm that male virginity was indeed considered a conundrum in the face of soteriology on the one hand and gender conventions on the other. Persons commissioning funerary inscriptions were in several cases illiterate and dependent on the stone cutter to provide the text. Standardized models may very well have been available and easy to pick out when the parents lacked the ability to formulate a text of their own.[173] As we do not know of any male virgin being consecrated by a rite similar to the one that female sacred virgins underwent, the virginity referred to in these inscriptions should perhaps rather be compared to those of non-consecrated female virgins.[174] In this sense, the inscriptions convey the existence of a religious belief in virginity's soteriological function and its beneficial effect on close relations, which, to some at least, was regardless of gender and attainable also to those outside the gradually more institutionalized order of virgins. In this sense, many of the virgins recorded in the epigraphic material pushes the limits of virginity's flexity. Although formal rites could function as a means to fix the concept of sacred virgins, virginity's soteriological benefits could apparently, at least by some bereaved parents hoping to advance their child's prospect of salvation, be extended beyond conventional borderlines.

Just like a virgin?

Jerome, in an attempt to explain the uneven balance of male and female virgins, wrote:

> Death came through Eve, but life came through Mary. And therefore the gift of virginity flows more richly among women, because it started in a woman.[175]

Nowhere nearly as present as the female virgins, who were extolled and admonished by Orthodox Fathers in numerous writings and who appear on several funerary inscriptions, it should be noted that male *virgines* are still not completely absent from the sources I have analyzed in this chapter. Jerome, for instance, is one of very few that calls attention to Christ's virginity,[176] which he presents as a model alongside that of Mary, thus offering his readers a celestial prototype for each sex.

Very rarely, however, is the term *virgo* applied to individual men of their own time. Neither do any of the Fathers themselves claim to possess the *virginitas* they praise – a rhetorical *topos* of humility, no doubt, but also an indication of the problematic gender ambiguity such a claim might convey. The extant inscriptions have therefore proved most helpful. Despite limitations regarding interpretation and context, the few epitaphs commemorating males described as *virgines* provide evidence that some young men or, more likely, the families of these deceased boys and men, found it beneficial to assert the sexual innocence of the departed in a commemoratory inscription by means of the term *virgo*. This practice, however rare, is in line with the same statements found on funerary inscriptions dedicated to young girls, and indicates that virginity, although not necessarily formally dedicated or consecrated, nevertheless was endowed with some kind of soteriological function. Perhaps it was the same kind of comfort found in the prospects of salvation that made Ambrose draw attention to the virginal aspects of his brother Satyrus, and Gregory of Nazianzus to describe Basil as a model for virginity in their funerary orations held for their brother and friend respectively.

Of significance, then, is what this absence of male virgins had for the idea of a genderless virginity, which was indeed conveyed in the texts by Christian authors. The spiritual virginity that was supposed to exceed purely physical virginity seemingly opens for such a "flexity" in the concept that could potentially lead to an inclusion of men despite potentially physical "shortcomings." It is therefore strange to find that, in this respect, the "fixity" – the notion of a very concrete and physical virginity located in the body of a sexually inexperienced female – is what ultimately seems to limit any truly innovative genderless virginity, however much desired by the Orthodox Fathers.[177] In other words, their attempts to ungender the concept by emphasizing metaphorical and spiritual readings of virginity eventually appear to be restricted by a cultural understanding of virginity as a site in a female's sexually untouched body. The virgin is undoubtedly gendered and apparently expressed in its "true" state only by a female virgin. Ultimately, as both Jerome and the fictitious Kleitophon would appear to agree on, what remains within men's capacity is merely to *imitate* virgins (whatever that might indicate),[178] and that is what some, as Jerome would have it, particularly priests and bishops, should strive to do. There is, however, a great difference between imitating and being and, when it comes to virginity, imitation is not always favorable, as the following chapter will explore further.

Approaching these texts by means of "inversed gender" in relation to the approaches of most prior studies on virginity, we thus find, perhaps not surprisingly, that the Early Christian texts display a deep tension between the desire to ungender virginity, to reach a flexible concept that could provide a universal road to salvation on the one hand, and the need to preserve the fixity of the concept as a bodily and explicitly female gendered/sexed quality on the other. This is tied to a physical understanding of virginity that becomes so crucial to the symbolic value that the consecrated virgins were to incarnate. Although virginity might be presented as a means for women to become more "male-like," a virtue of masculine rather than feminine character, the fundamental and intrinsic femininity of the concept still made it an unattractive virtue for men to be associated with. As Dale Martin has pointed out with reference to so-called Gnostic texts, it is repeatedly said that "women must become male in order to be saved, but nowhere is it claimed that men must become female."[179] The underlying ideologies at work here thus seem to be part of the tension that limits the flexity that would have been necessary in order for virginity to become a truly ungendered concept that in turn could be equally applied and valued when the virgin in question was embodied as male and not female.

The tension between the fixity and flexity of virginity is not only seen in the Christian writings. In a playful and experimental bending of sexuality and gender, we encounter discourses, especially in the Greek East, that challenge the gendered fixity of virginity, and it seems that such experimental flexity is carried further in the Greek patristic tradition than in the Latin West. However, it is evident that something more fundamental is at stake in the Christian discourses than in the non-Christian texts. The fumbling avoidance of explicit discussions of male virginity in Latin discourses reveals that this was not without embarrassment and difficulties for Ambrose and his contemporaries. John Cassian is, it appears, the only one who addresses this problem explicitly, only to conclude that perfect virginity is almost impossible to achieve and only bestowed upon a very few chosen ones – apparently regardless of gender.[180]

As long as bodily and spiritual virginity were understood to be interdependent, identifying a physical male virginity seems to have been the most problematic part in constructing a genderless virginity. McInerney turns the attention to how virginity was defined in terms of how it was lost:

> For Cassian, for Basil, and for Augustine, physical male virginity is measured not by contact with the opposite sex, or even the same sex, but by freedom from ejaculation and erection. The male virgin was thus a mythical beast.[181]

Augustine states that only a few women attain this physical virginity, and questions whether it is possible at all to speak of virginity in men; "to few men belongs a holy integrity even of body; yet such a man is a more honorable member."[182] Like Ambrose, he prefers *integritas* to describe the bodily state of sexual inexperience. By defining virginity as spiritual only and placing it in the mind and the will, rather than the body, or making it eventually achievable only by the grace of God, as Cassian and Augustine are often said to have done,[183] it gradually ceases to be an ideal confined to females – though not through a compromising "feminization" of men, but by transforming the virgins as such, making virginity equally as impossible to maintain (and prove) for women as it was thought to be for men.[184] Perfect virginity then, as it came to be defined in medieval times,[185] should eventually disappear out of reach for women as well as for men, and only the imperfect strive for perfection was left, a pursuit that at least in this respect should no longer be restricted by gender.

Notes

1   For an overview, see Clark 2001 and Wilkinson 2015.
2   Økland 2003: 130, cf. Oksala 2004: 102–3 "The prediscursive body is, by necessity, impossible to identify and theorize because as soon as we name it and start to talk about it we have already brought it into the realm of discourse."
3   Økland 2003: 139: "It may be that a more flexible Scandinavian concept of 'kjønn/kön' would have better captured the complexity of the various uses of *parthenos*, and would be more suited generally to grasp ancient Greek notions of men and women."
4   Kelly 2000: 16.
5   Hier. *Comm. in Ep. ad Ephesios* 28, (PL Vol. 26, col. 533): *Nec non et juxta litteram, quamdiu mulier partui servit et liberis, hanc habet ad virum differentiam, quam corpus ad animam. Sin autem Christo magis voluerit servire quam saeculo, mulier esse cessabit, et dicetur vir, quia omnes in perfectum virum cupimus occurrere.* The translation is from Bernau, Salih and Evans 2003: 3, cf. Martin 1995: 231, Kelly 2000: 98, Engh 2014: 20.
6   Cf. Castelli 1991, Vogt 1995. For critical questioning of these readings, see Davis 2002, Brakke 2003.
7   E.g. Cameron 1989: 192: "While for male ascetics asceticism itself was enough, for women who aspired to the ascetic life, the 'life of angels', far more was involved: it was a matter of denying their gender." Moxnes 2003: 77 on Philo's Therapautae: "described as having renounced their femaleness by becoming 'virgins'. They had sacrificed that which made them women, bodily pleasures and desire for children, and behaved like men in their yearning for wisdom (Philo *Contempl.* 68–9)." McNamara 1976: 153, Schulenburg 1998: 128. For the Vestals, Takács 2008: 83 sums up the legacy of Beard 1980 when she states that "the Vestals were anomalies in regard to womanhood" with their "state-ordered asexuality." See also Staples 1998: 148: "One of the ways that ideological virginity isolated the Vestal was by de-sexualizing her."
8   Elm 2003: 269: "the transformation of women into athletes and thus into men no longer remained solely a metaphorical concept or the momentary transfiguration of a vision. The transformation became real and permanent, in part quite simply as a result of the harsh life of the desert." Cf. Shaw 1998a: 135ff.
9   Shaw 1998a: 247, cf. Shaw 1998a: 241. "It is interesting that Jerome does not follow Basil of Ancyra and suggests that virgins affect a masculine appearance, nor does he tend to praise women for being 'manly', though the attribution of manliness to female ascetics is typical in the ascetic discourse of the fourth and fifth centuries."
10 Cass. *Conl.* 15.10: *Vade et apprehende nudam et pulcherrimam virginem; et si illam tenens, tranquillitatem tui cordis immobilem aestusque carnales pacificos in te senseris perdurasse, hujus quoque visibilis flammae mitis atque innoxius in modum illorum trium in Babylonia puerorum te allambet attactus.* Transl. NPNF2.

11 Cass. *Conl.* 15.10: *nec adhuc pondus castimoniae suae hujus probationis ponderi compensare conjectans.* Transl. NPNF2.

12 Ter. *Hec.* 140ff: *Quid ais? cum virgine una adolescens cubuerit. Plus potus, illa sese abstinere ut potuerit? Non verisimile dicis; nec verum arbitror.* Transl. Riley 1874: 263.

13 Rhea Ilia is of course the prime example in a Roman context (e.g., Ov. *Fast.* 3.11–80, Liv. 1.4.2–3, D.H. 1.77, cf. Hier. *Adv. Jov.* 1.43: *Ac ne nobis Dominum Salvatorem de Virgine procreatum Romana exprobraret potentia, auctores urbis et gentis suae, Ilia virgine et Marte genitos arbitrantur.*). Daphne, Cassandra, Sibylla, Semele, Leda, Io, Europa, Chione, Phylonome, Callisto and Thetis were just some of the most famous of these virgins to be desired by Olympian gods.

14 For the attempted rape of Athena, see Deacy 2002. The story of how Vesta was assaulted by Priapus is recounted by Ovid in *Fast.* 6.319–48, cf. Frazel 2003. According to some, Artemis/Diana also suffered such assaults by Orion and Buphagos (viz. Paus. 8.27.17). Actaeon, who was so unfortunate as to merely watch the goddess at her bath, suffered her wrath, cf. Ov. *Met.* 3.253–5: *Rumor in ambiguo est: aliis violentior aequo / visa dea est, alii laudant dignamque severa/ virginitate vocant;* [...].

15 Suet. *Aug.* 71.1: *circa libidines haesit, postea quoque, ut ferunt, ad vitiandas virgines promptior, quae sibi undique etiam ab uxore conquirerentur.*

16 Kelly 2000: 62. She quotes Adrienne Auslander Munich, according to whom "absolute virginity tells no story about itself, but enables the story to be told." Cf. McInerney 2003: 71, Burrus 1995.

17 Juv. 4.8–10: [*nemo malus felix, minime corruptor et idem*] */incestus, cum quo nuper uittata iacebat /sanguine adhuc uiuo terram subitura sacerdos?* The very same corruption, or perhaps hybris, is indicated in the references to the emperors Nero, Caracalla and Elagabalus, all counted among the bad ones, who were said to have had sex with Vestal virgins. Cf. Suet. *Nero* 28, D.C. 78.16,1–5, Lampr. *Elag.* 3–4, D.C. 80.9,3–4, Hdn. *Hist.* 5.6,1–2. These emperors saw themselves as gods, but were appropriately punished in the end. That the emperors had exclusive access to the Vestals was a titillating thought for eighteenth-century pornographers, and elaborated on, for instance, by de Sade and de Sales. See Delon 1995: 168–70.

18 Cf. above pp. 81–3, in particular Ch. 2 note 322.

19 Miller and Platter 1999: 451. They continue: "Hence the opposition between the Vestals and sexuality, plausibly asserted by Kraffert and others, turns out to be far less necessary than it seemed on the surface."

20 Martin 1995: 220.

21 Elm 2003: 269.

22 Attributed to Basil of Caesarea and quoted by John Cassian in *Inst.* 6.19: *et mulierem ignoro, et virgo non sum.* Transl. from McInerney 2003: 62.

23 Notable exceptions are Burrus 2000, Burrus 2005, McInerney 2003, Kelly 2000 and Laes 2013, all of whom will be discussed below.

24 E.g. Brown 1988: 243 and 383, Elm 2003: 29, McNamara 1976: 151, Evans 2003: 146, 149 and passim. See also McInerney 2003: 5, who criticizes Bugge 1975 and Brown on these grounds.

25 Cloke 1995: 60 states: "Most treatises on virginity from this period, whether addressed to men or women, are about women's virginity (Gregory of Nyssa is the only exception)."

26 McInerney 2003: 63.

27 Burrus 2005: 62, cf. Undheim 2012: 22.

28 McInerney 2003: 8.

29 McInerney 2003: 29 argues that this is the reason for Tertullian's high-strung anxiety in his treatise "On the veiling virgins" (e.g. *Virg. Vel.* 2.5). His fear, McInerney argues, is that unreserved praise of virginity would allow for women to claim an exclusive feminine avenue of access to the divine, one that is not open to men. See also Clark 2008: 16–18.

30   Kelly and Leslie 1999: 16–17 and Undheim 2012: 23. McInerney 2003: 5 criticizes Peter Brown for conflating the categories in his *Body and Society*. Cf. idem for the same critique of Bugge 1975.

31   Cf. e.g. Clark 1999: 113–15 for Jerome's practice of translating *sophrosyne* to *castitas*.

32   E.g. Kuefler 2001: 221. Skinner 2005: 7 and passim stresses the so-called "penetration model" (originally formulated by Dover), not tied to sex as such but a hierarchical distinction between active and passive, associated respectively with male and female qualities.

33   Transvestitism, androgynity and "sex change" in literature from Antiquity and Late Antiquity have been popular subjects for study. E.g. Davis 2002, Kuefler 2001, Moxnes 2003, Skinner 2005: 212.

34   Rousselle 1988: 5–23, cf. Harper 2013: 70–9 on the gloomy Stoic moralists.

35   Cf. Goldhill 1995: 22: "'virginity' is a term inapplicable to men in earlier Greek culture," and Kelly 2000: 91–2.

36   Caes. *De bello gallico* 6.21.3–4: *Qui diutissime impuberes permanserunt, maximam inter suos ferunt laudem: hoc ali staturam, ali vires nervosque confirmari putant.* Translation (slightly modified) from Perseus.

37   For other examples of *impubes* as *de rei veneriae experti*, see TLL, s.v. (b.γ).

38   Caes. *De bello gallico* 6.21.5: *Intra annum vero vicesimum feminae notitiam habuisse in turpissimis habent rebus.*

39   Nonius in Lindsay VI. p. 734–5: *Virgines non solum feminae dicuntur, verum etiam pueri investes: nam et quicumque ex ephebis excesserant, devirginari dicebantur.* [*Varro peri exagoges (409): 'quam sympathian lumbi ad oculos haberent, quid magnum interesset, puerum utrum essem devirginatum usurus an monokeros ac puros, dum cogito.'*] My transl. For the term *investis*, see note 172 below. The Varro quotation might indicate that "male virginity" often was lost by other means than sexual intercourse. Similar definitions concerning a monk's solitary and even involuntary loss of virginity/purity were explored and discussed by John Cassian, cf. Foucault 1988. The idea that female virginity could perish due to masturbation does not appear in any of the sources, but see Rousselle 1988: 65, indicating that Romans had difficulties imagining sex, at least when females were concerned, without penetration. Cf. Hallett 1997, Brooten 1996: 49 and passim.

40   Cf. TLL s.v. *devirgino*.

41   Two lost Greek tragedies by Sophocles (*Phaedra*) and Euripides (*Hippolytus Calyptomenus*), in addition to the existing one by Euripides (*Hippolytus Stephanephorus*). Cf. also Ov. *Her.* 4.

42   Serv. *Ad Aen.* 7.761: *tunc Diana eius castitate commota revocavit eum in vitam per Aesculapium [...] sed Diana Hippolytum, revocatum ab inferis, in Aricia nymphae commendavit Egeriae et eum Virbium, quasi bis virum, iussit vocari.* Cf. Verg. *Aen.* 7.761 and Ov. *Met.* XV, 478–546. Note that virginity is never an issue for these Latin authors, who prefer the term *castus*. *Castus* corresponds to the Greek term *hagnos*.

43   Lusching 1983: 117–18.

44   The term *hagnos* that appears here is a complex word, designating something forbidden, set apart, but also something or someone "ritually pure," cf. Parker 1983: 147–52. In this case, the term alludes to Hippolytus' sexual purity as well as his devotion to the virgin goddess. (Mason 1979: 201), cf. John Cass. *Inst.* 6.4: *Aliud enim est, continentem esse, id est, enkrate; aliud castum, et, ut ita dicam, in affectum integritatis vel incorruptionis transire, quod dicitur* hagnon: *quae virtus illis solis tribuitur maxime, qui virgines, vel mente, vel carne perdurant [...]*.

45   Euripides, *Hippolytus*, 1002–5, transl. David Kovacs, cf. Mason 1979: 200–1.

46   Euripides, *Hippolytus* 1005–6: *oude tauta gar skopein prothumos eimi, parthenon psuchen echon.*

47 Goldhill 1995: 22 states that "[Hippolytus'] transgressive withdrawal from the life of a citizen finds expression in the extraordinary description of his soul in such perverse gender-terms."

48 Greek mythology abounds with female devotees to Artemis who desired perpetual virginity, such as Cassandra, Calliope, Daphne and Atalanta. Apart from Daphne, who was transformed in to a laurel tree at a crucial moment, they were all forced somehow to give up their virgin status. In the story of Hippolytus, as well as in later novelistic and hagiographical literature, as we will see below, the narrative is in need of someone who wants to "take away" the virgin's virginity for her or him to be able to claim it.

49 Soranus, *Gynaikeia* 1.9 (Temkin:VII.30).

50 Discussed for instance by Foucault 1988, Brown 1988, Rousselle 1988, Hanson 1990, King 1993, Martin 1995, Kuefler 2001, Hanson 2007, *et al.*

51 Soranus, *Gynaikeia* 1.9 (Temkin:VII.30).

52 Soranus, *Gynaikeia* 1.9 (Temkin:VII.30). Similarly, Peter Brown translates a passage from Artemidorus writing about an athlete whose athletic career remained successful, "As long as he remained a virgin [*aphthoros*]"(Brown 1988: 19, quoting Artemidorus, *Oneirocritica* 5.95.). See also Goldhill's (1995: 22) comment on a fragment from *Ninus and Semiramis* where *adiaphtoros* describes Ninus as "uncorrupted," in the sense "from sex."

53 Cf. John Cass. *Inst.* 6.7.2 and Caelius Aurelianus 42.

54 See in particular Foucault 1988: 228–32, Goldhill 1995, Burrus 2005, Cooper 1996. For the novelistic character of Christian apocryphal acts, see Hägg 1983: 160–2.

55 Burrus 2005: 53.

56 *Joseph et Aséneth* 4.9, cf. Burrus 2005: 70.

57 Cf. Goldhill 1995: 119. Like Hippolytus, Charikleia's virginity is due to her dedication to Artemis, for whom she had "resolved to stay virgin all her life." (2.33, quoted from Burrus 2005: 73), whereas Theagenes is presented as being dedicated to Artemis' twin brother Apollo (Burrus 2005: 74). See also Parker 1983: 90–1 for some rare examples of male, virginal/"uncorrupted" temple servants, all in texts by Euripides.

58 Burrus 2005: 78.

59 *Ethiopian Story* 3.17, quoted in Burrus 2005: 74. For methods to assay male virginity in medieval hagiography, see Kelly 2000: 91–118.

60 *Kleitophon and Leukippe* 5.20, quoted from Burrus 2005: 61, cf. also Goldhill: 1995: 95.

61 *Kleitophon and Leukippe* 8.5, quoted from Burrus 2005: 62.

62 Burrus 2005: 62. Cf. Suet. *Ner.* 29, where Suetonius lists Nero's perversities, among which he played role games where he imitated a virgin being raped/taken by force by his freedman Doryphorus: *voces quoque et heiulatus vim patientium virginum imitatus.*

63 Goldhill 1995: 121.

64 See Goldhill 1995: 38–41, who remarks on the advice given to Daphnis for how to "initiate" Chloe, with particular regard to her potentially painful and blood-spattered loss of virginity.

65 For Theagenes and Charicleia, see Goldhill 1995: 119. The date of the Greek novels could indeed indicate that the religious aspect of these men's vow of virginity played on already existing practices, of which Christianity then would have been a prominent proponent. There are, however, no references to Christianity in these texts, although the story of Aseneth has been interpreted as Christian, partially because of its insistent focus on virginity.

66 Ambr. *Inst. virg.* 104: *Nunc ad te, decursis omnibus, Pater gratiae, vota converto, cujus pietati innumerabiles gratias agimus, quod in virginibus sacris angelorum vitam videmus in terris,*

quam in paradiso quondam amiseramus. My transl. Cf. Ambr. *De virgt.* 90–1, *De virgt.* 27, *De virgb.* I.52, *De virgb.* I.11, and Ambr. *Exh. virg.* 19.

67 Hier. *Adv. Jov.* 1.36: *In resurrectione mortuorum, non nubent neque nubentur, sed similes erunt Angelis* (Matt. XXII, 30). *Quod alii postea in coelis futuri sunt, hoc virgines in terra esse coeperunt. Si angelorum nobis similitudo promittitur (inter angelos autem non est sexus diversitas), aut sine sexu erimus, quod angeli sunt; aut certe quod liquido comprobatur, resurgentes in proprio sexu, sexus non fungemur officio.* Transl. NPNF2, with my amendments. For other examples of the notion that virgins are angels on earth, see Hier. *Adv. Helv.* 23, *Ep.* 48.14, *Ep.* 130.10, Greg Naz. *Or.* 37.11, *Or.* 43.62 and Greg. *Nys. De virg.* 13.

68 See Clark 2008: 21–2 on how Jerome changed his views on the nature of the bodily resurrection in the wake of the Origenist controversy.

69 Ambr. *De virgb.* (Marcellina), *Inst. virg.* (Ambrosiana,); Hier. *Ep.* 22 (Eustochium), Hier. *Ep.* 107 (Paula), Hier. *Ep.* 128 (Pacatula), Hier. *Ep.* 130 (Demetrias, cf. Augustine's and Pelagius' letters to the same), *De lapsu Susannae.* Cf. Rousselle 1988: 132–3.

70 The Pseudo-Clementine letter *Ep. I ad Virg.* is in the Syrian version addressed "to the blessed brother virgins, who devote themselves to preserve virginity 'for the sake of the kingdom of heaven'" (*Ep. I ad Virg* 1.) and "to the holy sister virgins," and "all virgins of either sex" (*Ep. I ad Virg* 2.). Transl. ANF. See, however, Caner 1997: 409–10, note 55: "Coptic fragments indicate its author originally addressed male virgins as eunuchs." See discussion on eunuchs below. To the extent that men are addressees in these texts, it is as fathers of female virgins, such as Gaudentius in Hier. *Ep.* 128 and as in the anonymous Greek *Homily on virginity.*

71 Cypr. *De hab. virg.* 2 writes: *Et quidem hoc tam viri quam mulieres, tam pueri quam puellae, sexus omnis atque omnis aetas observet, et curet, pro religione et fide quam Deo debet, ne quod sanctum et purum de Domini dignatione percipitur, minus sollicito timore teneatur.* Transl. ANF, with minor changes, cf. Evans 2003: 104.

72 Cypr. *De hab. virg.* 3: *Nunc nobis ad virgines sermo est.*

73 Cypr. *De hab. virg.* 3. For the virgin preoccupied with dress and jewelry as female, see, for instance, *De hab. virg.* 5.

74 Min. Fel. *Oct.* 31.: *Convivia non tantum pudica colimus, sed et sobria: nec enim indulgemus epulis, aut convivium mero ducimus; sed gravitate hilaritatem temperamus, casto sermone, corpore castiore; plerique inviolati corporis virginitate perpetua fruuntur potius quam gloriantur.* My transl.

75 Cf. TLL s.v. *inviolatus* 2. for the term used in regard to chastity and virginity.

76 This refers to what he has just discussed, namely how promiscuousness, adoption and infant exposure, as demonstrated in the tragedy of Oedipus, may lead to incestuous relationships.

77 Tert. *Apol.* 9: *Nos ab isto eventu diligentissima et fidelissima castitas sepsit, quantumque ab stupris et ab omni post matrimonium excessu, tantum et ab incesti casu tuti sumus. Quidam multo securiores totam vim hujus erroris virgine continentia depellunt, senes pueri.* Transl. ANF.

78 Tert. *Adv. Val.* 5: *Proculus noster, virginis senectae, et christianae eloquentiae dignitas.* My transl.

79 Hier. *Ep.* 128.3: *Quod loquimur, non in universum loquimur, sed in parte tractamus: nec de omnibus, sed de quibusdam dicimus. Ad utrumque enim sexum, non solum ad vas infirmum, noster sermo dirigitur.* Transl. NPNF2.

80 Hier. *Ep.* 128.3: *Virgo es, quid te mulieris delectat societas? quid fragilem, et sutilem ratem magnis committis fluctibus, et grande periculum navigationis incertae securus ascendis? Nescis quid desideres, et tamen sic ei jungeris, quasi aut ante desideraveris, aut (ut levissime dicam) postea desideraturus sis.* Transl. Rebenich 2002: 134.

81 Cf. Hier. *Ep.* 22.14 and Adkin 2003: 119–21.

82 Hier. *Ep.* 128.3: *Tu quoque virgo, vel vidua, cur tam longo sermone viri retineris? cur cum solo relicta non metuis? Saltem alvi te, vessicae cogat necessitas, ut exeas foras, ut deseras in hac re eum, cum quo licentius, quam cum germano: multo inverecundius, quam cum marito egisti.* Transl. NPNF2.

83 Burrus 2000: 188–9.

84 Burrus 2000: 148. See also the analysis of this passage in Boyarin 1999: 82–7.

85 Burrus 2000: 148, Ambr. *De virgb.* II.21: *Dicet aliquis: Cur exemplum attulisti Mariae, quasi reperiri queat matrem Domini quae possit imitari? Cur etiam Theclae, quam gentium Doctor instituit? Da hujuscemodi doctorem, si discipulam requiris. Hujuscemodi recens vobis exemplum profero, ut intelligatis Apostolum non unius esse doctorem, sed omnium.*

86 Kuefler 2001: 2423.

87 Note that this is where we encounter the only male explicitly identified as a virgin in Ambrose's corpus, in the virgin's prayer where she compares her seemingly hopeless situation to that of *Danieli virgini* in the lion's den. *De virgb.* II.27.

88 Ambr. *De virgb.* II.29: *Tua vestis me verum militem faciet, mea te virginem.* My transl. Note how "profession" and identity are merged here: in addition to both being faithful Christians, the soldier's identity relies on him being a soldier of Christ, the virgin first and foremost as virgin of Christ. Losing this identity will consequently be equal to giving up faith, which only martyrdom will thus preserve.

89 I.e. Iphigeneia in Aulis.

90 Ambr. *De virgb.* II.31. *Ecce non fabulosum illud cerva pro virgine, sed quod verum est, miles ex virgine. At etiam audieram et non credideram, quod aquam Christus in vinum convertit: jam mutare coepit et sexus.* (My transl.) Cf. Ap. *Met.* VIII.26: *non cervam pro virgine sed asinum pro homine succidaneum videre.*

91 Ambr. *De virgb.* II.32: *damnatus pro virgine, qui pro virgine comprehensus est.* My transl.

92 Ambr. *De virgb.* II.32: *At illa clamare coepit: Non ego te mortis vadem elegi, sed praedem pudoris optavi. Si pudor quaeritur, manet sexus: si sanguis exposcitur, fidejussorem non desidero, habeo unde dissolvam. In me lata ista sententia, quae pro me lata est.* […] *Moriar innocens, ne moriar nocens. Nihil hic medium est: hodie aut rea ero tui sanguinis, aut martyr mei.* […] *Est in virgine vulneri locus, qui non erat contumeliae. Ego opprobrium declinavi, non martyrium. Tibi cessi vestem, non professionem mutavi. Quod si mihi praeripis mortem, non redemisti me, sed circumvenisti. Cave, quaeso, ne contendas, cave ne contradicere audeas. Noli eripere beneficium, quod dedisti. Dum mihi hanc sententiam negas, illam restituis superiorem. Sententia enim sententia superiore mutatur. Si posterior me non tenet, tenet superior. Possumus uterque satisfacere sententiae, si me prius patiaris occidi. In te non habent aliam quam exerceant, poenam: in virgine obnoxious pudor est.* My transl.

93 Bloch 1991: 108.

94 Burrus 2000: 152 "… [Ambrose] both protects the hierarchy of gender established by relations of penetration and heightens the eroticism of an ascetic body that transforms a negation into affirmation – indeed a consummation – of desire. For the virgin martyr, 'no' means 'yes'." See also Burrus 1995: 31.

95 Ramsey 1997: 71 comments that the story of Damon and Phythias in the same book "has to do, of course, not with virginity, but rather with the self-sacrifice exemplified by the Antiochene virgin."

96 Ambr. *De virgb.* I.5–9, cf. McInerney 2003: 72–3. Burrus 2000: 150 refers to Ambrose's conclusion in *De virgb.* II.33, where it is stated: "Two contended, and both won. The crown was not divided but became two." In the Latin, however, there is no restriction to the number of crowns won in this contest: *Duo contenderunt, et ambo vicerunt: nec divisa est corona, sed addita.*

97 We should note that the last passage indicates that she was perceived as an adulteress by the spectators, although up until then she has been continually referred to as a virgin. After her stay in the *lupanar*, her preserved virginity is probably very unlikely to anyone else but the soldier, herself and God.

98   Undheim 2011: 187–8.
99   Cf. Consolino 1982: 473: "La lunga eshortazione rivolta da Giuliana ai figli, zeppa com'è di citazioni bibliche, compiaciuta di difficili esegesi, poteva essere pronunciata solo da Ambrogio o da qualche suo collega Greco."
100 E.g. Ambr. *Inst. virg.* 17: *Hanc igitur tentationem tantarum necessitatum, si vultis, filii, vitare, integritas corporis expetenda vobis est: quam ego pro consilio suadeo, non pro imperio praecipio.* Ambr. *Exh. virg.* 19: *Audistis, filii, quantum sit praemium integritatis.* Brown 1988: 354: "Ambrose's thought on virginity could be summed up in one word: *integritas.* This meant the precious ability to keep what was one's own untarnished by alien intrusion[…]," cf. Brown 1988: 357.
101 Ambr. *Exh. virg.* 13: *Sola fides utrique indiscreta sexui, census virorum, dos virginum.* My transl. Cf. Consolino 1982: 460.
102 E.g. *Homily on virginity* 2 (10): "Let the father persuade his son, and the mother her daughter, to live in chastity for Christ." Translation by Shaw. Other terms than *parthenos* are also here applied to "the son who is eager to consecrate his body," *Homily on virginity* 8 (110): *Tauta de kai epi huiou speudontos parastesai to soma.* See also Eus *Hist. Eccl.* III. 29. 3: "But I have learned that Nicholas had nothing to do with any other woman beside her whom he married, and that of his children the daughters reached old age as virgins, and that the son remained uncorrupted (*apthoros*)." Transl. Loeb.
103 As does Paul in his address to Corinthians, sometimes all, and sometimes gender-specific groups: 1 Cor. 7.
104 Hier. *Ep.* 55.3: *Statimque sub exemplo trium eunuchorum, virginitatis infert beatitudinem, quae nulla carnis lege tenetur.* (Ref. to Matt. 19:10–12). Transl. NPNF2.
105 Moxnes 2003: 74, Clark 1999: 90–2, 105–6 and passim. For some of Ambrose's readings of the passage, see above pp. 66–8 and *De vid.* 13.75.
106 Catholic Encyclopedia s.v. "St Melito" and Eus. *Hist. Eccl.* V. xxiv: *Melitona kai eunouchon.*
107 Tert. *De res. carn.* 61: *Ecce virtutis futurae liniamenta. Nos quoque, ut possumus, os cibo excusamus; etiam sexum a congressione subducimus. Quot spadones voluntarii? quot virgines Christo maritatae? quot steriles utriusquae naturae, infructuosis genitalibus structi?* Transl. ANF, with minor changes.
108 Cf. Tert. *Virg. vel.* 10, Tert. *Ad. ux.* 1.6. Hier. *Adv. Jov.* 1.12. See Adkin 2003: 156 for further references.
109 As pointed out by Caner 1997: 414, cf. Kuefler 2001: 97–9.
110 Kuefler 2001: 34–5.
111 Cf. Isidore of Seville, who notes that some eunuchs may have sexual intercourse, but that their semen is without strength. *Etym.* X.93.
112 Caner 1997: 412 and Brown 1988: 268, both with references to Basil of Ancyra's *De virginitate tuenda* (i.e. 62. 797 BC). Jerome warns Demetrias against electing eunuchs and male and female servants because of their appearances rather than their character, yet he seems to adhere to the belief that mutilation could ensure chastity: *Ep.* 130.13: *Eunuchorum quoque tibi, et puellarum ac servulorum mores magis eligantur quam vultuum elegantia, quia in omni sexu et aetate, et truncatorum corporum violenta pudicitia, animi considerandi sunt, qui amputari, nisi Christi timore non possunt.*
113 Basil Anc. *De virg.* 63 (797 CD), quoted and translated by Caner 1997: 413.
114 McInerney 2003: 34 with reference to Kelly 2000: 91–2.
115 Burrus 1996: 474 quoting *De vid.* 76.
116 Burrus 1996: 474.
117 Female eunuchs: Hier. *Ep.* 22.27 (*eunuchiae*), Kuefler 2001: 268 (note 101) lists some further examples, e.g. Hier. *Ep.* 55.4, Aug. *De sanct. virg.* 36, Prud. *Amarigenia* 1.957. Isaiah is explained with regard to virgins, for instance in Ambr. *Inst. virg.* 6.45 and *Exh. virg.* 3.171.

118 John Cass. *Conl.* 22. VI.9: *Illi namque sunt veri atque incorrupti virgines Christi, illi admirabiles atque egregii reputantur eunuchi, non qui metuunt, sed quibus non libet fornicari, nec qui impudicitiae reprimunt frena, sed qui ipsam quoque minimam mentis titillationem et tenuissima libidinis incitamenta vicerunt, et eo usque extenuaverunt illum carnis (ut ita dixerim) sensum, ut non solum ex commotione ejus, nulla oblectatione, sed ne exigua quidem titillatione tangantur.* Transl. Ramsey 1997: 771. Cf. Athenagoras, quoted in Brown 1988: 66: "[For] remaining in virginity and in the state of a eunuch brings one nearer to God."

119 Kuefler 2001: 231, with references to Hier. *Ep.* 107.7, 22.38, Ambr. *De off. min.* 1.18.69, Peter Chrysologus *Sermo* 80.

120 Tert. *Virg. Vel.* 7, cf. *Cult. fem* 1.2. D'Angelo 1995: 143ff., McInerney 2003: 29. For 1 Cor. 11:10, see BeDuhn 1999, Martin 1995: 229–49.

121 E.g. Ambr. *De virgb.* I.52. *Et quid pluribus exsequar laudem castitatis? Castitas etiam angelos fecit. Qui eam servavit, angelus est: qui perdidit, diabolus.* Ambr. *De virgt.* 87: *Ergo vos, sanctae virgines, et quicumque justi estis, et immaculatam animae geritis castitatem, cives sanctorum estis et domestici Dei. Sed tunc nobilitatem istam patriae possidebitis, si Christum intra civitatis hujus septa quaeratis, ingressi per fidem actusque pretiosos, patriarcharum clarificati lumine, fundati super apostolos, versantes inter angelos.*

122 *Ad Gall. Ep.* 2.5: *Quo enim pudore viduae aut virgini ausus est episcopus vel presbyter integritatam vel vel continentiam praedicare, vel suadere castum cubile servare, si ipse saeculo magis insistit filios generare quam Deo?* Text from Duval 2005: 32, Transl. Hunter 1999: 141.

123 McNamara 1983: 107, cf. Kuefler 2001: 230–1.

124 Similarly, Andrea Sterk 2004: 178 notes that the writings of the monk-bishop Epihanius of Salamis, "suggests that it was already customary to choose priests and bishops from among virgins if not monks."

125 Brown 1988: 359. Cf. Brown 1988: 157–9 and 1988: 243.

126 Note that McNamara 1983: 107 (quoted above) describes celibacy as "asexual."

127 *Passio Sancti Felicis Episcopi* 30 (Ed. Musurillo 1972): *Felix episcopus eleuans oculos in caelum, clara voce dixit: Deus, gratias tibi. quinquaginta et sex annos habeo in hoc saeculo. virginitatem custodiui, evangelia servaui, fidem et veritatem predicaui.* My transl. Cf. Kuefler 2001: 174 note 67. For other male virgin martyrs and rendering of trials of male chastity in medieval hagiography, see Kelly 2000: 91–118.

128 These issues are most fully discussed by Burrus 2000 and Kuefler 2001.

129 Hunter 1999: 139–52. Kuefler 2001: 236–7, on the other hand, sees the historical development to have started by the Church Fathers themselves "extending" their privileged title "brides of Christ" to include female virgins in order to control and make them conform to masculine authority.

130 Hunter 1987, Hunter 2003, Hunter 2007, cf. also Duval 2003.

131 Hunter 1999: 152 cf. Hunter 2003: 461–2, Hunter 2007, Brown 1988: 345, McLynn 1994, Lizzi 1990 *et al.*

132 Consolino 1982: 167–8. Cf. Ambr. *De excessu fratris* 54: *Quis igitur non miretur virum inter fratres duos alterum virginem, alterum sacerdotem,* referring to his sister and himself respectively. In this eulogy, however, as genre conventions allow, the virtues and sanctity of the lay brother are presented as no less than that of the two consecrated siblings: *magnanimitate non imparem, ita inter duo maxima munera praestitisse; ut alterius muneris castitatem, alterius sanctitatem referret, non professionis vinculo, sed virtutis officio?*

133 Hier. *Adv. Jov* I.34: *Aut permitte sacerdotibus exercere opera nuptiarum, ut idem sint virgines quod mariti: aut si sacerdotibus non licet uxores tangere, in eo sancti sunt, quia imitantur pudicitiam virginalem.* My transl.

134 Hier. *Ep.* 48.2: *Si saeculi homines indignantur in minori gradu se esse quam virgines, miror Clericos et Monachos et continentes id non laudare quod faciunt. Castrant se ab uxoribus*

suis, ut imitentur virginum castitatem; et id ipsum volunt esse maritatas, quod virgines?
My transl.

135   Likewise, in *Adv. Helv* 21 (23), Jerome states that widows and married women are
holy as long as they "imitate virgin chastity."

136   Hier. *Ep.* 24.5: *Viduae eam imitentur et virgines, maritae colant, noxiae timeant, suspiciant
Sacerdotes.* Cf. Hunter 1999: 142, with note 10.

137   Hier. *Adv. Jov.* 1.34: *Eliguntur mariti in sacerdotium, non nego: quia non sunt tanti
virgines, quanti necessarii sunt sacerdotes. Numquid quia in exercitu fortissimus quisque
eligendus est, idcirco non assumentur et infirmiores, cum omnes fortes esse non possint?*
[…] *Et quomodo, inquies, frequenter in ordinatione sacerdotali virgo negligitur, et maritus
assumitur? Quia forte caetera opera non habet virginitati congruentia, aut virgo putatur, et
non est: aut est virginitatis infamis: aut certe ipsa virginitas ei parit superbiam, et dum sibi
applaudit de sola corporis castitate, virtutes caeteras negligit. Non fovet pauperes: pecuniae
cupidior est.* My transl. See also Brown 1988: 377–8.

138   Hier. *Adv. Jov* 1. 34: *Evenit aliquoties, ut mariti, quae pars major in populo est, maritis
quasi sibi applaudant, et in eo se arbitrentur minores non esse virginibus, si maritum virgini
praeferant.*

139   Hier. *Ep.* 48.21: *Episcopi, Presbyteri, Diaconi, aut virgines eliguntur, aut vidui, aut certe
post Sacerdotium in aeternum pudici.* My transl. Cf. Hier. *Contr Vig.* 2: *Quid facient
Orientis Ecclesiae? quid Aegypti et Sedis Apostolicae, quae aut virgines Clericos accipiunt,
aut continentes: aut si uxores habuerint, mariti esse desistunt?* For other "male widows"
as somewhat analogous in status to female widows, see Hier. *comm in Matt* 1:
Josephum viduum, Tert. *Exh. Cast.* 3: *innuptos et viduos*, cf. *Virg. vel*.10, *Hermas* II.4.

140   Hunter 1999: 152.

141   Hunter 1999: 140.

142   Greg. Nys. *De virg.* 3, transl. NPNF2. Cf. Burrus 2000: 88.

143   Hier. *Ep.* 48.20: *Virginitatem autem in coelum fero, non quia habeam, sed quia magis
mirer quod non habeo.* (Transl: NPNF2, modified.)

144   Hier. *Ep.* 22.19: *Alium eunuchum necessitas faciat, me voluntas.* Cf. Kuefler 2001: 279.

145   Brown 1988: 159, viz. Aug. *Conf.* 6.3.3.

146   Ambr. *De excessu fratris* 52. My transl. This eulogy was written in 378, the year
after *De virginibus* and the same year as *De virginitate*. Cf. Cyprian's description of
Cornelius in *Ep.* 55.8, viz. Kuefler 2001: 145.

147   See note above.

148   Ibid.

149   For the concept of *pudicitia* as a valuable virtue for men, see Langlands 2006: 197
and 285.

150   Ambr. *De excessu fratris* 1.53.

151   Kuefler 2001: 151: "Bishops found in the language of humility (humilitas)
a perfect means to belie their ambition for social status and political authority."

152   *De viduis* and *De virginitate* were also composed in this period, i.e. 377/378.

153   John Cass. *Inst.* 6.19: *Fertur sancti Basilii Caesariensis episcopi districta sententia: Et
mulierem, inquit, ignoro, et virgo non sum. In tantum intellexit incorruptionem carnis
non tam in mulieris esse abstinentia, quam in integritate cordis, quae vere incorruptam
perpetuo sanctimoniam corporis, vel timore Dei, vel amore castitatis custodit.* My transl. cf.
McInerney 2003: 62.

154   Oration 43.62 (written in 379), Martin 2006: 98, note 25.

155   The text is given in Ferrua 1967: 357: *nat(us) kal. april ba(p)t. IIII non. april / Theusebio
virgini neofito / hic mihi caro, hic pio, hic igitur filio ecce sepulto / Theusebi sanctifico semper
sociato pudori. / bis senos menses deo qui pertulit annum / ter denos dies super ista luce
moratus est / immaculatus a pecc(at)o felici conditus dono est / natali completus et item
a Chr(is)to renatus / aeternam vitae penetravit Theusebius sedem / virginemq(ue) gerit,
dom(ino) tribuente, corona(m) / / Rufiinus et Severa parentes filio dulcissimo! Benemerenti
fecerunt in dom(ino) / quesquas in pace. dep(ositus) VI non. mai.* My transl.

156 Ferrua 1967 dates the inscription to 337 AD, but see now Arnulf 1989 and Jastrzebowska 1989 who both independently argue for dating the inscription to late fourth/early fifth century.
157 Ferrua 1967: 360–1: *HIC MIHI PRIOR FILIUS HIC VIRGO VIRGINEM DEDICAVI [T] HUNC LOCUM.*
158 This is not uncommon in funerary inscriptions, cf. CIL 6.25808 (*monumentum virginem*), AE 1950, 00038 (*purum virgin(eum) monumenti*), CIL 6.27857 (*virginem … locum*), (and CIL 6.33603? *soleum* [?] *virginem*).
159 Cf. Ferrua 1967: 359.
160 Cf. note 242 in Ch. 2 above.
161 ICUR VII, 19464: *Spes berecundo filio/ qui• bixit• an• xxx•birgo • bene /merenti in pace.*
162 ICUR IX, 25005: *[A]urel(io) Petro fil[io] / dulcissimo qui v[ixit an]n(os) XVII / mens(es) VII virgo Aur(elius) M[ari]nus et/ Ael(ia) Donata parentes Pelagiorum.* This is found in the cemetery of Priscilla and dated to the last half of the third century in EDB. Cf. Janssen 1981: 200, note 16.
163 ICUR IV, 10098: *Pontius / Athenago / ras, qui / vix an. / XXII / virgo.* This is from the catacombs of Callistus and is dated to the first half of the fourth century in EDB.
164 ICUR IV, 12459: *felici filio bene merenti qui vixit annos/ XXIII dies X qvi exivit virgo de saeculu et / neofitus in pace/ parentes fecerunt/ dep III nonas avg.* Cf. Janssens 1981: 199.
165 ICUR VI, 16173: *Eugamio l[ectori] virgini in p[a]ce / qui vixit annis [XXX]VIII me(nse)s II dies XXIII / cu[i titulum? pre]sbyter Generosus / una c[um patri]bus et frat[ribus posui]t / [depositus] XIII k(a)le(ndas) apriles.* The inscription is supposed to be in situ, (coem. ss. Marcellini et Petri), but not possible to date.
166 ICUR V, 14221: *Eusebi birgini.*
167 ICUR IV, 12093. Other inscriptions combining *virgo et neophyta* are inter alia CIL 11.02563 = CIL 11. *00315 = ILCV 1496: *Ulpiae Fausti/nae virgini n{a}e/ofytae / quae vix(it) / ann(is) XIII men(sibus) II / dieb(us) XXV de/posita VI Idus / Iul(ias) in pace,* ILCV 1489c: *Constantina virgo in pace neofita,* ILCV 1489d (=ICUR VII, 18631): *dp. Cyriacetis III idus Sep. que vixit/ annos XX, dies I / que neofita mortua / est virgo in p.,* ILCV 1489g: *inofita bir/go Suteres /in pace quies/quet (alpha et omega) per(it) a.III,* and ILCV 1500a: *b.m. /Prencepia, que fuit in /corpore annos plus m/enus XIIII et mensis IIII ver/5/go et neofita in Cristo.*
168 AE 1998, 00231.
169 Janssens 1981: 25=ICUR VII, 20300. See also Laes 2013 on male virgins in inscriptions from Rome.
170 CIL 13.2132: *D(is) M(anibus) / et quieti aeternae / Eutychiani fili(i) dulcissimi / pientissimi et prudentissimi / reverentissimique virgini(s) / qui vixit annis VIII m(ense) I d(iebus) IIII / Romanus pater ponendum / curavit et sub ascia dedi/cavit.*
171 CIL 10.03309 = ILCV 01746 = ICUR I, 02849: *Hic positus est / Iulius Marturius cibis / Co(n)stantinopolitanus / fidelis spiritalis virgo / qui vixit anno(s) plus min/us n(umero) L depositus die pri[d(ie)] / Idus A(u)gustas in pa{a}ce (chi rho).*
172 Janssens 1981: 202 also interprets *virgo super se* as an expression of the deceased's virginity in ICVR II 4348: *Iulius vernis venustus qui vixit / annos XXI et mensis X depositus / virgo super se IIII kalendas septembres,* cf. Note 26: MARANGONI, *Acta* 90: *dominie filie/ Leonine, que / vixit annis XXII / virg. super se b.m. in pa /ce fecit pater* and note 28: ICUR IV, 17932: *Maxentia /virgine super se / in pace.* Cf. also ICUR IX, 24020: *Domin(a)e fili(a)e / Leonin(a)e qu(a)e / vixit annis XXII / Virc(ini) super se b(ene) m(erenti) in pa/ce fecit pater.* Likewise, Janssens takes the expression *investis in pace* to refer to the virginity of an 18-year-old boy: ICUR VII, 18458: *v.a. n. XVIII, m. VII, d. XII. investis in pacae.* For *investis* in this sense, as a male equivalent to *virgo,* see, for instance, Tert. *Virg. vel.* 8 and 11 and *de orat* 21–2. According to Nonius

(I, p. 65): *sed melius intellegi potest investes appellatos quasi in Vesta, id est in pudicitia et [in] castitate*. Laes 2013 also discussed the more frequent term *virgineus* which appears in Christian epitaphs. This, however, seems to be the male equivalent of *virginea*, a term that semantically seems to overlap with *univira*.

173   Both Ferrua 1967 and Arnulf 1989 point out the similarity between the Theusebius inscription and other inscriptions, particularly ILCV 1685 as the model for the main text.

174   Cf. Janssens 1981: 202 and above p. 70.

175   Hier. *Ep.* 22.21: *Mors per Evam: vita per Mariam. Ideoque et ditius virginitatis donum fluxit in feminas, quia coepit a femina.* My transl.

176   Martin 2006: 98. For Christ as a virgin and other "biblical" male virgins, see Undheim 2011: 193–206 and Undheim 2012.

177   Cf. Kelly 2000: 7: "By defining virginity/chastity primarily as a spiritual quality, patristic and scholastic writers reconfigured the limits of the physical body. However, the fact that virginity may exceed bodily boundaries and actually reside in a given discourse did not prevent various writers from attempting to locate virginity in the flesh – female flesh, that is."

178   Cf. Burrus 2000: 169: "*vir* begins to mimic *virgo*, as Foucault describes it, and man is reformed as a maid."

179   Martin 1995: 231.

180   Cass. *Inst.* 6.

181   McInerney 2003: 63. As argued, however, inscriptions testify to different views and understandings.

182   Aug. *Tract. In Ioh.* 13.12: [*Ubi est ista virginitas? non enim in corpore. Paucarum feminarum est, et si dici virginitas in viris potest,*] *paucorum virorum sancta integritas etiam corporis est in Ecclesia, et honorabilius membrum est.* Adkin 2003: 184 comments upon this in a note to Augustine's skepticism towards Jerome's insistence on the virginity of Elijah.

183   Brown 2001: 631, Brown 1988: 421–3, Foucault 1985, McInerney 2003: 59–63, Jacobs 2000: 746, Kelly 2000: 114 with ref. to Tert. *Virg. vel.* 10.

184   Cf. McInerney 2003: 81. E.g. Hier. *Ep.* 22.5: *Perit ergo, et mente virginitas. Istae sunt virgines malae, virgines carne, non spiritu: virgines stultae, quae oleum non habentes, excluduntur a sponso.* Cf. *Ep.* 22.38 and *Adv. Helv* 20.

185   Cf. Arnold 2003, in particular 111–14, Riches 2002.

4   *De lapsu virginum consecratarum*

Crime and punishment of fallen virgins

The pontifex and the pope

Sometime during the last half of the fourth century, presumably before 382, the Roman senator and religious official Quintus Aurelius Symmachus dispatched two letters where he insisted on the fulfilment of an ancient procedure: the punishment of an unchaste Vestal virgin.[1] Primigenia, the Vestal in question, had, according to the content of these letters, polluted the sacred rites by her despicable crime. Symmachus therefore demanded that the priestess and her accomplice Maximus were to be executed according to the severity stated by the ancient laws:

> According to the tradition and principles established by our forefathers, an investigation by the high priest of our college[2] has discovered the *incestum* of Primigenia, who until recently was a Vestal priestess in Alba. The matter demonstrates what was made clear by the confessions both of she who has contaminated the sacred chastity, and of Maximus, with whom she committed the nefarious misdeed. What remains now is that the severity of the laws is carried out against those who polluted the public rites with their abominable crime, [a punishment] which is for you to carry out according to the example of recent times. Considering the laws and service of the commonwealth, you will therefore be deemed worthy to properly punish a misdeed which throughout all time and up til this day has been vindicated in the most severe manner. Farewell.[3]

A similar concern is expressed in an almost contemporary papal decretal, commonly called *Ad Gallos episcopos*. The letter was addressed to bishops of Gaul and gave rulings and regulations in reply to several questions regarding church discipline. After much dispute over authorship, in 2005 Yves-Marie Duval re-ascribed the letter to Pope Damasus.[4] Two of the paragraphs in this letter concern the punishment of girls who have committed the crime of acting against their promise to remain virgins consecrated to Christ:[5]

> [3.] It is inquired about the veiled virgins and […] which judgment should be applied [towards] she who has changed her promise.

If a virgin, already veiled to Christ – one who has professed her integrity by a public testimony and received the veil of blessings by the bishop after he has read the benedictions – committed her *incestum* either in secret or, wanting to cover over the crime, has placed upon her adulterer the name husband[6] and has taken the members of Christ and made them into the members of a prostitute;[7] so that she who was a bride of Christ (instead) will be called the wife of a man; in such a woman, there are as many reasons for condemnation as there are charges! She has changed her resolution of integrity, she has lost her veil, perverted her first promise and then withdrawn it to make it worthless.[8] Of what kind and for how long are amends needed? How severe is the penitence for her, who has brought upon herself the destruction of her flesh![9] It is not a small sin to have left God and gone after a man.[10] Therefore she has to lament for exceedingly many years, so that she may in time achieve forgivness, after she has received the dignified fruit of penitence,[11] if she indeed will do her penitence with repentance.

[4.] Likewise, the girl who is not yet veiled, but who has proposed to remain so, even if she had not received the veil in Christ, because she had professed [to remain a virgin] and is not veiled in marriage, [if she marries] her marriage is called clandestine,[12] for because of this, she could not keep the convention of marriage commanded from heaven, in [her] rushing to the blindness of desire.

And regarding these [girls], it is necessary to establish the amount of time for penance to be done. Whether she was taken by force [*rapta*] or she went willingly [*volens*], she consented contrary to all appropriate behavior, to go to the man, asking advice from neither her relatives nor her bishop with regard to the veil. These girls held their solemn rank with chaste *pudor*, yet they acted against the precepts of the Old Testament.[13] The law orders them to be killed by stones,[14] but now that this punishment is invalid, it is inflicted spiritually, so that they cannot enter the Church, as if they were dead.

They nevertheless have the possibility to do penance, but they will not obtain forgiveness easily, since, according to the law,[15] if the girl had cried [for help], and if she had contested and protested at length, she would certainly have been exempt from sin. It is therefore necessary for both of them to be suspended from communion for the same regulated period of time, to act out the proper penitance with lament, humility and fasts, and to redeem with compassion the crime that has been committed.[16]

The letters of Symmachus and the Roman bishop reflect, in two very different ways, the anxiety caused by lapsed consecrated virgins, and they exemplify different strategies to deal with this *crimen*. They demand punishments of the fallen consecrated virgins that at first glance appear to have very little in common. It may therefore be tempting to ascribe the differences in their treatment of this "crime" as reflecting the two authors' different religious

adherence. Symmachus, the Roman senator and antiquarian, often characterized as a reactionary nostalgic for the lost golden age of Rome,[17] is in this sense
opposed to the Roman bishop who represented the new Christian paradigm.
They both write as authoritative figures within their respective (religious)
communities; Symmachus as a member and on behalf of the Roman college
of *pontifices*, Damasus as Bishop of Rome in a phase when this office was about
to be established at the pinnacle of the hierarchy in the Western Church.[18]
While Symmachus argues that the old laws of the Roman forefathers should
be maintained, the decretal of Damasus claims that the old laws of the Christian
heritage, those of the Old Testament, have been deemed invalid, underlining
that new rules are to be applied from now on.[19] Symmachus solicits enactment
of the Roman laws in a very specific case, while the author of *Ad Gallos episcopos* provides disciplinary regulations in general terms for a distinct group
within the Christian hierarchy. Damasus addresses the question regarding the
lapsed virgins as one of several topics in his letter regarding Church discipline
in a reply to the bishops of Gaul.

Nevertheless, what is revealed in these rather brief passages is a deep concern
for the potential consequences should the crime in question not be atoned
properly. The rulings presented or referred to here also indicate the need for
admonitory sanctions, a call for measures to control and prevent[20] the consecrated virgins from temptations that might lead them to give up their solemn
profession, which, in both cases, is achieved by applying religious and juridical
authority of severe punishments.

The value placed upon the sacred virginity of the consecrated virgins must
therefore be said to be strikingly manifest in these sanctions that were meant
to punish such transgressions. This punishment would not only function as a
stern warning but also, by contrast, be a testimony to the elevated status of
those virgins who actually did manage to remain virgins. Where Symmachus
reveals no doubt whatsoever regarding the "non-virginity" of Primigenia,
having received a confession from both her and her accomplice, Damasus
mentions a few factors that could have been considered in a potential case of
this sort. For instance, he distinguishes between girls who have married legally
and those who have had secret affairs, between those who were formally veiled
and those who had merely promised to remain virgins, and between those who
went willingly and those who were raped. Eventually, however, Damasus seems
to find no extenuating circumstances that could free a consecrated girl or
woman from penitence once she was known to no longer be a virgin. The fact
that he brings up some of these factors does however suggest that such circumstances might be taken into consideration by others when the punishment was
to be meted out. By looking at different regulations on how lapsed virgins
were to be punished, and how this punishment was justified in the sources, it
will be more clear what was also thought to be at stake in these cases. Likewise,
presentations of potential consequences that could befall not only the virgin
herself, but also the community to which she belonged, if the crime was left
unpunished will appear more clearly from this perspective on borderlines and

the drawing of them. Using these letters of Symmachus and Damasus as a starting point, I will therefore look at both contemporary and earlier sources that exemplify different views on the "nature" of this crime and on the proper punishment, and thus also the ongoing negotiations over virginity and sacred virginity.

A relevant question to pose in this regard is how virginity, or lack thereof whenever doubted, was to be determined. As indicated earlier, it is exactly at the establishment and maintenance of such limits, i.e., at the very borders of transgression, that it perhaps becomes possible to grasp some of the key aspects in the different valuations of virginity. As we have already seen in a previous chapter, it was not all that clear whether virginity was perceived as something that could be identified visually, as a physical or behavioral quality of those possessing it. However, by turning to the *via negativa* and looking for how the lack of virginial qualities were believed to be detectable in so-called fallen virgins, I will argue that the descriptions of such signs of virginity present as well as of virginity lost help us understand the sacred virgins' qualities that were so necessary to preserve.

As argued in the previous chapters, the value of sacred virginity and the growing popularity of virgins in Late Antiquity allowed for some flexity in the understanding of who could be regarded and esteemed as a virgin, both in terms of social class, age and gender, *vis-à-vis* more traditional conceptions of what and who a *virgo* was. Such borderline flexity as seen in the variety of attempts to describe and define the (sacred) *virgo* appear, however, to have also drawn increasing attention to the seemingly fragile boundaries that needed to be redrawn and redefined in the face of this popularity. Identifying the very point where the *virgo* went from being virgin to non-virgin – which, as we have already seen, was not always as obvious as one might think – would therefore be important in these negotiations over value and meaning. Distinguishing virginity from non-virginity was very important, and the religious valuation of virginity can thus in many ways be said to be most clearly articulated in these conceptions of the potential consequences of the loss of vowed virginity and the subsequent need to penalize transgressions of the sacred virgins' vow and duty.

CRIME AND PUNISHMENT

> So how can the spritual bond made before the innumerable witnesses of the Church, before the angels and the armies of heaven, be dissolved by adultery? I don't know whether it is possible to come up with a suitable death or penalty for this offence.[21]

There is no doubt that the crime committed by a once consecrated and now lapsed virgin was considered a serious one. The questions that the Christian writers asked then was whether and how the punishment of this crime could at all reflect and express the gravity of the transgressions. Also, does what we know about the punishment of Vestals who were known to have lost their virginity shed some light on their sacred status as *virgines*? Starting with the vocabulary that describes these *crimina* and descriptions of how they were to be punished, I will look at terminology and symbolism linked to removal, purification and death. I will then move on to potential consequences that the crime was thought to incur, not only for the girl, but also for her family and society. This again reflects these virgins' socio-religious function beyond the question of individual salvation.

The name and nature of the crime: adultery and pollution

> Tremble along with me at the nature of this crime, which has been uncovered.[22]

Symmachus applies terminology that clearly evokes the idea of pollution. He writes that Primigenia had "contaminated the sacred chastity,"[23] and in the company of Maximus she had committed a "nefarious misdeed."[24] They had "polluted the public rites with their abominable crime."[25] The next letter maintains that she had "stained the secrets of the chaste divinity,"[26] and with "unspeakable crimes"[27] the couple had done "harm to the most chaste of times."[28] To Symmachus, the gravity of the crime seems to lie in the pollution, contamination and soiling of what was sacred and dedicated to the gods.[29] Primigenia had not only contaminated herself, a person dedicated to the gods, and thus her priestly office belonging to them. By this *crimen* she had also polluted the rites and the sacred sites she had been in charge of because of her sacred status.

As we have already seen, the letters of Symmachus refer to a specific priestess in a specific case, addressing general and ancient guidelines that he presupposes are already well-known. The papal decretal, on the other hand, provided general guidelines and mentions a number of possible concerns that could seemingly be of relevance to the assessment of punishment. The author of this letter deals with girls who have already been through the formal consecration ceremony (*velatae*), as well as girls who are not yet consecrated (*nondum velatae*) but had promised to become so; and he also distinguishes between girls who had committed their crime in secret and those who had openly married. Passages from the Bible are evoked to expose the nature and gravity of her crime, such as 1 Cor. 6:15, by which it is stated that the girl has "taken the members of Christ and made them into the members of a prostitute."[30] Likewise 1 Tim. 5:12, which originally concerned widows, is here applied to virgins, who will "be judged because they broke their first promise." The former virgin is said to have broken her vow to keep her integrity and as having lost her veil, which here obviously served as an indicator of her sanctity. By reference to 1 Cor. 5:5 it is stated that the girl has "brought upon herself the destruction of her flesh" by her deeds. In a seemingly sarcastic under-statement, perhaps alluding to Hosea's depiction of the adultery of Israel,[31] it is further made clear that it is by no means a small sin to have left God "to go after" a man.

As opposed to Symmachus, who emphasizes sacrilege and pollution as the core of the Vestal's crime, the former Christian virgin is in these paragraphs confronted with her broken promise to God. She is first and foremost presented as an adulteress.[32] Representations of fallen consecrated virgins as adultresses are abundant in the Christian literature from this period. In analogy with the *virgo velata* being regarded as the bride of Christ after her consecration, adultery follows as the logical consequence of any sexual relation with another man. But, unlike other adultresses, the *virgo velata* had been unfaithful to God himself. This divine status of the bridegroom to whom she has been unfaithful is often stressed in the texts dealing with fallen consecrated virgins, accentuating that her crime is much worse than "normal" adultery.[33] Likewise, in this letter, the girl who has proposed[34] to become a consecrated virgin (perhaps indicating a kind of novitiate) is also to be punished for her lapse. In analogy with the bride/adultress terminology, this girl seems to be thought of as something like a fiancée, whose promise is almost as binding as that of the girl who has been formally consecrated.

Both letters only allude to the sexual act, referring to it in a language proper to their formal contexts. There is no clear expression of pollution in the letter of Damasus, but several of the biblical allusions and citations could evoke such analogies. As we will see later, other contemporary Christian texts that deal with the same issue are more explicit regarding the pollution induced by a fallen virgin, as is also indicated in the prohibition of the penitents entering the Church. Thus, although Symmachus stressed pollution and Dasmasus adultery, it is clear in both cases that the crime is ultimately a religious offense – a crime against the divinity or divinities, which may carry grave consequences also beyond that for the individual perpetrator.

Crimen incesti

One striking thing about these letters is that both Symmachus and Damasus refer to the crime in question as *incestum*. This Latin term, which was most commonly used to denote illicit sexual relations between close family members (parents-children, siblings), did, however, carry a specific meaning to the Romans when it appeared in relation to lapsed sacred virgins.

According to the sources, Vestals who were suspected of no longer being virgins were charged with *incestum* and, if proven guilty, they were referred to as *incestae*. Symmachus' letter thus refers to the crime as *incestum* in line with established terminology in classical Roman literature. This terminology has for obvious reasons intrigued modern scholars, who have proposed a number of theories to explain the curious use of a term that otherwise denoted sexual relations with close kin (as the term "incest" is used today).[35]

The most widespread theory accepts the etymology proposed, for instance, by Isidore of Seville, who linked *incestus* to *incastus*.[36] Philippe Moreau provides a nuanced semantic analysis of the term *castus*, and points out its double etymology, pertaining to abstention on the one hand and to ritual regulations on the other. He demonstrates that several Roman authors employed it in the sense "rite" or "rule, regulation," as well as to refer to abstention from food and sexual relations. The negation of *castus* would thus, on the one hand, signify a notion of violation of a rule and impurity by failing to abstain and, on the other hand, the idea of impurity caused by contact with death or breaching ritual precautions.[37] A revealing example of how *incestum* is linked to impurity and pollution is to be found in Servius' commentary on the Aeneid, where Servius writes: "To incest is to pollute. And *incestum* is everything that is pollution."[38]

Because it is terminology linked to adultery that seems to have prevailed in Christian discourses of lapsed virgins, the term *incestum* as applied to the crimes of unchaste Vestals has been more extensively researched than the occurrences of such terminology for Christian virgins. In general, translations of Early Christian texts commonly render "unchaste" for *incestus* regardless of whether virgins or non-virgins are concerned.[39] Scholars who have encountered the terminology pertaining to *incestus* applied to consecrated virgins in Christian texts from Late Antiquity thus interpret the word in more general terms of unchastity and illicit sexual unions, and overlook the fact that in Roman terminology *incestus* referred to a very specific crime that already came with certain connotations and implications when the perpetrators were sacred virgins. In his commentary to *Ad Gallos episcopos*, Duval points out that the severity of the prescribed punishment seems to evoke Paul's condemnation of incest in his letter to the Corinthians,[40] and Gaudemet remarks *en passant* that the term *incestae* as used by Jerome and Cyprian "est pris ici dans le sens courant de la langue juridique de Bas-Empire, de mariage interdit."[41] Lucetta Desanti is indeed among very few scholars who have indicated a potential connection between the crime that was prosecuted against fallen Vestal virgins and similar accusations against Christian virgins. Desanti draws attention to the way the terminology of *incestae nuptiae* was applied in Justinian's legislation and other legal documents that concerned Christian virgins' marriage and/or sexual affairs.[42]

Regardless of authorial intent, that is, what kind of crime Damasus wanted to evoke by this word, it is my contention that an understanding of the meaning inherent in the term *incestum*, as it was used by Romans to specifically denote the well-known crime of Vestal virgins, will add to our understanding of how these texts were received and understood, and how they again added to the ongoing construction of what constituted sacred virginity. For any Roman with some acquaintance with Rome's history and religion, the term *incestum* as it was used in Symmachus' letter would clearly call to mind the gravity of the crime that Vestals had been condemned for; the severity of the punishment and the implications of sacrilege and pollution that were linked to the crime. Although the recipients of Damasus' letter were bishops in Gaul, there is no reason why his use of the term *incestum* in this context should not evoke the same connotations and semantic range as when Symmachus used it. In this respect, the two different kinds of sacred virgins would, if they lost the very principle of their sanctity, by means of terminology be held guilty of similar crimes.

A context for the case of Primigenia?

Symmachus' language in the letters concerning the crime of Primigenia indicates that he assumed the prescribed punishment was already known to the receiver.[43] As Mary Beard has pointed out, "the overwhelming preoccupation of ancient writers [writing about Vestal virgins] is the punishment of the Vestals, the Vestals who broke their oath of chastity, or those suspected of having done so."[44] Since the punishment of an unchaste Vestal virgin had no apparent parallels in Roman law or in specifically religious sanctions, the various and rather peculiar aspects of the process have engaged several scholars. Some have pointed out analogies to human sacrifice, in particular in connection with the episodes recorded from republican times.[45] The social dimension of the term *incestum* has also, as already noted, been explored, and the crime has been compared with punishment of incest between blood-relations.[46] Religious law was under the supervision of the pontefices, and it is as a pontifex that Symmachus addresses the prefect in the case of Primigenia.[47] Despite Symmachus' appeal to *mos maiourm*, religious law and the religious duties of the potifices, as well as those of the Vestals, went through many and major changes over the more than 1000 years that the cult of Vesta was tended in Rome. In order to make some sense out of these scarce sources that concern Primigenia, it might however be useful to sum up what is known about the punisment of *vestales incestae*. The best account is given by Plutarch, who described the procedure as part of a rather lengthy presentation of the priesthood:

> But the priestess who dishonours her virginity is buried alive near the Colline Gate. In this spot, just within the city, there is an embankment of earth stretching for some distance; it is called the 'agger' in Latin. Here a small chamber is constructed underground, with a way in from above. And in it is placed a couch, complete with covers, and a lighted lamp; there are as well small portions of life's necessities − such as bread, a jug of water, milk, oil − as if they were trying to escape the charge of starving to death a person consecrated to the greatest services of the gods. They put the offender herself on a litter, completely covering her over and fastening the covers down with straps, so that not even a cry can be heard from inside; then they carry her through the Forum. Everyone stands aside silently to let her pass, and without a sound they escort the litter with dreadful sadness. There is no other sight more awful than this; nor does the city experience a day more gloomy. When the litter has arrived at the spot, the attendants loosen the fastenings and the *pontifex maximus* utters mysterious prayers, stretching out his hands to the gods before the fatal moment.

Then he takes the priestess, closely veiled, and sets her on the ladder that leads down to the chamber below. Then he himself turns away, along with the other priests. But when she has gone down, the ladder is taken up and the chamber is buried with a great quantity of earth thrown down from above, making the place level with the rest of the embankment. This is the manner of punishment for those who abandon their sacred virginity.[48]

Plutarch also returns to the question concerning the punishment of unchaste Vestal virgins in his collection of *Quaestiones Romanae*, where he asks why the Romans punish with live entombment their sacred virgins who have been corrupted/seduced (*diaphthareisas*). He suggests that cremation by fire might be wrong for a person who had guarded the sacred fire. Perhaps, he asks, the Romans thought it impious and against divine law to destroy a body that had been consecrated to the gods by the most solemn rites. Did they fear they would upset the gods if they laid hands on a consecrated woman? This, Plutarch infers, was the reason why the Romans arranged that the priestess

> should die of herself, by putting her into a chamber made underground, in which was placed a burning lamp, a loaf of bread, and some milk and water; after which the top of the chamber was covered over with earth. Even this ritual does not rid them entirely of superstitious fears, but to this very day the priests go to that place and make offerings to the dead.[49]

In an intriguing interpretation of the ceremony leading up to the live interment, Augusto Fraschetti argues that the symbolism surrounding the condemned priestess conveys that she is already "socially dead."[50] Fraschetti notes that even the condemned Vestal retains her legal privilege to be buried inside the city, since the agger, as described by Plutarch to be just within the city boundaries, is the most marginal place of all, actually being neither inside nor outside the city wall, which otherwise marked the boundary between the living and the dead.[51] The *vestale incesta* is thus both dead and not dead, and the underground chamber dug out in this liminal space to where she is consigned underlines this status.

Prior to this fourth-century case of Primigenia, Vestals had, according to our surviving sources, only been charged with *incestum* at three different occasions in imperial times (two of which were prosecuted under Domitian), and a total number of eight Vestals received death sentences. Of the four Vestals who appear to have been convicted during the reign of Domitian, the ancient procedure of republican times was only followed in the case that was prosecuted sometime between 89 and 91 AD, when Cornelia, who was a *Virgo Vestalis Maxima*, was buried alive. Plutarch might very well have been in Rome at the time of Domitian, and his account of the procedures that are rendered above is likely to be based on information he had gained from others who had been present at the execution. In fact, the process might even have been

witnessed by Plutarch himself.[52] The details of the proceedings and the ceremony leading to the live interment of Cornelia are recorded in one of Pliny's
letters.[53] Pliny's version represents Cornelia as an innocent victim of the
emperor's unreasonable nature, but other versions claim that Domitian allegedly wanted to make a moral statement by enacting the traditional ritual
punishment for *vestales incestae*.[54] The last case we know of before Symmachus'
concern with the crime of Primigenia is dated to 212 or 213, and occurred
during the reign of Caracalla. According to Dio Cassius, three of the four
accused Vestals were executed, but one, Cannutia Crescentia, committed
suicide before her execution was carried out.[55]

The total number of Vestal virgins who according to the extant sources were
actually punished for *crimen incesti* is not very high, considering the amount of
attention they received in the historigraphical records, in other contemporary
texts, by polemical Church Fathers, not to mention posterity's interest in these
priestesses. There could be a number of reasons for potential under-reporting
in the sources from imperial times, without necessarily concluding that a
multitude of *virgines incestae* went unpunished.[56] However, as long as the Vestals'
virginity guaranteed divine benevolence, victory, prosperity and continuity, the
emperor and his subjects would certainly benefit from virgin priestesses who
served their rites with "chaste hands."[57]

Primigenia's crime

The two letters of Symmachus remain almost remarkably bereft of contemporary
context that could facilitate an interpretation. In fact, it is impossible to know
whether the punishment was even fulfilled in the end. Many have therefore taken
the reluctance of the city prefect that can be construed from the second letter as
an indication that the effectuation of the law was ultimately prevented (or maybe
somehow circumvented).[58] Other sources clearly state that the unchaste Vestal
was to be buried inside the city walls,[59] but as Primigenia is said to be in charge
of the Alban rites and *apud Albam*, other rules appear to have applied in her
case. Sergio Rhoda suggests that the prefect of Rome, in declining to effectuate
the punishment, claimed that the punishment should rather be carried out where
the crime was committed and thus found an excuse to avoid taking an action
that would indeed have been a delicate matter under a Christian emperor.[60]

But what is actually meant by the Alban rites? Apart from the case of
Primigenia, in which the outcome is not certain, we do not know of any
historical Vestal that has been punished outside of Rome. The evidence of
Vestals outside the city walls is on the whole very meager indeed. Parallel cults of
Vesta in other Latin cities (as well as in Athens[61]) are scarcely documented.[62]
A cult at Alba is, however, slightly more substantiated, yet the letters of
Symmachus are among the most important sources for our knowledge of such
a cult, and even these represent a somewhat ambiguous testimony.

Alba was an important site in the history of Rome, as it was there that the
usurper Amulius, according to legend, had forced his niece Rhea Silvia to serve

as a Vestal to prevent her from bearing children. It was here that she bore her twin sons Romulus and Remus, the famous founders of Rome.[63] According to Plutarch, when King Numa established the cult of Vesta in Rome, it was modelled after the one at Alba. At first, there had only been two priestesses, but the number had been increased to six under King Servius Tullius.[64] It has been suggested that the continued cult of Vesta at Alba consequently was maintained to honor Rome's origin and history.[65] The evidence for such a cult at Alba in imperial times is, however, very scant. Asconius mentions the *Albanae virgines*,[66] and an inscription dated to 158 AD likewise refers to a *Ma[nlia] Severina virgo Albana maxi[ma]*.[67] Another inscription records a *v.v. maximae ar[cis] / [A]lbanae*.[68] Juvenal's mention of *Vestam minorem* is referred to as additional evidence for a cult of Vesta in Alba, but this too is ambiguous and identified in analogy with the other sources.[69] Although some kind of cult of Vesta that included Vestal virgins must clearly have been upheld at Alba, we cannot say for certain whether this entailed an individual temple with permanent priestesses analogous to that which was established at the Forum in Rome.[70] As Symmachus' letters indicate, Primigenia, like the Vestals at Rome, was under the religious jurisdiction of the Roman pontifices. However, the religious circumstances of the last half of the fourth century appear to have posed difficulties for the priestly college in their effort to appoint someone willing to execute the punishment according to *mos maiorum*. What eventually happened to Primigenia and Maxentius, then, is only left to speculation.

Susanna's fall

Whereas Symmachus and the other sources on the *incestum* of Vestal virgins concern specific cases in which even the names of the culprits are often preserved, most of our Christian sources are of a general kind and, like the decretal in *Ad Gallos episcopos*, present authoritative rulings of bishops or Church councils on how to deal with fallen virgins. One of the few exceptions is a woman called Susanna, a "fallen virgin" to whom a long sermon was dedicated. The extant text is often attributed to Niceta of Remesiana, bishop in Dalmatia, and a friend and contemporary of Paulinus of Nola (355–431 AD).[71] It appears that it was originally delivered as a sermon. The text constantly shifts between addressing Susanna herself, her family, her accomplice and the rest of the congregation. Compared with Damasus' letter and other contemporary texts that were concerned with similar matters, the sermon on the fall of Susanna applies a much richer rhetorical repertoire. The author vividly expresses the lamentation, disappointment and frustration caused by the fallen virgin's grave offense.[72] As such, Niceta's sermon may provide a key to open up some of the more obscure aspects that were referred to in the letters of Symmachus and Damasus.

The sermon clearly relies on contemporary imagery evoked in the cases of fallen consecrated virgins in other texts, but seems to develop this imagery even further by applying more direct and explicit language. In this text on

Susanna's fall, we thus encounter perhaps the densest and most tense expressions of the repercussions a fallen Christian virgin brought with her. Death is an ever-present metaphor:

> If you had died of natural causes, your parents would have wept a bit for you on account of their love; but they had rejoiced exceedingly because they had sent forth an immaculate virgin, a living offering to the Lord, one who would surely atone for their own transgressions. But now they weep for you as dead, but not dead; they weep for you living and not living, dead surely to the glory of your virginity, alive in the dishonor of disgrace.[73]

Niceta explicitly contrasts Susanna's sin and its consequences with the positive effects her sacred virginity could have had for the rest of her family had she only remained a virgin. Niceta's question to Susanna and the congregation is thus, "Then how much, and what kind of penance do you think is necessary? That which equals the crimes, or, that which in fact, exceeds them?"[74] After comparing the sin with adultery, which he considers to be doubled by the secrecy of the crime, his answer is clear: "The magnitude of the penalty must be set in proportion to the quantity of the guilt."[75] Penance, he states, should be done not with words, but with deeds.[76] Once again, the death metaphor is applied to Susanna's condition. Penance is envisioned as death, and Niceta tells the girl to remind herself how her name has been erased from the Book of Life,[77] and how she will be handed over to infernal punishment and the fires of Gehenna, underlining that repentance is the only remedy that may free her from eternal damnation.[78] Susanna is told to "consider of yourself as if you were dead, as in a sense you are, and reflect upon how you may be restored to life."[79] The actual performance of this repentance is then thoroughly described. She is told to wear mourning dress and to punish her mind and every member of the body that deserves correction. She should also cut off her hair, constantly cry, wear her face pale, fast, and let her body be bent by fasting.

> Such a life, such a performance of penance, if you are perserverant, will dare to give you hope, if not of glory, perhaps of exemption from punishment. [...] Therefore, if a sinner does not spare herself, she will be spared by God. And if she will have made up for future eternal punishment in Gehenna in the short run of this life, she will free herself from eternal judgment.[80]

Turning slightly more hopeful, Niceta describes penance as combat, and Susanna is advised to cling to the penance like someone trying to stay alive by clinging to the remains of a shipwreck. If she maintains this penance until the very end of her life, Susanna may hope she can be freed from the eternal fire:

> Hold on to penance to the end of your life (*usque ad extremum vitae*) and do not presume to grant yourself any pardon in this life because anyone

who wants to promise you this is deceiving you. You who have sinned of your own will against the Lord, from him alone is it proper for you to wait for a relief on the day of judgment.[81]

Niceta then turns to the male lover of Susanna. This nameless "accomplice" is called a "son of the Serpent, minister of the Devil, violator of the temple of God."[82] His crime is described as twofold:

In one evil deed you committed two crimes, both adultery and sacrilege. And sacrilege it was when you with your insane rashness polluted the sacred vessel offered to Christ, dedicated to the Lord. [...] you who are ruined as much as you are a ruiner, you who impiously polluted the human vessel consecrated to Christ, sanctified by the Holy Spirit. You defiled her sacrilegiously, unmindful of your way of life, contemptuous of divine judgment. On the whole, it would have been better if you had not been born, but since you were born, that Gehenna should claim you for itself as its own son.[83]

That the crime is sacrilege is explained in terms of pollution of a person that had been dedicated to God. Adultery was, as already discussed, a crime that was considered serious enough on its own terms by early Christian standards, but this is, in Niceta's descriptions of the crime, somewhat overshadowed by it being sacrilege, an offense against God. The crime is seen as one committed against God's "property" and thus against God himself. Niceta admits that he cannot "deny medicine to a sick sheep much less to one dying,"[84] so some advice as to how Susanna's lover might still be saved for the afterlife is given with rather explicit descriptions of his penance.[85] At the end of the sermon, Niceta returns to Susanna, where he cites lamentations from the Psalms and places the words in the mouth of the repenting fallen virgin:

My sin and my iniquity are not like the offenses of other people, because they are sacrilege. When I promised that my flesh would serve as a virgin and I publicly professed chastity, I lied to the Lord. Now I have no confidence in invoking the Lord most high, because my mouth is blocked by transgressions.[86]

Sacrilege, as in *sacrilegium* and *impietas*, are in Niceta's sermon thus recurring terms used to describe the crime of both Susanna and her accomplice. The imagery of Susanna as a living dead, belonging neither among the dead nor among the living, recalls the language of Damasus' letter, where it was stated that the culprits were banned from entering the church "as if they were dead" (*tamquam mortui*). This kind of phrasing is not uncommon in writings on penitence. Jerome, for instance, writes in his letter to the lapsed deacon Sabinianus, among whose crimes was an attempted seduction of a consecrated virgin, that "what I lament is that you do not lament yourself, that you do not realize that you are dead, that like a gladiator ready for Libitina, you deck yourself out for your own funeral."[87] A little later, Jerome also quotes Ezekiel, stating that "the soul that sins shall die."[88] The specifically Christian soteriology, with its obsessive focus on sin and redemption, abounds with metaphors of death to describe the consequences of moral transgression. It is therefore necessary to further examine how this metaphor was expressed in the social context of the Christian community, and what was the effect of the spiritual sword on those against whom it was raised.

The spiritual sword and the living dead: punishment of unchaste Christian virgins

> Thus they are rejected and banished, those who do not want to be, but only want to seem to be virgins.[89]

Penance and excommunication were the most severe sanctions Church authorities could assign.[90] Niceta's description of how Susanna should repent thus appears to be in line with the canonical rulings. At the Synod of Elvira, held in Spain at the very beginning of the fourth century, a canon regarding those who had promised to remain virgins by dedication to God was recorded:

> It has been decided that virgins who dedicated themselves to God must not be given communion, not even at their death-bed, if they have broken their promise (*pactum*) of virginity, and have given in to their desire, not being aware of what they had committed. However, those women who have only once been persuaded and led astray through the fall of their weak body, if they repent all their lives by abstaining from sexual intercourse, so that the truly lost ones become through that all the more recognizable, they should be allowed to receive the communion at the end of their lives.[91]

The repentant sinner could thus, if the sin had happened only once and she demonstrated her regret by abstaining from sex for the rest of her life, receive communion and admission to the promised life in the hereafter. This seems to be in line with Niceta's prescribed penance for Susanna, where she is told she has to cling on to penance for the rest of her life if she wants to retain hope of salvation and eternal life.

Several versions of prescribed penance for lapsed virgins circulated in the fourth century, and the sanctions were clearly linked to interpretations of the gravity of the crime. Canons from various local and ecumenical councils, as well as later papal decretals, sought to regulate the conduct of consecrated virgins. To those formerly consecrated virgins who had married, there was no chance of salvation until the husband died or the "union was dissolved."[92] The language in these regulations is not necessarily lucid, and different opinions are certainly represented with regard to how lenient one could be in these cases. No matter how great the sin was, some believed, with reference to 1 Cor. 7:9, that a marriage was still better than adultery and fornication. According to most of the canonical rulings, however, an officially contracted marriage was held equal to a sexual relationship that had been secret, since both would count as adultery when one of the parties had already given promises as a bride of Christ.[93] According to this logic, adultery against a divine husband was an unparalleled crime that demanded severe repercussions.

Basil of Caesarea is perhaps the normative writer of this period who was most explicit as to the exact measuring of the punishment of fallen Christian virgins. According to him, penitence for lapsed virgins ought to be equal to that of adulterers, for whom he explicitly set the penitence to last for 15 years.[94] Thereby, Basil sought to replace the earlier rulings that had equalled virgins who married after their consecration with anyone who entered a second marriage, i.e. only one year of excommunication.[95] According to Basil, these former rulings were not only lenient but, as more virgins sought consecration, the more hazardous was the Church's position since the virgins could potentially retract their vow and consequently put the Church itself in a bad light. Restricting the regulations on penitance and excommunications was thereby an explicit means in order to cope with what, in Basil's rendering of the situation, seems to have become a problem that increased along with the growing number of virgins:

> A great sin indeed it is that even a handmaid giving herself over to secret marriage should fill the house with corruption, and through her evil life do an affront to her master; but it is far worse, of course, that the bride should become an adulteress and, dishonoring her union with the bridegroom, give herself over to licentious pleasures. Therefore, while the widow, as a corrupted handmaid, is condemned, the virgin lies under the charge of adultery.[96] Just as, therefore, we call him an adulterer who associates with the wife of another, not receiving him into the communion until he cease from the sin, so clearly shall we also decree in the case of him who keeps the virgin. [97]

A little further on, Basil shows himself more lenient towards lapsed virgins who professed their virginity when they were heretics, stating that they, if they had married, were allowed to continue to live as married and not be forced to break up their marital union. As a rule, Basil here declares that "in general such things as are committed in the catechumenical state are not called into account."[98]

Two of the next three popes that were to succeed Damasus also issued decretals that concerned lapsed consecrated virgins. Yves-Marie Duval has pointed out the similarities between these and Damasus' letter to the bishops of Gaul.[99] Siricius' letter to Bishop Himerius of Tarragona is dated 385. Like Symmachus' letters, this one obviously refers to a specific case, in which several monks and nuns had had "illicit and sacrilegious intercourse [...] under the cover of the monasteries" and had even "freely produced children with illicit partners." According to the Pope's ruling, these men and women were to be banished from the monasteries and from the Church and, after a life of repentance, it was only at death that they could receive "the grace of communion."[100] In 404, Innocent I sent a letter to Victricius of Rouen, giving general advice regarding Church discipline. Among this advice were some passages that concerned girls who had abandoned their sacred marriage for a secular husband. Like his predecessor Damasus, Innocent distinguishes between those who have spiritually married Christ and been veiled by the bishop, and those who "have not yet been covered by the sacred veil, but have promised to hold on to their virginal vow."[101] However, it is clear from the letter that they are both to be severely punished, the first because she broke her marriage contract with the immortal bridegroom in favor of human nuptials, the second because "she broke her first pledge of promise." In both cases, the crime is described in terms of adultery, either as public marriage or as "corruption in secret." Innocent refers to canonical laws for bigamists according to which the woman "is not allowed to do penitence unless one of them [i.e. the husband] dies." This then applies for the fallen veiled virgins, who are consequently not encouraged to dissolve their secular marriage. Instead, she seems to be excommunicated until the death of her husband, a severe punishment indeed if one, for instance, considers the possibility that she might die before him. The girl who had given her promise but had not yet been veiled is said to "do penance for a considerable amount of time" (*agendae aliquanto tempore paenitentia est*).[102] We see then that Damasus in *Ad Gallos episcopos* apparently had set some standards as to how the Church authorities ought to handle the delicate and troublesome issue of lapsed virgins.

The difference between canon 19 of Ancyra, which prescribed a year of penance, and that of Elvira, which only reluctantly would readmit the lapsed virgin after a lifetime of penance, demonstrates two extreme positions.[103] The later regulations of Damasus and Basil could thus reflect both the development of a growing "order" of sacred virgins and a continuation of concerns that seem to have been more culturally and geographically specific within the divide very generally drawn between the Greek and the Latin parts of the empire. Basil of Caesarea and the council of Ancyra use sexual crimes as the analogy to describe the crime and establish the punishment, while the more juridical approach found in the wording of Damasus and the council of Elvira appears to focus on the broken promise as the main offense. Gaudemet argues that there was a change in focus after Augustine, when it became the failure of keeping a vow and not adultery, based on the analogy with the virgin as *sponsa Christi*, that justified excommunication in the canonical rulings.[104] It appears, however, that the focus on the promise to God in the Latin sources preceded Augustine, and that there were geographical (and perhaps cultural) differences that also ought to be accounted for. What underlies all these regulations, however, is that the crime, which indeed was believed to affect the individual virgin as well as her family and community, first and foremost was seen as a crime committed against her divine husband/bridegroom and, as such, a crime against God. The language that is used in the Latin sources also indicates that sacrilege and pollution appear more frequently in the West than what perhaps was the norm in the writings of Eastern theologians on lapsed consecrated virgins, where it seems the closest analogy to this religious crime appears to have been bigamy and adultery rather than sacrilege.

Whether willing or raped

That the Christian virgin's own will and personal intent were seen as fundamental in her resolve to remain a virgin should be clear by now. Damasus' decretal indicates that will and intent might indeed play a role in how a potential loss of virginity should be judged, but his assessment of penance gives the impression that this eventually is of minor importance once a virgin has lapsed. The background for this somewhat surprising outcome is to be sought in contemporary secular as well as canonical law, but an example from Niceta's sermon addressed to Susanna can illustrate how this distinction between a girl who has willingly been seduced and one who has been the victim of rape would be of major importance:

> But you say: 'I did not will this evil; I suffered violence.' That most brave Susanna, whose name you falsely wear, will answer you: 'Placed between two elders, there between two judges of the people, set alone between the trees of the garden [Dan. 13:20ff.], I could not be conquered; because I did not will to be.' Could you not have shown some resistance against an inexperienced adolescent, there in the middle of the city, if you had not already wished to be corrupted? Then who heard your cries? Who observed your struggle?[105]

Like Damasus, the author of the sermon on the fall of Susanna refers to the passages in the Old Testament, advising how the potential innocence or compliance of a seduced girl ought to be determined.[106] The fact that Susanna had not revealed what had happened to anyone is taken as further evidence that she had willingly entered into a relationship with her lover. The burden of proof, then, is on the virgin herself.

The impact of the virgin's own collaboration in the act is thus considered both in the letter of Damasus and in Niceta's sermon. The rulings of Damasus regarding fallen virgins echo secular legislation that went back to Constantine. A law from 326 makes a similar distinction between a girl who was seized by a raptor unwillingly or led away willingly. According to Judith Evans Grubbs, this law did not concern rape but abduction marriage, a quite common and institutionalized practice that Constantine saw a need to restrict. She points out that in this law, "all variations of the bride theft scenario are condemned equally,"[107] and "a girl who actively consented was to suffer the same penalty as her abductor."[108] Evans Grubbs thus sees the most common legal application of the term *raptus* to be in the sense of "abduction," while what we today call rape was referred to as sexual violation by the verb *violare* and prosecuted as *stuprum per vim*.[109] There are of course blurred lines here. For instance, we may assume that an abduction would involve *stuprum* (illicit sex, considered so in this case because the couple is not (yet) officially married), and the *raptus* itself was often staged as a violent event. According to Evans Grubbs' analysis of this type of marriage, the girl's consent to the abduction was almost always assumed, and her "unwillingness" was only part of the mandatory performance. Constantius issued a law in 354 that specified punishment for men who abducted virgins or widows consecrated to God and insisted that the woman was to receive the same punishment as the male part of the couple if they later agree to marry.[110] A similar law issued by Jovian in 364 stated that not only should a man who raped/abducted a consecrated virgin or widow be punished by capital punishment, but the same punishment would also apply for anyone who proposed marriage to such a woman.[111]

According to Sozomen, these laws of Jovian were a reaction to the lawless sacrileges committed under the reign of the Emperor Julian, called the Apostate. Jovian therefore

> restored to the churches and the clergy, to the widows and the virgins, the same immunities and every former dotation for the advantage and honor of religion, which had been granted by Constantine and his sons, and afterwards withdrawn by Julian. He commanded Secundus, who was then a praetorian prefect, to constitute it a capital crime to marry any of the holy virgins, or even to regard them with unchaste desires and to carry them off. He enacted this law on account of the wickedness which had prevailed during the reign of Julian; for many had taken wives from among the holy virgins, and, either by force or guile, had completely corrupted them; and thence had proceeded that indulgence of disgraceful lusts with impunity, which always occur when religion is abused.[112]

With Evans Grubbs, we may assume then that such laws were meant to hinder virgins who regretted plotting such abductions (i.e., the *volentes*) to escape their vow. But if consent to marry her abductor was taken as a sign that the virgin had been willing, what other options did she have? If indeed she was abducted without her consent, or raped, was it possible for her to not marry, but to continue to live with her sacred status? Or was that status damaged beyond repair regardless of her being *volens* or *rapta*?

The doubt about a girl's true resentment and unwillingness towards her raptor obviously underlies the legal reasoning in both secular and canonical law, and it also obviously spills over to rape, or violation *per vim* (by force), so that the distinction between willingness and unwillingness was ultimately dissolved and became insignificant, just like Damasus' decretal demonstrates.

As Maud Burnett McInerney shows, the issues regarding rape of consecrated virgins became pressingly urgent when Alaric and his men, breaking through the city walls that had been unpenetrated by the enemy for more than 700 years, sacked Rome in 410:

> That Barbarians should have attacked Christian virgins and not been blasted by thunderbolts, that virgins should be sexually humiliated and left alive, bereft of what was to most people their defining characteristic of physical integrity, was enough to shake the faith of all but the most pious.[113]

McInerney demonstrates how Augustine in the *De Civitate Dei* tries to grapple with these theological challenges. His attempt to comfort those consecrated virgins who were no longer virgins left a bitter aftertaste, as he locates the holiness in the will, thus: "no matter what anyone else does with the body or in the body that the person has no power to avoid without sin on his own part, no blame attaches to the one who suffers it."[114] But then, according to Augustine, not only pain but also lust can be inflicted by force, and this is where also the virginity of the mind is demolished, as "shame is thrust in, shame for fear that the mind too may be thought to have consented to an act that could perhaps not have taken place without some carnal pleasure."[115] Although Augustine apparently agrees with Basil, who in 375 had stated that "Let women who have been corrupted by force stand guiltless. Thus even a slave, if she has been violated by her own master, is guiltless."[116] Augustine's lengthy discussion still reveals that, when it comes to lust, the will is feeble. As demonstrated by McInerney, "The possibility of having, at some level, consented to rape is always present in Augustine's discussion [...]."[117]

The question of whether sacred virgins would keep their sanctity when virginity was unwilfully lost appears to have been continuously discussed into the Middle Ages. About 25 years after Augustine finished his *De civitate Dei*, Pope Leo wrote to all the bishops of Mauritania Caesariensis in Africa concerning the handmaids of God who "had lost the integrity of chastity" by the violence of barbarians. According to Leo, if they refrain from daring to compare themselves with undefiled virgins, they will be all the more praiseworthy in humility and shame. The Bishop of Rome underlines that "although every sin springs from desire, and the will may have remained unconquered and unpolluted by the fall of the flesh, still this will be less to their detriment, if they grieve over losing even in the body what they did not lose in the spirit."[118] Just a few passages further, Leo returns to the same issue, specifying that these virgins who had been consecrated by a vow but then raped by barbarians and thus "lost their integrity of chastity, not in spirit but in body" should neither be

> degraded to the rank of widows, nor be counted among the number of holy and steadily persevering virgins: but, if they persevere in the virginal

mode of life, and in their mind guard the solidity of chastity, they shall not be denied participation in the sacraments. Because it is unfair that they should be accused or branded for what their wishes did not surrender, but was stolen by the violence of foes.[119]

Although the Latin Fathers and, perhaps most vehemently, Augustine himself, insisted that true virginity was located in the mind and will, and was not a physical asset, there were obvious limitations to such attempts to redefine virginity. In the end, true virginity, and particularly the sacred kind, was not fixed, as it was at the same time, both bodily and non-bodily, dependent on behavior and will as well as character and virtue.

Consequences of the crime

Both Damasus and Symmachus state the need to punish the crimes, yet the reason for such harsh methods seems to them to be evident and in no need of elaboration. The severity of the punishment and the language describing the crime indicate that the fallen virgin in question had not just harmed herself and, in the case of the Christian virgin, the prospect of her own salvation. In many respects, the consequences of the crime represent a reversal of all the positive sides of the "virgin effect" discussed above and, as such, the imagined outcome highlights the value assigned to virginity. Since the virgin's virginity was believed to work on behalf of the virgin's family, and even of the whole community, such a grave trespassing of her religious commitment would also cause great pain and grief for others than herself.[120] Niceta, supported by biblical authority, lays out the scenario depicting the devastating consequences of Susanna's crime:

> If the one who scandalized a single person ought to have a millstone hung aroung the neck and be thrown into the sea, what should I say about you, by whose transgression every soul is wounded and the name of the Lord blasphemed among unbelievers?[121]

More specifically, Niceta points at how Susanna's behavior will reflect badly on the Church as a whole by giving heretics and pagans reasons for damaging polemical attacks: "Paganism has opened its mouth among us: because of your dishonor, the Synagogue of the Jews has boasted against the holy Church."[122] The very same argument is found in Basil's letter to a fallen monk, where he states that "you have disgraced the promise of chastity; we have been made a tragedy of captives, and our story is made a play before Jews and Greeks."[123] Likewise, Basil had said that it was necessary to dissolve any marriage-like union of so-called canonical persons because such procedures would be "both advantageous for the safety of the Church, and will not give the heretics an opportunity to attack us on the ground that we have won men to ourselves by granting them license to sin."[124]

The embarrassment and exposed position Susanna has brought upon the Church *vis-à-vis* its potential opponents are not, however, Niceta's prime objection. He had already, at the opening of the sermon, stated that:

> She ruined herself and stained the Church. Because of her crime, the entire soul of Christianity suffers a severe wound (*grave vulnus*), because what was holy is given to the dogs and pearls were cast before swine ....[125]

Her crime thus seems to go beyond that of making the Church vulnerable to heretical and pagan attacks, as Niceta claims that "this is why there is an incurable sorrow, because no evil deed drags so much good away with it. The little cloud of one sinful woman obscures almost the entire light of the Church."[126] Niceta further portrays Susanna as:

> transformed from a virgin of God to a spoil of Satan, from the bride of Christ to a repulsive prostitute, from a dwelling place of the Holy Spirit to a shack of the devil, from the temple of God to a sanctuary of slime.[127]

Her fall is also depicted as a transformation from a dove to a lizard, from shining gold to dirt in the streets, from a star in God's hand into dead coals. The consequences, as they are laid out in this text, balance between the ruined prospects for the virgin's own personal salvation and her responsibilty on behalf of her family and the Christian community at large.

As several scholars have pointed out, the Christian virgins became a potent metaphor for the inviolability of the Church, both through the hagiographies of menaced virgin martyrs and by the presence of the consecrated virgins in the congregation and at the Christian rituals and celebrations.[128] Consecrated virgins' loss of virginity thus did not merely put the Church to shame in front of her mocking opponents. Just like *virgines intactae* signaled the eternity and integrity of the Church, *virgines incestae* would be signs of corruption and destruction. The potency of the symbol thus eventually depended upon its very fragility, as the very strength lay in the perpetuation of what was apparently so easily destroyed.

With this in mind, it is interesting to consider the Vestal virgins' virginity. Since traditional conceptions of a life after death in ancient Rome differed so much from that of the Christians, the individual Vestal's personal benefits from a preserved virginity were possibly believed to be rewarded first and foremost in this life on earth. The idea that virgins possessed religious "functions" that could serve the community at large, as was occasionally attributed to Christian virgins as discussed above, is brought even more sharply into relief when we consider the imagined consequences a lapsed Vestal could bring upon the city of Rome. The very meticulous performance of the peculiar ceremony that led to live interment of a *vestale incesta* is, according to Plutarch, an indication of the anxiety the crime would arouse in Rome and of the gravity of her crime.[129] Although theories describing the Vestals as a "depot" of virgins to be sacrificed in arduous times[130] in my opinion go too far in theorizing the material and the "scapegoat hypothesis," it is evident that the Vestals' virginity was considered a prerequisite for their service, which the state, and its safety in turn, depended upon. Tim Cornell and Augusto Fraschetti have convincingly illustrated that crisis and a high level of anxiety dominated the republican periods in which Vestals were convicted and buried alive according to the *mos maiorum*.[131] Likewise, periods of victory, prosperity and peace were related to exemplary behavior of the Vestals. This is well illustrated in Pliny's record of the *Virgo Vestalis Maxima* Cornelia's plea for justice, when she is said to have repeated, "How can Caesar believe me to be *incesta*, he who won and triumphed while I was tending the sacred rites?"[132] In Pliny's version, the well-being of the state is one of Cornelia's best evidences of innocence.[133] Ovid's statement that no Vestal will be buried under the rule of Augustus appears close to fawning when the chastity of the Vestals in this context becomes a testimony to the well-being and prosperity of the state brought by the ruler.[134] As such, *incestum* among the Vestals would signal a reversal of the beneficial "virgin effects," as we get an idea of the prosperity of the state that is upheld when Vestals are chaste. The republican episodes (as well as the case of Primigenia, possibly) may conversely illustrate the grave consequences imagined for the entire society when Vestals were guilty of *incestum*. However, the close link between prosperity in times of chaste Vestals and bad fortunes in times of *incestum* does occasionally appear to blur the ideas of cause and effect in some attempts to understand the different aspects of this crime. Would, for instance, impending crisis be an indication of *vestales incestae*? Or, as Pliny's Cornelia claimed, could the emperor's prosperity have ruled out the possibility of her guilt? This kind of circular argumentation, indeed taken up by some scholars, is not necessarily favored in the ancient sources, where the *incestum* of Vestals, as we will see, could and would be revealed by several and sometimes very different means and methods.

In terms of the dangerous pollution these fallen virgins represented and the subsequent harm they inflicted upon society, the sources depict the lapsed virgins as "dead." This status as "socially dead" is both conveyed in words and symbolically. For the Vestals, this social death leads to inescapable physical death but, for the Christian virgins, there is a possibility of "resurrection" and forgiveness through "the performance of penance." Their sacred status, however, can never be regained.

By approaching the sacred virgins of Late Antiquity as metonyms of a socio-religious community, and understanding their virginity as symbolizing the stability, unviolability and (eternal) continuity of this community, we also understand why so much was thought to be at stake when this virginity was no longer there.

Negotiating death: death as metaphor and death as reality

One of the most poignant juridical differences between pagans and Christians is often said to be the Christians' moral opinion upon mercy and capital punishment. Damasus stated that the laws of Moses were no longer valid, and the old punishment of death described therein was therefore to be inflicted spiritually, by denying the culprits entry to the church. There would no longer be a death penalty, but some kind of penalty was still needed. That excommunication often was presented as "spiritualization of the Law," was thus a motif that carried the meaning of death on in a highly symbolic way.[135]

For Christians, excommunication was, in this respect, not only equal to death or exile, but eventually a punishment that could extend beyond this earthly life. Despite the ruling of Nicaea that granted everyone communion at the deathbed, and thus access to eternal life,[136] there was still the constant danger of sudden death for those who were excommunicated. It might also be difficult to obtain a bishop to grant the last communion when needed. Such practical concerns resulted in further expansions of the Canon laws, and illustrate the gravity of punishments that could eventually prevent the salvation of an individual.

Although excommunication was a punishment that, unlike the punishment of the Vestal virgins, did not lead to the culprit's imminent death, we have seen that the texts of Niceta and his contemporaries abound with imagery of death. Reminiscent of Fraschetti's description of the desecrated and polluting Vestal who incurs danger upon the society as a whole, the former Christian virgin is depicted as socially dead and physically relegated to the outside of the Church, to the very margins where the penitents have to make themselves worthy of return to the lifegiving society. There seems to be an underlying danger that the fallen virgin's crime could pollute the Christian community, and so she had to be purified by penitence outside the gates of the Church, for some until the very end of their lives. Unlike the Vestals, the Christian virgins actually had a chance to "resurrect" from this temporary state of "social death," and to re-enter the Church and receive the life-giving communion. If they failed, however, it seems their punishment, in light of Christian soteriology, on the level of the individual was perhaps understood to indeed be even more grave. In the case of the Vestals, the pollution caused by the crime was beyond purification, at least on an individual level.[137]

VIRGINITATEM APPROBARE

Fake virgins and feigned virginity

> Rejoice sister; rejoice daughter; rejoice virgin: because you have truly begun to be what others imitate.[138]

Canons and laws quoted above seem to presuppose that it was obvious, or at least easily established, whether a girl was a virgin or not. Several other kinds of sources, however, indicate that this was not necessarily so. Considering that women, almost by definition, were often represented as sly and deceitful, how could one actually be certain – and that means absolutely certain – that the woman or girl in question really was a virgin? And by which standards? The tale of how Venus seduced Anchises, where the goddess, whose fame was linked to her amorous liaisons and by no means virginal behavior, feigned virginity in order to cunningly lure the young man into bed, could certainly work to alert men to the deceitful forms in which virginity could appear.[139] Because, if Venus herself could manage to pass as a virgin, a man could never be completely certain, could he? The uncertainty that is played with in such representations of Venus illustrate some of the epistemological challenges that the so-called *pseudoparthenoi*, the fake virgins, brought to the surface.[140] Because what were the "proofs" one could look for? As already discussed above, virgins, whether sacred or secular, appear to have displayed some kind of visible signs of their virgin status. This section will further explore these visible *insignia*, and the more deceitful forms the look of virginity was believed to take. Could the signs of virginity be trusted?

This is one of the problems that were adressed by Tertullian in his treatise *De virginibus velandis*. The virgins who refused to wear a veil, as their married female parishioners did, represented, according to Tertullian, a problem for many reasons. This manner in which they signalled their exceptional status, with their head uncovered, broke with gender conventions in a culture where it was expected that girls veiled themselves from the time they got married (which more or less coincided with the age at which they became sexually mature). Tertullian's text offers several interpretational difficulties in these passages,[141] but he at least makes it clear that the honor and charity that the community bestows upon the Christian virgins make it tempting for these girls to continue to appear as virgins even though they may no longer be so:

> If an uncovered head is a recognized mark of virginity, (then) if any virgin falls from the grace of virginity, she remains permanently with her head uncovered for fear of discovery, and walks about in a garb which then indeed is another's.[142]

Almost two centuries later, Jerome described pretend virgins at length in his letter to Eustochium, presenting them in this way:

> Their robes have but a narrow purple stripe, it is true; and their head-dress is somewhat loose, so as to leave the hair free. From their shoulders flutters the lilac mantle which they call "ma-forte;" they have their feet in cheap slippers and their arms tucked up [in] tight-fitting sleeves. Add to these marks of their profession an easy gait, and you have all the virginity they possess. Such may have eulogizers of their own, and may fetch a higher price at the market of perdition, merely because they are called virgins (*sub virginale nomine*). But to such virgins as these I prefer to be displeasing.[143]

Jerome remarks on how these so-called virgins may convince and deceive many as they pass under the "virginal name" (*sub virginale nomine*).[144]

Likewise, a few paragraphs later, he turns to those who do not want to be virgins, but only to appear as such.[145] Both Tertullian and Jerome give the impression of a highly esteemed status that attracted many impostors, and a trained eye was necessary in order to spot the frauds from the real and true virgins.

Jerome returns to the issue towards the end of the letter to Eustochium, when he writes that:

> it is because they know that the name [title] virgin brings glory with it, that they go about as wolves in sheep's clothing. As Antichrist pretends to be Christ, such virgins assume an honorable name, that they may better cloak a discreditable life.[146]

Also in Niceta's sermon to the lapsed Susanna, Susanna is described as an imposter, pretending to be what she was not. "She may be dressed like a virgin, but she has not acted like one. She is an adulteress twice over, both in deed and in appearance."[147]

Reminded of the false virgins depicted by the Fathers of the Church in their polemical writings on the Vestals, we return again to the crucial, but seemingly unsolvable, question of how to determine a true virgin. Unlike men as well as unlike other "true" female virgins who received praise for "imitating the exemplary virginity of exemplary virgins," the Christian virgin-imitators that Tertullian, Niceta and Jerome disapprove of are those that somehow do not live up to the virginal standards of the Church. The criteria by which these women failed to qualify as virgins are, however, not necessarily the same in these texts, and may be somewhat difficult to grasp in the midst of the rhetorical niceties flaunted by these writers. This again testifies to the different conceptions of virginity, or perhaps rather aspects of virginity, that these Church Fathers deemed as indispensable. To all three, the most evident breach of terms is nevertheless the lack of physical virginity. However, if these women are not revealed by swollen bellies or crying babies, they may never be known, and can "walk abroad with tripping feet and heads in the air."[148] A trained eye should still be able to identify them by their conduct, appearance and company. On the other hand, there are the flirtatious and vain virgins, who entertain inappropriate company, often to be confused with heretical virgins, who are mainly said to be false because of their false doctrines. The so-called *subintroductae*, or *agapetae*, are presented as false virgins, since the fact that they live with men obviously renders their proclaimed virginity untrustworthy.[149] These kinds of false virgins, however, often merge in the writings of the leading men of the Church, so that a heretical virgin, although she may physically be said to be a virgin, by no means can ever be a true virgin, as her mind clearly is polluted and "devirginized." At the same time, the mere fact that she is heretical indicated that she most certainly cannot be a real virgin in the physical sense either, as her depraved doctrine marks her conduct and her body. This kind of circular argument in the case of false virgins is the same as those we encounter in contemporary representations of Vestal virgins in Christian texts.[150]

The virginity of the mind and the virginity of the body – although in theory separable, with the former considered the most important – are interdependent, so that when one is lost, the other will not only be worthless, but also lost.

Locating virginity

Considering that morality and "spiritual" virginity has been claimed as a mark of true, Christian virginity, it might be useful to look at material highlighting the negotiations regarding Vestal virginity, and how the borders of virginity, sacred and secular, can shed light upon the difficulties the Church Fathers met when they needed to distinguish virgins from non-virgins.

The rhetorical exercises for students and schoolboys known as *Controversiae*, collected and published by Seneca the Elder, render pros and cons to imaginary legal cases, some of which are very creatively constructed. Although they are all fictitious, they may still give some idea concerning Roman logic and rhetorical ideals. As Mary Beard has convincingly argued, these texts are valuable sources for understanding the ongoing cultural concern for the virginity of the Vestal virgins.[151] Cases particularly negotiating the limits of virginity in relation to virginity as requirement for religious office are found in the so-called "prostitute priestess" and the *incesta de saxo*, "the *incesta* thrown from the rock," as well as the case, preserved only as a summary, regarding the Vestal who wrote a verse about the happiness of married women.

The story of the virgin in the brothel who "miraculously" escapes with her virginity intact, is, as we have seen, a theme that recurs in Hellenistic novels as well as in later *passiones* of virgin saints.[152] The brief story that introduces this particular declamation tells of how a virgin was captured by pirates and sold to a brothel. There, she managed to persuade her customers to let her remain a virgin, until she finally killed a man who would not agree on her terms and assaulted her. She then seeks a priesthood, and the discussion considers whether she is fit or not for such a sacred office.[153]

Among the arguments against her case are skepticism of her proclaimed virginity and chastity, as presented by the first speaker, Porcius Latro, who has her claim that "nobody took away my virginity." He goes on, arguing that "but everyone came intending to take it away, everyone went as though they had succeeded."[154] The next speaker, Fulvius Sparsus, then says that "we should not ask, and cannot know, what you did behind closed doors."[155]

Language of pollution and contamination from the pirates and the brothel, also from what she might merely have seen among the people of these places,[156] as well as pollution from the murder she committed, prevail in the declamations against her potential election as a priestess.[157] Cestius Pius concludes that although she claims nothing happened to her, and this might be satisfactory for someone who is to be married, it is not enough for a priestess,[158] who is obviously to be held to a different standard.

In the division, the question regarding whether she was chaste (*an casta sit*) is broken down to whether chastity is "to be judged merely by virginity, or by abstinence from all shameful and obscene things."[159] If she is indeed a virgin, she has still received kisses and "rolled about" with men,[160] but this argument is left more or less aside by the disclaimer in order to discuss the most crucial issue: Is she, or is she not a virgin?[161]

> [Latro] said that the followers of Apollodorus liked fixed themes that cannot be tampered with; but here the terms of the *controversia* did not clash with such a suspicion. It is not stated that she is still a virgin, and there are many reasons to make it credible that she is not. He added: "Finally, even if I do not persuade the judges she is no virgin, I shall ensure that they regard as unworthy of a priesthood one whose virginity is in doubt."[162]

Mere doubt about her virginal status, then, is enough to make her unfit for the office. On the other hand, for those defending her case, it is exactly the miraculous preservation of virginity against all odds that proves her to be chosen by the gods and fit for the priesthood. According to this line of reasoning, the gods must certainly have intervened in order to save this virgin and "not to violate, but to put on display the chastity of one destined to be a priestess."[163] Cestius states that "in the midst of so many dangers, the gods would not have saved her unless it was for themselves,"[164] and Pompeius Silo claims that, because of her incredible preservation of chastity through so many dangers, he "will guarantee you that she is a priestess who no Fortuna can make *incesta*."[165]

> You may say that all came to her as to a prostitute – so long as you say that they went away as from a priestess.[166]

The importance of divine interference is even more explicit in the following *controversia* titled *Incesta de saxo*. The brief introductory story that is the basis for the declamation is this: "A woman condemned for *incestum* evoked Vesta before she was to be thrown down from the rock. She was thrown down and survived. She is sought to pay the penalty again."[167] The following arguments explore whether she should go through the execution all over again, having survived her first punishment, or whether the fact that she survived lets her go free, whether she actually was saved by the gods for a particular reason or by haphazard and pure luck. The *controversia* alludes to the well-known stories of Tuccia and Aemelia, who were freed from charges because of divine intervention but, in this case, as the rhetorician states, the priestess appealed to the gods too late. Most of the speakers' arguments seem to rest upon the assumption that she was guilty, since she had already been convicted by a trial (perhaps by having pleaded guilty). The logic of the argument is thus that if she had been innocent, the gods would have intervened and saved her before she had become a condemned woman, and the fact that she survived is at most a dubious sign of her still being a virgin.[168] Another problem, throwing some light on the crime of *incestum*, is revealed in the claim that if she now was to return to her sacred duties, she would nevertheless pollute the rites because she had been polluted herself – if not from a sexual offense, then as *incesta* from the touch of the carnifex.[169] Pollution, as we have seen, is thus again at the crux of *incestum*, and it is the kind of pollution that offends and angers the gods that is at stake.

The third of Seneca's *controversiae* regarding Vestals and virgin priestesses is only preserved in an abbreviated version. It is titled "The Vestal's verse," and the introductory narrative goes as follows: "A Vestal virgin wrote this verse: 'How lucky married women are! Should I die if it is not sweet to marry.' She is accused of *incestum*."[170] Interestingly, the summary of points from the adversary side concludes that "she is *incesta* if she desires fornication, even if she has not had it."[171] Her defenders, on the other hand, claim that "no one can be convicted for *incestum* unless her body has been violated."[172] Her conduct and dress are also taken into consideration as evidence to her benefit: "She lived modestly and strictly; she wore no finery that was too luxurious, had no licentious conversations with men."[173] The notion that virginity is visually detectable through the virgin's conduct and her dress becomes an important point in later texts regarding Christian consecrated virgins, but it is evident that, despite the images of luxury and licentiousness reflected in the dress of the Vestals as described by the Church Fathers, Romans were likewise preoccupied with the dress of their sacred virgins and what it revealed about their true morality.[174]

Even more interesting is that for those arguing against her, the loss of virginity is located in the will or intent. It is reminiscent of Augustine's much later example of a virgin who is on the way to her lover with her mind set on seducing him. According to Augustine, it is not the bodily experience that changes her status from virgin to non-virgin, because she can no longer be said to be a virgin from the moment her mind is made up.[175] The very same point had been made by Jerome, who claimed that "a virgin is defined as one who is holy in body and in spirit, for it is of no good to have virgin flesh if she is married in her mind."[176]

The rhetorical dodges of Seneca's lawyers reflect the slippery flexity even in a seemingly either/or question of a girl's status as virgin. What emerges from these *controversiae* is the notion of some kind of degrees of virginity, in the main based on moral assessments with reference to what is physically detectable. Sacred virgins are clearly to be held to the highest standard, and be above any suspicion. Thus, virginity may not only be lost by intercourse and penetration, whether willingly or not. It is also severely imperilled, and probably even lost, by the company of the people in which the virgin has been, what she has seen, heard,[177] and experienced, whether it was indecent physical, yet not penetrative, sexual contact or indecent thoughts and desires. Likewise, it appears that close contact with death, either through murder or an executioner, was seen as another polluting factor that could make a priestess unfit for office.[178]

However, references to such activities were to be carefully phrased in court. That obscene and indecent language ought to be avoided by lawyers is indicated by Seneca, who mentions some arguments in passing towards the end of his treatment of the prostitute priestess, arguments he deems to be too obscene to be proposed in such a case, even if leaving them out means losing the case. These to some extent euphemistic (and certainly intended to make the audience laugh) "obscenities" illustrate once again how virginity was understood to possibly be negotiated and compromised, yet still be "virginity." The rhetor Murredius, for instance, was, according to Seneca, supposed to have said, "How do we know that she did not bargain with her visitors [in the brothel] to keep her virginity at the expense of some other kind of lust?"[179] and also, "Perhaps while she repelled his lust, she took it in her hands."[180] With an ironical twist, Seneca lists these and other examples, concluding that "some words are better left unspoken, even if it costs you the case, rather than spoken at the cost of your shame."[181] By focusing on what must be "unspoken" in this case, Seneca thus brings attention to the fact that the final answer regarding the priestesses' virginity will ultimately be left in the dark, beyond what suitable language, at least for a law court, may grasp.

Tangible evidence?

It is difficult to determine why manual "inspections" to verify the status of virgins are not mentioned in our non-Christian sources; whether it was because they were unknown by the Romans before the third century, or whether decency and religious respect simply made such physical inspections completely unthought of (or at least unspeakable). As is the case of the "historical" sources referring to trials against Vestals charged with *incestum*, there are no indications of a physical examination of the priestess whose virginity was questioned. The sources all indicate that the question of her guilt was settled by juridical processes, under supervision of the pontifical college and the pontifex maximus, where witnesses and confession, along with *prodigia* and other "evidence," were considered before the judgment was passed.[182]

Moving from Seneca's world of fictitious and imaginative court cases to one that has a better claim for historical accuracy, we return to Ambrose and his concern for consecrated virgins. The same kind of delicacy and rhetorical finesse that is urged by Seneca is used by Ambrose in his defense of the virgin Indicia, who was accused and brought before his contemporary colleague, Bishop Syragius.[183] Although only occasionally more explicit (yet by no means by obscene language), two letters of Ambrose shed additional light upon some of the many problems implied in establishing "the truth" when a virgin was accused of non-virginal activities.

Like so many of his peers, Ambrose concedes that pregnancy would be the most obvious sign of a lapsed virgin. "The belly swells, the burden of the fetus makes the person's gait heavy."[184] The Church Fathers were indeed not negligent of the possibility that a girl might conceal her pregnancy, particularly regarding those Christian virgins who lived secluded and with minimal contact with the outside world.[185] Ambrose also admits that some may cover up their crime by (self-obtained) sterility, but he does not explore this probability much further, as he concludes that when a child has been born, whether it is disposed of or killed afterwards, "freedom from calumny is absolutely impossible."[186] Knowledge of contraception and abortion was rather well dispersed in Antiquity,[187] and the Christian Church Fathers were obviously aware of this factor that might complicate their search for evidence and proof of virginity lost. This was, however, not relevant in the case of Indicia, where the accusations included giving birth to a child that she disposed of afterwards. Ambrose's argument thus concentrates on the impossibility of such a scenario. He maintains that Indicia lived in Verona and was frequently visited by virgins and women as well as priests, who would all have detected such a crime even if she had tried to conceal it. And if this is not enough evidence, the cries of pain from labor, he points out, would at least have given her away had she really given birth to a child.[188] In fact, Ambrose's warning against letting the midwives constantly visit the house of virgins points at the suspicion such visits might arouse in the neighborhood, since they would inspire rumors of birth and pain relief rather than confirmation of chastity.[189] His main objection to the use of midwives, however, is the fact that an inspection of the virgin's private parts would be a severe insult to virginal modesty. That poor midwives were prone to bribery and were, as such, untrustworthy, was one thing, but, as Ambrose states, even "medical experts say that the untrustworthiness of an inspection is not clearly understood, and this has been the opinion of older doctors of medicine."[190] According to Ambrose, also midwives disagreed and questioned the reliability of such examinations, and the result, in Ambrose's opinion, is thus "that there is more doubt about the one who has given herself to an inspection than of the one who has not."[191]

The use of midwives to ascertain virginity was clearly widespread, although problematic, according to the Church Fathers. Less negative than in his letter to Syragius, Ambrose had alluded to the practice some years earlier in *De viduis* from 377:

> For a virgin, though in her also character rather than the body has the first claim, puts away calumny by the integrity of her body. A widow, who has lost the assistance of being able to prove her virginity, undergoes the inquiry as to her chastity not according to the word of a midwife, but according to her own manner of life.[192]

Here, the chastity of a widow is only proven by her conduct and manner of life, while the virgin, it appears, is able to bring forth firmer evidence, attested by a midwife. Such inspections by midwives were referred to already by Cyprian in the second century as a method for attesting virginity. Like Ambrose and Augustine after him, Cyprian had also argued that such manual examinations were not to be trusted:

> Nor let anyone think that she can be defended by this excuse, that she may be examined and proved whether she be a virgin; since both the hands and

the eyes of the midwives are often deceived; and if she is found to be a virgin in that particular way in which a woman may be so, she may yet have sinned in some other part of her body, which can be corrupted although not be examined.[193]

A few passages later, however, Cyprian nevertheless demands that virgins, who have lived with men but now repented, are to be carefully inspected by midwives; and only if they still are found to be virgins are they to be readmitted to communion:

> But if they have repented of this their unlawful lying together, and have mutually withdrawn from one another, let the virgins meantime be carefully inspected by midwives; and if they should be found virgins, let them be received to communion, and admitted to the Church.[194]

Augustine, in his eagerness to demonstrate that true virginity is located in the mind and in the will, rendered an example where a clumsy midwife had destroyed the very thing she was meant to confirm and preserve.[195] Clumsiness, ignorance, medical uncertainty and the likelihood of midwives being bribed and thus not trustworthy are all factors that Ambrose considers in his defense of the accused Indicia. He fears that all brides as well as virgins about to take the sacred veil will have to be physically inspected. Still, like Cyprian, Ambrose concedes the need for bodily inspections by midwives, since many people only act rightly because they fear punishment, not because they love chastity:

> Let them then be present for inspection when they are maintaining custody of their body, provided this can be detected in those in whom the charm of modesty and training in chastity is faltering. The case is going badly when the body has to be consulted for stronger proof than the mind. I prefer virginity made manifest by the works of character rather than in the body's enclosure.[196]

Although the canonical as well as secular laws seem to assume there were manners in which one could achieve certainty regarding the virgin status of a girl or woman, the Church Fathers reveal that even the physical "evidence" provided by midwives was considered untrustworthy and, although a last recourse, one that needed supplementary evidence. That the Church Fathers refuted these methods indicates that they were used in Christian circles. Cyprian, Ambrose and Augustine's reservations against the use of midwives to examine potential and suspected fallen virgins serve to illustrate how the idea of the very tangibility of virginity, its fixity and physical "reality," is eventually constructed as so fragile that even attempting such verification may fracture virginity and make it disappear. Even at the point where one would expect virginity to be in its most "fixed" and tangible state, it thus evades firm attestation, which again has to be sought elsewhere.

Apparently, all references to this kind of manual inspection by midwives in the Latin sources belong to these kinds of Christian discourses regarding potentially fallen consecrated virgins. Judith Evans Grubbs discusses the possibility of a manual inspection of virgins in connection with a law issued by Constantine in 326, where it is stated that the guardian (*tutor*) of a girl who approaches marriageable age is to prove that her virginity is undefiled (*intemerata*).[197] Evans Grubbs' suggestion as to the reasons why such inspections were not performed on prospective brides is not unlike that of the Christian writers who opposed manual examination of Christian virgins, namely that it would have been a great insult to the girl and her family. She indicates that this kind of inspection could have been conducted more often than we may think, but that shame and discretion have left our legal sources near mute on the details of this topic.[198]

In the case of Christian virgins, this shame seems to extend to her spiritual family as well, namely the congregation and the Christian community at large, but perhaps first and foremost her spiritual father, the bishop who had consecrated her. As already pointed out, there are no indications that non-Christian Romans resorted to manual inspections, neither when the virginity of Vestals was under suspicion nor to affirm the virginity of a bride-to-be. As no evidence can be found in the sources, we therefore cannot know whether this kind of evidence ever played a part in trials against Vestals. However, the same reservations regarding the insult to Christian virgins' modesty may also have been considered for the Vestal virgins.

Virginity tests – or "how to recognize a virgin" 2

> What presumption, what impudence that your conscience should not haunt you! But you with your pretend virginity, you thought that you could deceive the Lord himself! [...] The One who does not lie revealed your secret crime in public, and in the sight of his sun he stripped your works of their shadows.[199]

Both Seneca's lawyers and the Christian Church Fathers apparently got caught in an epistemological conundrum: When all other marks of virginity ultimately prove to be untrustworthy, how then to know? Is pregnancy the only safe proof that she is *not* a virgin?[200] We have already encountered a test of virginity in the gridiron that Heliodorus had his hero and heroine pass in the Ethiopian story.[201] Tests or public trials of virginity and chastity are a quite common literary motif, found in Roman historiography and the Hellenistic novels, as well as in later hagiography. The staging of these trials is always initiated because someone's chastity or virginity is doubted, and these quite creative spectacles thus come about as a dramatically staged opportunity for the hero or heroine to demonstrate their inviolate virginity and receive the admiration and praise they were due. The proof can be all from the survival of a painful and/or impossible task, or, as in the case of the virgin martyrs, astonishing resistance against the most cruel execution methods, until death (most often by the phallic sword[202]) finally bestows the martyrdom upon her. In almost all these virgin tests, there are some magical or divine forces behind the revelation of the final proof.

Aelian, a writer and rhetorician who wrote in Greek but lived in Rome at the turn of the third century, recounts a rite from Lanuvium in which the aim was to expose girls who were no longer virgins. Holy maidens (*parthenoi te hierai*) entered the grove where a large serpent supposedly had his lair in a deep cavern. The girls were blindfolded and brought cakes as offerings to the snake and, if they were virgins, the food was accepted by the snake. Had any of them been deflowered, Aelian describes how the rejected cake was crumbled by ants and carried out of the grove as proof:

> And the inhabitants get to know what has occurred and the maidens who came in are examined,[203] and the one who has shamed her virginity is punished in accordance with the law.[204]

The context in which Aelian brings up this custom is his argument for the serpent's abilities in divination, yet the virginity of "the sacred virgins" as the object for this divination indicates both the serpent's skills in revealing what is beyond human knowledge and the importance of these girls' virginity. Propertius describes what appears to be the same rite in one of his poems, where the girls' proven virginity is presented as prophecy of a fertile harvest. "If they have been chaste (*si fuerint castae*), they return to embrace their parents, and farmers cry: 'Twill be a fertile year.'"[205] The tale of the chastity test in Lanuvium is of course an effective contrast to Propertius' description of his sexual liaisons in his girlfriend Cynthia's absence, and as historical evidence it is certainly no more trustworthy than Aelian's imaginative bestiary. Nevertheless, the two texts combined indicate that some virgins of Lanuvium/Lavinium had to publicly "prove" their virginity by some kind of ritual process that also depended on divination.[206]

That gods were concerned with virginity and willing to expose unchastity is also indicated by a story from Lavinium, told by Servius almost in passing. Here, two virgins are said to have slept in a temple of the nameless Lavinian gods. The unchaste one was killed by lightning, while the other felt nothing at all.[207]

In Rome there were well-known stories of Vestals who had been suspected of having committed *incestum* and who miraculously had been cleared from the accusations by divine aid. There are several versions of how the *Virgo Vestalis Maxima* Aemilia came under suspicion when the sacred flame had died under her supervision. (According to Valerius Maximus, one of Aemilia's apprentices was accused of the misdeed.)[208] The priestess prayed to Vesta for aid to clear her of these charges and, in her desperation, she tore off a piece of her garment and threw it at the cold, dead hearth. The sacred fire reignited immediately, which was taken as proof of Aemilia's dutiful and virginal service to her goddess.[209] Perhaps even more famous than Aemilia was Tuccia, who, when accused of *incestum*, had proven her innocence and thus virginity by carrying water from the Tiber to the temple of Vesta in a sieve, without spilling any water.[210] Another famous woman from Roman history whose chastity was first doubted and then proven, is Claudia Quinta. When the goddess Cybele (Magna Mater) was brought to Rome, the ship carrying the image of the goddess stranded and was impossible to move. Claudia Quinta tied her belt to the ship and miraculously pulled the ship up the Tiber all the way to Rome. Most versions of this story claim that Claudia was a Roman matron whose *pudicitia* was severely questioned[211] but, according to Herodian, Claudia was a Vestal who by this miraculous act freed herself from all accusations of *incestum*.[212] It is this version, where Claudia is a Vestal virgin, that seems to be the one that is transmitted by, for instance, the writings of Jerome.[213] As Denis Feeney remarks in his comment on Herodian's accounts of how Vestals had their virginity miraculously confirmed, "the fact that the Romans believe the stories and their historians have made so much of them is adduced, but subordinated to the strong moral point that the gods are concerned with human goodness and wickedness."[214] In Seneca's *controversia* on the prostitute priestess, Publius Vinicius argued against her case, claiming that the gods would eventually reveal the truth:

> Everyone's conscience is subject to the power of the gods quite otherwise than to our own judgement: we have seen only your overt actions, the gods have seen the secret too.[215]

This is quite in line with Niceta's description of how Susanna's deception could not be hidden from God, and was thus finally exposed for all to see.[216] Although loss of virginity might be hidden from human perception, it can never be hidden from the gods. Yet, since the answer to whether sacred virgins' virginity is preserved or lost so definitely is of public interest, it is important that the divine as well as the secular signs are perceived and understood in either case.

That scientific methods and what, in more modern empirical terms, might be termed "magic" were not necessarily understood as oppositions in Antiquity, becomes evident in treatises such as Pliny the Elder's massive work *Naturalis Historia*. Here we find a seemingly more prosaic method to detect virginity, one that included the use of fumes from burning jet (*gagates*): "The fumes of it, when burnt, keep serpents at a distance, and dispel hysterical affections: they detect a tendency also to epilepsy, and act as a test of virginity."[217] There are no indications that such or any other kind of test was used whenever the Romans suspected that their Vestal virgins were no longer virgins, yet *prodigia* could, it seems, set off a legal investigation.[218] This is in line with the general impression given in the sources, namely that a Vestal's virginal status was to be determined by trial or divine intervention. The best sign, however, was the well-being of the state and the testimony of the eternal fire in the temple of Vesta. As the story of Aemilia reveals, to the Romans the most well-known indication that something was wrong at the house of the Vestals was that the sacred flame in the temple died, which was interpreted as a most ominous sign. As stated by Dionysius of Halicarnissos:

> There are many indications, it seems, when a priestess is not performing her holy functions with purity, but the principal one is the extinction of the fire, which the Romans dread above all misfortunes, from whatever cause it proceeds, as an omen that portends the destruction of the city[219]

Acting the part: performativity and display

According to Prudentius' comparison between Vestals and Christian virgins, the Vestals were public priestesses and thus constantly in the public eye, whereas the sacred Christian virgins ideally ought to live in humble seclusion, shielded from the potentially harmful gaze of those less chaste and pure.[220] This seclusion, which was also meant to intensify the virgin's exclusive relationship with her bridegroom, was recommended by most of the Christian Fathers in their incitements to the life as virgins. Were the virgins to leave the house, proper action was required in order for their modesty to remain unimpeached in the encounter with others.[221] As Theresa Shaw has demonstrated, these sometimes quite detailed descriptions of correct virginal conduct were rhetorical strategies that "marked distance" and consolidated the virgin's status as different and indeed sacred.[222] According to Shaw, "Ambrose and the others instruct virgins to *become* virgins by *acting* like virgins, to claim the role by playing the role."[223] We have thus moved from the alleged private chambers of the virgin, where her status is mainly of soteriological importance on an individual level – an issue between herself and her bridegroom – to the Christian community and thus a public sphere, where her virginity had to be performed and displayed according to a prescribed ideal standard. The consecration ceremonies staged in the fourth century testify to this demand to put "virginity on display,"[224] where the very veiling of the virgins marked their honorary and publicly recognized status. The instructions on how true virginity ought to be properly performed in order for it to be recognized as such were, however, already discussed by Tertullian and Cyprian in the second and third century.

With reference to Judith Butler, Kathleen Coyne Kelly has focused on how virginity was performative, and how the epistemological negotiations did not necessarily evolve around physical "proof," but, perhaps precisely because of the unreliability of such proofs, were paradoxically interdependent on the "performance" of virginity:

> Virginity is constructed, consciously or unconsciously, as existing at the point at which the body and the social meet and intermingle, resulting in a kind of mixed metaphor or confusion of categories. *Verifying* virginity is

compromised by the possibilities of *performing* virginity: performing virginity both leads to and is caused by interrogating virginity.[225]

Just as a trial to prove virginity had to be public in order for the virgin's virginity to be recognized and valued properly, so the performance of virginity depended on some kind of public display, as Rebecca Langlands has argued was such a crucial part of the construction of Roman *pudicitia*. According to Langlands, "*pudicitia* is only visible against the background of sexual immorality and transgressive desire; when it figures merely as absence, there is nothing to see."[226] Its very existence depended on negations and transgressions, against which it could shine properly. In this respect, the gloom from the fallen virgins, and the constant impending danger that other sacred virgins might fall, made the "crown of virginity" [227] shine even brighter on those who performed their virginity satisfactorily. Although, as Denis Trout argues, "[q]uestions of sexual purity were [according to Augustine] not to be arbitrated spectacularly before the eyes of men, as Livy and Seneca preferred, but in the heart before the eyes of God,"[228] it is clear that the discourses on sexual morality in the Christian communities of Late Antiquity equally depended on some kind of public display and, at best, on spectacular divine interference, in order for true virginity (and chastity) to be recognized and valued. The display is indeed most evident in the erotically charged depictions of the exposed yet covered virgin martyrs in the arena, but the oscillating maneuver between visibility and invisibility was also central to the prescribed performance of consecrated virgins such as Eustochium and Demetrias.

LOSING WHAT CANNOT EVER BE REGAINED

'*Partheneia, partheneia*, where have you gone, deserting me?
Never again shall I come to you: never again shall I come.'[229]

In ancient Greek tradition there was a local myth about how Hera, the wife of Zeus, once every year restored her virginity and became *parthenos* again by a bath in the spring Kanathos in Nauplia.[230] However, ideas of such "restoration" of virginity seem to have been rare in pagan as well as Christian discourses. Some texts belonging to the latter might indicate an idea that baptism could provide this kind of restoration, since the person was thought of as completely reborn and so, as a logical consequence, a virgin when reborn. This idea is, for instance, expressed by Tertullian in *On exhortation to chastity*, where he divides virginity into three "species." The first, he explains, is the kind with which one is born, the second comes from the second birth "that is, from the font," which is then preserved by mutual consent between husband and wife or in chosen "widowhood." Tertullian also mentions a third species of "virginity," which is where he places exclusive monogamy that is not even dissolved by death.[231] He also goes on to describe the difference between these species, maintaining that the first is the virginity of happiness (or fruitfulness, *felicitatis*), because this virgin is ignorant about what is renounced. The second type of virginity is of virtue, because this virgin knows the powers of what he or she has to struggle against. The third type has, in addition to virtue, as with the second species, also modesty as a distinctive virtue. Tertullian's distinction reflects later hierarchies listing married, widows and virgins in order of increasing sanctity.[232] Tertullian's "virginities" in this context thus reflect some flexity of the concept in terms of metaphorical language, and in acknowledging the virtues upon which virginity can only with increasing difficulty persist. This flexity is still grounded in its fixed "physical reality" as the absolute criteria and the marker of the first species of virginity, and thus combines two hierarchies, one of physical purity and one of virtues,[233] in a topsy-turvy manner where top, middle and bottom are all conceded degrees of sanctity (and virginity).

The idea that baptism entailed renovation of virginity as part of the rebirth does not seem to have been explored by other Latin writers.[234] On the contrary, it is the irreparable damage that may be done to virginity – willingly or even unknowingly or unwillingly – that is most prominent in their constructions of the concept. As Ambrose rather sarcastically remarks in response to those who are afraid their wives will be affected by the Milanese wave of conversions to virginity: "and those who have wives should not fear: their wives cannot be virgins now."[235]

Jerome seems to be the originator of something that came to be a crux for later medieval theologians' understanding of the omnipotence of God when he stated:

> I will say it boldly, though God can do all things He cannot raise up a virgin when once she has fallen. He may indeed relieve one who is defiled from the penalty of her sin, but He will not give her a crown.[236]

Jerome's letter on the instruction of Pacatula likewise contains a reminder to the ones who have married: "Let him not seek the eternal nakedness of virginity and chastity (Gen. 3:12) which he has given up once for all."[237] Likewise, Jerome makes a point of Blaesilla's double misfortune, pointing to the fact that now that she is a widow, she has not only lost the crown of virginity, but the pleasures of wedlock as she has come to know them as well.[238] The same is stressed in his eulogy for Blaesilla, where it is said that Blaesilla mourned the loss of her virginity more than the loss of her husband. In this context, though, consoling Paula for the tragic loss of a 20-year-old daughter, Jerome cannot but grant Blaesilla some of the eternal bliss that he would otherwise only reserve for virgins:

> Be at peace, dear Blæsilla, in full assurance that your garments are always white. For yours is the purity of an everlasting virginity. I feel confident that my words are true: conversion can never be too late.[239]

Thus, despite linking the fixed and definite limits of virginity to the omnipotence of God, Jerome cannot even here avoid flexing and extending this limit in the face of death and the hope of salvation. Although it is not stated as explicitly as by Jerome in his letter to Eustochium, the idea that virginity was irrecoverable once it was lost is also found in Augustine's *De sancta virginitate*. Here, Augustine raises the question regarding who are supposed to "follow the Lamb" in his reading of Revelation 14:4. Others, who have lost their virginity, may follow the Lamb, Augustine concedes, but not wherever he goes and not in his immediate footprints, as there are certain joys reserved for virgins in which non-virgins cannot partake.[240] According to Augustine, there was no doubt that virgins were in a privileged position, since "virginity of the flesh is not for all, because they cannot have what makes them virgins, those, in whom it is done so that they are not virgins."[241] Augustine continues:

> But see, the Lamb walks a virginal road. How shall they go after Him, those who have lost what they can by no means whatsoever recover? For we can exhort married people unto any other gift of holiness, by which to follow Him, apart from this, which they have lost beyond repair. Follow Him, therefore, by holding persistently on to what you have vowed with ardor. Go when you can, so that the good of virginity does not perish from you, unto which you can do nothing, in order that it may return.[242]

Augustine, like Jerome before him, focuses here on how virginity is absolutely irreparable once it is broken/taken/lost, and it is exactly this characteristic that lends to its exclusiveness and thus potential for sanctity. Such sanctity is then, as a consequence, always fragile and only achieved with difficulty and care. It is its very carnality that gives it this exclusiveness. Augustine makes it perfectly clear that the rebirth of baptism is spiritual and not to be understood in carnal terms.[243] The miracle of baptism does thus not extend to the physical body and, therefore, if the sanctity of virginity is sought after, it must be preserved by one's first birth, as it cannot be renewed in the second. According to Averil Cameron, "The supreme miracle would lie in the restoration of virginity to one who had lost it."[244] The fact that such a miracle was never proclaimed by orthodox Christian writers is again a testimony to the unique status of those who actually preserved virginity, and to the fact that, however valued spiritual virginity was, it was worthless without its physical component. Even Tertullian's categorization of different virginities indicates that a virginity restored by baptism, "the virginity from the font," always comes second to the kind that is preserved from birth.

The value of virginity is thus throughout the classical sources poignantly expressed in its fragile and irrevocable nature. As conveyed by Valerius Maximus, virginity was valued precisely because the one to whom it is first given is the only one who will ever have it.[245] This idea is what is also conveyed in epitaphs where the virginity, in particular of the bride at the time of marriage (the so-called univira-ideal), is stated explicitly as part and proof of the wife's (and to a lesser extent husband's) virtues.[246] The notion that virginity is non-renewable was certainly not exclusive to Christian ideas. As phrased by

Apuleius, it is clear that this made the bride's virginity the most precious part of her dowry:

> A beautiful virgin may be poor, but she is still well enough endowed. For what she brings to her new husband is the fresh nature of her mind, her gracious beauty, her first blossom. Virginity itself is very rightly considered the best recommendation by all husbands. For whatever else you accept as a dowry, you can, if you want, return completely as you accepted it and so avoid obligations. Money can be paid back; slaves sent back, a house can be left, an estate vacated; only virginity, once accepted, can never be restored. It is the only element of a dowry that remains with the husband.[247]

In this sense, the virgin's virginity is something that can only be offered and given up once, which is exactly the core of its exclusivity. Transferred to the realm of religion, such a gift would certainly be no less precious when presented to the gods. In the human world, this "gift" can never be withdrawn or given twice, but for the consecrated virgins this is a constant possibility, as the material on fallen virgins illustrates. A virginity that is first dedicated to the gods and then to a human would certainly be an insult to the one to whom it was first given. This might be the reason why Vestal virgins seem to have been so reluctant to leave the priesthood and marry, even though they were legally granted this option. Taken to the extreme, as in Ambrose's account of the anonymous virgin of Antioch, virginity is only guaranteed by death; for as long as the virgin is alive, her virginity is in danger. This idea may also be reflected in the epitaphs dedicated to young deceased infants and toddlers, who, although obviously never formally consecrated while the child was alive, still were believed to be in possession of a state, or even "gift," which would prove fortunate in the face of death. This, then, is perhaps also what the parents of Theusebius recognized when they described their deceased boy as carrying his virgin crown into the eternal halls of the Lord. In terms of age as well as gender, Theusebius is indeed a most unusual virgin but, somehow, the way his virginity pushes towards some of the borderlines that define virginity in other contexts, allows us to see more individual expressions of what was at stake. The Theusebius inscription, as well as all the other male virgins recorded in the sources, thus also exemplifies the ongoing negotiations over virginity's fixity and flexity that in turn open for such borderline virginities.

A bodiless virginity? On flexity, fixity, and the identification of true virgins

> For fasting is not a complete virtue in itself but only a foundation on which other virtues may be built. The same may be said of sanctification and of that chastity, without which no man shall see the Lord. Each of these is a step on the upward way, yet none of them by itself will avail to win the virgin's crown.[248]

The tension between virginity as a physical characteristic and as performance makes definition difficult, and apparently caused much anxiety over how "real" virginity could be recognized.[249] In terms of flexity and fixity, one may say that the desire for flexity caused by a wish to make salvation through virginity attainable by all Christians, such as seen in Tertullian's hierarchy of virginity, called for rhetorical strategies that were able to both include and exclude those deviating from the stereotype or fixed notion of the virgin. Emulating or imitating virgins could thus be either positive or negative, depending not only on the motivation for such imitation, but also on the manner the imitation was performed according to standards increasingly more difficult to live up to. Defining such borderline virgins as either true or false according to theological truth, yet never wholly detached from conventional social classifications, becomes necessary in order for the "true virgins" to stand out and receive acknowledgement. In a comparative perspective, it is evident that Christian texts on virginity display the tension between flexity and fixity, with a continually challenging desire for flexity, which in turn can be understood as a natural consequence of the Church's focus on virginity as close to a guarantee for individual salvation. Still, I hope to have demonstrated that similar negotiations that extended the category of *virgo* to include both men and women, of all ages and social classes, had already been part of the cultural negotiations that featured these borderline virgins. Although not nearly as extensively, all these different perceptions of what constituted a virgin contributed to the ongoing construction of the Roman *virgo* in extant Latin discourses. However, the motivation for such negotiations should not be understood as specifically religious in the Roman context (although, as we have seen, some of the rare instances of male virgins in Greek texts were explained as personal expressions of devotion to a certain cult or god), but just as much a moral, social, juridical and cultural concern. Christian soteriology appears to have been the main inspiration for the spread of Christian virgin ideology, promising salvation on an individual level. This may, as we have seen, have led parents and relatives to stress the virginal status of a deceased person in commemorative practices, hoping that this would benefit the deceased in the next life. Even though there are occasional indications that a virgin's vow to Christ was a private affair, a pact between an individual and God, the virgin's alleged positive effects on the Christian community were too important to remain private. Thus, the tension between humble withdrawal and public display increases as the virgins' status increases within the community of Christians.[250] The Vestal virgins were tending the sacred and ancient rites on behalf of Roman society throughout most of the fourth century. They were public priests and, as such, their status was necessarily publicly displayed. As they became antagonists to the Christian virgins in the polemics of the Church Fathers, it appears that some kind of competition is launched when the Church Fathers seek to demonstrate their own virgins' superiority.

When there are many virginities, and many ways to perform virginity and define virginity, there are equally many ways to lose virginity. The very fact that

Vestals and Christian virgins were in constant danger of potentially losing their virginity is what heightens the value of virginity and makes it so apt for sanctity when it is properly performed and preserved. This is what both the rhetors of Seneca's *Controversiae* and the Church Fathers' epistemological conundrums reflect: virginity is extremely fragile – and sacred virginity, which has to be held to the highest standards, is the most fragile and precious kind.

Negotiating the value of virginity in Late Antiquity: borderline virgins and sacred virginity

The pimp values a virgin with different eyes than the priest.[251]

Returning to the question of comparison and continuity and change in Roman conceptions of virginity in general and sacred virginity in particular, the alleged watershed has been that early Christian ethics of sexuality differed radically from those of the pagans, who basically had no moral standards at all. This has, in turn, been exemplified in the distinction between the pagan Vestals, seen as anomalies because they are said to have represented an exception to a rule and had no relevance for the lives of "ordinary people," and a Christian ideal of virginity embodied by their virgin martyrs and their consecrated virgins, who were held up as ideals to be imitated by all Christians. The soteriological benefits conferred to this ideal implies a desire to make virginity universal, that all Christians ought to live as virgins, and that virginity as a sacred status thus ought to be attainable by all, regardless of age, gender and social status. This ideal is certainly present in the Christian texts concerned with virginity. However, what is perhaps even more evident is the constant stress on the exclusivity of virginity and its almost unattainable position. There is thus obvious tension between virginity as an ideal for all and the extremely restricted terms defining those who were said to live up to the ideal. As regards the concepts of flexity and fixity, there is indeed a desire for flexity, a strive towards an inclusive concept in terms of both social status and gender, yet the pulling power of fixity restrains any attempt to flex, and eventually returns to the young, aristocratic, morally impeccable and sexually untouched female body as the "fixed" stereotype that any other imitation will be measured against (and perhaps never be able to live up to).

The paradoxes of virginity are manifold, yet the most significant one in terms of sacred virgins' virginity is precisely its metaphorical value as a *pars pro toto*, where inviolate virginity guarantees the safety of society. Perpetual virginity is identified with firmness and impenetrable integrity; it signals stability and immutability. On the other hand, this perseverance is extremely fragile and, with the increasing importance of virgins in Late Antiquity, both as individuals and as a religious order, attention to this very fragility appears to be heightened. When virginity is lost, this fragility is indeed a weakness but, at the same time, the fragility is a result of the negotiations and need for a flexity in the concept in order to adapt it to the sanctity it manifests. The limits of virginity, although apparently obvious, still escape firm epistemological proof. This flexity of virginity, examined and negotiated in Antique as well as Late Antique discourses, also renders virginity less firm and fixed, and may eventually threaten to empty the concept entirely of its meaning. That is why Christian, but also pagan, discourses tend to return to the recurring attempts to fixate virginity in the female virgin's body. When does a virgin stop being a virgin? At what point is she (or he) devirginized? This is the question that could serve as a rhetorical exercise for the schoolboys who studied Seneca the Elder's declamations but which, according to much of the same lines of reasoning, came to be important in Augustine's definition of virginity. Eventually, both would seem to indicate that the answer would be beyond human verification, and thus the truth was only to be known by the gods and hopefully revealed by divine intervention.

As several scholars have pointed out, the fact that virginity was perceived as something more than merely a physical state, yet still never completely detached from the body, makes it an adaptable metaphor and a rich symbol of religious ideology. Despite limitations based on age, gender, social status, conduct, dress and religious adherence, in addition to sexual experience, these limits are always being pushed in the construction of sacred virginity. The very open approach of analyzing virgin ideology of Late Antiquity in terms of flexity and fixity may also work on other aspects of the sanctity of virginity that have only been touched upon in passing. For instance, the aesthetics of virginity is indeed forced to the limits of flexibility in some of the Fathers' vivid depictions of the devoted virgin's ascetic regime. On the other hand, the "eternal beauty of the virgin,"[252] so fundamental in the bridal imagery and in the equation to angelic life, operates as a "fixity" that nevertheless grounds the notion in terms of gender and age. Likewise, the paradoxical, yet with Christianity particularly significant, figure of the virgin mother similarly indicates a flexity that operates on the very limit, or bursting point, where virgin is about to become non-virgin. The Church Fathers, in their Mariological focus on the mystery of incarnation, are indeed aware that the image reaches its very limits of flexity yet, at the same time, this is what gives it religious value.

As Rebecca Langlands pointed out with respect to *pudicitia*, "when it figures merely as absence, there is nothing to see."[253] In the same manner, virginity, as the negation of sexuality, depends on transgression to be properly recognized and valued. Virginity in its stereotypical and ideal state is fixed and immutable, and will thus easily become invisible unless it figures against a background, not only of transgression but, as we have seen, of the constant negotiations over the limits of transgression. When we examine Late Antique texts that concern sacred virgins and the religious valuation of virginity, the attempts to fix the sacred virgin within Christian orthodox ideology are thus constantly compromised by aspects forcing flexity upon the concept, creating this tension that prevents a univocally defined virginity.

Where most recent studies have focused on either Vestal virgins or Christian consecrated virgins, keeping Roman religion and Christianity separate and only occasionally (mainly in studies of Christian virginal ideal) mentioning the Vestal virgins as potentially interesting for contrast or similarity, my approach, inspired by the more general studies in Late Antiquity and the so-called "cultural turn" that has blossomed in recent decades, has focused on the common cultural and social context of Rome in the fourth century. Looking at the history of comparisons between Vestals and Christian virgins, I have argued that the premises were to some extent set by the Church Fathers, and that, whether intentionally or not, it is almost impossible not to compare the two, since they have been intermingled and compared "from the very beginning." Can any conclusions then be drawn, apart from what has already been stated, that it is ultimately impossible not to compare them at one level or the other? The preceding comparisons have followed in some of the tracks that were set out by the Church Fathers, but hopefully also established some new directions that have not been equally explored before. Questioning the understanding of virginity as an ideal that in principle applied to everyone in the early Christian Church, I have looked at how cultural and social understandings of virginity in terms of social class, age and gender restricted the desire for flexity and a universally applicable virgin ideology. Likewise, significant motifs from the socio-/cultural-/religious context added to the understandings and valuations of virginity, which in turn contributed to, and were influenced by, the ongoing construction of "the sacred virgin" and her religious status. As my intentions were to disclose the importance of socio-cultural context in the construction of sacred virginities in Late Antiquity, certain motivating factors idiosyncratic to Christianity have only partially been discussed at relevant stages. That some of these were very different from pagan understanding of the significance of consecrated virginity and virgin priestesses is evident. For instance, the Church's battle against heretical deviation became a substantial factor adding to the Christian virgin ideal, where the need to define specific borderlines became important. The most obvious example is how Marian theology evolved alongside the dogma of incarnation as a response towards Neoplatonic devaluation of the physical world. Likewise, the soteriological benefits as deduced from biblical passages such as Rev. 14:4, Matt. 20:30 and Matt. 19:12 became important for the wish to be identified as virgins, as the numerous epitaphs over young children described as *virgines* seem to indicate.

Still, Vestal virgins and Christian virgins were also, in their own ways, prominent figures within contemporary religious communities in Late Antique Rome, communities that by no means were completely segregated from each other but that also took part in and related to the same socio-cultural context. Although the majority of the virgins themselves, according to the normative directions given by the Church Fathers, were rather sheltered from contact with most sides of Roman society, the men that wrote to and about these virgins related to the conceptions and ideals of a socio-cultural complex loosely framed by what may be called *Romanitas*, a common "Romanness." Since the sacred status of these girls and women was inextricably and explicitly tied to their status as virgins, Roman conceptions of virginity as such, in their very variety and similarity, has been the pivotal focus of the discussion. Although secular and sacred virginity clearly were measured by different standards, as the quote above from Seneca's *Controversia* on the prostitute priestess would indicate, they were also constantly negotiated in a mutual and interdependent relation. Between the two main categories of sacred virgins, the Vestals and the Christian virgins, there would necessarily be crossing paths as well as proclaimed oppositions and deviations. Some of these "similarities and differences" were, as stated above, already indicated by Church Fathers in their comparisons between the two kinds of sacred virgins. Others, I hope, have been brought to light and complicated rather than clarified the relationship between Christian and pagan virgins of fourth-century Rome. By the application of a wide selection of sources, I have analyzed some of the rhetorical strategies and ideological constructions that are present in a selection of texts from the Latin Church Fathers, mainly Ambrose and Jerome, whose insistence on the virginal ideal became decisive in the formation and consolidation of Christian ideology towards the Middle Ages. Supported by the theoretical framework loosely connected under the heading of "the cultural turn," and inspired by several studies on virginity, gender and sexuality that have appeared in recent years, my reading of these different sources open up a variety of understandings and valuations of virginity, demonstrating the tension between a somewhat culturally defined "fixity" – a mutual understanding of what a *virgo* was – and "flexity," the construction of meaning that became heightened in the exploration of the very "limits" or "bursting point," where the religious (and certainly also socio-cultural) significance and value of the virgin was negotiated and either became devoid of meaning or even more meaningful in its very paradox. Virgin mothers, virgin brides, virgin widows, *veteranae virgines* (as in *pueri senes*), slave virgins or *virgines libertae*, infant virgins: these are all examples of such virgins that could end up on either side of the demarcation line that separated virgin from non-virgin according to whether the flexity was deemed as stretched too far in the particular context. Of these apparently paradoxical virgins, the male virgin, in all his embodied (or bodiless) representations, is perhaps the most evident example of how different discourses in Antiquity and Late Antiquity expressed and negotiated the value of virginity. Although not solely, the majority of these discourses appear to refer to some kind of religious valuation of virginity as the very motivation for such identifications of male virgins. Some Church Fathers, notably Jerome and Tertullian among the Latin Fathers and possibly Greek Fathers more generally, wrote of male virgins as equal to the female virgins, and epitaphs also give evidence to such notions, even though, statistically, this evidence is not exactly overwhelming. Ambrose as well as other Latin sources indicate that the male virgin was a problematic figure in terms of status and gender, and as such they exhibit less desire for flexity in terms of gender than perhaps in terms of age and social status.

On the other hand, the fallen virgin embodied the stark contrast to which the sacred virgins' status was enhanced and further negotiated, not least because the different understandings of what could constitute "the loss" highlights the very flexity of virginity in terms of bodily and spiritual/moral qualities integral to the understanding of the virgins' sanctity. Although sexual intercourse was the most obvious reason for loss of virginity, a range of other factors could also, according to the discourses analyzed above, contribute to such loss and thus the claim to sacred status. Conduct, dress, intent, company, religious adherence as well as divine signs were all factors that could cause suspicion and thus eventually undermine the virgin's sacred status if they were not properly displayed. The meaning of virginity was therefore constantly negotiated and constructed, even though it would never become completely fluid, within this frame of tension between "fixity" and "flexity." By applying these two terms in my analysis, it has been possible to account for several variations both in continuity (or constancy) as well as change, and also make room for obvious tensions and variations in religious valuation and ideals, not only within the multi-religious society that Rome was in the last half of the fourth century, but also within different religious communities and between individual official representatives for these communities.

To sum up, what has been discussed here is how fourth-century notions of "sacred virginity" were construed and negotiated both in relation to specific religious ideas and ideals, as well as in an ongoing dialogical relation with a number of contemporaneous discourses in which conceptions of virginity in general were explored and consolidated in the tension between virginity's flexity and fixity. In addition to the comparisons between the sacred virgins of the pagans ("them") and the Christian sacred virgins ("us") made by Christian writers in Late Antiquity and the impact of these comparisons on modern scholarship, my focus has thus been issues concerning social status, religion, age, gender and the so-called "fallen virgins," which were all important in the construction and limitation of "the virgin" as a category of religious significance. The soteriological motivation in Christian virgin ideology made flexity more desirable and opened up an even wider variety of borderline virginities in the span between fixity and flexity. This is indicated, for instance, in the range of virgins challenging stereotypical representations of virginity, constantly punctuating the attempts to construe some defining borders that would make virginity fixed. However, the bulk of orthodox texts on virginity, with their rather detailed, normative descriptions of how "true" virginity is to be performed and recognized, still reveal that the concept of virginity was difficult to untangle from notions striving to fixate the virgin by embodying virginity in young aristocratic females with no sexual experience and of unimpeached behavior in terms of moral standards. In the end, the sacred virgins were to be no exceptions.

Notes

1 Symm. *Ep.* 9.147, and *Ep.* 9.148. PLRE I (s.v. "Symmachus 4," pp. 865–71") and Roda 1981: 318 date the letters with 382 as *terminus ante quem* because of the anti-pagan legislation of Gratian. Symmachus is said to have obtained his priesthood as *pontifex maior* sometime prior to 365 (PLRE p. 866 (d), cf. CIL 6.1699 = ILS 2946).

2   I.e. the pontifical college. See note above.

3   Symm. *Ep.* 9.147. *More institutoque maiorum incestum Primigeniae dudum apud Albam Vestalis antistitis collegii nostrii disquisitio deprehendit; quod et ipsius, quae contaminavit pudicitiam sacram, et Maximi, cum quo nefandum facinus admisit, confessionibus claruisse, gesta testantur. Restat, ut in eos, qui caerimonias publicas abominando scelere polluerunt, legum severitas exeratur, quae tibi actio de proximi temporis exemplo servata est; et ideo dignaberis, reip. utilitatem legesque considerans facinus cunctis usque ad hunc diem saeculis severissime vindicatum conpetenter ulcisci. Vale.* My transl. Text from Roda 1981: 369 Cf. Symm. *Ep.* 9.148.

4   Like the letter of Symmachus quoted above, the dating of *Ad Gallos episcopos* is disputed, as is the attribution of authorship. I follow Duval: 2005 and his (re)attribution of the letter to Pope Damasus, which supports the dating this letter to 383–4 AD.

5   And, although secondary in this ruling, also the men who contributed to the crime.

6   I.e. she has married her "accomplice in crime."

7   1 Cor. 6:15: *nescitis quoniam corpora vestra membra Christi sunt tollens ergo membra Chirsti faciam membra meretricis absit.*

8   1 Tim. 5:12: *habentes damnationem quia primam fidem irritam fecerunt.* This is a common *topos* in texts concerning unruly virgins, see, for instance, Bas. *Ep.* 199.18, Hier. *Ep.* 22.29, Hier. *Adv. Jov.* 1.13, Hier. *Ep.* 48.8, Hier. *Ep.* 79. 10, cf. Hier. *Ep.* 123. 3 and Hier. *Comm in Ezech.* 13. 44.17 seq, Innocentius I, *Ep.* 2,16.

9   Cf. 1 Cor. 5:5 *tradere huiusmodi Satanae in interitum carnis ut spiritus salvus sit in die Domini Iesu.*

10   A possible allusion to Hos. 2:13? (*et ibat post amatores suos et mei obliviscebatur dicit Dominus*), cf. Bas. *Ep.* 46.3.

11   In his commentary on the text, Duval 2005: 65 points out the allusion to Matt. 3:8 and Luke 3:8.

12   Duval 2005: 29 refers to Virg *Aen.* 4.171–2, an allusion that is to support Duval's hypothesis of authorship and Jerome's personal influence on this letter, cf. Duval 2005: 69 and 137.

13   Deut 22:22–9, cf. 22:16.

14   *Quos* indicates that this applies for the male accomplice as well, cf. *mortui.*

15   Deut 22:25–7.

16   *Ad Gall. Ep.*(I) 3–4: "*Quaeritur de virginibus velatis et, mutato proposito, (.†.) qui‹d› exinde iudicatum sit. Si virgo velata iam ‹in› Christo, quae, intergitatem publico testimonio professa, a sacerdote prece[t] fusa benedictionis, valemen accepit, sive incestum commiserit furtim, seu, volens crimen protegere, adultero marirti nomen imposu‹er›it, tollens membra Christi, faciens membra meretricis, ut quae sponsa Christi fuerit coniunx hominis diceretur, in eiusmodi muliere quot ‹c›ausae sunt, tot reatus: integritatis propositum mutatum, velamen amissum, fides prima depravata atque ‹in› inritum devocata. Quali[s] h‹a›ic et quanta satisfactione opus est! Quam magna paenitentia ei quae interitum carnis incurrit! Non est parva culpa requilisse Deum et isse post hominem. Unde, annis quam plurimis deflendum ei est, ‹ut› dignae fructu[m] pænitentia facto, possit aliquando ad veniam pervenire, si tamen paenitens paenitenda faciat.*

(4.) *Item, puella quae nondum velata eat, sed proposuerat sic manere, ‹si nupserit›, licet non sit in Christo velata, tamen quia proposuit, et in coniugio velata non est, furtivae nuptiae apellantur, ex eo quod matrimonii caelitus praecepti[o] non servaverit more‹m›, properante libidinis caecita[ta]te[m]. Et his paenitentiae agendae tempus constituendum est, quoniam, seu rapta, seu volens, ad virum ire perverso ordine consensit; nec propinquorum nec sacerdotum testimonio conrogato ad velamen, solempnitatis ordinem casto pudore tenuerunt, sed contra veteris testamenti praeceptum fecerunt. Quos lex lapidari praecepit, et nunc, cessante illa vindicta, spiritaliter feriuntur, ut ecclesiam, tamquam mortui, introire non possint. Habent tamen paenitentia agendae locum, cito non habeant veniam, quoniam, si, secundum legem, proclamasset puella et diu contestata se continuisset [et], utique fuisset inmunis a culpa. Utrisque ergo expedit, sub eadem temporis constitutione, a communione suspendi, dignam agere paenitentiam, fletu, humilitate, ieiunio, misericordia, redimere crimen admissum.* My transl. Ed. Duval 2005.

17 For Symmachus, cf. e.g. Hedrick 2000: 64–79, Matthews 2010: 215–53, Brown 2012: 93–119.

18 For Damasus' pivotal role in this process, and in the "Romanization" of Christianity, see Sághy 2000, Trout 2003, Lafferty 2003.

19 Symm. *Ep.* 9.147 (*More institutoque maiorum* etc,) *Ad Gall Ep.* 4 (*sed contra veteris Testamenti praeceptum fecerunt. Quos lex lepidari praecepit, et nunc cessante illa vindicta*), cf. Duval 2005: 66–7.

20 The preventive function of such regulations is explicitly stated, for instance, in Cypr. *Ep.* 62 and Bas. *Ep.* 188.6.

21 *De laps. Sus.* V.20: *quid, ubi inter innumerabiles testes Ecclesiae coram angelis, exercitibus caeli, facta copula spiritalis per adulterium solvitur? Nescio an posit ei condigna mors aut poena cogitari.* Transl. Tilley.

22 *De laps. Sus.* I.3: *detecti sceleris qualitatem mecum partier perhorrete.* Transl. Tilley.

23 Symm. *Ep.* 9.147: *contaminavit pudicitiam sacram.*

24 Symm. *Ep.* 9.147: *nefandum facinus.*

25 Symm. *Ep.* 9.147: *caerimonias publicas abominando scelere polluerunt.*

26 Symm. *Ep.* 9.148: *pudici numinis maculavit arcane.*

27 Symm. *Ep.* 9.148: *nefandi criminis.*

28 Symm. *Ep.* 9.148: *inuiriam castissimi saeculi.*

29 Fraschetti 1984: 120 underlines the pollution and thus danger that a *vestale incesta* represented as a major factor in the demand for such a severe and ceremonial punishment.

30 This is a common *topos*, e.g. Hier. *Ep.* 22.6: "*Si autem et illae quae virgines sunt, ob alias tamen culpas, virginitate corporum non salvantur: quid fiet illis, quae prostituerunt membra Christi, et mutaverunt templum Sancti Spiritus in lupanar?*" and *De laps. Sus.* II.8: *Quam tibi spem apud Christi Dominum requilisti, cuius membra tollens fecisti membra meretricis?*

31 Hos 2:13.

32 For adultery as a criminal offense in secular law, see, e.g., Gardner 1991: 127–31, Evans Grubbs 1999: 203–25.

33 Adultery was by no means considered a minor crime in early Christian canons. Unless heavy penance was paid and the "union" dissolved, it would result in excommunication, in some cases even at the death bed, i.e. with no chance of salvation.

34 For the term *propositum* in relation to sacred virgins and their status, see Adkin 2003: 33–4.

35 Cornell 1981, Fraschetti 1984, Mustakallio 1992, Lovisi 1997, Staples 1998: 131–5.

36 Isidore *Etym.* V.26.24, and X.1.148.

37 Moreau 2002: 18–19.

38 Serv. *Ad Aen.* 6.150: *Incestat polluit. Et incestum est quaecumque pollutio.* My transl. The passage he comments upon is the Sibyl's warning to Aeneas against entering the underworld: *Praeterea iacet exanimum tibi corpus amici, (heu! Nescis) totamque incestat funere classem.* The pollution that is referred to here is thus not connected to sexuality, but to death.

39 E.g., Cypr. *Ep.* 62. 3, Cypr. *Ep.* 62.15, *Optatus De schismate Donatistarum* II.19, Coelestin I, *Ep.* IV. 5, Gelasius *Ep.* IX. 20, Ambr. *De virgb.* II.27, Ambr. *De excessu fratris* I.32. These and other examples are discussed more fully in Undheim 2011: 304–10.

40 Duval 2005: 64–5.

41 Gaudemet 1980[1949]: 10, note 32, with ref to *Reg. Ulpiani* V,7.

42 Desanti 1987: 291–2, in particular note 106 and Desanti 1990: 480–3.

43   Symm. *Ep.* 9.146: *legum severitas, severissime vindicatum, Ep.* 9.147: *suppliciis vindicare.*
      For Late Antique sources testifying to knowledge of and interest in the republican
      cases, see, e.g., Oros. 4.5: *Capparonia, virgo Vestalis, incesti rea, suspendio periit: corruptor*
      ejus consciique servi, supplicio affecti sunt. Oros. 5.15: *Duas praeterea virgines Vestales*
      eadem Aemilia ad participationem incesti sollicitatas, contubernalibus sui corruptoris exposuit
      ac tradidit. Indicio per servum facto, supplicium de omnibus sumptum est.
44   Beard 1995: 172.
45   Cornell 1981, Fraschetti 1984, Lovisi 1997, Staples 1998, Mustakallio 1992, Martini
      1997b, Parker 2004, Undheim 2004. Human sacrifice was prohibited by law by the
      Senate in 92 BC, cf. Beard, North and Price 1998 Vol. II: 156–60.
46   See in particular Cornell 1981, who sums up some of the preceding arguments on
      this aspect.
47   Cic. *Leg.* II.22: *Incestum pontifices supremo supplicio sanciunto.* (Cf. Cornell 1981: 33.)
      For the emperor's title as *pontifex maximus* and practical cultic arrangements in
      the emperor's absence, see Beard, North and Price 1998 Vol. I: 372–4. Gratian
      apparently declined the title and position in 379 AD but, since the religious duties
      of the pontifex maximus normally were done by other members of the pontifical
      college in the emperor's absence from Rome, asking the emperor to preside over
      the punishment of Primigenia had probably never been considered, regardless
      of the current emperor's religious sympathies. From the reign of Aurelian, the
      traditional pontifices were called *pontifex Vestae.* Cf. Beard, North and Price 1998
      Vol. II: 213 (=CIL 6.1778).
48   Plu. *Num.* X.4–7. Transl. Beard, North and Price 1998 Vol. II: 203.
49   Plu. *Q.R.* 96. Transl. Rose 1974.
50   Frachetti 1984: 126.
51   See Serv. *Ad Aen.* 11, 206.
52   Jones 1971: 22–3. For dating and sources, see Mekacher 2006: 259.
53   Plin. *Ep.* 4.11.
54   In addition to Cornelia, three other Vestals are reported to have been condemned
      as *incestae,* the "sisters Oculatae" and Varonilla. According to Suet. *Dom,* 8.3–4, they
      were given the right to chose their own death, and their *corruptores* were exiled.
      The deviance from tradition is explained by Suetonius to be because these Vestals
      had committed their crimes before Domitian became emperor. Domitian is here
      presented as one who returns to the traditions that his predecessors had neglected.
      See also Dio Cass. 67.3.
55   D. C. 78.16.1–5. Caracalla sentenced four Vestals to death, one of whom, according
      to Dio, the emperor and *pontifex maximus* had himself raped. Cf. Herodian 4.6.4.
      For the date, see Mekacher 2006: 259 and note 249. From the republic, other Vestals
      were known to have committed suicide when faced with the grave charges. See
      Liv. 22.57.2 (Floronia). For Caparronia's death in 266 BC see note 5 in Fraschetti
      1984: 98 for further reference.
56   E.g. Min. Fel. *Oct* XXV, Wildfang 2006: 94–5; 105.
57   For the expression *castas manus* referring to the Vestals' ritual chastity, see Ov. *Fast.*
      VI.290, and Val. Max. VIII.1, absol.5. See also Ov. *Fast.* VI, 457–8, where the chastity
      of Vestals is linked to the prosperity of Augustus.
58   E.g. Lanciani 1967: 172. Exile was also regarded as capital punishment, cf. Plin. *Ep.*
      IV.11, where one of the men (Licinianus) who was involved in a case of *incestum*
      with a Vestal, apparently chose exile to avoid execution. This could perhaps also
      have been chosen in this case, at least for Maximus.
59   Serv. *Ad Aen.* 11, 206: *et meminit antiquae consuetudinis: nam ante etiam in civitatibus*
      sepeliebantur, quod postea Duellio consule senatus prohibuit et lege cavit, ne quis in urbe
      sepeliretur: unde imperatores et virgines Vestae quia legibus non tenentur, in civitate habent
      sepulchra. Deinque etiam nocentes virgines Vestae, quia legibus non tenentur, licet vivae,
      tamen intra urbem in campo scelerato obruebantur. Cic. *Leg.* II, 23 (58): '*Hominem*

mortuum' inquit lex in duodecim 'in urbe se sepelito neve urito'. Cf. Liv. 8.15.7–8 and D. H. 68 on *Campus Sceleratus* and *Porta Collina.*

60 Roda's edition of Symmachus' letters in Symm. (Roda 1981: 317–18).

61 Kajava 2001.

62 Cecere 2003.

63 E.g. D.H. I.76, Plu. *Rom.* 3.

64 Plu. *Num.* X, cf. Plu. *Rom.* 3 for others who argued that Romulus had been the one to establish the cult in Rome. Liv. I.20: *virginesque Vestae legit, Alba oriendum sacerdotium et genti conditoris haud alienum.*

65 McDaniel 1999: 22, cf. Serv. *Ad Aen.* 3.12.

66 Asc. *In Mil.* 40.

67 CIL 14.2410 = ILS 6190.

68 CIL 6.2172 = ILS 5011.

69 Juv. 4.61. See also Rhoda 1981: 316.

70 See Beard, North and Price 1998 Vol. I:51 and 322–4. And if there were permanent priestesses there, the number and terms of service may not have been the same as in Rome, see, e.g., Plu. *Num.* X.

71 Burn 1905: cxxxi–cxxiii.

72 Both as regards the expressions of (personal) disappointment and the *topoi* explored, the text has much in common with Basil's *Ep.* 44, 45 and 46, as well as with Jerome's *Ep.* 147.

73 *De laps. Sus.* IV. 16: *Et si fuisses communi sorte defuncta, flessent te modicum propter desiderium parentes; sed exultassent granditer, quia immaculatam praemiserant virginem, hostiam vivam Domino, propitiatricem suorum videlicet delictorum. At nunc plangunt mortuam et non mortuam, lugent vivam et non vivam: mortuam utique gloria virginitatis, vivam dedecore turpitudinis.* Transl. Tilley.

74 *De laps. Sus.* VIII.34: *paenitudo ergo est necessaria lapsis, sicut vulneratis necessaria medecamina. Sed quanta, putas, et qualis necessaria paenitentia? Quae aut aequet crimina, aut certe excedat.* Transl. Tilley, with small changes.

75 *De laps. Sus.* VIII.34: *Vide ergo si simplex hoc peccatum adulterii est, an duplex sit pro illa nece quae facta dicitur in occulto: et secundum conscientiae molem exhibenda est paenitentiae magnitudo.* Transl. Tilley.

76 *De laps. Sus.* VIII.34: *Paenitentia autem non verba agenda est, sed et actu.*

77 Cf. *De laps. Sus.* X.46.

78 *De laps. Sus.* VIII.34: *Haec autem sic agitur, si tibi ante oculos ponas de quanta gloria rueris, de quo libro vitae nomen tuum deletum sit, et sit e iam positam credas prope ipsas tenebras exteriores, ubi erit fletus oculorum et stridor dentium sine fine. Cum haec certa fide, sicut est, animo conceperis, quia necesse est praevaricatricem animam tartareis poenis et gehennae ignibus tradi, nec aliud remedium constitutum esse post unum baptismum quam paenitentiae solacium; quantam vis afflictionem, quantum vis laborem subire esto contenta, dummodo ab aeternalibus poenis libereris.*

79 *De laps. Sus.* VIII.35: *et quasi mortuam te existimans, sicut et es, quomodo possis reviviscere, cogita.* Transl. Tilley, with my changes.

80 *De laps. Sus.* VIII. 36: *Talis vita, talis actio poenitentiae, si fuerit perseverans, audebit sperare, etsi non gloriam, certe poenae vacationem; […] Peccator ergo si sibi ipsi non pepercerit, a Deo illi parcetur. Et si futuras poenas gehennae perpetuas in hoc parvo vitae spatio compensaverit, seipsum ab aeterno iudicio liberabit.* Transl. Tilley.

81 *De laps. Sus.* VIII.38: *Inhaere paenitentia usque ad extremum vitae, nec tibi presumas ab humana die veniam dari posse, quia decipit te quicumque hoc tibi polliceri voluerit. Quae enim proprie in Dominum peccasti, ab illo solo quaere remedium.* Transl. Tilley.

82 *De laps. Sus.* IX.39: *filio serpentis, ministro diaboli, violatore templi Dei.* For the virgin as a temple of God, see Hunter 2016.

83 *De laps. Sus.* IX.39: *In te autem quid dicam, fili serpentis, ministro diaboli, violatore templi Dei? Qui in uno scelere duo crimina perpetrasti, adulterium utique et sacrilegium,*

sacrilegium plane, ubi vas Christi oblatum, Domino dedicatum, dementi temeritate polluisti. [...] quid de te arbitraries, perdite pariter et perditor, qui vas rationabile consecratum Christo, sanctificatum Spiritui Sancto, impie temerasti, polluisti sacrilege, et tui propositi immemor et iudicii divini contemptor? Melius fuerat te omnino non fuisse natum, quam sic natum, ut te sibi gehenna proprium filium vindicaret. Transl. Tilley.

84 De laps. Sus. IX.40: tamen ne quid a pastore ovi morbidae vel moriturae medicaminis denegatum sit, do concilium. Transl. Tilley.

85 De laps. Sus. 40: Petas ultro carcerem paenitentiae, obruas catenis viscera, animam tuam gemitibus ieiuniisque crucies; sanctorum petas auxilium, iaceas sub pedibus electorum, ut non tibi cor impoenitens thesaurizet iram in die irae et iusti iudicii Dei, qui reddet unicuique secundum opera sua.

86 De laps. Sus. X.48. Meum peccatum, mea iniquitas, non sunt similia offensis hominum; quia impietas est. Carnem pollicita servare virginem, et castitatem professa publice, mentita sum Domino; ideo non est mihi fiducia invocandi Dominum altissimum, quia obstructum est os delinquentium. Transl. Tilley.

87 Hier. Ep. 147.8: Hoc plango, quod te ipse non plangis, quod te non sentis mortuum [al. esse mortuum]; quod quasi gladiator paratus libithynae, in proprium funus ornaris. Transl. NPNF2.

88 Hier. Ep. 147.10: Anima enim quae peccaverit, ipsa morietur (Ezek. 18: 4).

89 Hier. Ep. 22.15. Explosis igitur et exterminatis his quae nolunt esse virgines, sed videri. My transl.

90 Gaudemet 1980 [1949]: 64 draws attention to the difficult problems of determining ancient forms of excommunication and the extreme density in terminology and imprecise vocabulary.

91 Council of Elvira, Canon 13: Virgines, quae se a Deo dicaverunt, si pactum perdiderint virginitatis, atque eidem libidini servierint, non intelligentes quid admiserint, placuit nec in finem eis dandam esse communionem. Quod si semel persuasae aut infirmi corporis lapsu vitiatae omni tempore vitae suae huiusmodi feminae egerint penitentiam, ut abstineat se a coitu, eo quod lapsae potius videantur, placuit eas in finem communionem accipere debere. Quoted and translated by Elm, 2003: 26. The Council of Elvira was held at the very beginning of the fourth century.

92 Bas. Ep. 188.6. Note that Damasus does not make the same demand. It seems that, no matter under what circumstances it has been entered into, marriage is still considered a sacred union and ought not to be dissolved except by death, probably because a divorce would merely add another crime to the list.

93 Cf. Canons of Chalcedon, Canon 16 (dated 451 AD): "It is not lawful for a virgin who has dedicated herself to the Lord God, nor for monks, to marry; and if they are found to have done this, let them be excommunicated. But we decree that in every place the bishop shall have the power of indulgence towards them." Transl. NPNF2.

94 Cf. Bas. Ep. 217.58.

95 Cf. Council of Ancya, Canon 19: "If any person who profess virginity shall disregard their profession, let them fulfil the term of digamists." Transl. NPNF2. This canon is dated 314 AD Cf. Elm 2003: 25–9.

96 The hierarchical difference between a widow and a virgin is thus parallel to that between "a handmaid" and "a bride."

97 Bas. Ep. 199.18. Transl. Loeb. Unlike Damasus, Basil does not seem to demand punishment for those virgins who are "not yet veiled" but have "proposed to remain virgins." As we have already seen, according to Basil, only those who had been formally consecrated and proven to have taken on the vow by their own choice after they have turned 16 or 17, ought to be held liable for the crime. Cf. Bas. Ep. 199.19 regarding those who have taken up celibacy by a silent vow.

98 Bas. Ep. 199.20. Transl. Loeb.

99 Duval 2005: 140–1, where he reproduces the passages from these letters in an appendix.

100 Siricius *Ep.* 1.6,7: *Praeterea monachorum quosdam et monacharum, abiecto proposito sanctitatis, in tantam protestaris demersos esse lasciuiam ut prius clanculo, velut sub monasterii praetextu, illicita ac sacrilege se contagione miscuerint, postea uero in abruptum conscientiae desperatione perducti, de illicitis complexibus libere filios procreauerint, quod et publicae leges et ecclesia iura condemnabant. Has ergo impudicas detestabilesque personas a monasteriorum coetu ecclesiarumque conuentibus eliminandas esse mandamus quatenus, retrusae in suis ergastulis, tantum facinus, continua lamentatione deflentes, purificatorio possint paenitudinis igne decoquere ut eis uel ad mortem saltem, solius misericordiae intuitu, per communionis gratiam posit indulgentiae subuenire.* Ed. Duval 2005: 140, transl. Somerville and Brasington 1998: 39–40.

101 Cf. Gaudemet 1980: 5, who notes that the Council of Elvira in the same manner distinguished between those who were formally consecrated and those who had taken on a private vow (Can. 13 and 14). The private vow would still have been publicly known in order for the transgression to be known and subject to punishment.

102 Innocent I, *Ep.* 2 (*ad Victricium Rotomagensem*,) 13, 14–15, 16 (PL 20, col. 478–80) (date: 15/2/404) 13, 15. *Item, quae Christo spiritaliter nupserunt et velari a sacerdote meruerunt, si postea, vel publice nupserint, vel se clanculo corruperint, non eas admittendas esse ad agendam paenitentiam, nisi is cui se iunxerant de saeculo recesserit. Si enim de omnibus haec ratio custoditur, ut quaecumque, vivente viro, alteri nupserit habeatur adultera, nec ei agendae penitentiae licentia concedatur nisi unus ex eis defunctus fuerit, quanto magis de illa tenenda est, quae, ante, immortali se sponso coniunxerat, et, postea, ad humanas nuptias transmigravit! 14, 16. Hae vero quae necdum sacro velamine tectae, tamen in proposito virginali se promiserant permanere, licet velatae non sint, si forte nupserint, his agendae aliquanto tempore paenitentia est quia sponsio euis a Deo tenebatur. Si enim inter homines solet bonae fidei contractus nulla ratione dissolui, quanto magis ista pollicitatio quam cum Deo pepigit solui sine vindicta non debet! Nam, si apostulus Paulus, quae a proposito viduitatis discesserunt, dixit eas habere damnationem, quia primam fidem irritam facerunt* (1Tim. 5:12), *quanto magis virgines quae priori promissioni fidem frangent!*

103 Elm 2003: 26–8. She points out the difference in terminology and punishment as well as the geographical distance between Iberia and Asia Minor, but eventually her focus is on their common interest in *virgines Deo dicatae*. Cf. Evans Grubbs 1999: 76 on how the canons from Elvira and Ancyra probably reflect regional differences.

104 Gaudemet 1980 [1950]: 15.

105 *De laps. Sus.* III.12: *Sed dicis 'nolui hoc malum:[sed] passa sum violentiam.' Respondebit tibi fortissimo illa Susanna, cuius tu nomen fallaciter baiulas: 'Ego inter duos presbyteros posita, inter duos utique iudices populi, sola inter silvas paradisi constituta vinci non potui, quia nec volui'. Tu ab ineptissimo adulescente et in media civitate, quomodo vim perferre potuisti, nisi quia ultro vitiari voluisti? Quis denique tuas voces audivit? Quid obluctationem sensit?* Transl. Tilley.

106 I.e. Deut. 22.25–7.

107 Evans Grubbs 1989: 65, cf. Evans Grubbs 1999: 183 ff. and Grodinsky 1984.

108 Evans Grubbs 1999: 186.

109 Evans Grubbs 1989: 69, e.g. Liv. 1.4.2 on the rape of Rhea Silvia: *Vi compressa Vestalis.*

110 CTh 9.25.1.

111 CTh 9.25.2, cf. Desanti 1987: 272–6, Evans Grubbs 1989: 77 and Evans Grubbs 2001: 223–4.

112 Soz. H.E. 6.3, transl. NPNF2 cf. CTh 9.25.2, Evans Grubbs 1989: 77 and Evans Grubbs 2001: 223–4.

113 McInerney 2003: 78.

114 Aug. *Civ. Dei* I.16: *quidquid alius de corpore vel in corpore fecerit quod sine peccato proprio non valeat evitari praeter culpam esse patientis.* Transl. Loeb.

115 Aug. *Civ. Dei* I.16: *tamen pudore incutit, ne credatur factum cum mentis etiam voluntate, quod fieri fortasse sine carnis aliqua voluptate non potuit.* Transl. Loeb.

116 Bas. *Ep.* 199.49. Transl. Loeb.

117 McInerney 2003: 80, cf. Trout 1994: 66.

118 Leo I, *Ep.* XII. 8: *[Illae autem famulae Dei quae integritatem pudoris oppressione barbarica perdiderunt, laudabiliores erunt in humilitate ac verecundia sua, si se incontaminatis non audeant comparare virginibus.] Quamvis enim omne peccatum ex voluntate nascatur, et potuerit corruptione carnis mens invicta non pollui, minus tamen hoc eis oberit, si quod potuerunt animo non amittere, doleant se vel corpore perdidisse.* Transl. NPNF2, with some changes.

119 Leo I, *Ep.* XII.11: *[De his autem quae in sacro virginitatis proposito constitutae, ut superius dictum est, barbaricam pertulere violentiam, et integritatem pudoris non animo, sed corpore perdiderunt, ea nobis videtur servanda moderatio,] ut neque in viduarum dejiciantur gradum, nec in sacrarum et perseverantium virginum numero censeantur: quibus, si in moribus virginalibus perseverant, et castimoniae soliditatem mente custodiunt, sacramentorum non est neganda communio, quia injustum est illas in eo vel argui vel notari, quod non voluntas amisit, sed vis hostilis eripuit.* Transl. NPNF2, with some changes.

120 Cf. Fox 1988: 370.

121 *De laps. Sus.* VIII.31: *Quod si is qui unum scandalizaverit, mola circumligatus praecipitari debet in mari, quid de te pronuntias, per cuius scelus omnis anima sauciata est, et nomen Domini in gentibus blasphematum?* Transl. Tilley 2000. The allusion to Matt. 18:6, and Luke 17:2 also occurs in Basil's letter to a fallen virgin in *Ep.* 46.4.

122 *De laps. Sus.* VIII.30: *Aperuit in nos gentilitas os suum, adversum Ecclesiam Sanctam synagoga Iudaeorum per tuum dedecus exultavit.* Transl. Tilley. Cf. Jerome's warning to Demetrias in Hier. *Ep.* 130.19: *ut etiam si nihil mali perpetretur: tamen hoc sit vel maximum malum, frustra patere maledictis et morsibus Ethnicorum.*

123 Bas. *Ep.* 45.2. "You have disgraced the promise of chastity; we have been made a tragedy of captives, and our story is made a play before Jews and Greeks." Transl. NPNF2.

124 Bas. *Ep.* 188, 4: "The fornication of canonical persons [i.e. virgins] must not be accounted as marriage, but their union must by all means be dissolved. For this is both advantageous for the safety of the Church, and will not give the heretics an opportunity to attack us on the ground that we have won men to ourselves by granting them license to sin." Transl. Loeb.

125 *De laps. Sus.* I.3: *se perditit, et Ecclesiam maculavit. Hinc omnis anima Christiana grave vulnus excepit, quia datum est sanctum canibus, et margaritae missae sunt ante porcos.* Transl. Tilley. Winn 2003: 337 notes that Eusebius of Emesa also regards the consequences of a virgin's fall to affect the entire Church: *Virginis casus adversum omnem ecclesiam habetur.*

126 *De laps. Sus.* I.4: *hinc insanabilis dolor, quia una malum bona plurima secum trahit et unius nubecula peccatricis totam paene lucem obscuravit Ecclesiae.* Transl. Tilley.

127 *De laps. Sus.* II.7: *De Dei virgine facta es corruptio satanae, de sponsa Christi scortum exsecrabile, de habitaculo Spiritus Sancti tugurium diaboli, de templo Domini fanum immunditiae.* Transl. Tilley.

128 In particular Kelly 2000, whose study explores "how and why the virgin body comes to function as a metonym – a rhetorical shield – for the Church, particularly in the tale of circumvented rape," Kelly 2000: 13, cf. Kelly 2000: 42ff. Brown 1988: 354–7, Burrus 1995: 45, McInerney 2003: 67, Cameron 1994: 174.

129 Plu. *Num.* X, Plu. *Q.R.* 96.

130 In particular Lovisi 1997: 117, Staples 1998: 137. See also the critique of these theories in Gallia 2015.

131 Cornell 1981, Fraschetti 1984, cf. Kyle 2001: 37–9.

132 Plin. *Ep.* IV.117–8: *Me Caesar incestam putat, qua sacra faciente vicit triumphavit.*

133 Suetonius represents a different opinion on the question of guilt in this case: Suet. *Dom.* 8.3–4, see also Statius *Silv.* 1.1.32–6.

134 Ov. *Fast*.VI.455–8: *nunc bene lucetis sacrae sub Caesare flammae: / ignis in Illiacis nunc erit estque focis / nullaque dicitur vittas temerasse sacerdos /hoc duce nec vivam defodietur humo.*

135 Duval 2005: 67–9, with further references to Jerome, Cyprian and Augustine, who all present excommunication in terms of the spiritual sword versus the "real" sword. For Cyprian, cf. Clark 2008: 14.

136 Council of Nicaea, Canon 13.

137 Cf. Parker 1983: 98.

138 Hier. *Ep*. 22.38: *Gaude soror, gaude filia, gaude mi virgo: quia quod aliae simulant, tu vere esse coepisti.*

139 Skinner 2005: 26, cf. Verg. *Aen*. 1.315–16, where Venus appears before her son *virginis os habitumque gerens, et virginis arma/ Spartanae.*

140 On the *pseudoparthenoi* described by Herodotus, cf. King 1993: 119, Sissa 1990: 83.

141 Cf. Dunn's note 127 to his 2004 translation.

142 Tert *Virg. vel*. 14: *Si intectum caput virginitati adscribitur, si qua virgo exciderit de gratia virginitatis, ne prodatur, intecto permanet capite: et tunc jam alieno ambulat habitu, id est quem sibi vindicat virginitas: permanet nihilominus in habitu, vel tunc saltem alieno, ne scilicet mutatione prodatur.* Transl. ANF.

143 Hier. *Ep*. 22.13: *Purpura tantum in veste tenuis, et laxius, ut crines decidant, ligatum caput, soccus vilior, et super humeros hyacinthina laena Maforte volitans: succinctae manichae brachiis adhaerentes, et solutis genubus factus incessus. Haec est apud illas tota virginitas. Habeant istiusmodi laudatores suos, ut sub virginali nomine lucrosius pereant. Libenter talibus non placemus.* Transl. NPNF2.

144 Hier. *Ep*. 22.13, cf. *De laps. Sus*. II.5: *quae multipliciter misera cum gloria virginitatis nomen etiam perdidisti*; Bas. *Ep*. 55, Apul. *Apol*. 76.4: *Venit igitur ad eum nova nupta secura et intrepida, pudore dispoliato, flore exsoleto, flammeo obsoleto, virgo rursum post recens repudium, nomen potius afferens puellae quam integritatem.* cf. Adkin 2003: 117 for more references to "the name/title virgin."

145 Hier. *Ep*. 22.15: *nolunt esse virgines, sed videri.*

146 Hier. *Ep*. 22.38: *Sed quia sciunt virginale vocabulum gloriosum, sub ovium pellibus lupos tegunt. Christum mentitur Antichristus; et turpitudinem vitae falso nominis honore convestiunt.* Transl. NPNF2. Cf. Shaw 1998b: 496.

147 *De laps. Sus*.V.21: *et fingit se esse quod non est? Habitu virgo, facto non virgo: bis adultera, et in actu et in aspectu.* Transl. Tilley.

148 Hier. *Ep*. 22.13: [*Quas nisi tumor uteri, et infantium prodiderit vagitus*], *erecta cervice, et ludentibus pedibus incedunt.* Transl. NPNF2.

149 Cypr. *Ep*. 62, Hier. *Ep*. 22.14, cf. Clark 1977, Cloke 1995: 77–81, Shaw 1998b: 496–9.

150 Undheim 2017.

151 Beard 1995, cf. Langlands 2006: 252.

152 Sen. *Contr*. 1.2. Cf. Ambr. *De virgb.* II.22–33, and later parts of the Gesta of Saint Agnes. i.e. Denomy 1938: 23–4.

153 This case is thoroughly discussed by Langlands 2006: 253–64, and I follow her in her analysis and many of her arguments. For a similar case, see Quint. *Decl*. 252.

154 Sen. *Contr*. 1.2.1: *"Nemo" inquit "mihi virginitatem eripuit:" sed omnes quasi erepturi venerunt, sed omni quasi eripuisset recesserunt.* Transl. Loeb.

155 Sen. *Contr*. 1.2.2: *Quid inclusa feceris nec quaerere debemus nec scire possumus.* Transl. Loeb.

156 As opposed to Hippolytus, who still claims to have a virgin psyche even though he has seen images of the sexual act. Cf. above, pp. 111–12.

157 E.g. Sen. *Contr*. 1.2.3, 9–10 and passim.

158 Sen. *Contr*. 1.2.8: *"Nihil" inquit "passa sum." Hoc satis est nupturae, sacerdoti parum.* Transl. Loeb.

159 Sen. *Contr*. 1.2.13: *An casta sit, in haec divisit: utrum castitas tantum ad virginitatum referatur an ad omnium turpium et obscenarum rerum abstinentiam.* Transl. Loeb.

160   Sen. *Contr.* 1.2.13: *Puta enim virginem quidem essete, sed contrectatam osculis omnium; etiamsi citra stuprum, cum viris tamen volutata es.*

161   Sen. *Contr.* 1.2.13–14: *Etiamsi ad virginitatem tantum refertur castitas, an haec virgo sit.*

162   Sen. *Contr.* 1.2.14: *Aiebat Apollodoreis quidem placere fixa esse themata et tuta, sed hic non repugnare controversiam huic suspicioni: non enim ponitur adhuc virginem, et multa sunt propter quae credibile sit non esse. Illud adiciebat: denoque etiamsi non effecero ut credant iudices non esse virginem, consequar tamen ut non putent dignam sacerdotio de qua dubitari potest an virgi sit.* Transl. Loeb. Cf. Sen. *Contr.* 1.2.10: *Nulla satis pudica est de qua quaeritur.*

163   Sen. *Contr.* 1.2.18: *ut futurae sacerdotis non violaret castitatem <sed> ostenderet.* Transl. Loeb with small changes.

164   Sen. *Contr.* 1.2.19: *inter tot pericula non servassent illam dii nisi sibi.* My transl.

165   Sen. *Contr.* 1.2.20: *eam vobis sacerdotem promitto quam incestam nulla facere possit fortuna.* My transl.

166   Sen. *Contr.* 1.2.17: *Narrate sane omnes tamquam ad prostitutam venisse, dum tamquam a sacerdote discesserint.* Transl. Loeb. Cf. Ambr. *De virgb.* II.27 and II.30.

167   Sen. *Contr.* 1.3.1: *Incesti damnata, antequam deiceretur de saxo, invocavit Vestam. Repetitur ad poenam.* Transl. Loeb, with my amendments.

168   Sen. *Contr.* 1.3.6: *Ita dii damnatam maluerunt absolvere quam sacerdotem?*

169   Sen. *Contr.* 1.3.1. *Veniet ad colendum Romani imperii pignus etiamsi non stupro, at certe carnificis manu incesta.* For the idea that the executioner could pollute a chaste Vestal, see Plin. *Ep.* 4.11. Note that Plinius here quotes the very words used by Euripides to describe the death of Polyxena in *Hecuba* (569).

170   Sen. *Contr.* 6.8: *Versus Virginis Vestalis. Virgo Vestalis scripsit hunc versum: felices nuptae! moriar nisi nubere dulce est. Rea est incesti.* My transl.

171   Sen. *Contr.* 6.8: *Incesta est etiam sine stupro quae cupit stuprum.* Transl. Loeb, with small changes.

172   Sen. *Contr.* 6.8: *Incesti damnari nulla potest nisi cuius violatum corpus est.* Transl. Loeb, with changes.

173   Sen. *Contr.* 6.8: *Vixit modeste, castigate; non cultus in illa luxuriosor, non conversatio cum viris licentiosior.* Transl. Loeb, with changes.

174   This is also one of the main arguments of Kelly 2000: 134 who, in her analysis of contemporary material, draws the line back to Livy's descriptions of the trials of Postumia and Minucia, who were both initially suspected of *incestum* because of their conduct and dress: "It may be a tenuous thread that connects classical ideas about appearance and behaviors to modern ideas, [...] yet the belief that the secrets of the body are to be discovered in dress and speech is certainly a persistent one." See also p. 76 above for Postumia and Minucia.

175   Aug. *Civ. Dei* I.18: *An vero si aliqua femina, mente corrupta violatoque proposito quod Deo voverat, pergat vitianda ad deceptorem suum, ad hoc eam pergentem sanctam vel corpore dicimus, ea sanctitate animi per quam corpus sanctificabatur amissa atque destructa?*

176   Hier. *Adv. Helv* 20: *Virginis definitio, sanctam esse corpore et spiritu; quia nihil prosit carnem habere virginem, si mente quis nupserit.* Transl. NPNF2, with changes.

177   Cf. Plu. *Cato* 20.5, Ambr. *Ep* 63,34. Hier. *Ep.* 128.3. Cf. Adkin 2003: 212 for a long list of further references.

178   Cf. Fraschetti 1984: 125 on the need to protect the pontifex maximus from the pollution of death. Cf. Plin. *Ep.* 7.19, where he writes that Vestals, when seriously ill, are removed from the Atrium Vestae and nursed by matrons who are relatives or guardians appointed by the pontifices.

179   Sen. *Contr.* 1.2.21–2: *unde scimus an cum venientibus pro virgintate alio libidinis genere deciderit?* Transl. Loeb with small changes.

180   Sen. *Contr.* 1.2.23: *fortasse dum repellit libidinem, manibus excepit.* Transl. Loeb.

181   Sen. *Contr.* 1.2.21–3: *quaedam satius est causae detrimento tacere quam verecundiae dicere.*

182 E.g. Symm. *Ep.* 9. 147 and 9.148, cf. Plin. *Ep.* 4.9.6.

183 Ambr. *Ep.* 5, see Matroye 1929. Beyenka, in a note to her translation, refers to others who date the letter to post 380.

184 Ambr. *Ep.* 5.11: *Tumescit alvus, et incedentem fetussui onera gravant; ut praetermittamus alia.*Transl. Beyenka. Cf. Hier. *Ep.* 22.13,Tert. *Virg. vel.* 15. If interpreted as a general rule, however, this statement could have a particular relevance in Mariology, as it might reflect badly on Mary, the mother of Jesus, whose virginity was already dubious according to some (e.g. Orig. *Adv. Cels.* I.32). As treated by orthodox defenders of Mary's virginty *in partu et post partum* (which were crucial issues already in the Protevangelium of James), the impossibility of a pregnant virgin is exactly what asserts the unique status of the Christian mother of God.

185 If we are to take Soranus' comment on the physical state of the virgin priestesses seriously, a pregnancy might be difficult to detect just by the look of a virgin priestess, and thus not impossible to conceal, at least for some time. The eating regime for Christian virgins, however, might work the other way around in concealing pregnancy by malnutrition of both pregnant woman and fetus, at least for some time. Brown 1988: 8 refers to Soranus' assurance that virginity represented no harm to the health of the virgin priestesses; they might "have menstrual difficulties and become fat and ill-proportioned, but this was due to lack of exercise." See Brown 1988: 8 with note 13 for reference.

186 Ambr. *Ep.* 5.12. *At forte sterilitatis obtentu abscondi in aliquibus possit flagitium. Hic vero cum editus partus et expositus, vel necatus (dum invidiae magis, quam probationi consulitur) dissipatus sit per aures universorum, strangulata est libertas calumniarum, si peperit.*Transl. Beyenka. Cf. Hier. *Ep.* 22.13.

187 E.g. Juv *Sat*VI, cf. Gourevich 1984: 195–216.

188 Ambr. *Ep.* 5.12.

189 Ambr. *Ep.* 5.14: *partus putatur, et remedium doloris ducitur, non examen pudoris.*

190 Ambr. *Ep.* 5.8: *Quid, quod etiam ipsi archiatri dicunt non satis liquido comprehendi inspectionis fidem, et ipsis medicinae vetustis doctoribus id sententiae fuisse?* Transl. Beyenka. Ambrose appears here to be well read in ancient gynecology, cf. e.g. Sissa 1990: 172–4, King 1993, Hanson 2007, Lillis 2016. For current medical debate on virginity, and particularly the hymen as non reliable "proof" of virginity, see Blank 2007: 32–41, Kelly 2000: 119–41, Wogan-Browne 2003.

191 Ambr. *Ep.* 5.8: *Nos quoque usu hoc cognovimus, saepe inter obstetrices obortam varietatem, et quaestionem excitatam; ut plus dubitatum sit de ea, quae inspiciendam se praebuerit, quam de ea, quae non fuerit inspecta.*Transl. Beyenka.

192 Ambr. *De vid* 26: *Virgo enim, licet in ea quoque major sit morum praerogativa quam corporis, calumniam tamen integritate carnis abjurat; vidua, quae probandae subsidium virginitatis amiserit, non in voce obstetricis, sed in suis moribus habet castitatis examen.* Transl. NPNF2.

193 Cypr. *Ep.* LXII. 3 III. *Nec aliqua putet se posse hac excusatione defendi quod et inspici et probari possit an virgo sit, cum et manus obstetricum et oculi saepe fallantur, et si incorrupta inventa fuerit virgo ea parte sui qua mulier potest esse, potuerit tamen ex alia corporis parte peccasse quae corrumpi potest et tamen inspici non potest.*Transl. ANF.This is not unlike Murredius' insinuations in Sen. *Contr.* 1.2.21–3.

194 Cypr. *Ep.* LXII. 3 VI.1: *Quod si poenitentiam hujus illiciti concubitus sui egerint et a se invicem recesserint, inspiciantur interim virgines ab obstetricibus diligenter; et, si virgines inventae fuerint, accepta communicatione, ad Ecclesiam admittantur.*Transl. ANF.

195 Aug. *Civ. Dei* 1.18: *Obstetrix virginis cuiuedam integritatem manu velut explorans sive malevolentia sive inscitia sive casu, dum inspicit, perdidit.* McInerney 2003: 78–81, cf. Kelly 2000: 33–5, who also quotes John Chrysostom's skepticism towards midwives.

196 Ambr. *Ep.*5.14: *ut se offerant inspectioni, quo vel corporis probetur custodia; si tamen deprehendi potest, in quibus nutat pudoris gratia, et disciplina integritatis. Male tamen se*

habet causa, ubi potior est carnis, quam mentis praerogativa. Malo morum signaculo, quam corporis claustro virginitatem exprimi. Transl. Beyenka.

197   Evans Grubbs 1999: 193–202, CTh 9.8.1: *Imp. Constantinus a. ad Bassum vicarium Italiae. Post alia: ubi puellae ad annos adultae aetatis accesserint et adspirare ad nuptias coeperint, tutores necesse habeant comprobare, quod puellae sit intemerata virginitas, cuius coniunctio postulatur. Quod ne latius porrigatur, hic solus debet tutorem nexus adstringere, ut se ipsum probet ab iniuria laesi pudoris immunem. Quod ubi constiterit, omni metu liber optata coniunctione frui debebit; officio servaturo, ut, si violatae castitatis apud ipsum facinus haereat, deportatione plectatur, atque universae eius facultates fisci viribus vindicentur, quamvis eam poenam debuerit sustinere, quam raptori leges imponunt. Dat. prid. non. april. Aquileia, Constantino a. VI. et Constantino c. coss.*

198   Evans Grubbs 1999: 199 and 201.

199   *De laps. Sus.VI.26: Multum audax, multum temeraria, ut te conscientia tua non terreret, sed simulata virginitate, putares te etiam Dominum posse decipere. [...] ille qui non mentitur, furtivum scelus deduxit in publicum et in conspectu solis huius tenebrarum vestrarum opera denudavit.* Transl. Tilley.

200   A curious impediment to the identification of a fallen virgin by her growing stomach appears in Festus, who refers to Afranius' testimony of a stomach tumor called *molucrum* that could often afflict even virgins: "The stomach of a virgin grows just like that of a pregnant woman. This is called Molucrum, and it passes without pain." According to Afranius, this occurs often, and seemingly particularly to virgins, but he says nothing about how quickly it passed away. (Fest. 124: *Molucrum non solum quo mola verruntur dicitur [...] sed etiam tumor ventris, qui etiam virginibus <incidere> solet: cuius meminit Afranius in Virgine (336): Ferme virgini <tam crescit uterus> tamquam gravidae mulieri. Molucrum vocatur, transit sine doloribus.* Cf. *Pauli excerpta, idem* 125, Gourevich 1984: 158–60.) We could perhaps not assume that this medical condition was well known by the Fathers, but it is nevertheless one of the many complicating factors other bishops might have had to consider.

201   Cf. above pp. 112–13.

202   Cf. Burrus 1995, Kelly 2000: 56, McInerney 2003: 75.

203   The verb *elencho* indicates without further specification some kind of examination, either by cross-examination or by testing, but it also has a denotation in the sense "to disgrace" or "shame." Cf. Liddell and Scott s.v. *elencho*.

204   Ael. *N.A.* XI.16. Transl. Loeb.

205   Prop. IV.8.3–14: *si fuerint castae, redeunt in colla parentum, / clamantque agricolae "fertilis annus erit."* Transl. Loeb. The link between preserved virginity and agricultural fertility was, as we have seen, also one that Symmachus appealed to in his request to the Emperor to retain the Vestal priestesses' status and privileges, cf. above p. 54.

206   For this rite being related to a cult of Juno Sospita at Lanuvium, see Douglas 1913, in particular pp. 70–2, with several references to Frazer. See also Rose 1922, Aronen 1989 on the plausible connection to later legends of the Vestals and St Silvester killing the dragon-serpent allegedly in the custody of the virgin priestesses.

207   Serv. *Ad Aen.* 3.12: *dii penates [...] quod eorum nomina nemo sciat: quod praesentissimi sentiantur; nam cum ambae virgines in templo deorum Lavini simul dormirent, ea quae minus casta erat fulmine exanimata alteram nihil sensisse.*

208   Val. Max. 1.1.7: *Maximae vero virginis Aemilia discipulam extincto igne tutam ad omni reprehensione Vesae numen praestit.*

209   Val. Max. 1.1.7, D.H. II.68, Prop. IV.11,53.

210   Val. Max. 8.1.5: *Eodem auxilii genere Tuccia virginis Vestalis, incesti crimine reae, castitas infamiae nube obscurata emersit. Quae conscientia certa sinceritas suae spem salutis ancipiti argumento ausa petere est: arrepta enim cribro 'Vesta' inquit, 'si sacris tuis castas semper admovi manus, effice ut hoc hauriam e Tiberi aquam et in aedem tuam perferam.' Audaciter*

et temere iacitis votes sacerdotis Rerum ipsa Natura cessit. Aug. *Civ. Dei* X.16: *quod virgo Vestalis de cuius corruptione quaesito vertebatur aqua inpleto cribro de Tiberi neque perfluente abstulit controversiam.* See also Plin. *N.H.* 28.3.12, D.H. II.69 and VIII.8, Tert. *Apol.* 22.12. According to Liv. *Epit.* 20, a Tuccia was condemned for *incestum.* For modern scholars' interpretations of the *cribrum* of Tuccia, see Boldrini 1995, Sissa 1990: 127–8 and Richlin 1997.

211 Ov. *Fast* 4.291–348, Liv. 29.14.5–14, Tert. *Apol.* 22.12, Aug. *Civ. Dei* X.16.
212 Hdn. *Hist.* 1.11, 4–5.
213 Hier Adv. Iov. 1.41.
214 Feeney 2006: 26.
215 Sen. *Contr.* 1.2.3: *Aliter deorum numini subiecta uniuscuiusque conscientia est, aliter nostrae aestimationi: nos tantum quae palam feceras vidimus, illi etiam quae secreta sunt.* Transl. Loeb.
216 *De laps. Sus.* VI. 26, quoted p. 176 above.
217 Plin. *N.H.* 36.34: *fugat serpentes ita recreatque volvae strangulationes. deprendit sonticum morbum et virginitatem suffitus.* Albertus Magnus referred to the same method and elaborated on how this test was to be performed in his treatise *De mineralibus,* cf. note to this passage in Loeb, and Kelly 2000: 30–1.
218 Cornell 1981, Mustakallio 1992.
219 D.H. II.67.5. Transl. Loeb. The goddess Vesta was not represented by any cult image, she was only present in the form of the perpetual fire that was tended by her priestesses. E.g. Ov. *Fast.*VI.291 and Ov. *Fast.*VI.295–8.
220 Prud. *Contr. Symm.* II.1055–90.
221 Undheim 2015.
222 Shaw 1998b: 489.
223 Shaw 1998b: 493.
224 For the importance of public display, and the paradoxical tension with the demand to "be veiled" in the construction of the Roman concept of *pudicitia,* see Langlands 2006. For the performace of modesty, see also Wilkinson 2015.
225 Kelly 2000: 122. Cf. Langlands 2006: 264, commenting on Sen. *Contr.* 1.2: "to put *pudicitia* on trial is already to compromise it."
226 Langlands 2006: 211, cf. Miller and Platter 1999: 453
227 Cf. Adkin 2003: 124 for a long list of examples. For the "crown of *pudicitia*," see Langlands 2006: 38, 61–2 and 127–8, i.e. Val. Max. 2.1.3.
228 Trout 1994: 66, i.e. Aug. *Civ. Dei* I.19.
229 Sappho frag. 114V, quoted from Hanson 2007: 45. The poem presents a dialogue between bride and personified *partheneia.*
230 Dowden 1989: 143, Irwin 2007: 18, i.e. Paus. 2.38.2. Cf. Naguib 1992: 5, who states that "In antiquity, 'virginity' at a cosmic level was considered a grace perennially renewed and not intrinsic to chastity."
231 Tert. *Exh. cast.* 1: *Prima species, virginitas a nativitate. Secunda virginitas, a secunda nativitate, id est a lavacro, quae aut in matrimonio purificat ex compacto, aut in viduitate perseverat ex arbitrio. Tertius gradus superest monogamia, cum post matrimonium unum interceptum exinde sexui renuntiatur. Prima virginitas felicitatis est, non nosse in totum a quo postea optabis liberari. Secunda virtutis est, contemnere cujus vim optime noris. Reliqua species hactenus nubendi post matrimonium morte disjunctum, praeter virtutis, etiam modestiae laus est.*
232 The biblical source for this hierarchical classification is Matt. 8:8, which is explained in terms of this hierarchy of virgins, widows and married in, e.g., Hier. *Ep.* 48.2–3. See Adkin 2003: 126–7 for a long list of further instances in the corpus of Early Christian texts, especially in Jerome's writing.
233 This is even more explicitly expressed in *Virg. vel.* 10, where Tertullian apparently places chastity above virginity, because virginity is preserved by grace, while chastity is maintained by virtue. Cf. Kelly 2000: 114.

234 It has been suggested that the soul in the allegorical exposition in the Nag Hammadi text *The Exegesis of the Soul* is restored to virginal status as part of baptism and preparation for marriage to Christ. See Lundhaug 2007: 95, where it is also referred to Philo, whose theology posited that "God's intercourse with the soul renews its virginity."

235 Ambr. *De virgt* 38: *Si qui habent, timere non debent; uxores enim eorum jam virgines esse non possunt.*

236 Hier. *Ep.* 22.5: *Audenter loquar: Cum omnia possit Deus, suscitare virginem non potest post ruinam. Valet quidem liberare de poena, sed non vult coronare corruptam.* Transl. NPNF2. For the statement as contribution to medieval debate on the omnipotence of God, see Resnick 1988.

237 Hier. *Ep.* 128.3: *non quaerat virginitatis, et aeternae pudicitiae nuditatem, quam semel habere desivit.*

238 Hier. *Ep.* 22.15.2.

239 Hier. *Ep.* 39.1: *Secura esto, mi Blaesilla, sentiens omni tempore vestimenta tua candida. Candor vestium, sempiternae virginitatis est puritas. Confidimus probare vera esse quae dicimus: Nunquam est sera conversio.* Transl. NPNF2. For John Chrysostom reassuring widows that Christ is ready to welcome them as "pure virgins," see Clark 2008: 16–17.

240 See Undheim 2011: 198, i.e. Aug. *De bono conjugali* 31 and *De sancta virginitate* 27–9.

241 Aug. *De sancta virginitate* 27: [...] *virginitas autem carnis non omnibus; non enim habent quid faciant ut virgines sint, in quibus jam factum est ut virgines non sint.* My transl.

242 Aug. *De sancta virginitate* 29: *Sed ecce ille Agnus graditur itinere virginali; quomodo post eum ibunt qui hoc amiserunt quod nullo modo recipiunt? Vos ergo, vos ite post eum, virgines ejus; vos et illuc ite post eum, quia propter hoc unum quocumque ierit sequimini eum: ad quodlibet enim aliud sanctitatis donum quo eum sequantur, hortari possumus conjugatos, praeter hoc quod irreparabiliter amiserunt. Vos itaque sequimini eum tenendo perseveranter quod vovistis ardenter. Facite cum potestis, ne virginitatis bonum a vobis pereat, cui facere nihil potestis ut redeat.* Transl. NPNF1, with my changes.

243 Aug. *De sanct. virg.* 39: *Bonum est tibi, o anima virginalis, ut sic quomodo virgo es, sic omnino servans in corde quod renata es, servans in carne quod nata es, concipias tamen a timore Domini et parturias spiritum salutis* (Isai. XXVI, 18). See also Adkin 2003: 161.

244 Cameron 1994: 171.

245 Cf. above p. 9.

246 E.g. CIL 6.10867: *D(is) M(anibus) / memoriae / Ael(iae) Crescentinae / compari / quae vixit annis / virgo XII cum mari/to XXX et menses VI / Aufidius Secundianus / uxori fecit.* Cf. CIL 6.22657, CIL 6.17050, CIL 6.11939, CIL 6,07732, CIL 6.9810 (=ILS 7463) which all record Roman women who lived with their husbands "from" /"after" their virginity (*a/post virginitate*). See also Vogel 1966.

247 Apuleius *Apol.* 92.6–7: *Virgo formosa etsi sit oppido pauper, tamen [h]abunde dotata est; affert quippe ad maritum nouum animi indolem, pulchritudinis gratiam, floris rudimentum. Ipsa virginitatis commendatio iure meritoque omnibus maritis acceptissima est. (7) Nam quodcumque aliud in dotem acceperis, potes, cum libuit, ne sis beneficio obstrictus, omne ut acceperas retribuere: pecuniam renumerare, mancipia restituere, domo demigrare, praediis cedere; sola virginitas cum semel accepta est, reddi nequitur, sola apud maritum ex rebus dotalibus remanet.* Translation by Hunink in Harrison, Hilton and Hunink 2001: 110–11. Cf. Evans Grubbs 1999: 202.

248 Hier. *Ep.* 130.11: *Jejunium non perfecta virtus, sed caeterarum virtutum fundamentum est; et sanctificatio atque pudicitia, sine qua nemo videbit Deum, gradus praebet ad summa scandentibus, nec tamen si sola fuerit, virginem poterit coronare.* Transl. NPNF2.

249 Shaw 1998b: 496, cf. Kelly 2000: 122.

250 Undheim 2015.

251 Sen. *Contr.* 1.2.4: *aliis oculis virginem leno aestimat, aliis pontifex.* My transl.

252 Cf. e.g. Rousselle 1988: 136.

253 Langlands 2006: 211, see also Undheim 2015.

Bibliography

Primary sources: translations and editions

Where nothing else is stated, the Latin text is quoted from the Patrologia Latina or Loeb Classical Library. Apart from the Patrologia Latina editions, specific references are given in the bibliography below. When translations are quoted from a series, such as Ante-Nicene Fathers, Nicene, Post-Nicene Fathers or Loeb editions, the reference is to the series (for example, NPNF2), and not to the translator. In most of these cases, the translator can be identified in the bibliography below. Occasionally, translations are quoted from secondary literature or so-called "source collections," and thus, if not listed in the bibliography below, to be found in the subsequent bibliography of secondary sources. I have only provided my own translations of the texts in the cases where I have not been able to identify applicable translations elsewhere.

Achilles Tatius: *Leucippe and Clitophon*. Edited by Ebbe Vilborg, Elander Boktryckeri Aktiebolag, Gothenburg 1955
– *Leucippe and Clitophon*. Translated with notes by Tim Whitmarsh, Oxford University Press, Oxford 2001
Acts of Paul and Thecla: Acta Petri, Acta Pauli, Acta Petri et Pauli, Acta Pauli et Theclae, Acta Thaddaei (Acta Apostolorum Apocrypha, Vol. I). R. A. Lipsius (Ed.), Hermannum Mendelssohn, Lipsiae 1891
– *The Apocryphal New Testament: A collection of Apocryphal Christian literature in an English translation*. J. K. Elliott (Ed.), Oxford University Press, Oxford 1993
Aelianus: *De natura animalium* [*On the characteristics of animals*]. A. F. Scholfield, LCL, London 1958–9
Aldhelm: *De virginitate*. Michael Lapidge and Michael Herren (transl.), in *Aldhelm: The Prose Works*. D. S. Brewer, Cambridge 1979
Ambrose: *De virginitate: Liber unus*. Egnatius Cazzaniga (Ed.), Corpus Scriptorum Latinorum Paravianum, Paravia, Turin 1952
– *Écrits sur la virginité*. Dom Marie-Gabriel Tissot (Ed. and transl.), Abbaye Saint-Pierre de Solesmes, Solesmes 1980
– *Letters 1–91*. Mary Melchior Beyenka, O. P. (transl.), *The Fathers of the Church: A New Translation*, Vol. 26, The Catholic University of America, Washington, DC 2001
– *On virginity*. Daniel Callam (transl.), Peregrina Publishing, Saskatoon 1987
– *On virgins* in *Ambrose*. Boniface Ramsey O. P., Routledge, London 1997

– *On virgins* in *Ambrose: Select Works and Letters*. H. de Romestin (transl.), NPNF2 Vol. 10
– *On widowhood* in *Ambrose: Select Works and Letters*. H. de Romestin (transl.), NPNF2 Vol. 10
– *Opera Omnia di Sant'Ambrogio: Verginità e vedovanza*. Franco Gori (Ed. and transl.), Biblioteca Ambrosiana 14 (1–2) Città nouva editrice, Milan and Rome 1989
– *Scritti sulla verginità*. M. Bianco (Ed.), Edizioni Paoline, Roma 1954
– *Sulle vergini*. Pierfranco Beatrice (Ed.), Giovanni Coppa (transl.) Edizioni Messaggero, Padova 1982
Apuleius: *Apologia i.e., La Magia*. Biblioteca Universale Rizzoli, Milan 2000
– *Metamorfosi (l'asino d'oro)*. A cura di Marina Cavalli. Oscar Mondadori, Milan 1988
– *Rhetorical works*. Translated and annotated by Stephen Harrison, John Hilton and Vincent Hunink, Oxford University Press, Oxford 2001
Asconius: *Commentaries on Speeches of Cicero*. Translated with commentary by R. G. Lewis, with Latin text edited by A. C. Clark, Oxford University Press, Oxford 2006
Athanasius: *Apologia ad Constantium* in J.-M. Szymusiak, *Athanase d'Alexandrie. Apologie à l'empereur Constance. Apologie pour sa fuite Sources chrétiennes 56*, Éditions du Cerf, Paris 1958
– *First Letter to Virgins*. Appendix A in David Brakke: *Athanasius and the Politics of Asceticism*, Clarendon Press, Oxford 1995: 276ff
Augustine: *The Augustine volumes*. NPNF1 Vols 1–8
– *De civitate Dei. The city of God against the pagans, in seven volumes*. G. E. McCracken (transl.), LCL, London 1957–72
– *Marriage and Virginity. The Works of Saint Augustine: A Translation for the 21st Century*. Translation by Ray Kearney, edited with introductions and notes by David G. Hunter. John E. Routelle (Ed.), New City Press, New York 1999
Aulus Gellius: *Noctes Atticae* in 3 Vols. J. C. Rolfe, LCL, London 1961
Basil of Caesarea: *The Letters*. Translation by Roy J. Deferrari, LCL, London 1962
Caelius Aurelianus: *Gynaecia. Fragments of a Latin version of Soranus' Gynaecia from a Thirteenth Century Manuscript*. Miriam F. Drabkin and Israel E. Drabkin (Eds), Supplement to the Bulletin of the History of Medicine 13, John Hopkins Press, Baltimore 1951
Catullus: *The Poems of Catullus: A Bilingual Edition*. Translated with commentary by Peter Green, University of California Press, Berkeley 2005
Codex Theodosianus: The Theodosian Code and Novels and the Sirmodian Constitutions. Clyde Pharr, Princeton University Press, Princeton 1952
Church Councils (Ancyra, Elvira, etc.): *The seven Ecumenical Councils of the Undivided Church*. Henry R. Percival (Ed.), NPNF2 Vol. 14
Cyprian: *On the Dress of Virgins* in *Fathers of the Third Century: Hippolytus, Cyprian, Caius, Novatian, Appendix*. Ernest Wallis (transl.), ANF Vol. 5
– *The Epistles of Cyprian* in *Fathers of the Third Century: Hippolytus, Cyprian, Caius, Novatian, Appendix*. Ernest Wallis (transl.), ANF Vol. 5
De lapsu Susannae: Ad lapsam virginem libellus. A. E. Burn in *Niceta of Remesiana: His life and works*. Cambridge University Press, Cambridge 1905: 112–36
– "An anonymous letter to a woman named Susanna," Translation by Maureen Tilley, *Religions of Late Antiquity in Practice*. Richard Valantasis (Ed.), Princeton University Press, Princeton 2000: 218–29
– *Incerti Auctoris: De lapsu Susannae*. E. Cazzaniga (Ed.), Paravia, Turin 1948
Digestae: The Digest of Justinian. Alan Watson, University of Pennsylvania Press, Philadelphia 1998
Dio Cassius: *Roman History* in 9 Vols. E. Cary, LCL, London 1961

Dionysius of Halicarnassus: *Antiquitates Romanae* in 7 Vols. E. Cary, LCL, London 1960

Clement of Rome (Pseudo-Clement): *Two epistles concerning virginity*. B. P. Pratten (transl.), ANF Vol. 8

Euripides: *Children of Heracles, Hippolytus, Andromache, Hecuba*. David Kovacs (Ed. and transl.), LCL, Harvard University Press, Cambridge (MA) 1995

Expositio Totius Mundi et Gentium: Jean Rougé, Sources Chrétiennes 124, Cerf, Paris 1966: 299–360

Festus, Sextus Pompeius: *De verborum significatu quae supersunt cum Pauli epitome*. Wallace M. Lindsay, Teubner, Leipzig 1913

Homily: On virginity. Introduction and translation by Teresa M. Shaw in *Ascetic Behaviour in Greco-Roman Antiquity: A Sourcebook*. Vincent L. Wimbush (Ed.), Fortress Press, Minneapolis 1990: 29–44

– "Une curieuse homélie grecque inédite sur la virginité adressée aux pères de famille," David Armand and Mattheiu Charles Moons: *Revue Bénédictine* 63, 1953: 18–69

Innocent I: *Ep. 2, ad Victricium Rotomagensem*. Excerpt in Yves-Marie Duval, *La décrétale 'Ad gallos episcopos': son texte et son auteur: Texte critique, traduction française et commentaire*. Vigiliae Christianae Supplements 73, Brill, Leiden, 2005: 140–1

Isidore of Seville: *The etymologies of Isidore of Seville*. Translated by Stephen A. Barney, W. J. Lewis, J. A. Beach, Oliver Berghof, Cambridge University Press, Cambridge 2006

Jerome: *Letters and Select Works*. W. H. Fremantle (transl.), NPNF 2 Vol. 6

– *Letters* in *Jerome*. Stefan Rebenich (transl.) Routledge, London 2002

– *The Epistles of Cyprian* in *Fathers of the Third Century: Hippolytus, Cyprian, Caius, Novatian, Appendix*. Ernest Wallis (transl.), ANF Vol. 5.

Joseph and Aseneth: Joseph et Aséneth: Introduction, texte critique, traduction et notes. Par Marc Philonenko, Brill, Leiden 1968

John Cassian: *The Conferences*. Translated and annotated by Boniface Ramsey, O. P. *Ancient Christian Writers, The Works of the Fathers in Translation*, No. 57, Paulist Press, New York 1997

The Institutes. Translated and annotated by Boniface Ramsey, O. P. *Ancient Christian Writers, The Works of the Fathers in Translation*, No. 58, The Newman Press, New York 2000

Leo the Great: *The Letters and Sermons of Leo the Great*. Charles Lett Feltoe (transl.), NPNF2 Vol. 12

Macrobius: *I Saturnali*. A cura di Nino Marinone, Editrice Torinese, Turin 1967

Methodius of Olympus: *Le Banquet. Introduction et texte critique par Herbert Musurillo, traduction et notes par Victor-Henry Debidour*, Sources Chrétiennes, Paris 1963

Nonius Marcellinus: *De conpendiosa doctrina*. Libros XX, Wallace M. Lindsay (Ed.), Teubner, Leipzig 1903

Origen: *Against Celsus*. Frederick Crombie (transl.), ANF Vol. 4

Orosius: *Seven Books Against the Pagans*. Roy J. Deferrari, in *The Fathers of The Church: A New Translation*, The Catholic University of America Press, Washington, DC 1964

Optatus: *Against the Donatists*. Mark Edwards (Ed. and transl.), *Translated Texts for Historians*, Vol. 27, Liverpool University Press, Liverpool 1997

Ovid: *Fasti*. James G. Frazer, Classical Library, London 1989

– *Heroides – Heltinnebrev*. Thea Selliaas Thorsen (transl.) Gyldendal, Oslo 2001

– *Metamorphoses*. F. J. Miller, LCL, London 1966

Paulinus of Milan: *The Life of Saint Ambrose*, in *Ambrose*. Boniface Ramsey O. P. *Early Church Fathers*, Routledge, London 1997

Pausanias: *Descriptions of Greece*. Translated by W. H. S. Jones, LCL, London 1918–35

Philo: *De vita contemplativa*. In *Philo: Volume 9*, translated by F. H. Colson, LCL, London 1941

Propertius: *Elegiae*. H. E. Butler, LCL, London 1967

Prudentius: *Opera*, Vols 1–2. H. J. Thompson, LCL, London 1949–53

Seneca, M. Annaeus: *Controversiae*, Vols 1–2. M. Winterbottom, LCL, London 1974

Seneca, L. Annaeus: *Epistulae Morales*. John W. Basore, LCL, London 1965

Servius Honoratus: *In Vergilii Carmina Commentarii*, Vols I and III. Georg Thilo and Hermann Hagen (Eds), Georg Olms Verlagsbuchhandlung, Hildesheim 1961

– *In Vergilii Carmina Commentarii*, Vol. II. Georg Thilo and Hermann Hagen (Eds), Teubner, Leipzig 1884

Siricius: *Epistulae*. Patrologia Latina Vol. 13

– *Epistulum 1, ad Himerium Tarraconensem*. Excerpt in Yves-Marie Duval, *La décrétale 'Ad gallos episcopos': son texte et son auteur: Texte critique, traduction française et commentaire*. *Vigiliae Christianae Supplements* 73, Brill, Leiden, 2005: 140

– *Letter of Pope Siricius to Bishop Himerius of Tarragona* in *Prefaces to Canon Law. Books in Latin Christianity*. Robert Somerville and Bruce C. Brasington, Yale University Press, New Haven 1998: 36–9

Soranus: *Gynaikeia. Kvinnolära: om graviditet, förlossningskonst, spädbarnsvård och kvinnosjukdomar*. Sylvia Törnkvist and Ingrid Ursing, Åstöm 2001

– *Soranus' gynecology*. Translated by Owsei Temkin, John Hopkins Press, Baltimore 1956

Sozomenos, Socrates: *Ecclesiastical History*. Revised by Chester D. Hartranft, NPNF2 Vol. 2

Statius: *Silvae*. D. R. Shackleton Bailey (Ed. and transl.), LCL, Harvard University Press, London 2003

Sulpicius Severus: *The works of Sulpicius Severus*. Translated by Alexander Roberts, NPNF2 Vol. 9

Suetonius: *De vita Caesarum*, Vols I and II. J. C. Rolfe, LCL, London 1964 and 1965

Symmachus, Quintus Aurelius: *Commento storico al libro II dell'epistolario di Q. Aurelio Simmaco*. Giovanni Alberto Cecconi, Giardini Editori e stampatori, Pisa 2002

– *Commento storico al libro IX dell'epistolario di Q. Aurelio Simmaco*. Sergio Roda Giardini Editori e stampatori, Pisa 1981

– *Prefect and Emperor. The Relationes of Symmachus AD 384*. R. H. Barrow, Clarendon Press, Oxford, 1973

– *Symmaque, Lettres IV, livres IX-X*. Jean-Pierre Callu, Les Belles Lettres, Paris 2002

Terence: *Hecyra. Opera II*. John Sargeaunt, LCL, London 1965

– *The Comedies of Terence*. Henry Thomas Riley. Harper and Brothers, New York 1874. Available online, last accessed 27 April 2017: http://www.gutenberg.org/files/22188/22188-h/main.html

Tertullian: *Fathers of the Third Century*. A. Cleveland Coxe (Ed.). ANF Vol. 4

– *On the Veiling of Virgins*. Translated by Geoffrey D. Dunn in *Tertullian. The Early Church Fathers*, Routledge, London 2004

– *Latin Christianity: Its Founder, Tertullian*. Allan Menzies (Ed.). ANF Vol. 3

Valerius Maximus: *Facta et dicta memorabilia*. Vols 1–2. D. R. S. Bailey, LCL, London 2000

Zosimus: *Histoire Nouvelle*. François Paschoud, Société d'édition "Les belles lettres," Paris 1986

– *Historia Nova*. James J. Buchanan and Harold T. Davis, Trinity University Press, San Antonio 1967

Secondary sources

Adkin, Neil 2003. *Jerome on Virginity: A Commentary on the* Libellus de virginitate servanda *(Letter 22)*. ARCA 42. Cambridge: Francis Cairns

Ando, Clifford 2008. *The Matter of the Gods: Religion and the Roman Empire*. Berkeley: University of California Press

Arjava, Antti 1996. *Women and Law in Late Antiquity*. Oxford: Clarendon Press

Arnold, John H. 2003. "The labour of continence: Masculinity and clerical virginity," in *Medieval virginities*, Anke Bernau, Ruth Evans and Sarah Salih (Eds). Toronto: University of Toronto Press, 102–18

Arnulf, Arwed 1989. "Die Deckelinschrift des Berliner Kindersarkophages. Eine sardische Zweitverwendung eines stadtrömischen Sarkophagkastens," in *Jahrbuch für Antike und Christentum* 32: 141–50

Aronen, Jaakko 1989. "La sopravvienza dei cultu pagani e la topografia cristiania dell'area di Giuturna e delle sue adiacenze," in *Lacus Iuturnae I*, Eva Margareta Steinby (Ed.). Rome: De Luca edizioni d'arte, 148–74

Bauman, Richard A. 1992. *Women and Politics in Ancient Rome*. London: Routledge

Battaglia, Gabriella Bordenache 1983. *Corredi funerari di età imperiale e barbarica nel museo nazionale Romano*. Rome: Edizioni Quasar

Beard, Mary, North, John and Price, Simon 1998. *Religions of Rome: A History, Vol. I*. Cambridge: Cambridge University Press

– 1998. *Religions of Rome: A Sourcebook, Vol. II* Cambridge: Cambridge University Press

Beard, Mary. 1980. "The sexual status of the Vestal Virgins," *Journal of Roman Studies* 70: 12–27

– 1990. "Priesthood in the Roman Republic," in *Pagan Priests: Religion and Power in the Ancient World*, Mary Beard and John North (Eds). London: Duckworth, 19–48

– 1995. "Re-reading (Vestal) virginity," in *Women in Antiquity: New Assessments*, R. Hawley and B. Levick (Eds). London: Routledge, 166–77

– 1999. "The erotics of rape. Livy, Ovid and the Sabine women," in *Female Networks and the Public Sphere in Roman Society*, Päivi Setälä and Liisa Savunen (Eds). Rome: Acta Instituti Romani Finlandiae, Vol. 22: 1–10

BeDuhn, Jason David 1999. "'Because of the angels': Unveiling Paul's anthropology in 1 Corinthians 11." *Journal of Biblical Literature* 118.2: 295–320

Bernau, Anke 2007. *Virgins: A Cultural History*. London: Granta Books

Bernau, Anke, Salih, Sarah and Evans, Ruth 2003. "Introduction: Virginities and virginity studies," in *Medieval Virginities*, Anke Bernau, Ruth Evans and Sarah Salih (Eds). Toronto: University of Toronto Press, 1–13

Bjørnebye, Jonas 2007. *"Hic locus est felix, sanctus, piusque benignus": The Cult of Mithras in Fourth Century Rome*. Doctoral Thesis, University of Bergen

Blank, Hanne 2007. *Virgin: The Untouched History*. New York: Bloomsbury

Bloch, R. Howard 1991. *Medieval Misogyny and the Invention of Western Romantic Love*. Chicago: University of Chicago Press

Boldrini, S. 1995. "Verginità delle vestali: la prova," in *Vicende e figure femminili in Grecia e a Roma*, R. Raffaelli (Ed.). Ancona: Commissione per le pari opportunità tra uomo e donna della Regione Marche, 295–300

Boswell, John Eastburn 1984. "*Expositio* and *Oblatio*: The abandonment of children and the ancient and medieval family." *The American Historical Review* 89.1: 10–33

Bowersock, G. W. 2002 [1995]. *Martyrdom and Rome*. Cambridge: Cambridge University Press

Bowersock, G. W, Peter Brown and Oleg Grabar (eds.) 1999. *Late Antiquity: A Guide to the Postclassical World*. London: The Belknap Press of Harvard University Press

Boyarin, Daniel 1999. *Dying for God: Martyrdom and the Making of Christianity and Judaism*. Stanford: Stanford University Press

– 2004. *Border lines. The partition of Judaeo-Christianity.* Philadelphia: University of Pennsylvania Press

– 2009. "Rethinking Jewish Christianity: An argument for dismantling a dubious category (to which is appended a correction of my *Border Lines*)." *The Jewish Quarterly Review*, 99.1: 7–36

Boyarin, Daniel and Castelli, Elizabeth 2001. "Introduction: Foucault's *The History of Sexuality*: The fourth volume, or, a field left fallow for others to till." *Journal of the History of Sexuality* 10, 3/4: 357–74

Brakke, David 1995. *Athanasius and the Politics of Asceticism.* Oxford: Clarendon Press

– 2003. "The lady appears: Materializations of 'woman' in early monastic literature." *Journal of Medieval and Early Modern Studies* 33/3: 387–402

Brooten, Bernadette J. 1996. *Love Between Women. Early Christian Responses to Female Homoeroticism.* Chicago: University of Chicago Press

Brown, Peter 1986. "The notion of virginity in the Early Church," in *World Spirituality Vol. 17: Christian Spirituality: Origins to the Twelfth Century*, B. McGinn and J. Meyendorff (Eds). London: SCM Press, 427–43

– 1988. *The Body and Society: Men, Women and Sexual Renunciation in Early Christianity.* Columbia University Press, New York

– 2000a [1967]. *Augustine of Hippo: A Biography.* Berkeley: University of California Press

– 2000b. "The study of elites in Late Antiquity." *Arethusa* 33, 2000: 321–46

– 2001. "Christianization and religious conflict: Chapter 21," in *The Cambridge Ancient History, Vol. XIII: The Late Empire, A.D. 337–425.* Cambridge: Cambridge University Press, 632–64

– 2001. "Asceticism: Pagan and Christian. Chapter 20," in *The Cambridge Ancient History, Vol. XIII: The Late Empire, A.D. 337–425.* Cambridge: Cambridge University Press, 601–31

– 2003. "A life of learning," Charles Homer Haskins Lecture 2003. Available online, last accessed 2 April 2008: http://www.acls.org/uploadedfiles/publications/op/haskins/ 2003_peterbrown.pdf

– 2012. *Through the Eye of a Needle. Wealth, the Fall of Rome, and the Making of Christianity in the West, 350–550 AD.* Princeton: Princeton University Press

Buell, Denise Kimber 2005. *Why This New Race? Ethnic Reasoning in Early Christianity.* New York: Columbia University Press

Bugge, John 1975. *Virginitas: An Essay in the History of a Medieval Ideal*, International Archives of the History of Ideas, Series Minor 17. The Hague: Nijhoff

Burkert, Walter 2001. *Creation of the Sacred: Tracks of Biology in Early Religions.* London: Harvard University Press

Burn, A. E. 1905. *Niceta of Remesiana: His Life and Works.* Cambridge: Cambridge University Press

Burrus, Virginia 1987. *Chastity as Autonomy: Women in the Stories of Apocryphal Acts.* Studies in women and religion, Vol. 23. Lewiston: Edwin Mellen Press

– 1995. "Reading Agnes: The rhetoric of gender in Ambrose and Prudentius." *Journal of Early Christian Studies*, 3: 25–46

– 1996. "'Equipped for victory': Ambrose and the gendering of orthodoxy." *Journal of Early Christian Studies*, 4.4: 461–75

– 2000. *Begotten, not Made: Conceiving Manhood in Late Antiquity.* Stanford: Stanford University Press

– 2005. "Mimicking virgins: colonial ambivalence and the ancient romance." *Arethusa*, 38.1: 49–88

Cameron, Averil 1980. "'Neither male nor female'," in *Greece and Rome*. Second series, Vol. 27, no 1: 60–8

– 1986. "Redrawing the map: Early Christian territory after Foucault" (review). *Journal of Roman Studies*, 76: 266–71

– 1989. "Virginity as metaphor: women and the rhetoric of early Christianity," in *History as Text: The Writing of Ancient History*, A. Cameron (Ed.). London: Duckworth, 184–205

– 1994. *Christianity and the Rhetoric of Empire*. Berkeley: University of California Press

Caner, Daniel F. 1997. "The practice and prohibition of self-castration in early Christianity." *Vigiliae Christianae* 51, 4: 396–415

Castelli, Elisabeth 1986. "Virginity and its meaning for women's sexuality in early Christianity." *Journal of Feminist Studies in Religion*, 2.1: 61–88

– 1991. "'I will make Mary male': Pieties of the body and gender transformation of Christian women in late Antiquity," in *Bodyguards: The Cultural Politics of Gender Ambiguity*, Julia Epstein and Kristina Staub (Eds). New York: Routledge, 29–49

– 2004. *Martyrdom and Memory: Early Christian Culture Making*. New York: Columbia University Press

Cartledge, Paul 1997. "Getting after Foucault: Two postantique responses to postmodern challenges" (review), *Gender & History* 9.3: 615–19

Cazzaniga, Egnatius (Ed.) 1948. *Incerti auctoris: De lapsu Susannae (De lapsu virginis consecratae). Corpus Scriptorum Latinorum Paravianum*, Turin: Paravia

– 1950. *La tradizione manoscritta del 'De lapsu Susannae': Con nuovo apparato critico*. Turin: Paravia

Cecere, Maria Grazia Granino 2003. "Vestali non di Roma," *Studi epirgrafici e linguistici. Epigrafia e Storia delle religioni*, 20: 67–80

Clark, Elisabeth A. 1977. "John Chrysostom and the 'Subintroductae'." *Church History*, 46.2: 171–85

– 1986. *Ascetic Piety and Women's Faith: Essays on Late Ancient Christianity*. Lewiston, NY: Edwin Mellen Press

– 1988. "Foucault, the fathers and sex." *Journal of the American Academy of Religion*, 56.4: 619–41

– 1991. "Sex, shame and rhetoric: En-gendering early Christian ethics." *Journal of the American Academy of Religion*, 59.2: 221–45

– 1994. "Ideology, history and the construction of 'woman' in late ancient Christianity." *Journal of Early Christian Studies* 2.2: 155–84

– 1998a. "The lady vanishes: Dilemmas of a feminist historian after the 'linguistic turn'." *Church History* 67.1: 1–31

– 1998b. "Holy women, holy words: Early Christian women, social history and the 'Linguistic turn'." *Journal of Early Christian Studies*, 6.3: 413–30

– 1999. *Reading Renunciation: Asceticism and Scripture in early Christianity*. Princeton: Princeton University Press

– 2001. "Women, gender, and the study of Christian history." *Church History*, 70.3: 395–426

– 2004a. *History, Theory, Text: Historians and the Linguistic Turn*. Cambridge, MA: Harvard University Press

– 2004b. "Rewriting the history of early Christianity," in *The Past Before Us: The Challenge of Historiographies of Late Antiquity*, Carol Straw and Richard Lim (Eds). Bibliothéque de l'antiquité tardive 6, Turnhout: Brepolis Publishers, 61–8

– 2005. "Asceticism, class, and gender," in *A People's History of Christianity, Vol. 2: Late Antiquity*. Minneapolis: Fortress Press, 27–45

– 2008. "The celibate bridegroom and his virginal brides: Metaphor and the marriage of Jesus in early Christian ascetic exegesis." *Church History*, 77.1: 1–25

Clark, Gillian 1998. "Bodies and blood: Late Antique debate on martyrdom, virginity and resurrection," in *Changing Bodies, Changing Meaning: Studies on the Human Body in Antiquity*, Dominic Montserrat (Ed.). London: Routledge, 99–115

Cloke, Gillian 1995. *This Female Man of God: Women and Spiritual Power in the Patristic Age, AD 350–450.* London: Routledge

Cohen, David and Richard Saller 1994. "Foucault on sexuality in Greco-Roman antiquity," in *Foucault and the Writing of History*, Jan Goldstein (Ed.). Oxford: Blackwell, 35–59

Connelly, Joan Breton 2007. *Portrait of a Priestess: Women and Ritual in Ancient Greece.* Princeton: Princeton University Press

Consolino, Franca Ela 1982. "Dagli 'Exempla' ad un esempio di comportamento cristiano: il 'De exhortatione virginitatis' di Ambrogio." *Rivista storica italiana* 94.2: 455–77

– 1984. "*Veni huc a Libano*: La *sponsa* del Cantico dei Cantici come modello per le vergini negli scritti esortatori di Ambrogio." *Athenaeum*: 399–415

Coon, Lynda L. 1997. *Sacred Fiction: Holy Women and Hagiography in Late Antiquity.* Philadelphia: University of Pennsylvania Press

Cooper, Kate 1992. "Insinuations of womanly influence: An aspect of the Christianization of the Roman Aristocracy." *Journal of Roman Studies*, Vol. 82: 150–64

– 1996. *The Virgin and the Bride: Idealized Womanhood in Late Antiquity.* London: Harvard University Press

– 2007. "'Only virgins give birth to Christ': The virgin Mary and the problem of female authority in Late antiquity," in *Virginity Revisited: Configurations of the Unpossessed Body*, Bonnie MacLachlan and Judith Fletcher (Eds). Toronto: University of Toronto Press, 100–15

Cornell, Tim 1981. "Some observations on the 'crimen incesti'," in *Le délit religieux dans la cite antique.* Rome: Collection de l'école Française de Rome 48, 27–37

Corrington, Gail P. 1987. "The 'Divine woman'? Propaganda and the power of chastity in the New Testament." *Helios* 13.2, 151–62

Courtney, Edgar E. 1995. *Musa Lapidaria. A selection of Latin verse inscriptions*, American Classical Studies no. 36. Atlanta: Scholars Press

Curran, John 2000. *Pagan City and Christian Capital: Rome in the Fourth Century.* Oxford: Clarendon Press

D'Angelo, Mary Rose 1995. "Veils, virgins, and the tongues of men and angels: Women's heads in early Christianity," in *Off with Her Head! The Denial of Women's Identity in Myth, Religion and Culture*, Howard Eilberg-Schwartz and Wendy Doniger (Eds). Berkeley: University of California Press, 131–64

Davis, Stephen J. 2002. "Crossed texts, crossed sex: Intertextuality and gender in Early Christian legends of holy women disguised as men." *Journal of Early Christian Studies*, 10.1: 1–36

Deacy, Susan 2002. "The vulnerability of Athena: *Parthenoi* and rape in Greek myth," in *Rape in Antiquity: Sexual Violence in the Greek and Roman World*, Susan Deacy and Karen F. Pierce (Eds). London: Duckworth, 43–63

Delon, Michel 1995. "Mythologie de la vestale." *Dix-huitième siècle*, 27: 159–70

van Deman, Esther Boise 1912. "The value of the vestal statues as originals." *American Journal of Archaeology*, 324–42

Denomy, Alexander Joseph 1938. *The Old French Lives of Saint Agnes and Other Vernacular Versions of the Middle Ages.* Cambridge, MA: Harvard University Press

Desanti, Lucetta 1987. "Sul matrimonio di donne consecrate a Dio nel diritto Romano Cristiano." *Studia et documenta historiae et iuris* 53: 270–96

– 1990. "Vestali e vergini cristiane." *Atti del Accademia Romanistica Costantiniana, VIII Convegno Internazionale*. Naples: Edizioni Scientifiche Italiane, 473–88

Dillon, Matthew 2002. *Girls and Women in Classical Greek Religion*. London: Routledge

Douglas, E. M. 1913. "Iuno Sospita of Lanuvium." *Journal of Roman Studies* 3.1: 60–72

Dowden, Ken 1989. *Death and the Maiden: Greek Initiation Rites in Greek Mythology*. London: Routledge

Dubourdieu, Annie 1989. *Les origins et le développement du culte des Pénates à Rome*. CEFR 118. Rome, École Française à Rome

Dunn, Geoffrey D. 2005. "Rhetoric and Tertullian's *De virginibus velandis*." *Vigiliae Christianae* 59: 1–30

Duval, Yves-Marie 1974. "L'originalité de *de virginibus* dans le mouvement ascétique occidental: Ambroise, Cyprien, Athanase," in *Ambroise de Milan: XVIe centenaire de son élection épiscopale*, Yves-Marie Duval (Ed.). Paris: Études Augustiniennes, 9–66

– 2003. *L'affaire Jovinien: D'une crise de la société romaine à une crise de la pensée Chrétienne à la fin du IVè au début de Vè siècle*. Rome: Studia Ephemeridis Augustinianum, 83

– 2005. *La décrétale 'Ad gallos episcopos': son texte et son auteur: Texte critique, traduction française et commentaire*. Vigiliae Christianae Supplements 73, Leiden: Brill

Elm, Susanna 2003 [1994]. *'Virgins of God': The Making of Asceticism in Late Antiquity*. Oxford: Clarendon Press

Engh, Line Cecilie 2014. *Gendered Identities in Bernard of Clairvaux's Sermons on The Song of Songs: Performing the Bride*. Turnhout: Brepols

Evans Grubbs, Judith 1989. "Abduction marriage in antiquity: A law of Constantine and its social context." *Journal of Roman Studies* 79: 59–83

– 1999. *Law and Family in Late Antiquity: The Emperor Constantine's Marriage Legislation*. Oxford: Oxford University Press

– 2001. "Virgins and widows, show-girls and whores: Late Roman legislation on women and Christianity," in *Law, Society and Authority in Late Antiquity*, Ralph E. Mathisen (Ed.). Oxford: Oxford University Press, 220–41

– 2002. *Women and the Law in the Roman Empire: A Sourcebook on Marriage, Divorce and Widowhood*. London: Routledge

Evans, Roger Steven 2003. *Sex and Salvation: Virginity as a Soteriological Paradigm in Ancient Christianity*. Oxford: University Press of America

Eyben, Emiel 1972. "Antiquity's view of puberty." *Latomus* 31.3, 677–97

Faroult, Guillaume 2006. "Les Fortunes de la Vertu. Origines et évolution de l'iconographie des vestales jusqu'au XVIIIe siècle." *Revue de l'art*, 152.2: 9–29

Feeney, Denis 1998. *Literature and Religion at Rome*. Cambridge: Cambridge University Press

– 2006. "On not forgetting the 'Literatur' in 'Literatur und Religion': Representing the Mythic and the Divine in Roman Historiography." version 1.0 March 2006, *Princeton/Stanford Working Papers in Classics*

Ferrua, Antonio 1967. "Il sarcofago di un bambino del IVo secolo." *La civiltá cattolica* 118.1: 353–62

Flemming, Rebecca 2007. "Festus and the role of women in Roman religion," in *Verrius, Festus & Paul: Lexicography, Scholarship, & Society*, Fay Glinister and Clare Woods with J. A. North and M. H. Crawford (Eds). *Bulletin of the Institute of Classical Studies* Supplement 93, Institute of Classical Studies, School of Advanced Study, University of London

Foskett, Mary F. 2002. *A Virgin Conceived: Mary and Classical Representations of Virginity*. Bloomington: Indiana University Press

Foucault, Michel 1985. "The battle for chastity," in *Western Sexuality: Practice and Precept in Past and Present Times*, Phillipe Ariès and André Béjin (Eds). Oxford: Basil Blackwell, 14–25

212   *Bibliography*

– 1988. *The Care of the Self: The History of Sexuality*, Volume 3. New York: Vintage Books

– 1999. "Sexuality and solitude," in *Religion and Culture by Michel Foucault*, Jeremy R. Carrette (Ed.). Manchester: Manchester University Press

Fox, Robin Lane 1986. *Pagans and Christians in the Mediterranean World from the Second Century AD to the Conversion of Constantine*. London: Penguin Books

Fraschetti, Augusto 1984. "La sepoltura delle vestali e la cittá," in *Du chatiment dans la cité. Supplices corporels et peine de mort dans le monde antique*. Collection de l'école Française de Rome 79: 97–128

Frazel, Thomas D. 2003. "Priapus's two rapes in Ovid's Fasti." *Arethusa* 36.1: 61–97

Freudenburg, Kirk 2001. *Satires of Rome: Threatening Poses from Lucilius to Juvenal*. Cambridge: Cambridge University Press

Gallia, Andrew B. 2015. "Vestal virgins and their families." *Classical Antiquity*, 34.1: 74–120

Gardner, Jane F. 1991. *Women in Roman Law and Society*. Kent: Indiana University Press

Garrido, Mercedes Serrato 1993. *Ascetesimo femenino en Roma. Estudios sobre San Jerónimo y San Augustín*. Cadiz: University of Cadiz

Gaudemet, Jean 1980 [1949]. "Note sur les formes anciennes de l'excommunication," *Revue de sciences religieuses 83, 1949*, in *La société ecclésiastique dans l'Occident medieval*. London: Variorum Reprints

– 1980 [1950]. "Saint Augustin et le manquement au voeu de virginité," *Annales de la Fac. De droit d'Aix-en-Province, nouvelle série No 43. Aix-en-Province, 1950*, in *La société ecclésiastique dans l'Occident medieval*. London: Variorum Reprints, 5–15

van Gennep, Arnold 1981 [1909]. *Les Rites de Passage*. Paris: Picard

Goldhill, Simon 1995. *Foucault's Virginity: Ancient Erotic Fiction and the History of Sexuality*. Cambridge: Cambridge University Press

Gourevitch, Danielle 1984. *Le mal d'être femme: La femme et la medecine a Rome*. Paris: Societé d'édition "Les belles lettres"

Grodinsky, Denise 1984. "Ravies et coupables. Un essai d'interpretation de la loi IX.24.1 du code Théodosien." *Melanges de l'École française de Rome*, 697–726

de Gubernatis, M. Lenchantin 1916. "Ianuariae epitaphium." *Athenaeum* 4: 157–60

Hallett, Judith P. 1997. "Female homoeroticism and the denial of Roman reality in Latin literature," in *Roman Sexualities*, Judith P. Hallett and Marylin B. Skinner (Eds). Princeton: Princeton University Press, 255–73

Hanson, Ann Ellis 1990. "The medical writer's woman," in *Before Sexuality: The Construction of Erotic Experience in the Ancient Greek World*, D. M. Halperin, J. J. Winkler and F. I. Zeitlin (Eds). Princeton: Princeton University Press, 309–37

– 2007. "The Hippocratic *Parthenos* in sickness and in health," in *Virginity Revisited: Configurations of the Unpossessed Body*, Bonnie MacLachlan and Judith Fletcher (Eds). Toronto: University of Toronto Press, 40–65

Hanson, Ann Ellis and David Armstrong 1986. "The virgin's voice and neck: Aeschylus, *Agamemnon* 245 and other texts." *Bulletin of the Institute of Classical Studies*, 33: 97–100

Harlow, Mary and Ray Laurence 2002. *Growing Up and Growing Old in Ancient Rome: A Life Course Approach*. London: Routledge

Harper, Kyle 2013. *From Shame to Sin. The Christian Transformation of Sexual Morality in Late Antiquity*. Cambridge, Harvard University Press

Hastrup, K. 1978. "The semantics of biology: virginity," in *Defining Females: The Nature of Women in Society*, Shirley Ardener (Ed.). London: Croom Helm, 49–65

Hedrick, Charles W. 2000. *History and Silence: Purge and Rehabilitation of Memory in Late Antiquity*. Austin: University of Texas Press

Henry, Nathalie 1999. "The Song of Songs and the liturgy of the velatio in the fourth century: from literary metaphor to liturgical reality," in *Continuity and Change in Christian Worship: Papers read at the 1997 summer meeting and the 1998 winter meeting of the Ecclesiastical Historical Society*, R. N. Swanson (Ed.). Woodbridge: Boydell Press, 18–28

Hopkins, Keith and Mary Beard 2006. *The Colosseum*. London: Profile Books

Hunter, David G. 1987. "Resistance to the virginal ideal in late-fourth-century Rome: The case of Jovinian." *Theological Studies*, 48: 45–64

– 1999. "Clerical celibacy and the veiling of virgins: New boundaries in late ancient Christianity," in *The Limits of Ancient Christianity: Essays on Late Antique Thought and Culture in Honor of R. A. Markus*, W. E. Kingshirn and M. Vessey (Eds). Ann Arbor: University of Michigan Press, 139–52

– 2000. "The virgin, the bride, and the Church: reading Psalm 45 in Ambrose, Jerome and Augustine." *Church History*, 69.2, 2000: 281–303

– 2003. "Rereading the Jovinianist controversy: Asceticism and clerical authority in Late Ancient Christianity." *Journal of Medieval and Early Modern Studies*, 33.3: 453–70

– 2007. *Marriage, Celibacy, and Heresy in Ancient Christianity: The Jovinianist Controversy.* Oxford: Oxford University Press

– 2016. "Sacred space, virginal consecration and symbolic power: a liturgical innovation and its implications in late ancient Christianity," in *Spaces in Late Antiquity: Cultural, Theological and Archaeological Perspectives.* Juliette Day, Raimo Hakola, Maijastina Kahlos and Ulla Tervahauta (Eds). London: Routledge, 89–105

Irwin, Eleanor 2007. "The invention of virginity on Olympus," in *Virginity Revisited: Configurations of the Unpossessed Body*, Bonnie MacLachlan and Judith Fletcher (Eds). Toronto: University of Toronto Press, 13–23

D'Izarny, Raymond 1953. *La virginité selon Saint Ambroise: Thèse pour le doctorat en théologie.* Lyon: L'institut catholique de Lyon

Jacobs, Andrew S. 2000. "Writing Demetrias: Ascetic logic in Ancient Christianity." *Church History*, 69.4: 719–48

Janssens, Jos 1981. *Vita e morte del cristiano negli epitaffi di Roma anteriori al sec. VII.* Analecta Gregoriana, Vol. 223, 73. Rome: Università Gregoriana Editrice

Jastrzebowska, Élisabeth 1989. "Les sarcophages chrétiens d'enfants à Rome au IVe siècle", *Mélanges de l'École Française de Rome. Antiquité*, CI 1989, 101–2, p. 783–804

Jensen, Anne 1996. *God's Self-confident Daughters: Early Christianity and the Liberation of Women.* Louisville: Westminster John Knox Press

Jones, C. P. 1971. *Plutarch and Rome.* Oxford: Clarendon Press

Joshel, Sandra R. 1986. "Nurturing the master's child: Slavery and the Roman child nurse." *Signs* 12.1: 3–22

Kajava, Mika 2001. "Vesta and Athens," in *The Greek East in the Roman Context. Proceedings of a Colloquium Organised by the Finnish Institute at Athens May 21 and 22, 1999*, Olli Salomies (Ed.). Helsinki: The Foundation of the Finnish Institute at Athens, 71–94

Kelly, Kathleen Coyne and Leslie, Marina 1999. "Introduction: The epistemology of Virginity," in *Menacing Virgins: Representing Virginity in the Middle Ages and Renaissance*, Kathleen Coyne Kelly and Marina Leslie (Eds). London and Newark: Associated University Presses, 15–25

Kelly, Kathleen Coyne 2000. *Performing Virginity and Testing Chastity in the Middle Ages.* London: Routledge

King, Helen 1993. "Bound to bleed: Artemis and Greek women," in *Images of Women in Antiquity*, A. Cameron and A. Kurth (Eds). London: Routledge (1st Ed 1983), 109–27

– 2004. *The Disease of Virgins: Green Sickness, Chlorosis and the Problems of Puberty.* London: Routledge

King, Karen 2003. *What is Gnosticism?* Cambridge, MA: The Belknap Press of Harvard University Press

King, Margaret 2000. "Commemoration of infants on Roman funerary inscriptions," in *The Epigraphy of Death*, G. J. Oliver (Ed.). Liverpool: Liverpool University Press, 117–54

Kraemer, R. S. 1992. *Her Share of the Blessing: Women's Religions among Pagans, Jews and Christians in the Greco-Roman World.* Oxford: Oxford University Press

Kuefler, Mathew 2001. *The Manly Eunuch: Masculinity, Gender Ambiguity, and Christian Ideology in Late Antiquity.* Chicago: University of Chicago Press

Kyle, Donald G. 2001. *Spectacles of Death in Ancient Rome.* London: Routledge

Lafferty, Maura K. 2003. "Translating faith from Greek to Latin: *Romanitas* and *Christianitas* in late fourth-century Rome and Milan." *Journal of Early Christian Studies*, 11.1: 21–62

Laes, Christian 2013. "Male virgins in Latin inscriptions from Rome," in *Religious Participation in Ancient and Medieval Societies. Rituals, Interaction and Identity*, Sari Katajala-Peltomaa and Ville Vuolanto (Eds). Acta Instituti Romani Finlandiae 41: 105–19

La Follette, Laetitia 1994. "The costume of the Roman bride," in *The World of Roman Costume*, Judith Lynn Sebesta and Larissa Bonifante (Eds). Madison: University of Wisconsin Press, 54–64

Lanciani, Rodolfo 1883. "L'Atrio di Vesta. Con appendice del comm. Gio. Battista De Rossi," *Notizie degli scavi*, Dec.

– 1892. *Pagan and Christian Rome.* London: MacMillan

– 1967 [1888]. *Ancient Rome in the Light of Recent Discoveries.* New York: B. Blom

Langlands, Rebecca 2006. *Sexual Morality in Ancient Rome.* Cambridge: Cambridge University Press

Larmour, David H. J., Miller, Paul Allen and Platter, Charles 1998. "Introduction: Situating the history of sexuality," in *Rethinking Sexuality: Foucault and Classical Antiquity*, D. H. J. Larmour, P. A. Miller and C. Platter (Eds). Princeton: Princeton University Press, 1–41

Lazaire, Elisee 1890. *Etude sur les vestals d'apres les classiques et les decouverts du Forum.* Paris: Victor Palmé

Leveleux, Corinne 1995. *Des prêtresses déchues: l'image des Vestales chez les Péres de l'Eglise latine (fin IIe - début Ve siècle).* Paris: Université Pantheon-Assas (ParisII)

Lieu, Judith M. 2004. *Christian Identity in the Jewish and Graeco-Roman World.* New York: Oxford University Press

Lillis, Julia Keito 2016. "Paradox in partu: Verifying virginity in the Protevangelium of James." *Journal of Early Christian Studies*, 24.1: 1–28

Lizzi, Rita 1990. "Ambrose's contemporaries and the Christianization of Northern Italy." *Journal of Roman Studies* 80: 156–73

– 1991. "Ascetismo e monacheismo nell'Italia tardoantica." *Codex aquilarensis* 5: 55–76

– 1998. "Vergini di Dio – vergini di Vesta: Il sesso negato e la sacralità," in *L'eros difficile: Amore e sessualità nell'antico cristianesimo*, Salvatore Pricoco (Ed.). Rome: Rubbettino, 89–132

– 2007. "Christian Emperor, Vestal virgins and priestly colleges: Reconsidering the end of Roman Paganism." *Antiquité Tardive* 15: 251–62

– 2009. "*Augures et pontifices*: Public sacral law in Late Antique Rome (Fourth-Fifth Centuries AD)," in *The Power of Religion in Late Antiquity.* Andrew Cain and Noel Lenski (Eds). Franham: Ashgate, 251–78

Lovisi, Claire 1997. "Vestale, *incestus* et juridiction pontificale sous la République romaine." *Mélanges d'archéologie et d'histoire de l'école français de Rome* 109 (2): 699–735

Lundhaug, Hugo 2007. *"There is a rebirth and an image of rebirth": a cognitive poetic analysis of conceptual and intertextual blending in the Exegesis on the Soul (NHC II,6) and the Gospel of Philip (NHC II,3).* Doctoral Thesis, University of Bergen

Lusching, C. A. E. 1983. "The value of ignorance in Hippolytus." *American Journal of Philology* 104.2: 115–23

MacDonald, Margaret 1996. *Early Christian Women and Pagan Opinion: The Power of the Hysterical Woman.* Cambridge: Cambridge University Press

Markus, R. A. 1998. *The End of Ancient Christianity.* Cambridge: Cambridge University Press

Martin, Dale B. 1995. *The Corinthian Body.* New Haven and London: Yale University Press

– 2005. "Introduction," in *The Cultural Turn in Late Ancient Studies*, Dale B. Martin and Patricia Cox Miller (Eds). Durham: Duke University Press, 1–21

– 2006. *Sex and the Single Savior: Gender and Sexuality in Biblical Interpretation.* Louisville: Westminster John Knox Press

Martini, Maria Cristina 1997a. "Carattere e struttura del sacerdozio delle vestali: un approcio storico-religioso" (Prima parte). *Latomus* 56 (2): 245–63

– 1997b. "Carattere e struttura del sacerdozio delle vestali: un approcio storico-religioso" (Secunda parte). *Latomus* 56 (3): 477–503

Mason, H. A. 1979. "Key-words in Euripides' Hippolytus." *Cambridge Quarterly* 8.3: 197–203

Matroye, F. 1929. "L'affaire *Indicia*. Une sentence de saint Ambroise," in *Mélanges Paul Fournier.* Paris: Société d'histoire du droit, 503–10

Matthews, John 2010. *Roman Perspectives. Studies in the Social, Political and Cultural History of the First to Fifth Centuries.* Swansea: Classical Press of Wales

McDaniel, Mary Joann: 1999. *Augustus, the Vestals and the Signum Imperii.* PhD dissertation, University of North Carolina

McInerney, Maud Burnett 1999. "Rhetoric, power, and integrity in the passion of the virgin martyr," in *Menacing Virgins: Representing Virginity in the Middle Ages and Renaissance*, Kathleen Coyne Kelly and Marina Leslie (Eds). London and Newark: Associated University Presses, 50–70

– 2003. *Eloquent Virgins from Thecla to Joan of Arc.* New York: Palgrave MacMillan

McLynn, Neil B. 1994. *Ambrose of Milan: Church and Court in a Christian Capital.* Berkeley: University of California Press

McNamara, Jo Ann 1976. "Sexual equality and the cult of virginity in early Christian thought." *Feminist Studies* 3.3/4: 145–58

– 1983. *A New Song: Celibate Women in the First Three Christian Centuries.* New York: The Haworth Press

Mekacher, Nina 2006. *Die vestalischen Jungfrauen in der römische Kaiserzeit.* Rome: Deutsches Archäologisches Institut Rom (Palilia 15)

Mekacher, Nina and van Haeperen, Françoise 2003. "Le choix des vestales, miroir d'une société en évolution (IIIe s. a.C.- Ièr s.p.C)." *Revue de l'historie des religions*, 1: 63–80

Methuen, Charlotte 1997. "The 'Virgin Widow': A problematic role for the Early Church?" *Harvard Theological Review* 90.3: 285–98

Metz, René 1954. *La consecration des vierges dans l'église Romaine: Étude d'histoire de la liturgie.* Paris: Presses Universitaires de France

– 2001. *La consécration des vierges: Hier, aujourd'hui, demain.* Paris: Les éditions du Cerf

Miller, Patricia Cox 2005. "Is there a harlot in this text? Hagiography and the grotesque," in *The Cultural Turn in Late Ancient Studies*, Dale B. Martin and Patricia Cox Miller (Eds). Durham: Duke University Press, 87–102

Miller, Paul Allen and Charles Platter 1999. "Crux as symptom: Augustean elegy and beyond." *Classical World* 92 (5): 445–54

Mitchell, Robin N. 1991. "The violence of virginity in the Aeneid." *Arethusa* 24.2: 219–38

Moreau, Philippe 2002. *Incestus et Prohibitiae Nuptiae: Conception romane de l'inceste et histoire des prohibitions matrimoniales pour cause de parenté dans la Rome antique*. Paris: Les Belles Lettres

Moxnes, Halvor 2003. *Putting Jesus in his Place: A Radical Vision of Household and Kingdom*. London: Westminster John Knox Press

Murgia, C. E. 2004. "The truth about Vergil's commentators," in *Romane Memento: Vergil in the Fourth Century*, Roger Rees (Ed.). London: Duckworth, 189–201

Mustakallio, Katariina 1992. "The crimen incesti of the Vestal Virgins and the Prodigious Pestilence," in *Crudelitas: The politics of Cruelty in the Ancient and Medieval World*, T. Viljamaa, A. Timonen and C. Krötzel (Eds). Krems: Medium Aevum Quotidianum, 56–62

Musurillo, Herbert 1972. *The Acts of the Christian Martyrs*. Oxford: Clarendon Press

Naguib, Saphinaz-Amal 1992. "Mother of the God, daughter of the God, spouse of the God. The celibacy of priestesses in Egypt from 900 BCE to early Christianity," in *The Middle East Viewed from the North*, Bo Utas and Knut S. Vikør (Eds). Bergen: Nordic Society for Middle Eastern Studies, 1–14

Nielsen, Hanne Sigismund 1999. "Interpreting epithets in Roman epitaphs," in *The Roman Family in Italy: Status, Sentiment, Space*, Beryl Rawson and Paul Weaver (Ed.). Oxford: Oxford University Press, 169–204

Nock, Arthur Darby 1930. "*A diis electa*: a chapter in religious history of the third century." *Harvard Theological Review Vol. XXIII*, no. 4: 251–74

Økland, Jorunn 2003. "Sex, gender and ancient Greek: a case-study in theological misfit." *Studia Theologica* 57: 124–42

Oksala, Johanna 2004. "Anarchic bodies: Foucault and the feminist question of experience." *Hypatia* 19.4: 97–119

Osiek, Carolyn and Margaret Y. MacDonald 2006. *A Woman's Place. House Churches in Early Christianity*. Minneapolis: Fortress Press

Osiek, Carolyn 2003. "Female slaves, *porneia*, and the limits of obedience," in *Early Christian Families in Context: An Interdisciplinary Dialogue*, David L. Balch and Carolyn Osiek (Eds). Grand Rapids: William B. Eerdmans Publishing, 255–74

Palmer, Anne-Marie 1989. *Prudentius on the Martyrs*. Oxford: Clarendon Press

Panayotakis, Stelios 2000. "The knot and the hymen: a reconsideration of nodus virginitatis (Hist. Apoll. 1)." *Mnemosyne* 53.5: 599–608

Parke, H. W. 1988. *Sibyls and Sibylline Prophecy in Classical Antiquity*. B. C. McGing (Ed.). London: Routledge

Parker, Holt N. 2004. "Why were the vestals virgins? Or the chastity of women and the safety of the Roman state." *American Journal of Philology*, 125: 536–601

Parker, Robert 1983. *Miasma: Pollution and Purification in Early Greek Religion*. Oxford: Clarendon Press

Peyroux, Catherine 2001. "Canonists construct the nun? Church law and women's monastic practice in Merovingian France" in *Law, Society, and Authority in Late Antiquity*, Ralph W. Mathisen (Ed.). Oxford: Oxford University Press, 242–55

Pietri, Charles 1977. "Appendice prosopographique à la *Roma Christiana* (311–440)." *Mélanges de l'Ecole Française de Rome* 89: 371–415

Pomeroy, S. 1995 [1975]. *Goddesses, Whores, Wives and Slaves.* New York: Schocken Books

Potter, D. S. 1990. *Prophecy and History in the Crisis of the Roman Empire: A Historical Commentary on the Thirteenth Sibylline Oracle.* Oxford: Clarendon Press

Price, Simon 2001. "The place of religion. Rome in the Early Empire," in *The Cambridge Ancient History, Ch. 16, Vol. X: The Augustan Empire. 43. BC–AD 69*, Alan K. Bowman, Edward Champlin and Andrew Lintott (Eds). Cambridge: Cambridge University Press, 812–47

Raepsaet-Charlier, Marie-Thérèse 1987. *Prosopographie des femmes de l'ordre senatoriel (Ier-IIe siècles).* Lovanii: Aedibus Peeters

Ramsey, Boniface 1997. *Ambrose.* London: Routledge

Rawson, Beryl 2003. "Death, burial, and commemoration of children in Roman Italy," in *Early Christian Families in Context: An Interdisciplinary Dialogue*, David L. Balch and Carolyn Osiek (Eds). Grand Rapids: Eerdmans Publishing, 277–97

Rebenich, Stefan 2002. *Jerome.* London: Routledge

Resnick, Irven M. 1988. "Peter Damian on the restoration of virginity: a problem for Medieval Theology." *Journal of Theological Studies* 39: 125–34

Richlin, Amy 1997. "Carrying water in a sieve: Class and body in Roman women's religion," in *Women and Goddess Traditions in Antiquity and Today*, Karen L. King and Karen Jo Torjesen (Eds). Augsburg: Fortress Publishers, 330–76

– 1998. "Foucault's *History of Sexuality*: A useful theory for women?" in *Rethinking Sexuality: Foucault and Classical Antiquity*, D. H. J. Larmour, P. A. Miller and C. Platter (Eds). Princeton: Princeton University Press, 138–70

Riches, Samantha J. E. 2002. "St George as a male virgin," in *Gender and Holiness: Men, Women, and Saints in Late Medieval Europe*, S. Riches and Sarah Salih (Eds). Florence, USA: Routledge, 65–85

Rose, H. J. 1922. "Juno Sospita and St. Silvester." *Classical Review* 36 7/8: 167–8
1925. "The Bride of Hades." *Classical Philology* 20: 238–48

– 1974. *The Roman Questions of Plutarch. A New Translation with Introductory Essays and a Running Commentary.* New York: Biblo & Tannen

Roskam, Geert 2000. "Marriage ou Virginité? Le Carmen 62 de Catulle et la lutte entre deux ideaux de vie." *Latomus* 19.1: 41–56

Rousseau, Philip 2004. "The historiography of asceticism: current achievements and future opportunities," in *The Past Before Us: The Challenge of Historiographies of Late Antiquity. Bibliothéque de l'antiquité tardive 6*, Carol Straw and Richard Lim (Eds). Turnhout: Brepolis Publishers, 89–101

Rousselle, Aline 1988. *Porneia: On Desire and the Body in Antiquity.* Oxford: Blackwell

– 2000. "Body politics in ancient Rome," in *A History of Women in the West 1: From Ancient Goddesses to Christian Saints*, Pauline Schmitt Pantel (Ed.). London: Belknap Press of Harvard University Press, 296–336

Rüpke, Jörg 2007. *Religion of the Romans.* Cambridge: Polity Press

Sághy, Marianne 2000. "*Scinditur in partes populus*: Pope Damasus and the Martyrs of Rome." *Early Medieval Europe* 9.3: 273–87

Salzman, M. R. 1989. "Aristocratic women: Conductors of Christianity in the Fourth Century." *Helios* 16.2: 207–20

– 2001. "Competing claims to 'Nobilitas' in the Western Empire of the fourth and fifth centuries." *Journal of Early Christian Studies* 9.3: 359–85

– 2002. *The Making of a Christian Aristocracy: Social and Religious Change in the Western Roman Empire.* Cambridge, MA: Harvard University Press

– 2006. "Symmachus and the 'Barbarian' generals." *Historia* (Stuttgart) 55.3: 352–67

Saquete, José Carlos 2000. *Las vírgines vestales: Un sacerdocio femenino en la religión pública romana.* Madrid: Fundación de Estudios Romanos

Scatterlee, Craig Alan 2000. *Ambrose of Milan's Method of Mystagogical Preaching.* PhD dissertation, University of Notre Dame

Scheid, John 1992. "The religious role of Roman women," in *A History of Women in the West. I: From Ancient Goddesses to Christian saints*, Pauline Schmitt Pantel (Ed.). London: Belknap Press of Harvard University Press, 277–408

Schilling, Robert 1979. *Rites, Cultes, Dieux de Rome. Études et Commentaires XCII.* Paris: Klincksieck

Scodel, Ruth 1996. "Δόμων ἄγαλμα: Virgin sacrifice and aesthetic object." *Transactions of the American Philological Association*, 126: 111–28

Schulenburg, Jane Tibbetts 1986. "The heroics of virginity: Brides of Christ and sacrificial mutilation," in *Women in the Middle Ages and the Renaissance: Literary and Historical Perspectives.* M. B. Rose (Ed.). Syracuse: Syracuse University Press, 29–72

– 1998. *Forgetful of Their Sex: Female Sanctity and Society ca.500–1100.* Chicago: University of Chicago Press

Schultz, Celia E. 2000. "Modern prejudice and ancient praxis: female worship of Hercules." *Zeitschrift für Papyrologie und Epigraphik* 133: 291–7

– 2006. *Women's Religious Activity in the Roman Republic.* Chapel Hill: University of North Carolina Press

Scullard, H. H. 1981. *Festivals and Ceremonies of the Roman Republic.* London: Thames and Hudson

Sebesta, Judith Lynn 1994. "Symbolism in the costume of the Roman woman," in *The World of Roman Costume*, Judith Lynn Sebesta and Larissa Bonifante (Eds). Madison: University of Wisconsin Press, 46–53

– 1998. "Women's costume and feminine civic morality," in *Gender and the Body in the Ancient Mediterranean*, Maria Wyke (Ed.). Oxford: Blackwell, 105–17

Seim, Turid Karlsen 1994. *The Double Message: Patterns of Gender in Luke-Acts.* Edinburgh: T&T Clark

Shaw, Brent 1987. "The age of Roman girls at marriage: some reconsiderations." *Journal of Roman Studies* 77: 30–46

Shaw, Teresa M. 1998a. *The Burden of the Flesh: Fasting and Sexuality in Early Christianity.* Minneapolis: Fortress Press

– 1998b. "*Askesis* and the appearance of Holiness." *Journal of Early Christian Studies* 6.3: 485–99

Shuve, Karl 2016. *The Song of Songs and the Fashioning of Identity in Early Latin Christianity.* Oxford, Oxford University Press

Sissa, Giulia 1990. *Greek Virginity.* London: Harvard University Press

Sivan, H. 1993. "On hymens and holiness in Late Antiquity. Opposition to Aristocratic Female Asceticism at Rome." *Jahrbuch für Antike und Christentum* 36, 81–93

Skinner, Marilyn B. 2005. *Sexuality in Greek and Roman Culture.* Oxford: Blackwell

Smith, Jonathan Z. 2004. *Relating Religion: Essays in the Study of Religion.* Chicago: University of Chicago Press

Spiegel, Gabrielle 1990. "History, historicism, and the social logic of the text." *Speculum* 65: 59–86

– 2005. "Introduction," in *Practicing History: New Directions in Historical Writing After the Linguistic Turn.* London: Routledge, 1–31

Staples, Ariadne 1998. *From Good Goddess to Vestal Virgins: Sex and Category in Roman Religion.* London: Routledge

Stehle, Eva 1989. "Venus, Cybele and the Sabine women: The Roman construction of female sexuality." *Helios* 16: 143–64

Sterk, Andrea 2004. *Renouncing the World yet Leading the Church: the Monk-bishop in Late Antiquity.* Cambridge, MA: Harvard University Press

Stephens, Janet 2013. "Vestal Hairdressing: recreating the 'Seni Crines'." Available online, last accessed 16 March 2016: https://www.youtube.com/watch?v=eA9JYWh1r7U

Takács, Sarolta A. 2008. *Vestal Virgins, Sibyls, and Matrons.* Austin: University of Texas Press

Testard, Maurice 1996. "Les dames de l'Aventin, disciples de saint Jerome." *Bulletin de la société nationale des Antiquaires de France*: 39–63

Thomassin, Louis 1865. *Ancienne & Nouvelle Discipline de l'Église: Tome Troisième. Nouvelle édition, revue, corrigée et augmenté par M. André.* Bar-le-Duc: L. Guérin & Cie

Treggiari, Susan 1993. *Roman Marriage: Iusti coniuges from the Time of Cicero to the Time of Ulpian.* Oxford: Clarendon Press

– 1994. "Putting the bride to bed," *Echos du Monde Classique/Classical Views*, 38. n.s. 13: 311–31

Trout, Dennis E. 1994. "Re-textualizing Lucretia: Cultural subversion in the City of God." *Journal of Early Christian Studies* 2.1: 53–70

– 2003. "Damasus and the invention of Early Christian Rome." *Journal of Medieval and Early Modern Studies* 33/3: 517–36

Undheim, Sissel 2004. "Crimen incesti - vestalinnene og Roma." *Klassisk Forum*, 1. 38–50

– 2011. Sanctae virginitates: *Sacred and Consecrated Virginities in Late Roman Antiquity.* PhD thesis, University of Bergen

– 2012. "*Christus virgo*: Representations of Christ as a Virgin in Early Christianity and Late Antiquity." *Bulletin for the Study of Religion*, 41.2: 22–7

– 2015. "Veiled visibility: Morality, movement and sacred virginity in Late Antiquity," in *The Moving City. Processions, Passages and Promenades in Ancient Rome*, Simon Malmberg, Jonas Bjørnebye and Ida Östenberg (Eds). London: Bloomsbury, 59–71

– 2017. "The wise and the foolish virgins. Representations of Vestal virginity and pagan chastity by Christian writers in Late Antiquity." *Journal of Early Christian Studies*, 23.5

Visser, Margaret 2001. *The Geometry of Love: Space, Time, Mystery, and Meaning in an Ordinary Church.* North Point Press, New York

Vogel, Cyrille 1966. "Facere cum virginia (-o) sua (-o) annos ... L'age des epoux Chretiens au moment de contracter mariage, d'apres les inscriptions paleochretiennes." *Revue du droit canonique*, 16: 355–66

Vogt, Kari 1995. "The woman monk: A theme in Byzantine hagiography," in *Greece and Gender: Papers from the Norwegian Institute at Athens* 2, B. Berggren and N. Marinatos (Eds). Bergen: Paul Åströms förlag, 141–8

Warner, Marina 2000 [1985]. *Alone of all her Sex: The Myth and the Cult of the Virgin Mary.* London: Weidenfeld and Nicolson

Watson, P. 1983. "Puella and virgo." *Glotta* 61: 119–143

Wildfang, Robin Lorsch 2006. *Rome's Vestal Virgins: A study of Rome's Vestal Priestesses in the late Republic and Early Empire.* London: Routledge

Wilkinson, Kate 2015. *Women and Modesty in Late Antiquity*, Cambridge: Cambridge University Press

Wilpert, Joseph 1892. *Die gottgeweihten Jungfrauen in der ersten Jahrhunderten der Kirche: nach den patristichen Quellen und den Grabdenkmälern dargestellt.* Strassburg, Munich and St. Louis: Herder Verlag

Winn, Robert 2003. "The Church of virgins and martyrs: Ecclesiastical identity in the sermons of Eusebius of Emesa." *Journal of Early Christian Studies*, 11.3: 309–38

Wogan-Browne, Jocelyn 2003. "Virginity now and then: A response to *Medieval virginities*," in *Medieval Virginities*, A. Bernau, R. Evans and S. Salih (Eds). Toronto: University of Toronto Press, 234–48

Yarbrough, Anne 1976. "Christianization in the fourth century: the example of Roman women." *Church History* 45.2: 149–65

Index

Printed in Dunstable, United Kingdom

63622111R00138